Handbook of
Japanese Mythology

HANDBOOKS OF WORLD MYTHOLOGY

Handbook of Japanese Mythology

Michael Ashkenazi

OXFORD
UNIVERSITY PRESS

OXFORD
UNIVERSITY PRESS

Oxford University Press, Inc., publishes works that further
Oxford University's objective of excellence
in research, scholarship, and education.

Oxford   New York

Auckland   Cape Town   Dar es Salaam   Hong Kong   Karachi
Kuala Lumpur   Madrid   Melbourne   Mexico City   Nairobi
New Delhi   Shanghai   Taipei   Toronto

With offices in

Argentina   Austria   Brazil   Chile   Czech Republic   France   Greece
Guatemala   Hungary   Italy   Japan   Poland   Portugal   Singapore
South Korea   Switzerland   Thailand   Turkey   Ukraine   Vietnam

First published by ABC-Clio, Inc., 2003
130 Cremona Drive, Santa Barbara, CA 93116-1911

First issued as an Oxford University Press paperback, 2008
198 Madison Avenue, New York, NY 10016

www.oup.com

Oxford is a registered trademark of Oxford University Press

Library of Congress Cataloging-in-Publication Data
Ashkenazi, Michael.
Handbook of Japanese mythology / Michael Ashkenazi.
p. cm.
Originally published: Santa Barbara, Calif. : ABC-CLIO, 2003.
Includes bibliographical references and index.
ISBN 978-0-19-533262-9 (pbk.)
1. Mythology, Japanese.   I. Title.
BL2203.A86 2008
299.5'6—dc22
2007019403

1 3 5 7 9 8 6 4 2
Printed in the United States of America
on acid-free paper

To Zaf,
for, among many things,
first getting me interested in Japan

CONTENTS

PREFACE

A project of this magnitude contains numerous surprises. I had thought that I was fairly well acquainted with Japanese mythology, having spent years studying contemporary Japanese religion and beliefs. As the writing of this book progressed, so too did my horizons expand. Heretofore obscure figures took on flesh and color. Places I had been in and cursorily viewed, as tourist or researcher, took on new importance. In this volume I've tried to communicate some of the complexities and excitement of these (re)newed discoveries.

It is useful to start, too, by saying what this book is not. First and foremost, this is not an exhaustive description of Japanese mythology. Given the Japanese happy multiplicity of deities and other mythological figures, that would be impossible. The key word here is the Japanese concept *yaoyorozu-no-kamigami*: the eight million deities. Even with ruthless pruning, I ended up with more entries in the second section than my editor, Bob Neville at ABC-CLIO, was happy with. In a complex and conceptually rich culture such as the Japanese, that is not at all surprising.

What this book is, is a traveler's guide. It is here to point out the main features of the mythical landscape that is Japan and to relate it to the main actors, on the one hand, and to the anchor of the contemporary mundane world, on the other. The book thus has been organized into four main sections. Chapter 1, the Introduction, is intended to embed the main concepts of Japanese mythology in the historical, social, literary, and political matrixes from which it emerged. In this chapter, as throughout the book, I have taken the word *Japanese* in its broadest context, to refer not only to Japanese culture, but to the two other cultures that share the same land: Okinawan and Ainu. I have also, throughout the volume, made an attempt to relate features of these three cultures to one another, both in their similar features and in their contrasts. Japanese mythology itself is a composite of a number of elements, and the mythology derives from complex and varied sources. These too have been addressed in the Introduction.

Whereas Chapter 1 provides a context for Japanese myths, Chapter 2 describes the various myths themselves. The broad strokes of the description provide an overview without going into too many details. This chapter is thematically divided into two: a retelling of the Shintō myths, and then of Buddhist ones. It is immediately apparent that Shintō mythology is far more "coherent." That is, there is a continuous story into which specific myths fit, more or less, whereas Buddhist mythology is far more fragmented. The reader must keep in mind, however, that this is to a very large degree the effect of editing. The original recorders of myths selected and edited the myths they wrote. In the interest of providing a coherent description for the reader, so did I. Neither time nor space in myth is constrained by physical time, space, or causality. Things happen simultaneously, and prime causes are obscure or are told in different ways by different persons. And, inevitably in a print medium, some sort of order must be imposed if only to be able to put it down on a page. The time and space of all myths must therefore be seen as mythical time and space: They are congruent with "real" time and space only in a limited sense.

Chapter 3 contains an alphabetical listing of the major concepts and figures in Japanese mythology from all three cultures. Though I have devoted a great deal of thought to choosing those entries, the list, as all such lists are, is probably idiosyncratic to some degree. Nonetheless, most of the central mythological figures are noted. At this point it is worth warning the reader that many Japanese figures, mythological as well as historical, have numerous names and are referred to under several names in the same source. Thus the deity Ōkuninushi is referred to throughout most of his adventures as Onamuji. To compound this problem for the writer and the reader is the issue of orthography. There is no single, agreed-on way to spell most Japanese classical names in English (nor, for that matter, in Japanese in some cases!). After a great deal of consideration, and in the interest of simplicity, I have compressed all lengthy names (many of them descriptive) into a single word, and then hyphenated the titles added to the name. Thus Ōkuninushi's name might also be spelled O-kuni-nushi, Okuninushi, and Ōkuni Nushi in different sources. Here I've elected to choose Ōkuninushi.

The fourth chapter of this book is concerned with sources for further and detailed study of the features of Japanese mythology. Here too, the list of sources is not exhaustive. More obscure English-language sources, as well as those that are highly technical, have not been included. Because this book is for English-language readers, I have included only a scattering of references from non-English European languages, choosing those that are either absolutely necessary as references or that might be easily accessible to the reader. Finally, some Japanese sources, a mere mouthful of the plenitude available, have been selectively included for those willing (and able) to pursue that avenue. The reader is warned, however, that some of the issues in Japanese mythology are still "hot," politically and socially speaking, in Japan, and the views the reader will encounter will often be contentious and conflicting.

The advent of information technology has been both a blessing and a curse to the researcher. On the one hand, the World Wide Web has allowed wide access to an enormous pool of data and information. On the other hand, the Web is a catch-all: Anyone can post anything, and much of the information posted is uncritical. I have included a number of significant websites in Chapter 4, but the reader is warned that (a) some of these are misleading, and (b) websites come and go: New ones will emerge, better than the ones that existed when this book went to print. Some of those listed here will, in the nature of things, disappear.

As with all books, several people have contributed or assisted in the preparation of this manuscript, though, as all authors do, I take responsibility for all omissions and commissions within. My editor, Bob Neville, who commissioned this book, supported the writing cheerfully and ensured that even when I felt I was being overwhelmed, I was kept on an even keel. Michelle Asakawa, the copy editor, did a sterling job of untangling my often convoluted sentences and keeping an eagle eye on the minutiae of naming conventions, hyphenation, and syntax. Many thanks are owed her for a painstaking and professional job that greatly improved the book. Great thanks, as usual, are owed to my wife, Jeanne, who put up with blank stares, mumbled replies, and screams of "Amatsumikaboshi? Who the hell is Amatsumikaboshi? I can't keep track of all these people!" that were emitted irregularly from my study. Steve Fletcher and Sven Griesenbeck, librarians at Regent's College, tracked down a number of obscure works and provided them for me. My friend Asakura Hisashi took time from his own work to help with providing Japanese material, as did Mrs. Taketomi Yoshiko, a friend of my mother's who provided a very necessary Japanese book. My mother, Dr. Zafrira Ashkenazi, has, as always, been an intellectual foil and goad and, in the case of this book, provided encouragement and material assistance for which I give many inadequate thanks. And finally, I'd like to thank all those many ordinary Japanese people, who over the years have provided me with information and support concerning their beliefs and religious habits. Minasama, dōmō arigatō gozaimashita.

Leamington, 2003

1

INTRODUCTION

"**B**e careful of the snake," Mr. Takayama said conversationally. We were passing beneath a large cryptomeria on our way back from a purification ritual he had conducted in a small shrine set among ripening rice fields.

"Where?" I looked down, expecting the snake to appear, fangs dripping venom, from between the gnarled roots.

"Oh, he's around somewhere," Mr. Takayama said vaguely. "I just didn't want you startled. I've already warned the people at the shrine."

Behind us, a small group of people—farmers mostly—milled around the little wooden model building that served as a shrine. Before it two rather ratty banners fluttered in the breeze.

"It's very bad to hurt one of these snakes, the ones that live in the cryptomerias near shrines. They are always messengers of Ryūjin." Mr. Takayama led the way along the narrow path that headed for his car. It was a ten-minute ride to the city, whose buildings were clearly visible before us. During the ride, he told me the story of Ryūjin, how this dragon *kami* (deity) lived in a lake crater in the extinct volcano about thirty-two miles away. He dropped me off in front of an electronics store, where a neon dragon flashed on and off, advertising the shop.

For many modern Japanese, the relationship between myth and life is a complex one. Myth consists of stories about nebulous and concrete beings and items. It also consists of beliefs about origins—of the Japanese people, of their customs and culture—which are unquestioned, often unquestionable. And few Japanese will admit to "believing" in these myths. They simply act as if they do. To complicate things still further, religion and ritual, household practices and national ones blend in subtle and unpredictable ways. Mr. Takayama, my priest friend, was at one and the same time a serious believer in the dragon *kami* and dismissive of what he called superstition and superstitious practices, which he decried very strongly. To him, the foundations of his ritual practice were not mythical: They simply were, and he wished every person that came into his orbit, to perceive things as simply as he did himself: an unbroken continuity between humans and deities, and between humans and other forms of life on the planet.

Myths, as understood in this volume, stand at the intersection of a number of narrative forms. On the one hand is the category of the folktale, oral stories that are repeated in some traditional format. Quite often they are mythical in character (speaking of deities, causes for things, and morals), and sometimes they are mere entertainment. Many such folktales were collected by Japanese folklorists, particularly in the first half of the twentieth century, when the oral traditions started disappearing with the advent of radio, television, and other forms of entertainment. Another narrative form popular in Japan is the ghost story. Traditionally told in midsummer in order to send a chill down the listener's back (a simple form of air-conditioning!), ghost tales often came from a Buddhist tradition concerned with the afterlife and with the consequences of acts in one's lifetime. A third important narrative form are "official" myths, often recorded by, or at the instigation of, persons in power with the intent of creating charters for political and social circumstances. All of these forms contribute to a culture's mythology. The mythology in this volume acknowledges the many sources, oral and written, folk and elite. To keep things fairly consistent and clear for a nonspecialized audience, many "alternative" versions have been ignored, or merely mentioned briefly in order to provide a coherent picture.

TRANSLITERATION OF JAPANESE TERMS

The Japanese language is easily transcribed into English. All the consonant and vowel sounds of Japanese are common to the English alphabet, and there are also fairly regular rules about the relationship between consonants and vowels: No consonant except "n" can appear on its own after a vowel. All consonants except "n" must be followed by a vowel. There are five vowels: a, e, i, o, u, pronounced roughly as they would be in English. The only difficulty for the English speaker is the existence of double vowels: oo (a long "o" sound, not the "u" sound), ou, and ee (double "e," not "iy"). These have been indicated in the text with macrons: ō, ū, ē.

Japanese names given in the text are given in the Japanese order: surname, then personal name, thus Minamoto (surname) Yoshitsune (personal name). Historical names usually have the possessive "no" between the surname and personal name: Minamoto no Yoshitsune. To make reading easier, hyphens have been used to join the parts of a single name: Amaterasu-ō-mikami.

MYTHOLOGY AND THE JAPANESE WORLD

Japanese mythology is a misnomer in at least two ways. First, rather than there being one coherent mythology of the Japanese people, there are in reality a multitude of them. There are a number of different mythological traditions, some recorded in writing (and of use to politicians and ideologues), others stories that individuals tell one another, and which the experts often dismiss as "folk traditions" rather than "proper" mythology. The mythologies of small villages, and of minority peoples of the Japanese islands—the Ainu and the Ryukyuans—are sometimes not considered, in some fashion, "properly" Japanese or "properly" mythology. Second, even recorded "proper" Japanese mythology—whatever that means—is a compendium of mythologies of local origin and those that come from other traditions, largely India and China, but even the West.

To complicate matters, the term *myth* itself can be confusing. For our purposes here, myths consist of two elements. One element is the story-telling part. Myths almost always consist of stories with a supernatural (i.e., the intervention of powerful, autonomous entities) component. These stories can be lengthy epics or brief anecdotes. In this, it is difficult to distinguish between myths, legends, ghost stories, and fairy tales. Myths, however, have a second component as well: They generally have an intellectual component that provides a structure to people's lives. The people concerned might be individuals, or they might be an entire culture. Myths are ways in which people explain *to themselves* who they are, what they are doing, and why. Though no myth does all of these things, the corpus of myth, however contradictory and fragmented, offers individuals an inventory of explanations about how things come about, and why and how they themselves came into being as the end product of a lengthy (therefore, respectable, worth adhering to and defending) process. Many of the myths dealt with throughout this book are in a familiar narrative structure: Some individual, under certain circumstances in the misty past, performed some action, whose social, physical, material, and/or ideological consequences are visible to us here, today. Other myths, however, have no narrative. They are descriptions—in verse, sculpture, painting, or architecture—of features of the universe, the culture, the history. To give an example, there are no "stories," in the conventional sense, of one of the main Buddhist figures, Kannon. There are, however, lengthy descriptions of her qualities and nature. And, of course, Kannon appears in numerous myth stories about other people, usually as savior and supporter. To understand these different types of myth in the Japanese context, we discuss their emergence at greater length below.

In more mundane terms, Japanese myth, particularly in its function as a social and political charter, has been extremely important. In the early ninth century two families, the Takahashi and the Imbe, vied for the position of imperial family chef. To bolster their claims, each cited their clan myths as justification. Far more recently, in the 1980s, a Japanese government minister cited the Japanese uniqueness myth as justification for limiting imports of meat. Perhaps none of these parties were "believed" by their audiences, but the cited myths, nonetheless, were conceived of as powerful and compelling arguments.

Great Tradition and Little Traditions

In the early twentieth century, Yanagita Kunio, and later Origuchi Shinobu, started collecting the folklore of the peasants and common people, which Yanagita believed were rapidly disappearing. Yanagita in particular felt that this folklore was the "original" and "authentic" folklore of the Japanese people, and thus was the essence of the traditional and real Japaneseness that formed the Japanese nation. Many of the myths Yanagita and Origuchi collected were unique to specific locales, stories that did not necessarily reflect the things taught about and repeated in schools that were becoming *the* traditions of Japan, at least according to the government. Surprisingly, many of these myths contradicted the established myths that are recounted in monumental compilations of Japanese traditions such as the *Kōjiki* and the *Nihonshōki.* These had been republished and republicized in the eighteenth century as part of an ideological effort to "renovate" Japanese society. To explain these contradictions, it is useful to turn to a set of terms credited to American anthropologist Robert Redfield. More or less a contemporary of Yanagita's, but working in Mexico, Redfield coined the terms "Little Traditions" and "Great Tradition," which will be of use to us here.

"Little Traditions" are sets of local beliefs and practices that are to be found in all human groups, but which are particularly prevalent in communities that are relatively self-contained, even if not isolated. Little Traditions vary from one community to another, tend to be very flexible and changeable, and are rarely recorded since those repeating them are often illiterate. They focus on the immediate concerns of these communities: family, social responsibilities, agriculture, and health. The Little Traditions are in effect the mythology of the common people.

In contrast, the "Great Tradition" of a nation or culture tends to be written, printed in books, codified, almost frozen. It is controlled by the elite (who are generally literate, and always powerful) and tends to serve their purposes: the glorification of the nation, the religion, the culture in terms that they, the elite, determine for their own ends.

The relationship between Little and Great Traditions is dynamic. The Great Tradition tries, through its main supporters, the literate elites, to mobilize people for the ends of the entire society that they lead. The Great Tradition incorporates elements of local stories and myths insofar as they can be used to support the central myths of the elite and of the nation. Little Traditions feed into the Great Tradition but often deal with themes that are not central to the Great Tradition—hunger, local patriotism, the concerns of farmers and producers—or even antithetical to it, through themes of rebellion. At the same time, Little Traditions may take and adapt myths that derive from the Great Tradition for their own local purposes.

Little Traditions and Great Tradition in the Japanese Context

In the Japanese context, localism has always coexisted uneasily with "Japanism." That is to say that it was in the local community—the *buraku* (hamlet) and the *ie* (household)—that most personal interest was focused on and most emotional investment was given to. The larger community—the nation or the *han* (feudal domain)—were of less concern to most individuals except those in power. As a direct result of this dichotomy, the central government (when it was powerful and able to do so) was at pains to try and "nationalize" local myths to engender and strengthen a nation rather than a collection of separate communities. In such a ferment, it is not surprising to find that the same deity may play several different roles and have several different identities and names, or that different deities will be subsumed into the same one and different myths "amalgamated" into one myth that serves the interests of those in power.

External Sources of Japanese Traditions

Japanese traditions, including the mythical, were influenced by a number of external sources. Two of these, because they were traditions of literate cultures, are well documented and relatively easy to trace. Both India and China contributed to Japanese myths and enriched them substantively, largely through the vessel of Buddhism. There are also traces—less well documented, far more diffuse—of two other traditions: Ainu mythology is a crystallization and expression of traditions that can be found in many neighboring cultures such as the Okhotskian and Tungus cultures to the north and northwest of Japan. It is also possible to trace similarities between Japanese myths—for example, the myth of the creators of the land, the brother-sister combination of Izanagi and Izanami—and myths from the proto-Polynesian cultures of the island chains that stretch southward from Japan, through the Ryukyus, Taiwan, and the Philippines, where this myth (along with others) is retold in many variants.

Chinese Sources

One of the greatest influences on Japanese mythology has been the mythology of neighboring China. Chinese mythology was composed, itself, of a blend of two traditions. One was the native tradition of gods (*shin*) arranged in great arrays of heavenly officials, princes, and generals, headed by a supreme Jade Emperor, or Celestial Emperor, who ruled the heavens, as the earthly Chinese emperor was supposed to do on Earth, with virtue and benevolence. A large number of local deities and saints—some of them historical persons of verified existence, whose virtues impressed their peers—were assimilated into this pantheon in the form of celestial officials.

The other tradition was that of Buddhism, itself a distillation of earlier Hindu traditions mixed with some Central Asian and even Persian myths. Buddhism introduced new deities and concepts, new sages and saints into China, and they too assumed the form of a celestial bureaucracy, coexistent with, or identified as, the native one.

As all mythologies, Chinese conceptions of the mythical world were based on people's perception and understanding of the social world that surrounded them. One of the major social features of the traditional Chinese world was the imperial government system. Although the emperor was supreme, he was expected to govern by virtue, and he was in principle the head of a bureaucracy whose office-holders acquired their posts by merit. In formal terms, a system of strict (and difficult!) examinations open to all males allowed every individual the chance to become an official. The humblest farmer's son, could, in theory, become the chief minister of the empire. Thus Chinese mythology expresses official positions within the celestial government's bureaucracy. This bureaucracy was divided into departments and bureaus, just as the material world's imperial government was.

For all its adherence to parts of the Confucian ethic, Japan never evolved a meritocratic examination system. Clan and family membership and relationship to the ruler were far more important. Moreover, outlying parts of the Japanese state, though always expressing deep loyalty to the emperor, owed actual fealty to their immediate clans, and later feudal lords.

The mythological differences between the two sociopolitical systems are reflections of this. When Japanese borrowed mythological figures from China (as, for example, the conversion of Ch'ung-chuan into Shōki Demon-queller), much of the rationale for the person's deification vanished, because Japan had no comparative bureaucratic system. As a result, mythological figures in Japan assumed different degrees of importance and even play different roles than their Chinese originals.

Indian Sources and Buddhism

India had a thriving literate culture well before the emergence of the Japanese as a nation. Indian Buddhism had adapted and built upon the earlier mythological tradition of Hinduism. Indian mythology included references to a pantheon of powerful, well-defined gods. Many of the chief deities of Hinduism—Brahma the Creator, Vishnu the Preserver, Indra the Fort-Breaker, and even many of the demons—were harnessed as Buddhist figures: lower than the Buddhas themselves, but nonetheless powerful and worthy of respect. Introduced into Japan via China, these figures and deities became figures in Japanese mythology as well, under Japanese names and with Japanese attributes, but clearly sourced from a rich Hindu and Indian tradition. Here too, social differences between India and Japan—the absence of a caste system, for instance—meant that the imported deities are found in different niches than in their original homeland, with corresponding differences in the myths told about them.

The Myth of Japan

One of the primary myths the Japanese ascribe to is the myth of Japan. In this view, Japan is a nation alone, unique as to culture, special as to its place in the world, inscrutable and homogenic. This is, of course, part of the Great Tradition, and it is what has come down to us in the form of written documents; the *Kōjiki* and *Nihonshōki* texts, which we discuss later, are two examples of that. The Great Tradition of Japanese myth is very much alive in modern Japan. Most Japanese will still subscribe to some version of the following:

- Japanese language is unique, without any similarities beyond the slight traces to other languages.
- Japanese culture, and particularly the way of thought of the Japanese, is incomprehensible to other people. This is particularly true with regard to Japanese communication, which relies strongly on unspoken, felt emotions transmitted between people who share them: the Japanese people.
- The origin of the Japanese people is unique.
- The course of Japan's cultural development was largely unrelated to developments elsewhere in the world.

And quite a few will agree that the complex of physical traits Japanese people have is homogeneous and unique. Thus, over the past five decades, books have come out in Japanese explaining the uniqueness of the Japanese by their supposed unique gut length, hair color, blood type, or physical brain structure.

None of these views, it so happens, is true. These beliefs are, however, held because the elite—the bureaucracy, academics, religious figures, even show-business figures and foreign reporters—will often repeat these mythical details as if they are true. To a certain extent they are, but only if one adds numerous qualifications. For our purposes in discussing Japanese mythology, they are mythological facts that derive from, and sustain, the presence of many of the detailed "story" myths we shall examine here. To do so, we must now turn to some of the features of Japanese society that give birth to Japanese mythology.

JAPANESE TOPOGRAPHY AND GEOGRAPHY

Japan is a large archipelago running from tropical seas to arctic ones along the east coast of Asia. The archipelago is composed of four major islands—Honshu, the largest and most populous; Kyushu; Shikoku; and the most recently "Japanized" one, Hokkaido—along with numerous smaller ones. The islands are volcanic in origin, and active volcanoes still erupt from time to time. Significantly, mountain ranges criss-cross the country, isolating some communities, and these mountains have always been a locus of mythical activities.

The land is also very fertile as a whole, and early Japanese (as well as their modern descendants) rightly view it as a source of plenitude and bounty, which it generally is, notwithstanding historical famines and infertile rocky areas. The topography is not all benevolent. A Japanese saying, "Kowai mono yotsu: jishin, kaji, kaminari, oyaji" (There are four frightening things: earthquake, fire, thunder, and daddy), exemplifies the feeling that nature was dangerous as well as benevolent (and, of course, that the *pater familias* was the dominant figure in everyone's life).

Although from a social or economic viewpoint Japan's most important geographic features are its fertile plains and river valleys, which produced wealth in the form of grain for food surpluses, the most important features from a mythical viewpoint are its mountains. The most famous of these is Mt. Fuji, a near-perfect, snow-tipped cone that is visible (pollution and weather permitting) from Tokyo, over sixty miles away. This and many other mountains are associated with mythical events and beings, and mountain deities feature prominently in ritual and myth—probably because, though often impenetrable and difficult to reach, mountains loomed close to centers of population.

Another geographic feature that has been traditionally important, both culturally and for myths, is the sea. As an island people whose livelihood and lines of communication were often associated with the sea, the Japanese unsurprisingly made the sea a locus of belief, practice, and art. The Seto Inland Sea, locked between the islands of Kyushu, western Honshu, and Shikoku, is particularly important, because many of the events of the national foundation myth happen on its shores, islands, and many bays.

The Japanese islands are sufficiently close to the Asian mainland that they can be reached by four land bridges—that is, by moving from land mass to land mass via relatively narrow water passages. Just off the western tips of Kyushu and Honshu islands one can reach the Korean Peninsula in a modern ship in twenty-four hours. To the south, Kyushu dwindles into a series of fingerlike peninsulas from which one can island-hop through the chain of Ryukyu Islands to Taiwan and on to Southeast Asia via the Philippines. To the north, a string of islands visible from the northern tip of Hokkaido stretches via Sakhalin Island to the Asian mainland at Kamchatka, and another arc of islands off the eastern corner of Hokkaido leads to the Kuriles and the Arctic Ocean. These island bridges have been the highways across which the prehistoric settlers of Japan moved to the islands. One of these bridges—the passage to Korea—has been particularly important in providing cultural influences throughout history. It thus also features heavily in myths.

Besides the mountains and the Seto Inland Sea, the most important area for Japanese myths is the Yamato Plain (around the modern city of Nara) and the mountains and valleys surrounding it. This is a lush area that runs down from mountains on all sides to the usually quiet Inland Sea. To the southeast are the wild forested mountains of Kumano and the Kii Peninsula. To the east, beyond a range of high mountains, is the largest lake in Japan. Named Lake Biwa for its resemblance to a Japanese lute, its shores and the valleys around it have been the source of stories and lore for centuries. To the north and northeast are other ranges of mountains bisected by valleys. Both forested mountains and cultivated valleys provide the backdrop to many of the country's myths.

Far to the east lies another huge, fertile plain: the Kantō. Though this is the economic and political center of Japan today—one small fishing village named Edo evolved into the de facto capital and, finally, changed its name to Tokyo in the nineteenth century—in the past it was the source of opposition to imperial control, a land of vagabonds, rebels, and the headquarters of the warriors who eventually wrested all real power from the imperial court. The wide Kantō Plain runs for 180 miles almost due north, and its villages and towns provided both economic and military power for Japan's rulers after Japan's Middle Ages.

The rest of the country replicates the geography of the Kantō and Yamato (now part of the Kansai) areas: wide alluvial, fertile river valleys bordered by forested mountains, some of them quite impenetrable. Even in the twenty-first century, some areas of the mountains are relatively unvisited, and there remains room for mythical occurrence.

The northernmost island of Hokkaido is slightly different from the other three main islands. Most significantly, it was the last to be settled by the Japanese proper. Until the nineteenth century its forests were prowled by bears and deer, and its rivers teemed with salmon. It was also far colder, covered by a boreal forest of pines and other needle-leafed trees. Besides the giant brown bear (a relative of the American grizzly) it was also home to giant owls and sea eagles, and not very well suited to rice agriculture. Its Ainu inhabitants, unsurprisingly, spent their lives hunting and gathering for a living.

In contrast to the boreal northern island, the southern islands that are strung like pearls between Kyushu Island and Taiwan were quintessentially tropical. Now Okinawa prefecture, the Ryukyu Islands grow pineapple and sugar cane like many other tropical islands. In the past, their inhabitants relied heavily on fish and on rice farming, and the difficulties of making a living in such restricted landscapes led to poverty and inequality. Beautiful as the islands are, they support a large population with difficulty. Speaking a different language (about as close to Japanese as Provençal is to French), the Ryukyuan culture developed in a different form than the Japanese, though incorporation into the Japanese state obscures this.

POPULATION

The population of Japan is probably a fusion of people who used all four of the land passages (the Kuriles, Sakhalin, Kyushu-Korea, and the Ryukyus) to reach these fertile shores. There is some evidence of linguistic, cultural, and genetic ties to peoples from the west—Koreans, Manchus, and Chinese—the south—proto-Polynesians who arrived in prehistoric times, and whose descendants were probably the Kumasō of Japanese myth—and the north—the Emishi and Ezo natives, ancestral to the Ainu as well as to the Japanese. The homogenization of the Japanese people was the result of political expansion of one central state—the Yamato—which, for political reasons, was loath then (as the current Japanese government is loath today) to acknowledge internal heterogeneity. "Strange" or "foreign" groups were incorporated into Yamato social forms and forced to politically, socially, and culturally join the Yamato state. Groups that did not do so were marginalized or destroyed, as happened to nomadic groups of hunters, gatherers, and craftsmen, and to the Ainu.

The cultivation of rice has great importance culturally and mythologically. It has also had a major effect on the population of the Japanese islands (and, of course,

Rice, still considered "The Staff of Life," being harvested and piled into stooks on a family farm near Mount Fuji. (A. Tovy/ArkReligion.com)

on other places as well). Briefly put, growing rice permits greater population growth than most other grains. This has meant that notwithstanding occasional famines, the Japanese islands were and are able to support a large population.

Japanese society emerged from small local groups who had to depend heavily on group effort to survive. Space in river valleys is limited, rice requires careful water management, and horizons can be restricted both emotionally and economically. These local groups were often isolated in their river valleys. Strangers and outsiders were a class apart, whether as *hinnin* (outcast wanderers) or as wandering deities (*marebito*). In any case, powerful and dangerous itinerant strangers feature prominently in the Japanese consciousness.

The fact that agriculture could be practiced very successfully in the river valleys has also had an important political consequence. Surpluses garnered by primary producers—that is, farmers—could be converted to cultural artifacts and thus gave rise to privileged nonproducing classes. Thus several versions of social history could exist simultaneously: one for farmers on the land; one for city dwellers, made possible by surplus from farming; and for the ruling classes, enjoying surpluses created by farmers and townspeople alike. Quite often, the mythologies that emerged served as part of the glue to keep the whole system together, forging a single national entity. For example, the existence of a single prosperity god—Inari—across most of Japan helped make possible a certain national unity. And many other myths reflect the population realities of Japan: Hunger, rebellion, the lives of urban dwellers, and many other themes are reflected in myth.

JAPANESE HISTORY AND TRADITIONS

Like many other mythologies, Japanese mythology takes place against a background of real events. In fact, at least some of the heroes of Japanese myth are real historical personages. The following brief history emphasizes two aspects: the social and political context, and the evolution of Japanese religion. For convenience's sake, Japanese history has been divided into periods that more or less coincide with the types of myths encountered, rather than the more common divisions used by historians.

Archaic Period: Jōmon, Yayoi, and Kofun (Approximately 1000 B.C.E. to 650 C.E.)

The coasts of Japan are littered with huge mounds composed of sea-shells—the detritus of thousands of years of Neolithic hunter-gatherer dinners. Some of them are about five acres in extent. That's a lot of sushi dinners. These Neolithic people entered Japan along the chains of islands that link it to the mainland, finding a welcoming and fertile ecology. They mainly lived in pit dwellings that were probably communal. A large pit about six feet deep was dug in clay and roofed over with a system of posts and grass thatch.

This culture evolved into a more sedentary farming population called by anthropologists the Jōmon culture. Sources of food were expanded, and agriculture—perhaps developed indigenously, perhaps influenced by migrants from the continent—started being practiced. Larger villages came into existence in some places. This culture lasted from about 1,000 B.C.E. to about the third century B.C.E. Jōmon culture is reflected in a rich assortment of artifacts and probably was very heterogeneous. There are remains of pit dwellings, of long-houses, and of villages. Large shell mounds and other middens indicate the Jōmon survived on a mixture of dry farming and hunting-gathering, much like the Ainu of later centuries. The

Jōmon also produced pottery in amazing variety and quality. (The name *Jōmon,* meaning "rope-mark," was given them by archaeologists who noticed the many pieces of pottery marked with a ropelike pattern. We do not know what, if anything, they called themselves.) Much of this pottery includes animal- and human-shaped masks and dolls. Presumably they had an elaborate mythology, and possibly that mythology was the forerunner of the Japanese mythology we know today.

Around 250 B.C.E., new groups of Asian immigrants entered the Japanese islands, largely from Korea and the northeastern Asian mainland, or else internal developments in Jōmon society brought about a radical social and cultural change. Called the Yayoi by archaeologists, the new culture or people were a different kettle of fish entirely. They had bronze and iron technology and, no less important, the use of the horse. They had learned about irrigated agriculture, which meant they had the knowledge to produce a surplus far greater than the more hand-to-mouth Jōmon people. Most important, they were organized into clans composed of mounted warrior-aristocrats, common people, and a lower stratum of slaves. Perhaps the Jōmon people found themselves at the bottom of the heap, and this made for some strong resistance. Perhaps development was uneven in the Japanese islands, or perhaps there was (as some archaeologists claim) a lengthy period of population movement. Certainly the myth of Yamato-takeru (which we will discuss in the next chapter) indicates that the Jōmon culture people did not accept the impositions of Yayoi culture lying down! The Yayoi clans contested for territory, and an early Chinese record of Japan notes the large number of independent sovereignties into which southwestern Japan, at least, was divided at that time.

The arrival of this new culture brought about significant changes. The new political system was far less egalitarian than the Jōmon culture. The new culture also brought with it a network of ties to the more politically complex Korean kingdoms, and through them, to the mighty Chinese empire with its culturally sophisticated ideas. It was a short step from squabbling clans to the establishment of complex kingdoms, with palaces, courtiers, and the varied apparatus of state. By about 250 C.E., large tumuli tombs called *kofun*, echoing Chinese and Korean models of the time (similar mound tombs can be seen in Kyongju, Korea, and near Xian, China), were erected to commemorate powerful kings in several of the small kingdoms that divided up much of Kyushu and the Inland Sea coast of Honshu. The Kofun period thus is named for these large keyhole-shaped and moat-girded tombs established by the Japanese monarchic states.

Yamato emerged as a powerful kingdom in central Japan. It had located itself on a fertile, wide plain not far from the sea. Having a great deal of surpluses at their disposal, the Yamato rulers were able to dominate their neighbors. Yamato did so both militarily, as the myths of Jimmu Tenno and Yamato-takeru show us, and by political alliances, cooptation of neighboring clan chiefs, and the practice of impressive rituals. When all else failed, it even resorted to assassination.

When it began expanding, the Yamato kingdom was organized as little more than an enlarged clan. The emperor or empress (until the arrival of the patriarchal Chinese political system, one was as likely as the other) was the head of the dominant clan and therefore the head of the state. There were few courtiers or officials, and clans of warrior-aristocrats were relatively free to control their own domains and, in fact, impose their own economic or political systems. These clans were supported by estates worked by attached peasants. Some of the clans, notably the clan that ruled Izumo, brought their gods with them when they joined the Yamato kingdom, and room had to be found for those deities in the official accounts.

The proximity to the Asian mainland brought about changes. As the kingdom expanded and became richer, the demand for luxuries grew. Specialist craftsmen immigrated from Korea and China. These did not fit into the clan pattern, and the solution was to establish special autonomous corporations of craftsmen, sometimes with grants of land, so they could practice their crafts. These craft corporations produced pottery, cloth, and other luxury items and built the aristocrats' palaces. There was the beginning of a standing army, as well as written laws, taking over from customary tribal law. The influence of the mainland, particularly China, did not end there: It extended to political and legal models, and, no less important, to the importation of a whole new religion: Buddhism.

The Roots of Empire (Approximately 500–781 C.E.)

Toward the end of the Kofun period, in the sixth century C.E., the capital—which had moved from one place to another with the death of each reigning emperor— was established at Nara. The cost of moving the entire court, dismantling the great halls and rebuilding them, was possible in a small clan-dominated system but impossible in an administrator-centered government, with its attendant officials and records. Great palaces and temples were built, based on Chinese models. One of these, the Tōdaiji, houses to this day an enormous bronze Buddha, tribute both to the craftsmanship of that era and to the penetration and dominance of Buddhist theology in the court's life. Court life was regulated by rituals managed by a clan of ritual specialists, the Nakatomi. Other clans specialized in administration or warfare. All of these required an elaborate economy to support them.

Seventy years after the establishment of the court at Nara, the transformation of the Yamato kingdom into the Japanese empire was complete. A new capital, designed on a grid pattern and arranged in accordance with *feng-shui* principles, was established to the north of Nara, in an auspicious cup of mountains facing south, and called Heian-kyō: Tranquil Capital. A proper bureaucracy based on the Chinese model was established. Laws were codified. Land was made the property of the emperor, and he—from this point on, virtually all emperors were males—granted its use as he felt necessary. Slavery, never a prominent social feature, was in effect abolished. And Buddhism became a major religious, literary, ethical, political, and even military influence.

In the early sixth century (521 according to some sources, 528 according to others), a Korean king of Paekche introduced the Japanese court to Buddhism, sending an image of the Buddha, some priests, and copies of the sutra (Buddhist canon) to the Japanese court. One of the aristocrat-administrator clans, the Soga, promoted the new practice, building several temples. The indigenous ritual specialists, headed by the Nakatomi clan of priests and ritual specialists, were concerned about their possible loss of power and influence. So were the Mononobe clan of royal guardsmen: If the Chinese model of government would be adopted, they would become bureaucrats and retainers, rather than a free clan giving military and other service to a paramount chief. A running battle of several decades and two generations ensued. The Soga (their motives were more political than religious), aided by a certain Prince Umayado, second son of a previous emperor, finally defeated the Nakatomi-Mononobe coalition in battle, aided, it is said, by the appearance of two Buddhist warrior-deities. Buddhism, which was in general favor at court (its rituals were impressive, it had written books, and its promises of a better afterlife were extravagant compared to the native belief in a dark, cold underworld that local myths spoke about) was supported openly, and eventually became, in effect, the court religion. Unsurprisingly, the Soga clan chief immediately deposed the emperor and put his own puppet, Suiko (who was also his niece), on the throne. Surprisingly, Prince Umayado not only broke with his Soga relatives but actually, through a combination of political acumen and sheer magnetic personality, blocked the Soga grab for power and established a reasonable and balanced governmental system based on Buddhist ethics (which he published in a seventeen-article rescript, or public announcement) but giving scope for native observances. Prince Umayado, better known to millions of Japanese as Shōtoku Taishi (his posthumous Buddhist name), a brilliant scholar and skilled administrator, became chief minister and regent to Empress Suiko and oversaw the massive overhaul and Sinicization of the government system.

Native Japanese religious beliefs became known as Shintō, or Way of the Gods, to distinguish them from Butsu-dō, or the Way of the Buddha. Contrary to the practice with religions in the West, this new religion neither superseded nor was expected to supersede traditional ritual and religious practices. Instead, the two religions were gradually blended, place being found for both. The end of the religious contest was marked by the emergence of two bodies of writing. One consisted of translated and native Buddhist writings, including the seventeen-article rescript and translations of the sutras. The other was the recording in the early seventh century of compilations of chronicles of the Japanese nation, its myths and history (though the two were not distinguished), the *Kōjiki* and *Nihonshōki* compilations (of which more later) being the most prominent. These two bodies of literature allowed for the development of both Buddhist and Shintō traditions. And along with them came several theories that accounted for the blend of Buddhism and Shintō. These, generally known as *honji-suijaku* theory, eventually agreed that the Japanese *kami* (deities) were the local-national aspects of the Buddhas, who were the universal aspect of the *kami*. All nice and tidy.

Religiously this period is characterized by the gradual domination of Yamato myths and religious practices over those of other states and polities, and by the introduction of Buddhism. The states overcome by Yamato in its gradual rise to supremacy in the islands had their own tutelary deities, myths, and supporting rituals. In very broad terms these were similar to those of the Yamato, if different in detail. Some vestiges of these myths can be found in Little Tradition practices; others, such as the mythology of Ōkuninushi (whose cult is centered at Izumo-taisha, a major shrine northwest of Yamato), were incorporated into the Yamato mythology. The struggle for dominant mythologies was also a political one: Ritual and its motivating myths were embedded in the state apparatus, and whomever controlled the rituals the emperor carried out had a great deal of control of the emperor himself, a feature that reemerged from time to time to the present century.

The Aristocratic Period (Approximately 650 c.e.–1185)

As mentioned earlier, the Yamato state established a stable capital at the new city of Nara in 712 c.e. and then in 781 c.e. moved the court to a new city named Heian-kyō. The period of foundation of these cities marked the gradual emergence of the Japanese empire from the Yamato state. The city of Heian was built according to Chinese principles—its back to a northern mountain, a square-grid pattern of streets, a central palace following *feng-shui* geomantic principles—and this, the Heian period to historians, was the high point of emulation of things Chinese. More significant than the buildings, however, were the bureaucratic and administrative changes.

The emperor headed a state bureaucracy modeled on the Chinese one in all respects save for the all-important one of promotion by examination and merit. The aristocratic clans were converted into a civil bureaucracy, with administra-

tive offices in government they were entitled to fill. The Heian aristocracy numbered little more than 20,000 to 30,000 people. Outlying provinces were considered the wilderness, and one of the worst punishments for an aristocrat was
banishment to Kyushu or the wilds of northern Honshu. The precarious hold of
the central government on outlying provinces, some of which were controlled by
the central government in name rather than in fact, is reflected in the mythology of that time. It is a mythological period of heroes who, (usually) operating
under imperial license, set out to restore order in the world. Heroes such as
Tawara Toda and Raikō, either by themselves or together with bands of no-less-
famous retainers, subjugate rebels and bandits (the two terms are often synonymous) and add to the emperor's dominions. Things are not, of course, so simple:
Tawara Toda toys with the idea of joining the rebels but is repelled by the rebel
leader's perceived meanness. Very clearly loyalty to the emperor takes second
place to personal success. Nonetheless, most of these myths are very similar,
and they are summed up in a legend known to every Japanese: the legend of
Momotarō.

An elderly childless couple, after living a virtuous life and praying to the
gods, find a giant peach floating down the stream. From the fruit pops a baby,
whom they raise. When he is older, the child—now named Momotarō (Peach
boy)—hears of an island of evil demons who terrify and dominate the countryside. Taking his wooden sword, a store of millet dumplings, and a banner made
by his mother saying "First in Japan," he sets off to find the island. Along the
way he encounters a bird, a monkey, and a dog, whom he treats kindly and with
whom he shares his food. He and his loyal retainers reach the island and defeat
the demons. Some of them agree to become peaceful beings, and Momotarō is
rewarded for his victory.

The heroic mythology of the aristocratic period frequently repeats this story
line, indicating perhaps that not only was the country unsettled and wild but
there was plenty of scope for individuality and individual action, so long as it was
away from the court. For, back at the capital, the Heian period was a period of
intense cultural flowering. Poetry, painting, literature, and ritual flourished. The
world's first novel, *Genji monogatari* (Tale of Genji), was written in this period
by a court lady. Reminiscences and diaries, and new forms of poetry and painting
prospered during this period. The court and the aristocrats isolated themselves
from the reality of the countryside, concentrating on ritual and aesthetic pursuits.
So long as the rent in rice and labor from the domains continued to arrive, they
could ignore anything outside the capital. Most tried to avoid traveling more than
a hundred miles from the court. Many considered distant Ugo (modern Tohoku
in the far northeast of Honshu) and the island of Kyushu to be the outer darkness:
a realm of bandits and uncivilized boorish and savage warriors.

A Kobako (small box) in the shape of a fan with sticks of inlaid silver. Decorated lid depicts the mansion and gardens of Prince Genji, the mythological hero of the 11th century novel The Tale of Genji. *(Spinks/ArkReligion.com)*

Like many such enclosed environments, the Heian court created the seeds of its own destruction. The Heian period ended with squabbles between aristocrats, which escalated as the squabbling parties brought in their own "barbarians": the warrior descendants of exiles, lower-class aristocrats, and the mythological heroes who had maintained their military abilities on the peripheries of the empire. The rural warriors—referred to somewhat contemptuously as *samurai* (temple servitor)—hardened by fighting among themselves and by wars of subjugation against the Emishi (Ainu tribes on Honshu) and the Kumasō (other native tribes in Kyushu), were hard to control. So when the aristocrats entered into squabbles among themselves, some were careless enough to invite their country-bumpkin cousins to do their fighting for them. The results were predictable. In the Onnin War the capital and imperial palace were burned. Further squabbles made the situation worse, and the Gempei war between two powerful coalitions of rural families spelled the end of the Heian period and its elegance.

The Medieval Period (1185–1600)

By the twelfth century, squabbling Heian aristocrats had called their own doom upon themselves. Accustomed to calling in their rough country cousins to help settle disputes, they discovered to their horror that the rough warriors—the *bushi*—had no intention of relinquishing control. To add to the aristocrats' woes, Buddhist monasteries, the supposed embodiment of peace and harmony, had established their own armies of *sōhei* (monk-soldiers), who terrorized the aristocracy to the point that Heian, the capital itself, became a ghost town at one stage.

The fighting *bushi* (warriors) eventually resolved themselves into two coalitions. One, the Taira (known also as the Heike), more refined than others (they lived closer to the capital and in the eyes of the aristocrats were at least semi-domesticated), gained the advantage at first and seized control of the ultimate symbol of rule: the person of the emperor. The Taira's opponents, the Minamoto (known also as Genji), after having been almost exterminated in the early twelfth century, roared back triumphantly. Led by Minamoto no Yoritomo, son of the defeated and executed Minamoto chief, the clan in the five years of the Gempei War (a contraction of Gen[ji] and Hei[ke], 1180–1185), swept the Taira before them. Yoritomo was aided by several able generals, among them his younger brother Yoshitsune (birth name Ushiwakamaru), who in 1185 decisively defeated the Taira at a sea battle at Dan-no-Ura, in the far west of Japan, where the child emperor Antoku lost his life. Minamoto no Yoritomo was appointed *shogun*, an ancient military title—somewhat like the republican Roman "dictator"—given temporarily to generals with a commission to suppress Ainu/Emishi forces in western Japan.

The Minamoto were not about to repeat Taira mistakes. Not to be taken in and weakened by the seductions of aristocratic living in Heian, they established a new capital at Kamakura (near modern Tokyo, in eastern Japan) away from the influences and intrigues of the court. A new form of government, the *bakufu* (tent government)—headed by the *shogun*—was established. This military regime persisted in one form or another until 1868.

The Minamoto were heads of an alliance, and thus each domain, headed by a family of one of the alliance members supported by its retainers—they had adopted the epithet *samurai* for themselves—assumed a great deal of autonomy. This period brought into the foreground tales of heroism and bravado of individual, sometimes historical, personages whose mythical exploits, like those of

Yoshitsune/Ushiwakamaru, victor of Dan-no-Ura, became models of propriety for future generations. National myths did emerge, but as the country descended into civil war, and as domains became isolated and xenophobic, so they also concerned themselves with creating their own local myths and practices.

The major national myth to emerge in this period was to have lasting consequences. In 1274 Kubilai Khan, grandson of the Mongol conqueror Genghis Khan, mobilized a massive fleet of some 450 ships manned by 15,000 Korean sailors and 15,000 Mongol troops. These landed in Hakozaki Bay in Kyushu. The local forces mobilized but were on the verge of defeat when the Mongols returned to their ships. A storm was brewing, and they did not want to be cut off from their means of maneuver. In the event, a typhoon blew up, dispersing the fleet and drowning about half its manpower. By the time the Japanese relief column had arrived, it was all over. Kubilai was busy finishing off the Chinese Sung dynasty and did not turn his attention to Japan again for several years. In 1281 the blow fell. A Korean fleet of 50,000 Mongol soldiers and Korean sailors landed in Kyushu. A second fleet of 100,000 Mongols and Chinese arrived from Southern China. The two fleets landed men at Hakata Bay, one of the expected landing points that the Japanese had fortified with a wall. The fighting lasted for about fifty days. At the end of that period another typhoon arose. Both invading fleets were heavily damaged, losing over two-thirds of their ships and manpower. The repeatedly miraculous nature of the Mongol defeat, combined with the claims by the clergy that the Japanese victory was due to divine intervention, meant that the idea of the *kamikaze*, the divine wind that helps Japan defeat its enemies, became enshrined deeply as a national myth.

The medieval period ended with a century-long civil war, the *sengoku jidai* of the historians, in which fiefs and clans battled one another for supremacy or survival while the shogun's government became as powerless as the emperor's court, which was still resident in Heian-kyō. The civil war ended with the establishment, after years of fighting, of a suzerain (though not supreme) government based in Edo. This small fishing village in Eastern Japan emerged as the capital of a premodern Japan unified under the shogunal government of the Tokugawa family. The exploits of the years of the civil war (roughly, the fifteenth and sixteenth centuries) were well documented and yielded more in the realm of personal myth-making than national myths. Many of these myths fall into the realm of what we call today image management and public relations: The various domain lords were well-versed in psychological warfare, and most were fully conscious of the need to appear invincible, or at least highly successful.

The Premodern and Modern Periods (1615–)

The Tokugawa government in Edo issued in a period of unprecedented peace from about 1615 to 1868. This was characterized by ultimately unsuccessful attempts to keep out foreign (read, Western) influences. A major, though often overlooked, myth of samurai virtues and strengths, which has become the national myth of economic Japan, emerged from this period, when the virtues of the samurai were codified, glossing over their actual practices. They were pictured as the perfect warrior, dedicated absolutely to their lord even at the expense of themselves and their families. An event occurred in the middle of the Edo period that, though factual in outline and many details, must also be considered as a major myth. This event, known subsequently as the Forty-Seven *Rōnin* and illustrated in a famous play as *Chūshingura* (Treasury of Loyal Retainers), had a major effect on the ideology of Japan in subsequent centuries. The forty-seven *rōnin* exemplified in their actions everything the Japanese wished to believe about themselves: loyalty beyond death, acceptance of misfortune without flinching, ability to face insurmountable odds. It dovetailed nicely with a previous national myth—the *kamikaze*—that showed how, in practice, the *kami* were ready to defend their land, but only if the Japanese themselves rallied to its defense without thought of personal survival.

The outline of the events is fairly straightforward. Lord Asano of Akō, a *daimyō* (lord of a domain; the closest English concept is baron) of modest standing, was fulfilling his duties at the shogunal court. While receiving instruction in court etiquette, he was insulted by his instructor, Lord Kira. (Kira, it is said, had told Asano to wear the wrong kind of trousers to a court function.) Asano drew his sword on Kira. Drawing a sword in the shogunal palace was an act of treason, and Asano was ordered to commit *seppuku* (honorable suicide), which he duly did. His fief was confiscated and his retainers disbanded, becoming *rōnin* (masterless samurai). Forty-seven of these retainers pledged to extract vengeance. After three years of secret preparation, during which they abandoned their families and friends and proceeded by subterfuge to throw the authorities off track, they struck. In the winter of 1703 they assembled and forced their way into Kira's mansion in Shinagawa, a suburb of Edo. After taking the villain's head, they placed it upon the gravestone of their dead master. They surrendered to the authorities, and after a year of debate (most of the public were hugely delighted by the romance and passion of the events, as was the shogun himself), they were ordered to commit *seppuku*, which they promptly did. It was great drama, and it contributed immeasurably to the Japanese sense of who and what they were.

The Tokugawa state, through a combination of bribery, threats, hostage-taking, and elaborate ceremonialism, managed to perform two major feats. It kept the two-hundred-odd domains isolated from one another, so that even the most hostile of them needed a couple of centuries to band together to remove the Tokugawa shogunate. And, overall, it kept Japan peaceful and free of annexation by rapacious Western colonial powers. The settled lives of the townsmen and *bushi* brought forth a renewed Great Tradition of literate discussion by philosophers as well as artists, of myths in the context of national mythologies rather than regional or local ones. Such myths were incorporated into theatrical works, paintings, popular cheap "penny dreadful" books, and formal story-telling arts. They formed a *national* mythology, the hallmark of a mature Great Tradition. The Little Traditions still flourished in the shade, often the object of satire by sophisticated urbanites and the educated.

In the latter half of the nineteenth century Japan started a rapid program of modernization and part-Westernization. This culminated in World War II, when Japan attacked and its forces occupied most of its neighbors. The myth of the *kamikaze* was revived during the war: the idea that with nothing more than spirit and self-sacrifice, the deities would save Japan from defeat.

The Japanese adapted rapidly to the situation after their defeat in World War II, and within a couple of decades, they were directing their energies to surviving in a capitalist, reasonably peaceful (from their perspective) world. In the process, new myths started emerging: myths built on Japanese successes, and explaining Japanese failures as well. Many of these myths—collectively called by foreign scholars "myths of Japanese uniqueness" and by Japanese scholars *Nihonshugi* (Japaneseness) or *Nihonjin-ron* (Japanese thinking), were initiated and spread by academics and politicians. They also had impact on diverse fields such as fashion. The idea of Japanese uniqueness, based on some physical distinction of the Japanese as a race, is particularly prominent. Thus in the past twenty years alone, several such myths have emerged: that the Japanese, being largely vegetarians, have gut lengths shorter than most other humans. That the prevalence of one blood type in Japan is responsible for the communitarianism and self-sacrifice in Japanese society. That Japanese brains are structured differently from other nations, and therefore Japanese language can be imprecise and vague without limiting intra-Japanese communication. There is even a modern myth that brown-haired people (as opposed to black-haired or blond) are warmer, more sociable, and kinder than other people, leading to a rash of younger Japanese people dying their hair brown!

SOCIAL HISTORY

While all the political history described above was going on, the vast mass of the population were living much as their ancestors had. Hamlets, usually of farmer-tenants, lived in close proximity to their landlords, who also worked the land. Small manufacturing and service towns, often clustered around castles that offered some protection in times of unrest, were scattered about the countryside. In the larger cities of Sakai, Osaka, Edo, and others, a large class of workers and small entrepreneurs emerged from the fourteenth century onward. These populations, often isolated from others (there were major travel restrictions imposed by fearful local governments starting in the fourteenth century), sometimes marginalized, created their own myths and the rituals that bolstered them. These myths were sometimes transmitted from one community to another by way of wandering monks and priests, pilgrims, sailors, medicine sellers, and other itinerants. And some of these myths were incorporated, one way or another, into the myths of the Great Tradition.

But more than that, each hamlet, each area, had its own myths associated with their way of life, which they perceived to be unique and markedly different from those of their neighbors. These local myths were of varied and diverse origins, but they shared one major element: They reflected local experience and fears. The ferocious *Bimbogami*, the deity of poverty, was always knocking at the door. Sprites and demons lurked at particular local places where real dangers to the unwary—precipices and deep rivers, falling trees and landslides—were to be found. Wizards lurked in the mountains, and if they were properly addressed and solicited they might provide a relief from the hardships of life.

The social world of the Japanese individual throughout "traditional" history (that is, up to the end of World War II) was intensely circumscribed and formalized. For much of history, peasants (whom the rulers knew, even if they did not admit it, were the real wealth of the land) were forbidden to travel without permission. And when they did travel, it was in supervised groups visiting pilgrimage sites. Formally and informally the population was divided into four classes: warrior-administrators, farmers, craftsmen, and merchants. They were discouraged from interacting with one another socially. The prohibitions were not airtight, and there was some overlap, but unsurprisingly, different traditions did emerge.

Whatever the formal social divisions in Japan, the source of myths during the middle ages and the premodern age of Japan can be attributed to three social categories: powerful, powerless, and outsiders.

The Powerful

The early aristocracy, those connected with and directly serving the imperial court, were a tiny proportion of the population, never numbering more than twenty thousand or so. Nonetheless, under the aegis of the emperor, they exemplified power. Originally the aristocrats were clan members and landowners, but with the entrance of the Chinese bureaucratic system they became administrators paid for by domains granted them by the emperor. By the twelfth century the court aristocrats had lost power to the warrior-aristocracy from the provinces, the *bushi*. These warrior-knights had a different ethos and different myths from those of the imperial aristocracy. But, together, these power-holders had a shared interest in maintaining and supporting the Great Tradition and in emphasizing the unity and greatness of Japan. Later, when the country was semi-unified under the Tokugawa rulers, these warriors became mainly official-bureaucrats, still later metamorphosing into the civil-servant bureaucrats and managers of the modern state. It was their ideals and ideas that find reflection in many myths: ideas about loyalty, about masculinity and the power of perseverance, and about forthrightness and battle.

The Powerless

The powerless made up more than 90 percent of the Japanese population. They included farmers, craftsmen, and merchants. During the archaic period they were in effect the clients, if not the virtual property, of the powerful. Later, under Chinese ideological influence, they were expected to defer to their betters, and when a national ideology emerged, they were exhorted to sacrifice their all for emperor and nation. Aside from that, they were often left to their own devices. Their myths and interests reflected these facts. By and large, their interests were local and immediate. In their myths foxes and mysterious spirits, ghosts, and goblins inflicted themselves upon individuals, but in ways that the central government or powerful samurai could not deal with. Only prayer, reliance on the wits of others (humans and Buddhas), and a certain sharpness could extricate a person from his troubles. And sometimes, as in most ghost stories, there was no solution but to part from the dead on amicable terms: *inochi wa tsurai-yo* (life is difficult).

Outsiders and Rovers

The powerful and the powerless in Japan both had a vested interest in promoting stability, as well as in resisting outside influences. But outside influences were inevitable, even in the smallest hamlet. Japanese traders and travelers had been frequenting Korea, China, Indochina, and what were to become the Philippines. A Japanese rover had become high admiral to the Siamese court. Japanese embassies and scholars had been visiting China for centuries. Japan's rulers, as a group, were fully aware of international developments in East Asia. They were thus very cautious about foreigners. But the caution of foreigners went far deeper, to the days, perhaps, when the Jōmon lived in isolated bands. Villages and domains abhorred strangers, and they were proscribed or controlled. Nonetheless, there was a tradition of wanderers and itinerants throughout the islands. The Emishi, inhabitants of northern and eastern Japan against whom the Yamato conducted a series of campaigns, might have been wandering hunter-gatherers like their Ainu cousins. There were bands of hunters, of foresters, of weavers of *akebi* vine baskets making a living in Japan until the early twentieth century. They lived in the forests and mountains, coming into contact with settled villages only occasionally. And there were wanderers who deliberately came into contact with settled areas. *Kebōzu* (hairy priests; unlike most Buddhist priests, they did not shave their heads) and *bikuni* mendicant nuns visited remote villages on a regular basis, offering rituals and exorcisms. Wandering medicine sellers would stock a household's medicine chest once a year, receiving payment for what had been consumed since the previous visit. Slave dealers would purchase children for household service and brothels. Pilgrims passed through on their way to remote sites, as did poets on inspiration-seeking travels. Occasionally seamen and sailors washed onto the beach. No one was completely isolated from these visitors. Unsurprisingly they became the source for much myth, and while many were considered outcast and dangerous, many others were considered holy and dangerous: worthy of worship, of hospitality, and of the wish that they retire, benevolently inclined toward their hosts, after being properly entertained.

Essential and central to all these social groups, powerful and powerless alike, was a shared concept of language and of kinship.

JAPANESE FAMILY RELATIONS

The Japanese kinship and family system differs in some crucial regards from families in most other societies. First and foremost, the significant element is the *ie* (household), and the foremost traditional responsibility of its members was to maintain it in perpetuity. Normally, an *ie* would be composed of a married couple and their unmarried children. Nonmaterial social categories were also members of the *ie:* the ancestors (called *hotoke* and *kami*) and unborn generations of members. The living members had responsibility toward both these categories of nonmaterial members. Unmarried members, both male and female (except for the one intended to inherit the *ie*), were members on sufferance only, sometimes on a temporary basis until they married out and often severed all ties with their natal *ie*.

Nominally, inheritance of all productive property went wholly to the senior male child. The overriding necessity for ensuring *ie* continuity, however, meant that in practice, the eldest son *could* be replaced by another son. This was rarely done but existed as a normative and legal possibility. If no qualified son were available, a married daughter could take on the inheritance, and her husband would be adopted by her father into the family and take on the surname of the *ie*. This is still relatively common in families who own productive property (farmland, family manufacturing businesses, even Kabuki acting families). About 15 percent of marriages in rural Japan were of this sort during the twentieth century.

Another peculiarity of the traditional family, though less observed during the modern period when most family economies are based on wage earning, is that the inheriting son (or daughter) inherited *all* the *ie*'s property. As a consequence, wealthy families "spun-off" junior or branch houses, giving them their own productive resources. The junior families owed fealty and ritual and sometimes economic obligations to the senior, or main or "stem" *ie*. A branch house could, if it became wealthy, spin off a number of branches of its own. This sort of branched inter-*ie* system is known as a *dōzoku*.

In mythical terms, the Japanese people constitute a super-*dōzoku*. The imperial household, descended from the foundress Amaterasu-ō-mikami through her grandson Ninigi-no-mikoto, is the *honke* or main *ie*; other households are distantly or more closely related to the imperial household through a process of continued branching of *ie*. Some members of the sets of deity or ancestor arrive there by adoption, others through birth. Whatever the case, some form of amorphous familial feeling is engendered in many of the myths. This also means that the precise familial relationships are not at all clear, nor particularly important. After all, the main concern is membership in, and protection of, the entire system, not how any individual case fits into it. What mattered was that the individual acted responsibly as a representative of his/her group.

THE MYTHIC TRADITIONS

As noted before, a number of cultural traditions make up Japanese mythology. The two dominant influences are the mixed and often intertwined religious elements from Shintō and Buddhism. To that we need to add the two "outrider" cultures in the Japanese islands: the Ainu in the north, and the Ryukyuans in the south. We'll discuss the religious traditions of Shintō and Buddhism at some length, since they are the matrix within which much Japanese mythology was embedded.

Shintō

Shintō, the native religion of Japan, did not acquire its name until it became necessary for the Japanese to distinguish their native practices from the imported *Bukkyō* or *Butsu-dō* (Buddhism). The local religion was based largely on the veneration of, and appeal to, local spirits that resided in material objects, usually natural or peri-natural. Mountains, unusual trees, waterfalls, water, peculiarly shaped rocks, and other objects were considered to have a power—*kami*—of willfully influencing people's lives. The spirits of the dead were of that sort too, though the dead were also considered to live in a dark and dank place, somewhat like the classical Greek concept of hell. *Kami* could and did reside in everything and anything that inspired awe or even great interest. To this day in Japan there are trees, rocks, waterfalls, and oddly shaped stones that are *kami*. This is in addition to the sun, mountains, and other major geographical and natural features.

The native religion heavily emphasized personal purification as an element in worship, along with direct communication with the *kami* and the offering of gifts: There was no clear division between the mundane and the *kami* worlds. As we shall see, much of this has been retained in Japan's various Little Traditions. Indigenous belief was local and unwritten. There was no effective limit to the number of *kami*. Some of the *kami* became specialized, as for example the rice-field *kami*, or the water *kami*. Indeed, when I lived in northern Japan, our garden was graced by a small spring surmounted by a stone carved only with the word *suijin* (water *kami*). My landlord urged us to keep the stone clean "and make occasional offerings," which we duly did: saké and flowers, easy to come by and enjoyable in their own right (as in all Shintō rituals, we shared the *kami*'s saké and enjoyed looking at the flowers as much as s/he did).

As the Yamato state grew larger and stronger it was faced with the need to centralize and control its populace, resorting, as many states do, to religion, among other devices. Thus the local cult of the Yamato state became the paramount religious system in the Japanese islands, and local *kami*, their myths and rituals, became absorbed into or made to align with the imperial Great Tradition. This resulted in two somewhat contradictory features. On the one hand, a series of "constructed" myths—derived from attempts to amalgamate disparate traditions—became "the" standard Japanese mythology, particularly when they were eventually written down. Often incorporating local myths and inevitably containing contradictions, these are the written mythology published in such

Shintō priests at a Lily Festival in Nara, Japan. (B. A. Krohn Johansen/ArkReligion.com)

works as the *Kōjiki* and *Nihonshōki*. Such mythologies are charter myths for the Japanese state. On the other hand, underlying these Great Tradition myths are the myths of the Little Traditions, fitting more or less comfortably into the overarching structure of the Great Tradition. The saints and goblins, the *kami* and demons of local mythology had to adapt themselves, happily or not, to the ruling viewpoint: All of them, in some fashion, were and are *kami*.

The Kami

The term *kami* used throughout this book is a complex one. For our purposes (and to avoid a lengthy discussion) the term functions as both noun and adjective. As a noun, kami means a powerful being with an interest in the lives of humans and the ability to intervene in human affairs, either directly or indirectly, by influencing the activities of other kami, animals, or natural events and features: in short, a deity. As an adjective, the term means something close to "holy": a mysterious and elevating quality that various living beings, including animals and humans, possess to varying degrees. Kami (the noun form) possess kami (the adjectival form) in very great degrees, though they too, as the story of Susano-wo shows, can lose some, even much, of the quality. Kami (the adjective) is closely associated with purity. Polluting oneself or others lowers one's "store" of kami. Contrariwise, purifying oneself— by austerities, washing in pure or sea water, use of salt or fire, and avoiding polluting substances such as the dead, feces, and blood—will add to one's store of kami.

The Shintō mythological actors are individuals—deities, humans, or animals—who have greater or lesser degrees of *kami*. The deities among them often have intensely human characters. All actors require purity in order to retain their position, whether they are deities or humans. In fact, the borderline between the two classes, human and divine, is a very thin one. Humans can be purer, and thus possess more *kami*, than certain deities.

Many Japanese deities help and protect people (mainly from their own locality or lineage) as long as they are properly honored. These *matsurareru kami* (celebrated deities), as Yanagida calls them, can become angry and fierce when appropriate offerings are not made. And when angered, such deities will take action, often violent, to express their feelings.

Though many of the Japanese *kami* are identified as "deity of X," where X might represent thunder, wind, fire, or some other phenomenon, this is not strictly accurate. Many Japanese *kami* are *associated* with some natural phenomenon, or perhaps embodied in them or it. The vagueness of this association means two things: Many *kami* may be associated with one phenomenon, and the nature of the association may well be obscure. Thus both Raiden and Takemikazuchi are "thunder deities" quite independently of one another.

Shintō acknowledges the presence of *yaoyorozu-no-kami* (the eight million *kami*) as an indication that the number of *kami* was effectively infinite. In reality, a far smaller number of *kami* are named in the myths. However, this number is complicated by the fact that many *kami* have several names, which were changed according to circumstances (as were the names of individuals throughout their lives and after death in traditional Japan). Sometimes a particular *kami* was given several names at birth in the myth. In this volume I have tried to use the most commonly used and most familiar names.

Small shrine at crater of Mount Aso. (D. Harding/ArkReligion.com)

The names of *kami* are further complicated by the fact that they are descriptive and always incorporate one or more titles, such as *no-kami* or *o-mikoto*. Each *kami* is considered to have three *mitama* (souls or natures): *aramitama* (rough and wild), *nigimitama* (gentle and life-supporting), and *sakimitama* (nurturing). Obviously, one or another of these natures might predominate in any particular myth: Susano-wo usually expresses his *aramitama*, whereas Amaterasu usually expresses *nigimitama*. Under different circumstances, however, for example, when not sufficiently honored, another of the deity's natures would express itself: when forced to confront Susano-wo's apparent rebellion, Amaterasu very quickly assumes her *aramitama*, arming herself as a warrior and performing aggressive rituals.

A brief word is necessary about Shintō as a religion. Ritual practices and beliefs of what we call Shintō existed in Japan well before the name was created. The practices came under two headings: propitiation and divination. Propitiation involved acts of purification—water, sparks, and salt were the best purifiers—the recitation of a prayer or request, and offerings of foods that were considered pure, mainly vegetables, fruit, and wine from various sources. More elaborate rituals involved some form of entertainment, whether a dance, a magical play, or some music. (Keep in mind that rituals in all simple societies are a great source of entertainment, as well as awe and worship.) Divination was carried out using a number of devices: hot-water cauldrons, possession-trance, and dances, many of which are still performed today.

With the emergence of the Yamato state, these rituals became formalized, and groups of specialists such as the Nakatomi assumed responsibility for "proper" ritual organization within the state. Upon the arrival of Buddhism, Shintō went into a lengthy period of somnolence. The *kami* were worshiped, often within the confines of Buddhist temples. Large rituals were conducted for the grandees of the land, while the common people, as they do, continued performing the rituals to the *kami*, led by whatever local ritual specialist they could find, be it a Buddhist priest, local ritual expert, or wandering *kebōzu* ("hairy priest," usually a wandering mendicant member of the Shugendō sect who did not shave their heads; also called *yamabushi*). Then in the eighteenth century, as a result of political events, some Japanese scholars started taking an interest in the "Japanese" elements of their religion, trying to separate it from the "foreign" elements, notably Buddhism. The *Kōjiki* became fashionable again. When the shogunal government was toppled by middle-class samurai of non-Tokugawa fiefs in 1868, part of their motivation was derived from the ideology of Shintō/Japanese nationalism started in the eighteenth century.

Very quickly—in 1873—the new government forcibly separated Buddhism and Shintō, forcing Ryōbu Shintō (Two Schools Shintō) and its *honji-suijaku* theories to abandon all Buddhist ties and ideology. The process was neither immediate nor completely thorough. There are still many Shintō shrines served by Buddhist priests, and many boddhisatvas are the *kami* of Shintō shrines. Nonetheless, a separation was created where none existed before. Large Shintō shrines were supported by the government, and a new ideology—Kokutai Shintō (National Shintō)—emerged. In this theory, Shintō was more than a religion: It was the expression of the Japanese people's inner spirit and way of life. Shintō priests became in effect government functionaries on a salary. Shintō was directed toward national glorification and support of government activities. In 1946, after the Japanese defeat of World War II, the Occupation authorities instituted a new religious law that separated religion and government absolutely. Shintō shrines became independent once more. All are today supported by donations, and they are free to worship whichever *kami* they choose, in the ways that please them. There are several confederations of shrines and priests, but there is some degree of variation between shrines and localities.

Shintō Kami Classification

The large number of named kami (not all of them mentioned in this handbook, because of sheer numbers) can be classified in a number of ways. The following classification is an attempt to clarify the concepts used here in a way that is accessible to the average reader. However, you should be aware that a number of scholars have classified the deities in other ways. For example, all the Shintō deities can fall into "job" classifications, that is, by their responsibilities and functions: agriculture, war, health, and so on. For us the problem is that many kami cross these divides and thus will appear in more than one category. Another classical category much beloved by folklorists is to classify kami by their nature. There are thus sea and water kami, mountain kami, field kami, and storm/thunder/fire kami. Again, the cross-boundary problem is evident here as well, and much of this identification is on the basis of speculation about the "original" nature of a particular kami during prehistory. In the spirit of cooperating with the idea of multiplying the number of classifications, the following classification is offered. It has two virtues: First, it is as simple and comprehensive as possible; and second, it relates directly to the entries in the next section of the book.

1. The Classical Kami   This category includes three subcategories, the heavenly kami and the earthly kami, and a small group of named *marebito* (visiting kami), all of whom are named in one of the classical works such as the Kōjiki, the Nihonshōki, and the Engishiki. Many of these kami were included in those works in order to bolster the political status of one of the many aristocratic clans, including the imperial house, which ruled Japan during the eras before the Heian period. The assignation to one of the subclasses depended heavily on historical events: whether they were Yamato clans (and therefore, in most cases, their ancestor kami was defined as a heavenly kami), or were from one of the clans that were absorbed or conquered by the Yamato, such as clans from Izumo. In such a case, the ancestor kami were identified quite often as earthly kami and their status was, in general, lower.

1.1. The Heavenly Kami The named heavenly *kami* include those who appeared in heaven before the earth was created and those who are the descendants of these original *kami*. The relative status of these *kami*, and the degree to which there are myths about them, does not reflect their origin: It is a "second-generation" *kami*, the Sun deity Amaterasu, who is the chief deity. Next after her is a male, Takamimusubi-no-kami, who is one of the originals but who features far less, perhaps because he was the patron deity/ancestor of a lesser, or losing, clan in some long-forgotten internecine squabble.

1.1.1. The Original Kami Many of the *kami* of this category are barely defined in the myth beyond their name. These *kami* all come into existence from nothing, springing into being without any explanation. Some of them appear as single deities, while others appear as pairs (with the implication of male and female). The three exceptions to the barely defined characteristic are Takamimusubi, who seems to be (almost) equal to Amaterasu-ō-mikami, and the two founder deities, Izanagi and Izanami. Certainly Takamimusubi features as decision-maker and as major mover in a number of myths, notably in the work to pacify the Central Land of the Reed Plains. Izanagi and Izanami are, of course, the creators of the land, the true demiurges, bringers of both life and death, as well as the parents of a number of *kami*.

The male-female couples are often spouses as well as siblings. The ancient Japanese apparently saw nothing wrong in sibling incest, and marriages of siblings, half-siblings, and aunt and nephew are recorded in the *Nihonshōki* and the *Kōjiki*. This sat very uneasily with the Confucian-trained Japanese of later times (incest was strongly abhorred by the Chinese), and Motoori Norinaga, the popularizer and interpreter of the *Kōjiki* in the eighteenth century, had a hard time explaining the phenomenon in his *Kōjiki-den* (Commentary on the Kōjiki). He concluded by stating that since Japan's gods were unique and special, so too were their marital arrangements (and no backtalk from incredulous foreigners wanted!).

1.1.2. The Descendant Kami These are the children and descendants of the original *kami*. Most, though not all, are the descendants of Izanagi and Izanami, including Amaterasu-ō-mikami, the chief deity and Sun goddess, and her brother, Susano-wo, ruler of the netherworld and hero in his own right. Various of these descendant *kami* are named ancestors of Yamato clans, as they accompany the various expeditions that ensured the dominance of the heavenly *kami* over the land of Japan.

1.2. The Earthly Kami   As the heavenly *kami* interact with the denizens of the Earth, they discover a host of local *kami* has taken up residence, though, apparently, mismanaging their trust. Some of them, such as Ōkuninushi, are descendants of heavenly *kami* (in this case, Susano-wo), but they are clearly identified in the texts as earthly, not heavenly *kami*. The attitude in the classical writings was that they were more or less fine for their place and time but that they needed to learn a lot more respect, which the heavenly *kami* duly taught them. Many of the earthly *kami* were hospitable and supportive of the expeditions to subdue the land, and many such minor *kami* appear from rivers, the sea, and inside rocks or caves to support the triumphal progression of the heavenly grandson, Ninigi-no-mikoto, the heavenly *kami*'s representative.

1.3. Marebito: The Overseas Connection   The final class of *kami* found in the classical texts are visiting *kami* from over the sea. The two most notable ones are associated both with the creation of the land and its subjugation: Sukunabikona, who helps Ōkuninushi in creating the land, and Sarutahiko-no-kami, who helps to guide the heavenly grandson when he descends to subjugate the land. The idea of mysterious gods from over the sea is a recurrent theme in Japanese myth. It occurs as a Buddhist theme as well as a Shintō one, and similar features can be found in Ryukyuan myth and in Ainu tales, though in the latter case the overseas visitors are rarely benevolent.

2. The "New" Kami

More kami emerged (that is, were acknowledged and worshiped) after the classical texts were written. They may well have been worshiped before this time but did not have "official" recognition. They can be subdivided into two categories, neither mutually exclusive.

2.1. Officially Established Kami   This category includes *kami* that emerged, or were added to the list of known and officially acknowledged *kami* maintained by the authorities, after the classical writings had been finished. The two most important such deities are Hachiman, *kami* of war and culture, and Inari, *kami* of prosperity, grain, and commerce. Although both of these deities existed in local forms from a fairly early period, their continuing worship is due very largely to the establishment of major shrines in their honor during the Heian period by Buddhist priests. Hachiman became important to warrior families during the latter half of the Heian period, and his worship was intensified by the *kami* identification with Emperor Ōjin, who, it appears from the sources, was a formidable man (both intellectually and martially), and his mother, the Empress Jingū (a no-less-formidable woman, it appears). One myth recounts that Ōjin, then an elderly man, drank heavily of some excellent wine at a party. Later that night he walked tipsily home. He tripped on a stone that had been lying in the road. The enraged emperor shouted so fiercely at the stone that it got up and ran off the road! His mother, being engaged in the conquest of Korea while she was pregnant with the future emperor, tied a girdle hung with stones tightly around her waist and so delayed the birth for three years. It is possible that the Korean connection was also partly responsible for the renown of Hachiman: The rise of his popularity coincided with the loss of the Japanese colonies on the Korean Peninsula, and someone perhaps saw the need for a bit of spin-doctoring.

A second important *kami* in this category is Inari, who rivals Hachiman in the number of shrines erected to worship him. Rice deities were probably worshiped in many communities, and there is some argument that the main *kami* of the Yamato state may have been a food *kami*, displaced only later by the totemic deity of the imperial clan. Even so, Inari's emergence as a *national* deity of rice and prosperity was probably due, paradoxically, to Buddhist influence. By establishing temples that supported both Buddhist figures and a *kami* of prosperity, Buddhism ensured greater acceptance among the laity and commoners.

2.2. Upgraded Kami This category blends with the previous one. It includes a number of *kami* who were officially upgraded by the imperial court for one reason or another—political appointees, one might say. The most prominent of this category is Tenjin, *kami* of scholarship. His promotions (he was upgraded a number of times) were due to calamities that beset the imperial capital at Heian after the death in exile of a courtier, Sugawara Michizane. Sugawara was then deified as the *kami* Tenjin, and when the calamities did not stop, was upgraded in rank until he appeared satisfied, and the plagues and fires ceased. Recently deceased emperors, such as the Meiji emperor and the Shōwa emperor (better known outside Japan by his personal name, Hirohito), are also members of this category. Even retired politicians can receive this honor: Tokugawa Ieyasu, founder of the Tokugawa shogunal dynasty that ruled Japan for seventeen generations (1603–1868), was deified as a *gongen*, a *kami* who is recognized as avatar of a boddhisattva, and is worshiped at the magnificent shrine of Nikko Toshogū.

2.3. Kami from Buddhist Sources   A number of *kami* owe their existence to borrowings from the Buddhist pantheon. Thus both the Indian gods Indra and Brahma are worshiped as *kami* in Ryōbu Shintō (syncretic Shintō) rituals. So is the boddhisattva Kannon, seen by some as a Shintō *kami* who chose a Buddhist guise "because Buddhism is more feminine," as one worshiper said to me.

3. Local Kami

The final class of kami is a residual one. It contains all those kami who were not assimilated into the national cult. Sometimes they are identified with one or another of the formally recognized deities, often not. Various forms of Dosôjin (kami of the crossroads and of the phallus) and of Ryūjin (the dragon kami) are worshiped in rural areas throughout Japan, often in household or family contexts. Priests will conduct rituals at tiny field shrines, sometimes claiming that the deity worshiped is "really X-kami" (insert kami name of choice), while others, more humble, perhaps admit they have no idea which of the yaoyorozu-no-kami the kami is. Nor does it matter. The locals, meantime, happily continue to repeat the myths of "their" kami, usually relating to local events and places, that they heard from their grandparents.

All in all, the Japanese are remarkably laissez-faire about the myths they embrace or are prepared to embrace and accept. Although there are instances of people dismissing these stories as *mukashi banashi* (old legends, fairy tales), few people dismiss the myths entirely.

Buddhism

Buddhism emerged as a response to social and religious features of northern India in the fifth century B.C.E. Transmitted via a number of routes to China, it found its way to Japan as well. The transmission to Japan was not straightforward. The first injection of Buddhism into Japan came from the Paekche kingdom of Korea in the fifth century C.E. The Koreans were interested in "taming" their overseas Japanese cousins, both to avoid piratical and raiding pressure and to enlist them in their own fight against the rising power of Silla, another Korean kingdom. Not surprisingly, the major emphasis in this early Buddhism was on magic and material efficacy. Later, Japanese scholars—Ennin, Kūkai, and others—traveled to China, each one bringing back a different version of Buddhist belief, practice, and myth, which were incorporated both into local traditions and the traditions of the Japanese courts, depending on local presence and current political fashion and prestige.

Buddhism brought with it a number of important features. The most important one, perhaps, was the Buddhist focus on the afterlife and on salvation. In traditional Buddhist thought (i.e., that of Shakyamuni, the founder of Buddhism), death was a prelude either to rebirth or, if the believer practiced the right path (*dharma*), to a condition of Buddhahood where one was relieved from the burden of rebirth. In the Chinese context, these beliefs became embroidered into native Chinese beliefs of hell and retribution, and it was these beliefs and their associated practices that arrived in Japan. As a consequence, Buddhist practice was strongly focused on dealing with the afterlife and the dead.

A second feature is closely related to the first. In its migration from India to China via Tibet and Mongolia, Buddhism acquired large canons of elaborate rituals. Many of these rituals had to do with the dead (funerals, obsequies, memorials), but many of these rituals were concerned with efficacy, that is, with causing material changes in the world through the practice of the "right" ritual formula, of which there were many. The significant element here is that Buddhism brought with it the idea that one could, if one knew the correct formula, *directly* influence material outcomes.

Buddhism differed radically from Shintō in a number of ways. First, it was a "revealed" religion. It had a definite founder in the person of Shakyamuni Siddharta, a prince of the Sakya clan in what is now Nepal. Second, it was concerned with personal morality, salvation, and the afterlife. Third, it was a world religion, in the sense that its message was deliberately aimed at all humankind, not at a specific nation or culture. Not only that, but Buddhism has always acknowledged that life is widespread throughout the universe of time and place, and can take many local forms in different worlds. Fourth, as a consequence, it introduced the Japanese to a number of new philosophical and political concepts that had a major impact on their institutions and thinking.

Individual salvation is the core of Buddhist belief. The question of how an individual can be saved was solved in two different ways. Some Buddhist thinkers argued that individuals could not attain salvation by their own efforts. This "Other-salvation" party holds that it is by the mercy of a special person—a Buddha or boddhisattva—that an individual can reach paradise, or *nirvana*. Other thinkers argued that individuals can only be saved by their own efforts. This "Self-salvation" party, in contrast, therefore requires an individual to follow a rigorous regime of denial and discipline in order to be saved: something that not every person is capable of. This in effect means that *most* people will never reach the goal outlined by Shakyamuni. The "Other-salvation" party, it should be noted, argues that this is a contradiction: The Buddha could hardly be all-compassionate if he was only interested in saving himself, could he? Both of these viewpoints are supported, in different places, in the canon of Buddhist writings. Unsurprisingly, the "Other-salvation" party became more popular and is the basis for most Buddhist sects in Japan and in China. The "Self-salvation" party, popular today in Sri Lanka and Southeast Asia, nonetheless finds an echo in Japanese Buddhism in the form of Zen.

Buddhist Cosmology

The fundamental cosmological idea of Buddhism consists of two related syllogisms. First, that actions, good or bad, bring about consequences for the individual. Second, that the individual's ego or soul—some immaterial component of the self—lives, dies, and is then reincarnated in a form that is the consequences of that soul's previous actions. The fundamental truth that the Buddha preached, and which Buddhism as a religion adheres to, is that this process can be stopped, albeit through great effort. The trick, as we all know, is in the details.

There are three different types of realms in which this action takes place. The most exalted realm is the Realm of Formlessness, which has no material component. This is the realm of nirvana, the release from the recurrent cycle of birth. To reach that realm, one must be entirely in tune with the fundamental principles of the Buddhist Law. Below that exalted realm, which is characterized in different ways by different Buddhist sects, is a realm of fundamental material truths. This, the Realm of Form, has only some material qualities. In this realm the forces that underlie the material universe are played out. Its inhabitants are still part, albeit a detached part, of the process of birth, destruction, and rebirth of universes and living beings. Below these realms is the Realm of Desire. This is where all the action takes place. In it are six destinies corresponding to six classes of being, all of whom are struggling and living within the wheel of birth and rebirth.

The six destinies/classes of existence in the Realm of Desire are all related in that their inhabitants can, through the cycle of birth and rebirth, migrate from one to another, according to their deeds in a previous life. The first destiny is that of the gods, myriad of them, living in a multitude of heavens. The second is that of humans, both good and bad, saintly and otherwise. The third is that of the *shura*s, a class of spirit. The fourth is that of animals, both zoologically existing and mythological. The fifth and sixth levels, or destinies, are those of the hungry ghosts (those who have died an untimely death, or who have no one to care for them in the afterlife) and hell, where those who have been utterly evil suffer great torments.

The destiny of the gods contains a variety of heavens each presided over by a Buddha. Thus Miroku, the future Buddha, resides in one awaiting his time. Four heavenly kings, the Myō-ō, inhabit another. The Pure Land Paradise of the West may be a third: It is there that good people would go, awaiting Amida Buddha's mercy for final salvation in nirvana, that is, ascending to the Realm of Formlessness.

Six Jizō protecting the six destinies of living beings. (Courtesy of the author)

Buddhist cosmology also accepts the existence of an infinitude of universes, each unbounded, each open to salvation by its own Buddha. The Lotus Sutra (one of the main books in the Buddhist canon), for instance, mentions 3×10^{18} Buddhas. That's three billion billion. Most of these are faceless and nameless. In *this* universe, on *this* world, the Buddha is (or in some versions, is heralded by) the historical Buddha Shakyamuni. Shakyamuni, who now resides in the Realm of Formlessness, was in previous lives a boddhisattva, a resident of the Realm of Form who in his infinite compassion returned to the Realm of Desire in order to assist others to free themselves from that Realm. Born in some unknown eon as a man, he gradually made his way to the Realm of Formlessness. In some traditions he is thought of as the seventh, and final, in a series of Buddhas to have appeared; in others he is considered the twenty-fourth (the numbers reflect Indian numerology more than any reasoned figure).

Brief History of Buddhism in Japan
The peculiarities of Japanese Buddhism owe much to two sources: the influence of Shintō, and the freedom with which Japanese chose from the vast mass of beliefs, practices, and philosophies offered to them under the name Buddhism. Though the main cosmological points are more or less agreed to by all, differences

Buddha Amida in contemplative pose: the Kamakura Daibutsu. (Courtesy of the author)

in nuances of interpretation have led to the creation of a number of different forms of Buddhism—sects—that still flourish today in Japan.

The arrival of Buddhism in Japan was a gradual process. Starting with personal importation of images and books, by the time the king of Paekche had sent his famous image of Dainichi to the Japanese emperor there already was a substrate of people who were sympathetic to the new religion. As mentioned earlier, Buddhism was formally introduced into Japan in the sixth century from Korea in an attempt at political and cultural pacification. The king of Paekche, a Korean kingdom with linguistic, cultural, and blood ties to the Yamato court, sent several Buddhist images, a number of teachers, scrolls, and artists to the Yamato court. This was an attempt to mitigate the raids of Japanese corsairs on Korea, as well as to initiate closer political and military cooperation against the rising power of Silla, Paekche's rival on the peninsula. Several decades of opposition in Japan were insufficient to dampen the enthusiasm for the new doctrine. After a period of some fifty years of resistance by major imperial clans, notably the Mononobe warriors and the Nakatomi priests, Buddhism was adopted as the court religion. Buddhist practices were adopted at court and were formally supported by Shōtoku Taishi, the imperial regent. By the seventh century several Buddhist sects were operating in Japan, though only one of those early sects, the Hosso, is still extant today.

These sects were largely established in the capital of the time, Nara. But by 741, the government had decreed the establishment of *kokubunji* (provincial branch temples) in each province. These began to spread Buddhist doctrine, and, what was no less important, gradually took over two government functions: They became the registrars of birth (because support of the temples was allocated to local families, this was at first limited to the gentry only, but in later centuries all households were registered) and of death (because the temples also took over the performances of rituals for the dead, which Shintō generally lacked).

Japanese Buddhism is divided into a number of "schools," or sects, more or less the equivalent of different Christian denominations, which arrived in Japan, or were formulated in Japan, at different points in history. The period 550 to 850 C.E. was a period of importation. Different Chinese Buddhist sects were brought back by visiting scholars from Japan. The two most important and influential sects that have come down to us from that period are Tendai and Shingon. Zen was brought to Japan some time later. The last of those importations was the Zen Ōbaku sect, which was imported in the seventeenth century. Jōdō, a major Buddhist sect, though based on Chinese ideas, was essentially a Japanese sect. Certainly this is true of its large and fractious offshoot, Jōdō Shinshū. Last on the scene of the large Buddhists sects was Nichiren-shū, in the fifteenth century.

Differences between sects are the effect of emphasis on one or another aspect of Buddhist doctrine—a very complex subject well beyond the scope of this book. Each sect has selected particular constellations of important sutras and writings, and with them particular deities and rituals. Each such school tends to define a "central" Buddha (Amida is the most popular) but in a slightly different (but significant to the practitioners) way. For our purposes, it also means that different Buddhist schools will emphasize different mythological beings. Nonetheless, most schools (Nichiren-shū and Jōdō Shinshū being the major exceptions) will acknowledge the importance of most other deities or figures, whether or not they consider the figure central to their doctrine, since there is a potentially infinite number of Buddhas.

Each one of these sects draws from the same, or at least a similar, pool of anecdotes, myths, and images, but lays emphasis on a segment of this vast pool. The *religious* differences between the sects may be profound, but the *mythological* differences are more a matter of selecting one myth rather than another as being worthy of repetition.

The strong influence of Buddhist ideas and symbology, including myths, was due to another institution that the Buddhist temples, particularly in the countryside, took upon themselves: education. Virtually every town and moderately sized village from the seventeenth century onward had a *teragoya*, a temple school, where the local commoner boys (the *bushi* boys were educated in their own schools) could get an excellent education, albeit one permeated by a Buddhist flavor. The graduates of these schools often went on to become successful merchants, landowners, and craftsmen, and, no less significantly, as Bellah (1957) argues, were inspired, like the Protestants of late Medieval Europe, to go forth and succeed as a way of glorifying God.

The following paragraphs are a brief introduction to the major existing Buddhist sects in Japan, more or less in order of their historical appearance.

Tendai

The Tendai (Heaven's Peak) school of Buddhism was introduced from China, together with the Shingon school, at the beginning of the ninth century. In China, Tientai was a thriving sect, but in Japan it became a powerful independent organization, threatening, at times, the emperor himself from its headquarters on Mt. Hiei, northeast of the capital Heian-kyō. The various temples of the school did not necessarily get along, and the long feud between Miidera on the shores of Lake Biwa and Enryakuji on Mt. Hiei broke out into violence from time to time.

Tendai was founded on the basis of the Lotus Sutra by Saichō, a monk who had been ordained in 785, collected a small band of monks on Mt. Hiei not far from the capital, and was eventually sent to China in 804 by the emperor. There he studied Zen, Shingon, and Tendai (to give these sects their Japanese names), eventually choosing the last to propagate in Japan when he returned to found a temple at the site of his old monastery. Other temples and monasteries were soon founded nearby, and Mt. Hiei eventually became a complex containing three thousand temples and about twenty thousand monks. Many of these were *sōhei,* or monk-soldiers. Originally temple guards, by the thirteenth century and after they had become marauders and bullies, ever ready to riot and descend upon the streets of the capital below at the slightest excuse. The most famous of these fighting monks, one who became a figure of myth, was Benkei, who not only stole the bell of Miidera (he was himself a partisan of Enryakuji) but disrupted traffic in the capital itself.

Tendai teaches that any individual can become a Buddha. They can do so by following the eightfold path of the Buddha. Tendai accepts all the Buddhist scriptures and writings, viewing their complexity as a developing and unfolding truth: As one achieves one stage of wisdom, a further stage beckons. In the ninth century, Tendai came under the influence of Shingon (another sect, described below) and became more mystical, describing these development stages in mystical and artistic terms.

Tendai also recognizes four paradises, each one for a different type of inhabitant. There is a paradise in which ordinary people and saints live together, there is a paradise of those who have freed themselves from rebirth and attained per-

sonal nirvana, there is a paradise for boddhisattvas, and there is the final paradise of Dainichi Nyōrai, inhabited by Buddhas and those who have rid themselves of ignorance.

Shingon
Shingon (True Word) was introduced from China by Kūkai, better known by his
posthumous Buddhist title as Kōbō Daishi. Probably the most celebrated figure
in Japanese Buddhism, he is reputed to have invented the katakana and hiragana
syllabaries and was a miracle worker, writer, painter, and sculptor. He studied in
China from 804 to 806 at the Golden Dragon temple of the Qen-yen ("True
Word") sect. When he returned to Japan he founded a monastery on Mt. Kōya,
away from the capital Heian-kyō, perhaps because he did not want to compete
with Saichō, who had established himself and the Tendai sect on Mt. Hiei at
about the same time. Upon Saichō's death, Kōbō Daishi was appointed the
emperor's chaplain. He died at Kōyasan in 835.

Shingon is characterized by two features: a reliance on magical formulae by
which an individual may acquire power, and the worship and acceptance of a
large host of deities of Hindu, Buddhist, and Shintō origins. In fact, many Shingon temples were constructed to protect and honor local popular deities in Japan.
Shingon has an outer (exoteric) and inner (esoteric) doctrine. The first is to be
found in the teachings of Shakyamuni; the latter is communicated secretly to
Shingon adepts. Only a person who has been properly indoctrinated and who performs the proper Shingon rites can ascend to the true consciousness of Dainichi
Nyōrai, who is the supreme Buddha.

Shingon is a very cosmotheist sect: The whole universe is regarded as the
body of Dainichi Nyōrai. His body is composed of six elements: ether, air, fire,
water, earth, and consciousness. These are symbolized in *sotoba*, small pillars
found on the grounds of Shingon temples, consisting of a ball, crescent, pyramid,
sphere, and cube placed one atop the other, standing for ether, air, fire, water,
and earth, the surrounding atmosphere standing for consciousness. Shingon also
allocates a place for the Pure Land, or paradise, of Amida, saying that it is located
everywhere that people meditate on Amida in the Shingon way!

Shingon is the source for some of the most popular Buddhist deities in Japan:
the Myō-ō, particularly Fudō Myō-ō, who are widely worshiped in Shingon. The
same is true of the boddhisattvas Jizō and Kannon. A large number of Hindu
deities have also found a place in Shingon in the form of boddhisattvas and gods.
Because all are considered reflections of Dainichi, it is not surprising that Shingon is a very broad and accepting church.

An important graphic feature of Japanese Buddhism that owes much to
Shingon propagation is the use of *mandara* (mandala), a schematic illustration

of Dainichi's power and virtue. A *mandara* usually shows illustrations of deities and saints confined within a circle or other geometric figure upon which one can focus one's meditations. Two of these *mandara* are particularly important in Shingon: the *Kongōkai* (Diamond mandala) and the *Taizōkai* (Womb mandala). The Diamond mandala is bright and eternal, like the ideas of Dainichi. All the saints and deities are contained within the universe of Dainichi like children in their mothers' wombs in the Taizōkai. The Diamond mandala is mainly white in color, the Womb mainly red. The deities and saints portrayed have specific headdresses, attitudes, positions, and objects in their hands, all of which have esoteric significance. Some of these symbols have become translated into general mythology and are associated as physical (rather than symbolic) elements with particular deities.

Jōdō

Founded by Hōnen (1133–1226), the Jōdō (Pure Land) sect is based, as is Jōdō Shinshū, on the worship of Amida, the merciful Buddha of the Pure Land. The focus of the sect is to show the common person how to be reborn into Amida's paradise. The only way to do so is to trust solely and wholly in the benevolence of Amida. Amida himself became a Buddha by making a series of vows to save humankind. The salvation consists of being reborn in the Pure Land of the West. The way to enter paradise is simply to recite the nembutsu prayer: the formula Namu Amida-butsu, or "Hail Buddha Amida." The prayer should be repeated as often as possible to ensure salvation, and repetitions of ten or a hundred thousand during a day or week are not uncommon. Though Jōdō mythology centers around Amida, the founder, Hōnen accepted that other beings, deities, and boddhisattvas were worthy of respect and even worship, just so long as the faithful repeated the nembutsu.

Jōdō Shinshū

Founded by Hōnen's disciple, Shinran (1173–1262), Jōdō Shinshū (True sect Pure Land) takes the belief in Amida a step further. Worship is offered only to Amida, and salvation is to be attained solely by faith. In fact, even without reaching paradise, which one does after death, the true believer in the salvation of Amida immediately receives the benefits and is saved. Unlike previous sects and religions, Shinshū introduced a new element into Japanese religion: the scourge of religious particularism. Thus Shinshū members are expected to reject other religious practices and works and devote themselves to belief in Amida. Nonetheless, there are several persons considered worthy of veneration by the faithful: Shinran, who founded the sect; the seven preceding patriarchs, including Jōdō's Hōnen and Shōtoku Taishi, the minister and scholar who introduced Buddhism into Japan;

and Amida himself. Shakyamuni (Shaka in Japanese), the historical Buddha, is regarded as a reincarnation of Amida, in his form as Teacher. And though no other deities are worshiped or addressed in prayers or rituals, it is recognized that the numberless Buddhas, boddhisattvas, and deities are all contained in Amida.

Zen

The Zen (Emptiness) sect has several subsects that agree on principles and aims, and disagree on methods. In Japanese (and Chinese) tradition, Zen was brought to the Shōrin temple in China by a Buddhist monk and master named Boddhidarma. Known as Daruma in Japanese, he may be entirely mythical. Zen was introduced into Japan from China by Eisai (1141–1215) and by Dōgen (1200–1253). Under the Hōjō steward-regents who ruled in Kamakura, the administrative capital, during the Japanese Middle Ages, it was patronized by members of the bushi (warrior) caste. Zen was antiintellectual and surprisingly practical-oriented though it supported monasteries, and it claims to be based more on feelings and emotions than on rationality.

Zen has three major divisions—Sōtō, the largest, Rinzai, and Ōbaku—which agree on most points of doctrine. Sōtō emphasizes gradual enlightenment through training, and Rinzai emphasizes sudden enlightenment (often quite abrupt: a quick smack to the top of the head is considered one excellent way to attain enlightenment). Ōbaku, the latest to be introduced (in 1654), favors sudden enlightenment like Rinzai but also through meditation on the *nembutsu* (calling on Amida's name—a Jōdō practice). *Satori* (enlightenment), unfortunately, is not an easy term to explain. Basically, Zen thinking holds that those who have experienced it cannot teach it, and those who have not experienced it cannot understand it. An analogy from a common Zen parable is useful here:

> In a pond were many tadpoles. They swam about in their watery world, puzzled, sometimes, by the glow that rose, progressed across the ceiling of their domain, then disappeared. The glow was warm, bright, pleasant. One day, one of them turned, as tadpoles do, into a frog. Reveling in its new freedom, the frog hopped onto a lotus leaf, and observed the dry world outside the pond. When he hopped back and dove into the water, the tadpoles asked him to explain, at last, the mystery of the glow they had so yearned for.
>
> "It is a perfect circle" said the frog.
>
> "Circle?" queried the tadpoles.
>
> "It is bright enough to bring tears to your eyes," said the frog after some thinking.
>
> "Tears?" asked the tadpoles.
>
> Whatever explanation the frog gave, he found that the tadpoles lacked the basic concepts to understand his explanation. Finally, the exasperated frog

Rinzal Zen "Leaping Tiger Garden," Nanzen-ji Temple, Kyoto. (C. Rennie/ArkReligion.com)

growled that there was only one way the tadpoles could possibly understand what the sun was: to turn into frogs themselves.

Satori is thus whatever a Zen adept is searching for. It has been compared to reaching nirvana, and also to a complete unification of the inner person. *Satori* may arrive suddenly and in the most mundane of circumstances (it came to Battabara as he was entering the bath), or after many years of intensive study and meditation, as it came to the Buddha Shakyamuni. Many Zen practitioners follow a monastic way of life in which hard conditions and regulated lifestyles help in shedding the distractions of this world and achieving *satori;* others live entirely mundane lives.

Any deity is acceptable in a Zen temple because all are either equally worthless and unimportant or equally valuable. The Buddha venerated (though not prayed to) is Shaka, the historical Buddha.

Nichiren-shū
Founded in 1255 by Nichiren (1222–1282), a bellicose priest from the Kantō (the area around modern Tokyo), this is the most extreme case of particularism in Japanese religions. Nichiren preached that only the worship of Dainichi Nyōrai through the medium of the Lotus Sutra is the proper Buddhism. He identified Dainichi, Buddha of the Sun, with Amaterasu-ō-mikami, and the religion he preached was intensely nationalistic. His fanaticism was so extreme that he predicted that calamities would befall the Kamakura shogunate unless other sects were suppressed. Those prophecies proved (somewhat) true when Japan was invaded in 1274 and again in 1281 by Mongol fleets that were defeated only by apparent divine intervention, for which Nichiren claimed credit. His sect took off after that. Nichiren-shū teachings emphasize the adoration and study of one single sutra—Hokke-kyō (the Lotus Sutra), and adherents are expected to repeat the formula Namu-myoho rengei-kyō (Hail to the sutra of divine law) as the only way to eternal life. To this day a number of very large socioreligious movements are based on Nichiren teachings: Rissho-koseikai and Sōka Gakkai number millions of members each.

Buddhist Deities
The mythological figures of Buddhism all fit, more or less, into the cosmological scheme described above, and their popularity or lack of it relates to support and "official" recognition and adoration by one or more of the sects. In a real practical sense, there are five central Buddhas—one for each of the five cardinal directions (in Asia this includes the center)—of whom Amida (Buddha of the West), Dainichi Nyōrai (of the Center), Yakushi Nyōrai (of the East), and, of course, Shakyamuni himself are the main figures in Japan. Either the five Celestial Buddhas are considered aspects of the one Buddha Shakyamuni, or he is considered a reflection of one (or all) of them: The details differ according to the sect.

In Buddhist tradition, Shakyamuni, an Indian prince, became enlightened into Buddhahood. Before the death of his corporeal form, he instructed his followers in a set of reasonably simple ethical and behavioral practices. Buddhas have no interest or need to intervene in mundane affairs: They have no desires nor wants. To overcome the need people have for help in their daily lives, Buddhist thinkers came up with the idea of the *boddhisattva:* someone capable of achieving Buddhahood, who has decided to delay this state in order to assist in the salvation of others. With time, some Buddhist schools also proposed the idea of Buddhas as active players in the world: creators, saviors, rulers, of heavenly realms. These entities functioned in much the same way as the Gods of the Western world. In fact, in both Chinese and Japanese thought, they were often *identified* with local gods/*kami*. The Buddha, in some doctrines, has three bodies: A human form in which he appears to humanity; a body of bliss, in which he manifests in paradise or nirvana; and a body of law, which is the true body and cannot be described as having existence or nonexistence. In another view of the same concept, the Buddha Shakyamuni has, by his good deeds (in revealing the Law) acquired a spiritual power that allows him to appeal to humankind, and has become the "perfect man." He can also appeal to those like the boddhisatvas, who are on a higher plane of existence, revealing the true Buddha nature. These two bodies are provisional, assumed for the purpose. His real body is pure "suchness" without taint, imperfection, or emotion. Much more elaborate schemes of ten, twenty, and more bodies of the Buddha are also extant among Buddhist philosophers and theologians. An analogy in the West is the Kabbalah, a Jewish mystical system much studied by Christian theologians, in which the monad nature of the Creator and God is divided into subunits following a logical progression of functions and opposites.

Disregarding for a moment the extensive scholarly analysis and enumeration of the different Buddhas and deities in Buddhist mythology throughout Asia, we shall try to make sense of the plethora of different deities mentioned in the Japanese context. Doing so, we must keep in mind that this description is necessarily a vast simplification of the qualities and the nature of the Buddha. It is also necessary to remember four other features of Buddhist mythology:

- The deities mentioned here are not universal. Some Japanese Buddhist sects do consider them part of the pantheon, others do not.
- Many Buddhist sects consider particular figures to be reflections, or *avatars*, of a limited number of, or even one, "original" or "central" Buddha. Nonetheless, the laypeople, even of that sect, will consider these avatars to be wholly functioning, independent entities.
- The term *god* or even *deity* is inappropriate, because many of these figures are more similar to the saints and miracle-workers of Western tradition. In actual common usages, the Buddhas, gods, saints, and abbots are *shoson* (venerated persons), and they, in effect, following the doctrine of transmigration, can and will metamorphose from one to the other.
- There is no one authoritative statement of creed, as there is in Christianity, Islam, or Judaism, to name but a few.

Bearing the above in mind, we can, nonetheless, try to establish some sort of classification of the various figures. This classification is a modification, for reasons of clarity, of the commonly accepted (keeping the first feature from the list above in mind!) classes of venerated beings.

1. The Buddhas: Butsu and Nyōrai. A Buddha is a being who has detached himself (it is possible for females as well, but because females are generally held in low regard in Buddhism, they usually become males first, before being able to attain this status) from the Wheel of Being and has entered nirvana, where he is not touched by the passions of the world or by the need for action. Buddhas reside/exist in the Realm of Formlessness. They are highly compassionate, but because of their state, do little in the world directly: They act through their reflections/avatars or lesser beings. Three of the Buddhas—Dainichi, Yakushi, and Shaka—traditionally have the title *nyōrai* (lord) appended to their names. Others have the title *butsu*. A number of other mythological figures are mentioned as having attained the status of butsu (Buddha). As butsu, they rarely interact with humans (or even with one another, at least mythologically). They merely exist in the timeless frame of the Realm of Formlessness.

The four Buddhas named below are the central Buddhas in Japanese mythology. That is to say, they tend to be worshiped more than others, are commonly represented in art and sculpture, and are worshiped in person. This is not to say that, with the exception of Shaka, they feature heavily in mythological texts. If and when they do appear, it is at the climax, as proof of their mercy and compassion.

Amida-butsu (Sanskrit: Amitabha), Amida Nyōrai: Probably the most commonly worshiped Japanese Buddha of all, Amida is formally the Buddha of the Western Paradise. Worship of Amida, the Buddha of salvation and faith, is accomplished by meditating on his name or by reciting a simple formula: *Namu* (or *Namo) Amida-butsu* (Hail the Buddha Amida), called the *nembutsu.* Amida is barely mentioned in the Lotus Sutra, and his worship probably originated in central Asia, perhaps based on an Iranian original. He may well have emerged from Zoroastrian scriptures, which worship him in a similar way to the Amidists. In Zoroastrianism, those who pray to Ahura-Mazda and rely on his mercy will end in the Paradise of Boundless Light, which they may attain if they repeat the proper formula. In Amidist thought, Amida is to be found everywhere, and all other Buddhas and deities are merely reflections of the one central reality. Shakyamuni, the historical Buddha, is little more than a forerunner, a sort of John the Baptist to Amida's Christ. According to Amidists, humans are too weak and foolish to save themselves, and only reliance on Amida's boundless mercy can bring them into his paradise. The giant seated bronze Buddha of Kamakura, which often adorns travel brochures and other "things Japanese," is of Amida.

Dainichi Nyōrai, also known as *Roshana Butsu (Sanskrit: Vairocana):* The Buddha of the sun and of the origin of the universe, Dainichi may be the original creator as well. He is the principle object of worship in Shingon, and the large statue at Nara—the largest bronze statue in existence until the modern era, housed in the Tōdaiji temple—is of him. Like Amida, he is viewed by his adherents as the original Buddha, with all other Buddhas being his reflections. This is particularly true of the Nichiren sect, which does not recognize other Buddhas at all.

Shaka Nyōrai (Sanskrit: Shakyamuni; also *Siddhartha,* his personal name, and *Gautama Buddha):* The historical Buddha Shakyamuni is honored by the Nichiren sect but largely ignored by Jōdō and Jōdō Shinshū, where he is eclipsed by Amida. Nichiren regards Shaka as the only manifest Buddha, the avatar of Dainichi Nyōrai. Shaka's life has been described in brief above. In most sects he is seen at least as the great teacher, the Buddha of his age. He is one of the central Buddhas for the schools of the Zen sect.

Yakushi Nyōrai (Sanskrit: Baishajyaguru): The Buddha of healing and of restoration, Yakushi is Lord of the Eastern Paradise. His power is to heal ills, not only of the body but of the soul. Given his healing powers, he is obviously important to laypeople, though he is eclipsed by most other central Buddhas.

2. The Bosatsu (Boddhisattvas). The second class of beings addressed in Japanese Buddhism are the bosatsu. A Buddha is someone who has attained enlightenment and has entered nirvana. A boddhisattva is, by definition originating in India, a being who though capable of attaining Buddhahood, has decided to remain in the Wheel of Life (that is, will be constantly reborn, and has the will and ability to act) in order to assist others to attain enlightenment and start the process toward Buddhahood themselves. This does ignore the issue of Amida's infinite mercy and his active benevolence, but there you are. Successful religions do not have to be consistent, only glorious. Boddhisattvas in effect miss perfection by a hair, albeit a deliberate hair.

Unsurprisingly, the various *bosatsu* tend to be the most venerated and adored figures in Japan. Statues of Jizō and of Kannon, in one of the recognized formal variants, can be found everywhere in Japan, and new ones are still erected today. Several giant statues of Kannon carved of stone or concrete have been erected in Japan in the past two decades.

In theory there can be innumerable *bosatsu,* but in practice Japanese mythology considers a limited number of named ones. Most of these are of Indian origin. The four most important *bosatsu* (in terms of their interest to the Japanese) are beings without antecedent or historical-scriptural context. They are:

Jizō-bosatsu (Sanskrit: Kshitigarbha): Protector of the dead, and particularly

Twelfth-century Boddhisatva. (J. Stanley/ArkReligion.com)

of dead children and aborted embryos, Jizō is portrayed as a saintly baby-faced monk carrying a *shaku* (priest's staff topped with rings) and sometimes holding the Jewel of Mercy. Statues of Jizō can be found throughout Japan, often dressed in a red bib and cap—the sign of childhood. These are donations from anxious parents who have lost a child, or whose child is ill. Quite often these statues have small piles of pebbles before them, as one of Jizō's tasks is to aid the spirits of dead children in building these small mounds.

Kannon-bosatsu (Sanskrit: Avalokiteshvara): The personification of absolute mercy. Kannon originated in India as a young man, but along the way to Japan, through China, he underwent a sex change and became a female. Kannon is the fount of mercy, but she can also bestow immortality on the deserving, sprinkling them with the bottle of Waters of Life she carries. One common way of portraying her is as a willowy woman in monk's robes, with a tall headdress, carrying a vase (usually interpreted by laypeople as a bottle of Waters of Life) and a lotus bud, indicating that mercy is the foundation of the Buddhist Law (the lotus).

Miroku-bosatsu (Sanskrit: Maitreya): This is the Buddha of the future, who waits, hidden, until the right time to appear, and who will save all living things. In common with other Buddhist figures, Miroku has many guises, among them Hōtei, one of the seven gods of good fortune.

Monju-bosatsu (Sanskrit: Manjusri): The boddhisattva of learning and of the law, Monju supports those engaged in earnest effort to be good Buddhists. He is often featured in monasteries and temples dedicated to learning and repeating the scriptures.

Other Bosatsu: A number of other *bosatsu*, less commonly portrayed than the five above, also feature in Japanese consciousness. They include:

Fugen-bosatsu. Riding a white six- or nine-tusked elephant, Fugen is likely to appear to those who are engaged in meditation upon the Law. The elephant represents the earthly presence of the Buddha, that is, Shaka Nyōrai.

Hōkai Kokūzō-bosatsu. He is the Buddha of wisdom and is usually dressed as a pilgrim and sage, carrying a ring-topped staff. He appears in five manifestations as the Go Dai Kokūzō. He is particularly important because of his association with Kōbō Daishi, the most important Japanese saint.

Seishi-bosatsu. In most representations of Amida, the deity is flanked by Kannon on one side and by the lesser known and less-worshiped Seishi-bosatsu on the other. Seishi-bosatsu (Sanskrit: Vasubandhu) and his brother, Muchaku-bosatsu, were sages in India. Seishi founded the Yogacara school of Buddhism, which eventually led to the belief in Other-salvation. Muchaku ascended to heaven and acquired the Buddha Law from Miroku.

3. The Gods.   In the Buddhist scheme of things, the deities rank lower than the Buddhas and boddhisattvas. Unlike the two previous categories, deities are still enmeshed in life, and it is by their efforts to protect the Law that they aspire to reach membership in the higher categories. Thus they serve as protectors and defending deities. In Buddhist mythology their function is to protect the Buddhist Law, or particular aspects of it. In many cases they have made a vow to live in the world in this way.

This category can be split into a number of subcategories based more on their popular associations than on their nature (ferocious or tranquil) or history. We thus have a number of groups of deities that often occur together in statuary, paintings, or myths. Many of these have manifold identities: Some are the more martial aspects of the gentle *bosatsu*, the Buddhist equivalent of the *aramitama* of the Shintō *kami*. Some appear in more than one group, assuming different names and attributes, but considered (at least according to priests and scholars) to be "the same as" one in another group.

Ten (Sanskrit: Devas; protective gods): This subcategory includes a number of deities, mostly of Indian origin, who command armies of gods and lesser spirits devoted to protecting Buddhism and the Buddhist Law. The most important of the *ten* are the four heavenly kings who have taken a vow to protect Mt. Meru, the home of the gods and the symbol of the ascent to Buddhahood. The four, generally called the *shitenno* (four heavenly kings), are:

- Bishamon-ten (Sanskrit: Vaisravana), also called Tamon-ten. He is the defender of the North and appears in full Chinese armor, carrying a reliquary and a spear.
- Jikoku-ten (Sanskrit: Dhrtarastra) carries a trident and rests his foot on the head of a demon. He is the defender of the East.
- Zōchō-ten (Sanskrit: Virudhaka). Armored like his peers, he carries a polearm or holds a drawn sword and stands on a demon. He defends the West.
- Kōmoku-ten (Sanskrit: Virupaksa). Armored as well, he carries a scroll and wields a baton. His domain is the South.

Two other *ten* (out of a larger list) are of great importance and originate with major Hindu gods. They are:

- Bon-ten. Originally Brahma, the Hindu god of creation. In Japan he protects warriors who fight in his name and follow the Law.
- Taishaku-ten, originally Indra, the Hindu god of warriors. Like Bon-ten, he is a deity of warriors who defend the Law.

The Myō-ō (bright kings): Developed mainly in esoteric Buddhist sects such as Tendai, these beings are the personification of the essences of Buddhist law. They are active principles in the lives of individuals, and reflections, as it were, of the Buddhas. They are the martial counterparts of the mild *bosatsu.* The distinction between *bosatsu* and these gods is a thin one. *Bosatsu* tend to be more personal, and "softer" or "feminine," whereas the Bright Kings tend to be more aggressively male and to be the defenders of principles rather than of persons. There are, of course, exceptions, and the *bosatsu* can be powerful warrior protectors (as Jizō was protector of Shōtoku Taishi), just as Maha Mayuri, one of the Myō-ō, is generally portrayed as a gentle supporter.

The Myō-ō are nonetheless generally regarded, and portrayed as, fierce deities. Two of them, at least, have been borrowed from Hinduism. They have sworn oaths to protect Buddhism, or specific aspects of it. Fudō Myō-ō (Sanskrit: Acala) is probably the most popular of the Myō-ō and is often the center of worship in Tendai temples. In Shingon temples, Fudō Myō-ō is the protector and patron of the *goma* fire ritual. Aizen Myō-ō is another popular member of this group. Gundari Myō-ō (Gundari) has eight arms and is surrounded by flames. He carries a *sanko* (three-pronged diamond weapon), spear, wheel, and battle-ax, and performs the crossed arms *mudra* (hand gesture) with the remaining two arms. Maha Mayuri (the only one of the Myō-ō who is not ferocious) is generally portrayed as a woman, or at least a feminized figure. Other Myō-ō are Batō Myō-ō, Buteki Myō-ō, Dai-Itoku Myō-ō, Dairin Myō-ō, Gozanze Myō-ō, Munō sho Myō-ō, and Shozanze Myō-ō.

The Myō-ō are often the central images in temples of the Tendai sect. In other sects they may have separate halls established for their worship within the grounds of a larger temple. They can be regarded as personifications of attributes necessary for the protection of Buddhism. This means that though there might be myths associated with them ("Fudo appeared to me in a dream . . .") there are very few myths in which they feature as major protagonists, unlike the Shintō deities. Their ferocity (Maha Mayuri excepted) is an iconic representation of the power of protection they offer in their particular "area of expertise."

The Ni-ō (two guardian kings): The Ni-ō are the two guardians of temple precincts. They are giants, exhibiting fierce scowls, and can be seen as statues or paintings at the gates of almost all major temples in Japan. Sometimes they are identified with Aizen Myō-ō and Fudō Myō-ō. More often they are thought to be deities in their own right. They have Shintō counterparts in the form of depictions of armed Heian-period generals who sometimes flank the entrances to major Shintō shrines.

Hachi-bu-shu (Sanskrit: Ashura; eight messengers of the Buddha): These are the eight classes of supernatural beings converted by Buddha to be his disciples. They are usually arrayed with the *Ju Dai deshi* (ten major disciples) around the Buddha Shakyamuni. This class of beings is generally undifferentiated. They feature, if at all, as figures that surround the Buddha while he sleeps or preaches.

Gongen (local deities, avatars): Most of the deities and Myō-ō are transformations, into the Buddhist canon, of extant Hindu or Buddhist deities from India. They came to Japan already part of the vast Buddhist array of worthy beings. The *gongen* category, in contrast, is made up of deities who are protectors, or essences of a particular place in Japan, most commonly a mountain. The *gongen* are *kami* considered to be the avatars of boddhisattvas. They, like the Myō-ō, are fierce figures, martially attired, and are called upon in times of war and trouble. They include the deification of real historical persons such as Tokugawa Ieyasu, founder of the Tokugawa dynasty of shoguns, who after a century of warfare brought stability and peace to Japan in the early seventeenth century; Amaterasu-ō-mikami; and other *kami*.

4. *Kōsō soshi* (Eminent Religious Figures).   A number of historical figures—predominately the founders of Buddhist sects and disciples of the Buddha Shakyamuni—have become mythologized through the devotion of their disciples or the fame of their magical acts. Of those, the most important is undoubtedly Kōbō Daishi, the founder of the esoteric Shingon sect, but popular in Japan as the devisor of the syllabary alphabet, founder of a major pilgrimage route, civil engineer, and sculptor. Others include En-no-Gyōja, a wizard and legendary founder of the Shugendō sect; Nichiren; and the founders of other major Buddhist sects.

Of perhaps lesser religious importance, but often greater popular reverence and prominence, are a large number of minor Buddhist functionaries—abbots, disciples, hermits, and the like—who feature in stories that have struck the imagination of the populace. Examples are Battabara, usually titled *bosatsu*, who is the patron of the bath in Buddhist monasteries; Fu-Daishi, patron of libraries; and Binzuru-sonja, a disciple of the Buddha who through a bizarre twist of fate became the patron of healing.

DEMONS, GOBLINS, WITCHES, GHOSTS, HERMITS, AND WIZARDS

The story of Japanese mythology would not be complete without accounting for the plethora of figures—demons and witches, goblins and ghosts—that, though interwoven with the "religious" mythology, do not have any "official" existence in religious consciousness. These figures are nonetheless very important as myths, or elements in myths.

These figures derive from the interaction of local people with the mysterious and unexplained in their lives. Some of them owe their existence to popular Japanese interpretations of Chinese stories that were fables of Daoist, Buddhist, Chan (Zen), or popular origin. They are in no sense systematized, though in many instances such persons or creatures feature (often as the villains) in the Great Tradition myths. They are "outlying" myths in the sense that though they were very real and feature prominently in the myths of the common people, they rarely had any official existence. On occasion the elite who control the Great Tradition would adopt one or another of these elements into the Great Tradition myths. In a very rough division, these figures can be divided into human and nonhuman figures, though the division is often very blurred. Another possible categorization is between classes of creatures on the one hand—ghosts, *tengu*—which are not generally personalized—and actual personalities—Gama-sennin and Yuima Kōji—from Japanese, Chinese, or Indian traditions.

Humans

Many of the human figures that are described in myth are of Chinese Daoist origin. Philosophical Daoism, which coalesced after the publication of Lao-tze's *Tao-te Ching* and the *Chuan-tze,* was a sociophilosophical belief at whose center stood the individual hermit. Daoism has always been heavily permeated by Chinese religious beliefs in ghosts and demons, and with the transfer of these beliefs to Japan, these mythological creatures came along for the ride. Thus one character, Shōki, reputedly a wronged official in China who had vowed to fight all demons after his suicide, became popular in Japan as a suppresser of *oni* (demons).

Quite a few of these mythical characters have more of an existence in art than in actual mythological discourse. But they were available, as it were, in Japan's traditional but highly literate society, to fill mythical niches as required.

Non-humans

Several "tribes" of nonhuman creatures also populate Japanese myths. The four most prominent of these are *gakki* (ghosts), *tengu* (forest goblins), *oni* (demons), and *kappa* (water sprites). They generally figure as nonpersonalized creatures or groups of creatures. Rarely personally named (the Kurama tengu is one exception), they may be the victors or the butt of a particular story.

Ghosts are a large category of nonhumans who afflict humanity. The appearance of ghosts in Japanese myth coincides with the arrival of Buddhism, and they may have been a Buddhist introduction from China. Ghosts tend to be the souls of those who have passed away without being allocated proper care by their families. However, certain categories of ghosts were prominent in Japan. One of the most notable is the caring ghost: for example, a mother who has died but returns to care for her infants or children. Most ghost stories are, or have, a Buddhist moral attached to them.

Tengu are a form of goblin (the word itself is not exact, because *tengu* are amoral rather than evil) who reside in the deep woods, and who can cast spells upon the unwary. They particularly afflict those who do not show them proper respect. The reverse of the coin is that they are able to provide the well-behaved, determined individual with great gifts.

Oni are usually translated as demons in English, though this too is a misnomer. On the one hand, *oni* are misguided, wild, anti-Buddhist individuals who can be converted to the good if they meet the right person. On the other hand, their wildness, mischief, and lack of morals means that they are the cause of numerous calamities that befall individuals. At the same time, they also serve in the Buddhist hells in a manner similar to some Christian concepts, as the stokers who torment the souls of sinners—a concept borrowed from Buddhism and Daoism.

Kappa, as well as other types of monsters, can bring about calamities, but can also be exploited to learn from or to acquire skills and gifts. And, like all nonhuman mythical figures, they can be banished or killed by the determined, the powerful, or those equipped with the proper spells and procedures.

Many of these creatures are "monsters," in the sense that they attack or menace humans or their doings. Nonetheless, it is useful to remember that these creatures are not "evil" in the Western sense. They are, at most, misguided, and as a consequence are suffering the penalty of this lack of law, whether the law is seen from the native Japanese viewpoint of obedience to higher authorities or through the Buddhist lens of obeying the Buddhist Law. Though occasionally it is necessary to kill such creatures, they can just as well be converted or subjugated by the proper authority.

SHUGENDŌ

Shintō and Buddhism merged and melded on many levels and in many different ways. During the Japanese Middle Ages (roughly twelfth to sixteenth centuries), a series of philosophical-religious systems broadly called Ryōbu Shintō emerged. The driving idea behind these movements was *seishin-ichi*, the idea that the *kami* and the Buddhist deities were one and the same. This adds a layer of complexity to the mythological actors in both religions. One expression of Ryōbu Shintō was a syncretic religious movement called Shugendō, which consisted of four main features, both historically and in popular imagination: ascetic practices drawn from both Shintō and Buddhism (fasting, bathing under waterfalls); mountain worship and pilgrimage; wandering priests; and magical rituals. Mountain worship was a central element in many Shintō practices, and the transference to Buddhist practice was, of course, very easy. The *shugensha* (Shugendō practitioner), *gyōja* (ascetic), *yamabushi* (mountain monk), or, colloquially, *kebōzu* (hairy Buddhist priest) and *bikuni* (wandering nuns) would appear from out of the mountains, practice their magic spells, and disappear again. This relates to the concept of *marebito* (visiting deity) so prominent in Japanese mythology.

The *shugensha* were also important because, as the only religio-medical figure many common people saw in their isolated hamlets, they were also the bearers of news. That is, mythological ideas and stories were carried by the *shugensha* and nuns (and other wandering figures like players and puppeteers) from place to place. Their patron saint was En no Gyōja (En the Ascetic), considered to be founder and first practitioner of the *yamabushi* (mountain monk; that is, ascetic) way of life.

Shugendō priests and nuns fulfilled a number of roles, not all religious and not all even highly moral in character. In addition to organizing prayer meetings and exorcisms in remote villages and communities, they organized and participated in pilgrimages, sold charms and medicines, and provided fortune-telling and prostitution services along the road. Many of these activities did not endear them to the authorities, and they were banned or suppressed from time to time in the history of Japan. Even so, the entire set of Shugendō beliefs, which focused on a number of different famous mountains, has survived, altered and modified, to this day. The *yamabushi* tradition, and more than that, the stories the *yamabushi* and *bikuni* told their rural audiences as Buddhist morality tales, became one of the origins of wondrous stories, legends, and myths in Japan.

OUTLYING MYTH COMPLEXES

Japanese national and imperial mythology tried to foster the idea of a politically and culturally monolithic Japan. This reflected the aims and interests of the central elite, and ignored and blurred the interests of local communities and the Little Traditions. But the Japanese nation is not as homogeneous as the authorities tried to make out. Two other distinct cultures—perhaps the sole two remnants of a richer and more varied cultural quilt that used to exist in the Japanese islands before Yamato's rise to dominance—still retain some vestiges of their cultural past, including their mythologies. These two cultures—the Ainu of the north, and the Ryukyuans of the south—are significant not only for their own sake, which is significance enough, but also for the comparative light they shed on Japanese (here read to mean that of the Yamato tradition) mythology as well.

Okinawa and the Ryukyu Islands

Okinawa prefecture in southern Japan consists of the Ryukyu archipelago, including the largest island, Okinawa. Indigenous language and culture differ from the Yamato (that is, standard Japanese). An independent kingdom until conquest by the Japanese Satsuma clan early in the seventeenth century, Okinawa was influenced by both China and Japan, and it often served as a bridge between the two cultures. Okinawan culture and religion have been maintained as distinct entities in many ways to this century. The Ryukyu Islands stretch for four hundred miles between the southern tip of Kyushu and the northern coast of Taiwan. Okinawa is about seventy miles long, situated more or less in the middle of the island chain. The population currently numbers about 1.3 million, excluding American troops.

The Ryukyuan economy was based on subsistence farming and fishing. Perhaps under the influence of Chinese envoys, the small independent polities that existed in the islands were amalgamated by Shō Hashi in 1429 into a single kingdom. One of his successors, Shō Shin (1477–1526), consolidated these conquests and established a Confucian-based government, forbidding the carrying of arms and institutionalizing the separation between nobility and commoners. In the late sixteenth century, the growing power of the southern Japanese domain of Satsuma brought the Okinawan kingdom more and more into Japan's orbit than China's, and the kingdom became a part of the Satsuma domain in the seventeenth century.

In contrast to the Japanese on the main islands, Ryukyuans have been recorded by almost all researchers as being singularly uninterested in mythology. Mythological figures are amorphous and undefined, and discussions of legends and mythology seem to have little or no interest for the average Okinawan. In many cases what has been touted as a Ryukyuan myth was a reworking by a mainland Japanese scholar in search of some affinity between Okinawa and Japan, usually to justify Japan's ascendancy. Such myths that do exist and are retold are generally origin myths, and even those are often abbreviated and localized. The Ryukyuans are religious in the sense that most individuals recognize the importance of participating in rituals and in carrying out ritual require-ments. But their religion is not focused on, nor dependent on, clear enunciation of the gods they refer to. The focus is rather upon the proper conduct of rituals, which are deeply embedded in Ryukyuan life and interpersonal behavior. Unusually too, Ryukyuan religion is one of the few female-centered religions in the world: The majority of ritual specialists (priests and mediums), and all the senior ones, are female. Whether this is the relict of an earlier matriarchal type of religion or a peculiarity of Ryukyuan culture is impossible to say.

The main Okinawan mythological figures are the *kang*. These are conceived of as very similar to humankind, if much more powerful. Where portrayed, they are seen as figures dressed in Chinese robes and hats: the clothes assumed by the nobility of Okinawa. The *kang* are generally neutral so long as the rituals are car-ried out and people behave "properly" in their relations with others and with the sacred groves and caves the *kang* inhabit (or rather, through which they travel to the mundane world). The *kang* are powerful and possess abilities that people do not have. They will interfere in human lives if the rituals are not carried out. Even so, they can be manipulated, even cheated, by human actions and deceit.

In the vague mythology that is expressed, there are a number of identifiable categories. The senior group are the *ting nu kang* (heavenly *kang*). Like the Japanese *kami*, these are vaguely felt to be superior. Among them are *unjang* (sea *kang*), *miiji nu kang* (water *kang*), and *tiida-kang* (solar *kang*). Again, like the Japanese system, there are a plethora of local *kang*: well *kang*, house *kang*, and paddy *kang*. There are also occupational *kang*: fishermen, net-makers, and boat builder *kang*. The final category is composed of the *futuki*, the ancestors, who might mediate between living individuals and the *kang*. All of these conceptu-alizations are blurred and vague, and few Okinawans can distinguish (or are even interested in distinguishing) between these figures. It is sufficient, in Ryukyuan eyes, to behave properly and make the offerings via the *nuru* (village priestesses).

The mythological timeline, vague as it is, starts with the Age of Heaven. During that age, the heavenly *kang* (or, in some versions, Nirai Kang, the heav-enly creator deity) instructed a brother and sister *kang*, Shinerikyu and Amaikyu, to create the land and the people on it. The two of them descended from heaven and created the mythical paradise of Kudaka Island out of the waters. Another version of the same myths (in the *Chuzan Seikan*) recounts that the two descended with building materials—stones, earth, trees, and plants—with which they held back the waves and formed the archipelago's islands. They then gave birth, without sexual intercourse, to three offspring: the first ruler (a son), the first priestess, and the first farmer (again, a son).

After several generations a descendant of these first people was born. Ten-teishi, as he was named, divided humankind into proper classes: kings, nobles, farmers, high priestesses, and village priestesses. Each of his five children assumed one of these positions. The people were then many, and they crossed the sea, landing at Seefa Utaki (the sacred grove of Seefa) on the south shore of Okinawa island. Seefa Utaki is still the main pilgrimage site in Okinawa.

Every village or community normally has an *utaki* where the local priestess communes with the *kang*. The world was ordered so that temporal power in Ryukyuan communities is wielded by men, while the spiritual power that supports them is wielded by their sisters. The same is true in most families. With the establishment of the unified Okinawan kingdom in the early fifteenth century (the kingdom also controlled, with greater or lesser effect, the outlying islands), the female-male system was formalized, and village *nuru* (priestesses) were trained and appointed by the central government.

The generalized creation story recorded in the main island of Okinawa is repeated on other Ryukyuan islands, with local, rather than "national," referents. Ouwehand recorded a similar story on the island of Hateruma, which makes no reference to Okinawa. And the foundation myth of sister-brother founder deities can also be found further south, in Taiwan and the Philippines, as well as further north, echoed in the Japanese foundation myth.

For the Ryukyuans there are two distinct realms: The first, of humans (that is, the mundane world), occupies most people's interest. The other realm, of the *kang*, is poorly identified, diffuse, and not clearly conceptualized. The *kang* inhabit that realm, but they are able to manifest themselves in the mundane world. The portals between the two worlds, at least insofar as humans are concerned, are the sacred groves (*utaki*), springs, and caves through which the other realm may be accessed. Above all, however, it is the hearth through which information on the doings of individuals and families reaches the *kang*.

Ainu

The other of the indigenous cultures of Japan, now absorbed almost wholly by Yamato culture, is that of the Ainu. Speaking a language distinct from the Japanese language, they populated northern Honshu and the island of Hokkaido during the early history of Japan. On Honshu they (or a closely related culture whom the Japanese called Emishi) gradually merged into the general Japanese populace as a result of the Yamato kingdom's expansion before and during the Heian period. By the Kamakura period, Ainu culture in northern Honshu had virtually disappeared, leaving behind place names and some indefinable cultural influences. Ainu culture continued as an independent culture in Hokkaido and in the southern Sakhalin islands. Never very numerous (about 16,000 lived in

Hokkaido), the Ainu came once again under cultural, demographic, and political pressure from the Japanese in the nineteenth century, when Hokkaido was opened to Japanese settlement. They have today virtually disappeared as a distinct culture. Remnant communities maintain some aspects of the culture, notably for the tourist trade. Those tracing themselves to Ainu descent today number around 18,000.

The Ainu were an element in the much larger circumpolar arctic culture. Their economy was based on a mix of gathering and hunting with some subsistence farming of millet, until forced to abandon their practices by the Japanese and become full-time farmers. An important element in their political economy was sea-borne trade, and their large, clinker-built boats plied the waters between the northeast Asian islands and possibly the mainland as well. In this they were not unlike their cultural relatives in Siberia and Tunguska in Asia, and the Northwest Coast cultures of North America.

A warlike people, the Ainu struggled against their Sea People neighbors—probably members of what anthropologists call Okhotskian Culture, who inhabited the island chains to the north of Hokkaido—and later against the Japanese, who subdued them only in the eighteenth century. Many Ainu myths tell of struggles against the Sea People, or of the treachery of the Japanese, to whom the Ainu turned for valued goods such as lacquerware and metalwork.

Politically, the Ainu were organized into small bands or communities of about a hundred people divided into several households. These communities laid claim to a *kotan* or domain, where they, and only they, exercised the right to hunt, fish, and gather. Each *kotan* was centered on a river valley, running up to the ridges between. Raiding and conflict were, to judge by the evidence of the sagas, quite common. Communities were generally quite isolated from one another, though the need to marry outside one's matrilineage brought about a certain amount of intercourse between communities, and thus a certain cultural uniformity.

Men were warriors and hunters. Women were gatherers and shamans providing visions to guide the people. Though spheres of activity were different, women were not inferior to men, and they possessed a great deal of power of their own, resting often in their matrilineal lineage, or "girdle group": women of the same matrilineal descent wore a *kut*, a narrow girdle of recognized weave peculiar to that group. A woman's daughters-in-law could not be of the same girdle group, and it was thus the women who controlled Ainu fertility, since men were forbidden from seeing or even discussing the girdles. Women in Ainu myths are generally portrayed as powerful, even warlike. They fight alongside their menfolk and are perfectly capable of fighting off intruders, or handling the tasks of daily life, including hunting and fishing, on their own.

Two concepts are fundamental to understanding Ainu religion: *ramat* and *kamui*. *Ramat* is an immanent power possessed by all living things, both plants and animals, and by objects, particularly those associated with humankind. *Ramat* is a nonsentient force that can occupy an object that is whole and functional, and that leaves it upon destruction and death. In this *ramat* is very similar to Polynesian *mana*, as well as, unsurprisingly, Japanese *kami*. The destruction of an object results in its *ramat* leaving it, as does the death of a being. Larger, more complex beings such as humans, have more *ramat* than do simple implements and beings such as tools or seeds.

Kamui are the deities of Ainu religion. They include several subclasses, some more powerful, some less powerful. There is a fundamental difference between *pirika kamui* (good *kamui*), *wen kamui* (hostile, malevolent), and *koshne* (neutral). Again, there is clear similarity between the Ainu and Japanese conceptions, and it is clear that they either share a common origin or have been mutually influencing one another for a long time. The *kamui* are no different from human beings. They live, love, even die as human beings do. However, they are, or can be, extremely powerful once they leave their homeland and visit the homeland of the Ainu. The *kamui* and the Ainu have a reciprocal relationship. Central to Ainu religious behavior were offerings to the *kamui*. Offerings consist of wine, food, and items of value, the most important of which are *inau*. Every *kamui* has a type of *inau* specific to that deity. *Inau* can only be made by humans. Using a thick wand of willow or other tree, the craftsman would carefully shave curling strips from the wand. Still attached to the tip of the wand, these were formed into shapes appropriate to the *kamui* in question. The *inau* were *kamui* in their own right, though their only activity was to convey the respect and gifts of the person making them. *Inau* would be stuck in the ground in appropriate places—before the hearth, on a river bank, at an ill person's bedside—and offerings of food and drink, song, and dance were made there. As we learn from the *yukari* poems, *kamui* are highly dependent upon the offerings and the *inau*. Without the food, wine, and other offerings, the power of the individual *kamui* will wane, and he or she might eventually become moribund. Without the *inau* to convey the gift, either the recipient *kamui* will not get it or having got it, will not know who is responsible for it.

The *kamui* could assume any shape, and when they reciprocated the offerings of human beings they would "dress" in animal, or tree, or vegetation "clothing." A fish or a whale, a tree, or an animal were the outer garments of a *kamui*, who provided these things to the Ainu when the deity returned to the *kamui* homeland. These outer garments were shed by the *kamui* and became gifts to the person being visited. The *ramat* of the deity was still associated with the object, which needed to be treated with great respect. A hunter who caught a good prey or a gatherer who found succulent lily bulbs was receiving a present from the *kamui.*

This practice was exemplified in the bear ritual, practiced until the early years of the twentieth century. A young bear cub was raised for a year, then killed with arrows. The meat eventually was eaten and the fur used, but for a week the bear was displayed and offered wine and entertainment; finally the bear deity was sent back to his homeland, minus his "clothes": the empty husk of the bear cub's body, which he left behind as a gift to his hosts. Bears in general were very important to the Ainu. The largest land predator (the Asian brown bear *Ursus arctos,* of which the Hokkaido brown bear is a subspecies, is related to the American grizzly) in their experience, bears were generally considered benevolent and well disposed toward humans. They were, in effect, the outer clothing worn by the mountain god Nuparikor Kamui when he came to visit humankind, soliciting offerings of wine and *inau,* and leaving his earthly husk, or covering— the fur, meat, and bones of the bear—behind for the humans to enjoy. Monster bears—*ararush*—existed as well, usually because people did not treat the bears with proper rituals and offerings. *Ararush* were feared because not only did they not yield their garments gracefully to the hunters but they actually would stalk and attack people, dam up the rivers to keep the salmon to themselves, and frighten off deer and other food animals.

In Ainu cosmology there were four realms. Two of those, the realm of the land, or land mass (Hokkaido) and the realm of the sea islands over the horizon, were populated by people: the Ainu in one, and their enemies—Japanese and Okhotskians—in the other. The *kamui* lived in their own realm, similar in every way to that of humans, and often portrayed as being up in the sky. The fourth realm was the deep dank realm of those who had misbehaved in life. Such sad souls, whether human or *kamui,* were doomed to wander that clammy and dark realm, whereas those who behaved properly, having reciprocated hospitality and performed rituals, would be kept in the hearth by the Hearth Goddess until released to be reborn.

JAPANESE MYTH IN THE MODERN WORLD

Japan has been a modern state, and in some ways an ultramodern state, since at least the 1950s. Though many of its institutions might look odd to someone from North America, they are modern expressions of historical Japanese culture. Most of the population is literate (over 99 percent, one of the highest rates in the world). All modern technological devices are available to the population. There is a reasonably equitable distribution of wealth. Transportation facilities are unsurpassed.

Even in this modern milieu, however, myth has a place. Myth is one expression of religion, and though most Japanese might claim they are irreligious, they do, at the same time, perform religious rituals at a frequency that is very high. And most people are aware of the general thrust of Japanese mythology. Whether they accept the myths as true or not is a different issue.

Certainly many Japanese have a sense of *Nihon-damashii* (Japanese spirit). Whether they support the actions of Japan before and during World War II or not, they are nonetheless conscious of the fact that Japan fought bravely against huge odds. And fundamentally, in the Japanese view expressed in many myths, winning is not all: Fighting with style is far more important. The great heroes of Japanese myth are often the losers, but they lost with their eyes open and died in style.

Japanese myth thus is viewed as relevant to the modern world in that it provides a template for doing. Whether one is a samurai or a *sarariman* (salaried office worker), one is expected to fight tenaciously, to be loyal, and if necessary to be ready to sacrifice all. That few people actually live up to this behavioral template is immaterial.

At the same time, Japanese myth has plenty of examples, or behavioral templates, for other types of life: sly foxes, wild deities, contemplative scholars and recluses who acquire power for ends of their own. These thematic myths occur and reoccur in modern Japan in the form of films, historical series, samurai dramas, advertisements, and comic books.

The most powerful and enduring myth is still the myth of Japanese uniqueness. This includes the physical, mental, cultural, and familial qualities of the Japanese. In the physical realm recurrent ideas are floated by scholars and writers about some unique characteristic Japanese are supposed to have. In the familial realm, the feeling still persists among a large segment of the population that the Japanese are special because each family is the *bunke* (branch house) of the imperial family, and thus descendant from the heavenly deities. All of these feelings are based upon a substrate of myth that has originated from the dawn of Japanese culture.

SOURCES OF JAPANESE MYTHOLOGY

There are two main types of sources from which we get information about Japanese mythology. Both Shintō and Buddhism have textual canons from which myths have been drawn. Few of these written works have the same status of irrefutable truth attributed to, say, the Christian Bible. Nonetheless, like the Bible, they recount the myths of deities and heroes, along with moral precepts, ritual requirements, and explanations of the world.

A second source is the work of ethnographers who have recorded oral myths, usually those of the Little Traditions. Starting with Yanagida (also Yanagita) Kunio, and Origuchi Shinobu, Japanese ethnographers have been diligent in recording the myths and folktales, rituals, and traditions of far-flung, often remote villages. Others such as Kindaichi Kyōsuke and Chiri Mashiho did the same for the Ainu.

The Shintō Canon

The major works recounting Shintō mythology are compilations of purported histories compiled during the Heian period. Two are of primary importance: the *Kōjiki* (Record of Ancient Matters, compiled circa 712 C.E.) and *Nihonshōki* (Chronicles of Japan, compiled circa 720 C.E., often referred to as *Nihongi*). Both provide a mixture of mythical (or at least, unverifiable) and historical accounts of the Japanese nation, from mythical times to the reign of the first emperors. Until the eighteenth century, neither work was held in particularly high regard (*Nihonshōki* slightly more than *Kōjiki*). But in the middle of the eighteenth century, the *Kokugaku* (National Learning) scholar Motoori Norinaga started on his massive (49 volume) *Kōjiki-den*—a commentary on the *Kōjiki*. In his view, the traditional myths of Japan, untainted by Confucian or Buddhist influences, were the charter history of the Japanese people. The elevation of the *Kōjiki*, and with it, of the *Nihonshōki*, thus derive quite clearly from political ideologies associated with the decline of the Tokugawa shogunate.

Both books are similar in character and cover much of the same material in slightly different formats. The *Nihonshōki*, however, provides a number of alternative versions of myths along the lines of "Some say this, others say otherwise . . .." The *Nihonshōki* also shows much more of a Chinese influence and borrows terms and explanations from that source, whereas the *Kōjiki* is more self-consciously Japanese. Both books consist of brief chapters, the earliest describing the activities of the deities, the later describing the events during the reigns of named emperors. In the *Nihonshōki* the emphasis is slightly more on the latter, and it includes events relating to the introduction of Buddhism, which is deemphasized in the *Kōjiki*. There are also a number of other compilations of lesser importance and renown. One such is the *Engishiki*, a collection of *norito* (declamatory prayers). Another are the *Fudoki*, collections of local myths, records of customs, and gazetteers from various areas of Japan collected in the Heian period. Of these, only fragments remain of many, and only small parts of some have been translated into English.

The sources of heroic and later myths have been recorded, or mentioned, in a variety of formats. Song-recitation texts, plays, and novels provide rich sources for Japanese myths, though they often contradict one another. Some, though by no means all of this literature—for example the *Heike Monogatari* (Tale of the Heike)—have been translated into languages other than Japanese.

Another rich source is available: the graphic arts. Japanese painting and sculpture, as well as arts such as lacquering and enameling, quite often express mythical themes. Favorite images such as Buddhist sages, heroes, and deities are often replicated and portrayed in art, sometimes with commentaries in prose or poetry. These portrayals provide an essential source for understanding how the Japanese in any particular period thought about mythical events and personages. Some portrayals, such as those of Daruma (the mythical founder of Zen) and the Ni-ō temple guardians, are still "mythicized" by people today: People still make Daruma dolls to ensure effort, and still offer the giant Ni-ō straw sandals for their bare feet.

Buddhist Literature: The Sutras and Commentaries

Buddhist literature is vast. Soon after Shakyamuni's death, an attempt was made to write down what he had said in his forty-five years of preaching. Even then there were disagreements, with some followers essentially arguing "Yes, you are right, the Buddha probably did say such and such at a particular event, but he *told me* something else under other circumstances."

A second pan-Buddhist conference about one hundred years later added more material, but neither reduced the disagreement nor brought about a unified canon of work, or any statement like the essentials recorded for Christianity in the Nicene creed. As the Buddha's followers spread throughout East and Central Asia, they wrote still more books, trying to explain or resolve problems they thought were central. And they came into contact with other ideas—Zoroastrianism from Persia, Bon in Tibet, and even Christianity—and tried to interpret the Buddha's preaching in light of what they encountered.

The central Buddhist writings are organized into sutra (meaning "thread" in Sanskrit). These sutra were either brief expositions of the main points of Buddhist doctrine or lengthy essays on the topic, including the preaching of Shakyamuni. Two sutra play a central part insofar as Japan is concerned: the Diamond Sutra and the Lotus Sutra. Most Japanese versions of Buddhism see one or the other as central to their thought. The problem from our point of view is that quite often the mythological characters mentioned are found, if at all, only marginally in these works.

Other writings, including a variety of exegeses from Hindu, Chinese, Tibetan, and no-longer-available Central Asian texts, are the sources from which much of the Buddhist mythology in Japan is constructed. A more or less agreed upon canon of texts exists in the form of the *Daizō kyō* (Collected Buddhist writings), which, though vast, encompasses only part of what can be considered Buddhist source writings. Many of these writings have been adapted from works that have vanished, or that had little popular distribution, but caught the eye of some scholar or priest.

Folktales and morality tales told by or about Buddhist miracles and miracle workers are also sources of Japanese Buddhist mythology. These tales, many of which have been complied into collections such as the *Konjaku Monogatari* (but only some translated from Japanese), offer a good source of ideas about the deities and Buddhas, and of myths about them and their powers.

Ainu *Yukari*

The Ainu did not have a writing of their own. They did, perhaps as a consequence, manage to maintain an extensive oral tradition of poetry that was performed publicly. Much of Ainu mythology is retained in *kamui yukar*, or "deity epics," in which a singer recounted a deity's adventure in verse. These epics, some of great length (over 7,000 verses), were sung at gatherings by a singer who appropriated the persona of the *kamui* or the culture hero. A person who could recite a story in poetic format was highly honored. These poems—passed on from father to son and mother to daughter—concerned the doings of the deities and heroes. They were recited in formal gatherings and served as entertainment when time and other activities permitted. In the late nineteenth and early twentieth centuries, Western missionaries and Japanese ethnographers (and eventually some Ainu trained in those disciplines) set about recording these poems—*yukari*—with the object of preserving them. The strong interest the Ainu have maintained in their own religious practices, as well as the tradition of memorizing the *yukari*, has ensured that a great number have been preserved. What this means is that many of the extant poems have been filtered through non-Ainu sensibilities. Even so, we get a feel for the major concerns of Ainu life: the nature around them, social relations, and family issues.

Yukari are usually classified as deity *yukari*, hero *yukari*, and human *yukari*, essentially repeating tales of these three categories of individuals. They tend to be lengthy sagas of the lives and activities of humans and deities, usually told in the first person. *Yukari* sometimes contradict one another, assigning the same events to different actors, or describe a particular character in opposite terms. This is unsurprising in the oral literature of a culture organized into small, relatively isolated bands.

Ryukyuan Myths

The Ryukyuans, as noted earlier, are probably the least myth-inclined people in the world. Very few Ryukyuans, including ritual specialists of various sorts, show any interest in discussing myths of origin or of the deities, or in discussing metaphysical issues in any way. As was discussed earlier, some myths of origin have been gathered on some of the islands, similar to origin myths found elsewhere, both to the south (Taiwan and the Philippines) and to the north (Japan). Discrete scraps of myth are recorded here and there in various works, but there is in effect no "body" of Ryukyuan mythology comparable to Japanese or Ainu mythologies.

Ryukyuan mythology is difficult to characterize because the sources themselves are contradictory and sometimes suspect. Two main categories of sources are available. A number of ethnographers and anthropologists have studied the religion of the Ryukyus at firsthand (these include Norbeck, Ouwehand, Sered, and Robinson, and a large number of Japanese scholars that have not been translated into Western languages). In most cases the study has been limited because it has focused on one of the small island communities, and the degree of generalization possible is restricted. However, these studies have provided firsthand information directly from the people concerned.

The second source of information are written records, of which three are paramount. One, *Omoro Sōshi*, was collected between 1531 and 1623. The *Omoro Sōshi* was an anthology of poetry and literature but includes mythological themes. By 1609 the Okinawan kingdom had become a vassal of the Satsuma lords of southern Kyushu, and this collection no doubt reflects Japanese concerns. The same is true of the second source. Taichu-shōnin, a Buddhist monk, wrote the *Ryukyu Shindo-ki* in 1638. This reflected his Buddhist point of view, which sought to make parallels between his Japanese Buddhist concerns and Okinawa, where he acted as missionary. Finally, Tomohide Haneji, a politician and scholar, wrote *Chuzan Seikan*, a compendium similar to Taichu's, but more detailed.

LANGUAGE AND WRITING

One important aspect of Japanese culture that is relevant to myths is the Japanese language. Japanese is part of the Ural-Altaic family of languages that includes Korean and Manchu. These languages are agglutinative, that is, words are modified by meaningless particles to indicate aspects of the language such as verb, politeness levels, tense, and so on. Japanese is written, however, in *kanji* (Chinese characters), which are ideographic in nature. Chinese does not have the agglutinations of Japanese, and the Japanese people, of necessity, eventually developed two sets of syllabaries (characters indicating a consonant and a vowel) to write these agglutinations (one of these, *katakana,* was invented to simplify reading Buddhist scriptures for women, who were considered too weak-minded to read proper Chinese characters). The consequence, however, is that many concepts in Japanese are expressed by two words: one of Japanese native origin, and another of Chinese. Moreover, though each Chinese character has a unique meaning, its "reading"—the sound it is indicated by—can have many meanings in Japanese.

All this has consequences for Japanese mythology. The names, and often the characteristics of mythological beings and articles, may be derived from alternative readings/interpretations of their names, their location, or actions. A name that might have had one meaning in the *on yomi* (Chinese reading) of a word might be read deliberately as if it were *kun yomi* (Japanese reading), and meaning then read into the sound. Here is an example: Most people are familiar with the three monkeys, Hear No Evil, See No Evil, and Speak No Evil. In Japanese mythology they are associated with the road *kami,* Sarutahiko-no-kami. The word *saru* in Japanese means monkey, and *ta* means rice paddy. In the Chinese character rendition of the *kami*'s name, it is written with the characters for monkey and for field, which sound like the *kami*'s name. This associates the deity with monkeys, though there is no such association in the *Kōjiki* or in the *Nihonshōki* where Sarutahiko is mentioned. In old Japanese the verb suffix *-saru* or *-zaru* is the negative imperative suffix of a verb ("do not . . ."). Thus the exhortation, probably from a Buddhist source, to hear no evil, see no evil, and speak no evil, can by a visual pun be illustrated as three monkeys, effectively associating these three monkeys with Sarutahiko.

INTERPRETING JAPANESE MYTH

How does Japanese myth fit into other myth systems, and into a general understanding of myth and of Japan? The original recorders and interpreters of Japanese myth were the two Japanese ethnologists, Yanagida (also Yanagita) Kunio and Origuchi Shinobu, and their students. Yanagida, in particular, was interested largely in trying to reconstruct "the original circumstances of life of the Japanese people." He, in effect, concentrated, as noted earlier, on the "Little Traditions" of the hamlets and villages of Japan. There are varied interpretations of (and methods of interpreting) Japanese myths. Quite often no single interpretation is "the right" interpretation, since much rests upon speculation and some esoteric pattern comparisons: Multiple explanations perhaps hit closer to the mark. Some of the more prominent interpretations are described and explained briefly below.

Universal Types

Many Japanese myths follow patterns that are clearly discernible in stories that have been told around the world. They represent, in a sense, Japanese expressions of archetypal themes. To cite but one example, the legend of the descent of Izanagi into the land of the dead in search of his wife, her refusal to come because she has eaten of the food of the underworld, and his violation of his oath to her are paralleled by the myths of Persephone and Hades, and of Orpheo and Eurydice. Now, whether or not these stories and images come from some common source is not as important as the fact that this myth type is so significant that two peoples, separated by hundreds of years of history and thousands of miles, will nonetheless retell these myths and feel they are important.

What this means is that many Japanese myths repeat themes that are sociopsychologically important to all humankind. Both human hopes and human fears are represented and re-represented in culturally acceptable guises. It should not therefore surprise us at all that some myths seem familiar.

Structuralist Interpretations

Structuralist interpretations are related to the search for universal types. In this technique the interpreter seeks to establish patterns relating themes—items, types of actions, descriptions of protagonists, relationships between all of these three elements—to one another in different myths. For example, Ouwehand (1964) and others have related the thunder god and the catfish in this way.

Many of the themes of Japanese mythology can benefit from this kind of structuralist treatment, which then allows them to be compared to myths and more universal themes found elsewhere. The repeated occurrence of swords, and the contexts in which they are found, as well as the repeated contrasts between high/low and heavenly deities/earthly deities, are simple relations of this type. Not all myths yield to this kind of analytical treatment, but over the years of interpretation, a number of analyses of this kind have been made.

Diffusion

Very little is really known (as opposed to speculated upon) about the cultural and genetic exchanges and changes during Eurasia's prehistory. Yes, we know some of the gross facts, but these tend to be the result of *post-hoc ergo propter hoc* thinking: This is the way it is now, therefore everything must have led up to it. The myths, if the attempt to trace them cross-culturally is correct, seem to paint a more ambiguous picture. Littleton (1995) has shown how two myths from either side of the Eurasian continent (a distance of over ten thousand miles!)—Arthur and Yamato-takeru—show great homologies that may very well mean they are the result of *cultural diffusion:* a tribe or culture that split in prehistoric times, part of the culture moving east, the other west. The same can be said of the story of Ho-ori's sea-wife. Known to European folklorists as a Melusine myth, it is found throughout Europe: the silkie or mermaid wife marrying a nobleman, who then spies on her in her bath, whereupon she flies away to her home in the sea. Ōkuninushi's escape from his father-in-law is another case in point. The "escape from the giant's castle" myth can be found in numerous European folktales, even to the specifics of the harp (or other musical instrument) waking the sleeping victim, and the use of various magical items to create a barrier from pursuers—a theme that is also present in the myth of Izanagi's descent into the underworld.

There are other indications of diffusion that can be traced, somewhat less ambiguously than the Arthur/Yamato-takeru story. The myth of the brother-sister founder can be found throughout the island chains south of the Japanese islands all the way to the Philippines. The stories are, if we discount ecological and cultural differences, very similar. It is reasonable to speculate, under those circumstances, that somehow or other these stories come from a common source or sources, and that they have arrived either by contact between peoples or because the same people have spread throughout a much greater geographic area than is known today.

Interpretation on the Basis of Archaeo-Anthropology: The Attempt to Extract Prehistory from Myth

Many Japanese students of mythology have been concerned about trying to understand the prehistory of the Japanese people by looking at the myths. This is of course a dangerous business, not least because there is a difference between those who recounted the myths and those who, many years and often centuries later, wrote them down. This is not only because the literate people were not living in the archaic times they were recording but also because the writers, members of the elite, had, as we know, their own ideological and political axes to grind.

Even so, by comparing the different versions of foundation myths recorded in the *Kōjiki,* the *Nihonshōki,* and the *Engishiki,* to name but a few, we can get a sense of the political and social life the people of early Japan led. It does not require much analysis to see, for instance, that the conquering Yamato had a different social makeup from the people they "subdued," nor that a variety of different social customs were familiar and common. For example, Yamato-takeru approaches a communal pit dwelling, and yet he lives, and his ancestors live in "Heaven-reaching halls." We know from archaeological evidence that both sorts of structures were used, and we can see that the communal pit dwellers, often ruled by an elder-brother, younger-brother combination of rulers, were supplanted by the clan- and family-oriented Yamato social structure. We can also get a glimpse of the relations between the sexes. Women are far more powerful in archaic than in traditional (or even modern) Japan. They rule, often achieving their aims by force, supported by brothers or husbands. Primogeniture (inheritance by the eldest son) is the exception rather than the rule in most cases. It is usually the younger sibling who inherits (Amaterasu, Jimmu-Tenno, Yamato-takeru, to name but a few), whereas the reverse became true in traditional Japan, presumably because of Chinese Confucian influence. Interestingly enough (and unsurprisingly), these two features of archaic societies—female equality and ultimo-geniture—were features that neither Motoori nor Yanagida—the two central proponents of Japan's traditional practices, but both the products of paternalistic Confucian-derived morality—definitely did *not* promote.

Many of these interpretations are valid because we find support for them from another quarter. Archaeological excavations in Japan have uncovered the remains of pit dwellings, of weapons and tools described in the myths, and of different foods consumed during this period by the mosaic of people who populated the Japanese islands during the archaic period.

Japanese Uniqueness Myths

Motoori Norinaga, the eighteenth-century scholar of the National Learning School, was, in effect, an interpreter of myths. He very strongly believed that the Japanese foundation myths were unique to Japan and that they demonstrated the primacy of Japan in the world. He (and his many followers) attempted to explain the nature of Japanese myths based on linguistic associations, construction of elaborate tables of genealogy and chronology, and relating ideas common in his own era to scraps of items found in the classics.

With a very similar view, Yanagida Kunio attacked the problem from the opposite direction, methodologically speaking. Convinced that the uniqueness of the Japanese people was to be found in the practices of the common people and the peasants in remote villages, he set out to collect these customs firsthand.

Yanagita believed that the peasants had not been contaminated by the Confucian, Buddhist, and Chinese influences that the elite writers of the Great Tradition (including, presumably, Motoori) had been touched by. The essence of Japanese tradition and culture was therefore to be found among the peasants: Motoori would have thought that a ridiculous notion.

Notwithstanding the different political stances of these two (and many of their colleagues and students), the idea behind this form of interpretation was the enhancement of "pure" Japanese culture. Both schools, that of Motoori and that of Yanagida, were partly attempts to buttress Japanese culture against assumed cultural threat from outsiders: the Chinese and Europeans.

2

MYTHIC TIME AND SPACE

The two dominant mythical timelines of Japanese thought, from Buddhism and from Shintō, are radically different in their origins as well as their beginnings, but they converge and eventually meld into a single progression centering on Japan and the Japanese people. One reason, perhaps, why the Japanese had no difficulty in reconciling Shintō and Buddhist myths is that each of these mythical traditions leaves large sections of the account blank, or at best, sketched in rather perfunctorily, so that it can be "filled in" by the other.

The Shintō mythical timeline can be divided into four eras. The first is the mythical era of the heavenly and earthly *kami*. This is the time for the creation of the heavens and earth, and for their population and organizing. The end of this era sees the earth created in all its aspects, and the earth *kami* subdued by the proper authority of the heavenly *kami*. The second era is that of the emperors. It details the lives of the emperors and their rule from the earliest and most mythical to the historical. The third era, of heroes, deals with the activities of a string of powerful warriors and heroes, many with a grain of historical fact. Some of the heroes fought to extend the imperial reign, and others fought for their kin and clan.

Finally we come to an extensive era of more localized myths, ghost tales, and belief paradigms that include modern times. This blends Shintō and Buddhist myths into a mix of Great and Little Traditions that make up the modern world and include a number of modern myths relating to the nature of modern Japan.

Buddhist mythic timelines are not easily compartmentalized in this way. Very roughly, they can be divided into (1) myths that have a continental, mainly Indian origin, which essentially deal with the ages of the Buddha, and (2) those that concern the establishment of Buddhism in Japan. As noted above, this timeline blends with Shintō in the settled periods of the Edo and modern ages.

A word, too, about the Japanese calendar. The traditional Japanese calendar was a complex affair. This is not surprising, given that both native and Chinese ideas gave great importance to the seasons, the stars, and the association of portents with days that could be used for divination. The calendar was modified several times during the early history of Japan. It was modified again when Japan became a modern state and adopted the Gregorian calendar, albeit with simple numerical months (First Month, Second Month, . . .) rather than the Western names. One peculiarity, however, remains: Years are often indicated not by the Common Era indicators used worldwide but by imperial reign names. Thus 1925, the first year of the reign of the Shōwa emperor (most non-Japanese know him as Hirohito) became Shōwa 1. Hirohito's son assumed the throne in 1989, taking the reign name Heisei, and the year promptly changed to Heisei 1, though it can still be referred to as Shōwa 63. Significantly, this system has ensured that many mythical dates avowed as authentic are probably inaccurate.

CREATION AND CONSOLIDATION: THE FOUNDATION MYTHS

In the beginning, says the *Kōjiki*, five single deities (that is, they had no spouses) came into existence. The land itself was formless, like a jellyfish. Six more generations of gods came into existence after the first five, some of whom had spouses. The last of the seventh generation were a male and female pair, called Izanagi-no-mikoto and his spouse, Izanami-no-mikoto. The *Nihonshōki* provides a number of versions that are roughly similar.

By unanimous voice of all the *kami*, the last two were given the Heavenly Jeweled Spear and told to solidify the land. This they did by standing on the Heavenly Floating Bridge, and stirring the liquid with it. Raising the spear, droplets fell from the tip and formed solid islands.

The two creator-*kami* descended to the islands and built a heavenly pillar and a palace to live in. Having completed the palace, they noted that their bodies were constructed somewhat differently. As Izanagi is said to have told Izanami, "My body, formed though it be formed, has one place which is formed to excess. Therefore, I would like to take that place in my body which is formed to excess and insert it into that place in your body which is formed insufficiently, and give birth to the land" (*Kōjiki*, as cited in Phillipi, 4:4). Izanami agreed, and the two deities resolved to walk around the pillar, he from the left, she from the right, meet again, and have conjugal intercourse. They circled around, but when they met, Izanami exclaimed, "How wonderful! Such a handsome lad!" Izanagi too was delighted to see her, but he reproved her, saying it was unseemly for the woman to speak first.

They commenced procreation, but gave birth to a leech-child without arms or legs (in the *Nihonshōki* this is the last, rather than the first, child), then to an island. Distressed, they consulted the senior deities, who informed them that the problem was the result of Izanami having improperly spoken first after they circled the pillar. They repeated their actions, this time getting the greetings in the right order. As a consequence, Izanami gave birth to the eight islands of Japan. Then she gave birth to many deities.

Izanami died after giving birth to the fire deity, who burned her genitals as he was born. In her dying throes she gave birth to many other deities, created from her organs and discharges. In total she gave birth to fourteen islands and thirty-five deities. The enraged Izanagi killed the newly born fire deity. The dead fire-deity's organs yielded more deities, as did the blood collected on Izanagi's sword.

After her death, Izanagi wished to visit his wife in the land of Yōmi (the underworld). He met her in her great hall in the underworld, and she agreed to come with him to the land of the living if she received permission from the *kami* of hell. Izanagi broke his word to wait patiently, spied on her, and discovered her putrefied body being eaten by maggots. He fled, and she, accompanied by the maggots who had turned into snake-thunder deities and her servants, pursued. He blocked the way after him with a rock, but Izanami cursed Izanagi and his people that one thousand people would die every day. Izanagi averted the curse by blessing humanity with 1,500 births every day.

Izanagi purified himself from the taint of the underworld by washing. From each element of his dress came forth several deities, both pure deities and polluted deities. The same happened when he washed his body: From each part he washed came forth a *kami*. Seeing his children, he assigned them to rule various dominions. The three last—Amaterasu-ō-mikami, Tsukiyomi-no-mikoto, and Susano-wo—were especially blessed and so were assigned the rule of heaven, night, and the ocean. All the *kami* obeyed their father's orders and took up the duties of their office, except the last, Susano-wo. He lamented the loss of his mother, Izanami, and as a consequence was reassigned by his furious father to rule over Yōmi. Izanagi then retired to a palace he had built in Izumo.

Susano-wo's Crimes and the Sun Goddess

As was only proper, Susano-wo came to take leave of his sister Amaterasu before leaving for his kingdom in Yōmi. Not unnaturally suspicious, she armed and armored herself, tied up her hair in a masculine manner (women of the archaic period would have let their hair fall free; men tied it up in bunches), and took a plentiful supply of arrows. As he approached, she performed a war dance, kicking the earth up into the air and stamping it down so she sank to her thighs in the hard ground. Susano-wo protested that his intentions were completely benign and her suspicions unfounded. He then said he would prove his words: He and his sister would undertake a trial by ordeal. Trials by ordeal were apparently a familiar feature of life, and Amaterasu agreed. She requested her brother's sword, broke it into three pieces, rinsed them in the Heavenly Well, then chewed and spat them out. The spray from her mouth brought forth three deities.

Susano-wo requested his sister's string of *magatama* jewels (which, as a chieftain, she had taken care to wear into battle). She gave him those from the right hair bunch on her head. He rinsed them, chewed, and spat. From the spray emerged a deity. He then borrowed the jewels from her left hair bunch, her hair band, her left arm, and her right arm, chewing and spraying each time, bringing forth five deities in all.

The account in the *Kōjiki* is that Amaterasu conceded defeat: The first three deities were female, and because they had come from Susano-wo's possession (his sword), they were his children. The *Nihonshōki* account is the reverse: Because the first children were *male,* victory went to Susano-wo, and his innocent intent was proven.

Susano-wo, never gracious, gleefully ran amuck, emitting the equivalent of "I've won! I've won!" He tore down the dikes between the rice paddies in heaven, covered up the ditches, and finally defecated in the Hall of First Offerings.

Amaterasu was too indulgent with her younger brother. "He only did it because he was drunk," she said. "And perhaps he thinks that growing rice is wasteful."

Alas, indulging bullies is never a good strategy. Susano-wo's mischief continued, until one day he caught a heavenly dappled pony, skinned it alive, then threw the corpse into Amaterasu's weaving hall. One weaving girl was so shocked, she hit her genitals with a shuttle and died.

Amaterasu herself, whether from fear or disgust, closed herself into a cave. The consequences of the solar deity's retreat were serious: Heaven and earth became completely dark. The myriad deities called out, and many calamities cursed the land. The eight million heavenly *kami* resorted to their usual practice in time of trouble: They assembled to discuss the issue in the dry bed of the Heavenly River. Then, taking the necessary materials, they commissioned the smith *kami* Amatsumara to make a metal mirror. They commissioned Tamanoya-no-mikoto to make long strings of *magatama* beads. They ordered the proper deities to perform divination to ensure the success of their efforts. Uprooting, then replanting, a sacred evergreen *sakaki* bush, they hung offerings on its branches: the jewels and mirror, along with blue cloth and white cloth. They performed rituals of offering.

Then Amanotachikara-ō-no-kami, the strong deity, hid himself behind the rock closing the cave entrance. The wily deity, Ama-no-uzume bound up her sleeves and hair, exposed her breasts and genitals, and, standing on a bucket, danced a loud and rowdy dance. The eight million *kami* burst out laughing. Thinking this behaviour strange (for, after all, she had brought darkness and gloom to heaven and earth by her retreat), Amaterasu opened the cave door and demanded what the levity was about. Ama-no-uzume retorted that they were happy because there was a better deity than Amaterasu around. Then the two ritual specialist deities showed Amaterasu her own image in the mirror. Amaterasu, intrigued, opened the cave further and peered out at the mirror. Ameno-tachikara, whose name means "heaven's strength," then seized her hand and pulled her out of the cave. Amenofutotama-no-mikoto, one of the ritual-expert *kami*, then closed the entrance to the cave with a sacred rope, which she could not pass. And light came back to heaven and onto the land.

As for Susano-wo, the source of all this trouble, he was sentenced by the assembled *kami* to a fine of one thousand tables of offerings, his beard was shaved, his nails pulled out, and he was expelled from heaven (and, the *Nihonshōki* says, from the Central Land of the Reed Plains as well; some say he went to Korea). The one thousand tables of offering—cloth, jewel strings, paper, bronzeware, and foods, such as are still offered at shrines and at ceremonies to the emperor today—were presumably distributed among the *kami*.

The Creation of Food for Humankind

Amaterasu heard of a *kami* named Ukemochi-no-kami living on the Central Land of the Reed Plains. She sent her brother Tsukiyomi-no-mikoto to inquire after her. When he arrived at her dwelling, Ukemochi-no-kami took rice and other foods from her mouth, placed them on offering tables, and gave them to the visiting *kami*. Tsukiyomi-no-mikoto was insulted at what he saw as a polluting act, and he killed the food goddess. Amaterasu was furious at her messenger, vowing never to set eyes upon him again and making him the deity of the moon, which always rises at night, when the sun is down. She sent to see the body of the murdered food deity. In the corpse's head there came to be cattle and horses. Millet was found in her forehead, and silkworms in her eyebrows. Rice was in her belly, and wheat in her genitals. These were presented to Amaterasu, who declared they would be used by humanity for its living.

Although the former story is told by the *Nihonshōki*, the *Kōjiki* tells the story differently. In that version the offending *kami* was Susano-wo, who in his exile asked for shelter from Ugetsu-hime. She took various foods out of her nostrils, mouth, and rectum, and offered them to him. Insulted by the seeming pollution, he killed his hostess. Various foodstuffs and other things useful for humankind grew out of her eyes, and so on.

The two myths illustrate two important contradictions that would have been apparent to the Japanese of that age. First, that growth, and the very livelihood of humankind, was dependent upon death and decay. With the change of seasons, plants would die only to spring forth later and yield their seeds, just as animals would die to make way for their young. No less important was the sociopolitical commentary. Food was the source of life, but men were socially dependent upon women to prepare food for them: as a consequence, it is female deities that are the source of food. Yet, in the male-dominated culture of early (and modern!) Japan, women were more polluted then men. The food they offer the male visitors is suspected of contamination and pollution, as, presumably, can any food be. As neat a put-down of women as can be found anywhere.

Susano-Wo and the Eight-Tailed Dragon

In his wanderings, Susano-wo encountered an elderly *kami* couple, seven of whose daughters had been eaten by the eight-tailed dragon of Kushi. Only the eighth daughter remained, and Susano-wo arrived the eve before the dragon was expected again. Susano-wo volunteered to slay the serpent (not before extracting a promise to have the remaining daughter for his bride). They brewed specially strong wine at his order, and Susano-wo had a strong fence constructed with eight doors. Inside the doors he laid eight barrels of wine, strongly tied to sturdy platforms. The dragon arrived, pushing one head through each door and drinking the wine, then falling into a drunken stupor. Susano-wo drew his sword and chopped the dragon into pieces. When he cut into the middle tail, his sword broke, and, digging deeper, he found the sword Kusanagi, which he presented to Amaterasu, possibly in apology for his previous misdeeds.

He then built a magnificent palace in Izumo, at Suga, and lived there with his wife, Kushinada-hime. He took another wife as well and fathered a number of children, who, in turn, fathered their own.

Ōkuninushi and His Eighty Brothers

One of Susano-wo's descendants was named Ōkuninushi. Though he had eighty brothers and was reckoned the least among them, he finally became master of the land (*kuni-nushi*). This is how it came about: All the brothers wanted to marry Yagami-hime, a great beauty from Inaba. They went to court her, taking Ōkuninushi along as baggage carrier. At Cape Keta they found a rabbit who had lost its fur. Jokingly, they told the rabbit to cure itself by bathing in the sea, then lying in the sun. The rabbit did so and found its skin cracking and the salt seeping in with painful results. Ōkuninushi, presumably still struggling with luggage, and at the time still named Ō-Namuji-no-kami, passed by. Taking pity on the rabbit, he asked what had happened.

"I was on Oki Island and wished to visit the mainland," said the rabbit. "I tricked the sea crocodile to cross the sea. I told him I would count his relatives (to show how powerful the crocodile clan was, presumably) by having them lie side by side from Oki Island to Cape Keta. The crocodiles assembled, and I skipped from one to the other, counting as I went. Just as I was on the last crocodile, I boasted about how I had fooled them. The last crocodile seized me and skinned me of my fur. Then your brothers came by."

Ōkuninushi instructed the rabbit to bathe in fresh water, then roll in the pollen of a certain grass, which would restore his fur. The rabbit, in gratitude, prophesied that of all the brothers, Ōkuninushi would win Yagami-hime's hand. And so it was.

The eighty brothers were not pleased at this development and plotted to kill Ōkuninushi. At the foot of Mt. Tema they tried their hand at boar hunting, placing Ōkuninushi in ambush, to which they would drive the red boar from above. Instead, they took a large rock, heated it until it glowed, and rolled it down the mountain. When Ōkuninushi caught the boulder he was burned to death. His mother ascended to heaven and pleaded for his life. Two female deities were dispatched and restored him to life as a beautiful young man.

Once again the eighty brothers tried to kill him. They split a tree, shoved him inside, then removed the wedge holding the tree open. It snapped shut, crushing him to death. Again his mother revived him, this time telling him to flee. His brothers pursued, but as they were about to shoot him, he managed to slip away.

Ōkuninushi Is Tested by Susano-wo

Ōkuninushi was counseled to go to see Susano-wo, his great-great-great-grandfather, who was living in his palace in a distant country. Upon arrival at the palace, Suseri-hime, Susano-wo's daughter, met him. They fell in love and married. Then she went in to talk to her father, who greeted Ōkuninushi by one of his five birth names (that is, not as Ōkuninushi). Susano-wo, to try his new son-in-law's mettle, invited him to sleep in a chamber of snakes. Suseri-hime gave her new husband a snake-repelling scarf. He waved the scarf about, and the snakes went to sleep, as he did himself. The following night Susano-wo put him to sleep in a room full of centipedes and bees. Again his bride gave him a scarf, and again he slept the night peacefully. Then Susano-wo shot a humming arrow (the shaft had a bone whistle attached, and it was used to frighten enemies) and made Ōkuninushi fetch the arrow. While Ōkuninushi searched in a bed of tall grass, Susano-wo set fire to the grass all round. A mouse came and showed Ōkuninushi a narrow cave in which he hid until danger had passed and the mouse could bring him the arrow.

Ōkuninushi returned the arrow to Susano-wo, who graciously allowed his new son-in-law to pick lice from his head. But the deity's head was crawling with centipedes (he was, after all, the ruler of the underworld as well). Ōkuninushi tricked Susano-wo into believing he was removing the centipedes and biting them to death (thus proving his immunity to poison), and the older deity fell asleep, whereupon the younger deity took his elder's hair and tied it to the rafters, blocking the door of the chamber with a boulder.

With the father-in-law asleep and immobilized, Ōkuninushi put his bride on his back and escaped, not forgetting to steal Susano-wo's sword, bow and arrows, and jeweled *kōtō* (zither, a harplike instrument). As he fled, the *kōtō* brushed against a tree and its sound awakened the sleeper. As Susano-wo jumped up, he pulled the hall down with his hair, and by the time he had gotten himself out of the ruins, the young couple were far away. Susano-wo pursued them to the borders of his land, but they escaped. From the distance he blessed them, saying Ōkuninushi should assume his proper name, and, using the weapons he had stolen, subdue his brothers. He should make Suseri-hime his chief wife, and raise a great palace. Susano-wo ended his blessing (either under his breath or in an exclamation for approval for a crafty rival and descendant) "You scoundrel!"

Ōkuninushi did indeed subdue his brothers. He then raised his great hall, and took over the task of creating the land.

Versions of this myth should be very familiar to readers of European legends, and there are numerous variants, with or without the giant's/witch's/god's daughter (for example, Jack and the beanstalk). It has been suggested by Littleton (1995) that another common Japanese myth, that of Yamato-takeru, is very similar to the legend of Arthur, and he has managed to trace the legend to a source of Central Asian nomads, from whom it dispersed east and west as those people split and migrated into Europe and Siberia. The similarity of the story of Ōkuninushi and his father-in-law may well reinforce the case, and may have first been told by those same people.

Ōkuninushi and Sukunabikona Finish Creating the Land

Ōkuninushi married several times, arousing the ire of his chief wife, Suseri-hime, and causing his first wife Yagami-hime, the beauty of Inaba, to abandon her husband and child and return home. Possibly because of the press of the great number of offspring that resulted from his many marriages, the deity continued the process of creating the land started initially by Izanami and Izanagi. While he was busy in Izumo, a dwarf deity approached Ōkuninushi, carried across the waves on a boat made of a tree pod wearing the skin of a wagtail (or, according to one version of the *Nihonshōki*, a goose, which would have made him slightly larger). The dwarf deity would not speak, so the toad deity suggested they ask the scarecrow *kami* Kuyebiko, who, though without feet, was out in all weather and all seasons and knew everything under the skies. It was revealed to them that the dwarf deity, Sukunabikona by name, was one of the thousand sons of one of the heavenly deities, Kamimusubi-no-kami (says the *Kōjiki*) or Takamimusubi-no-mikoto (says the *Nihonshōki*). The two deities, Ōkuninushi and Sukunabikona, then set forth to solidify and create the land, which Izanagi and Izanami had left unfinished.

The substance of this myth, with the complex genealogy that is described, is closely related to the following story of the conquest of earth by the heavenly deities. There are several versions of these myths, in the *Kōjiki* (which is the source most strongly advocated and made "authoritative" by supporters of the Imperial status-quo and the Great Tradition) and *Nihonshōki*, but also in the *Engishiki*, another compendium of myth and prayer. In the latter versions, the Izumo partisans are painted much more favorably. This supports the view that historically, there must have existed a body of myth/history of the Izumo people, which was substantially different from that of the Yamato people. When the latter's state expanded at the expense of the former, the two mythological/historical accounts were blended. The Yamato scribes or scholars, having the more dominant position, naturally tended to belittle the personalities and accomplishments of the Izumo deities.

The Heavenly Deities Subdue the Land: First Attempt, with Weak Son

The procreative actions of Susano-wo and of Ōkuninushi, which are detailed in extensive "begat" lists in the *Kōjiki* and the *Nihonshōki*, seemed to have alarmed the deities of heaven. Most of the earthly deities married several times, either happily or unhappily (as Ōkuninushi), and many important deities of specific locations—as well as of specific functions, such as the hearth deity—were born.

Amaterasu commanded her son Ame-no-oshi-homimi-no-mikoto (who was one of those born in her struggle with Susano-wo) to go down to the land and take possession. However, as he stood outside heaven, on the Heavenly Floating

Bridge from which the earth had originally been formed, he saw that the earth was in an uproar (as result, presumably, of the actions of Ōkuninushi's large family). There were gods flitting to and fro, lighting up the night sky like fireflies. Evil spirits buzzed like flies, and trees and rocks talked and could move about. He returned in some fear to report to his mother.

As was their custom, the heavenly deities assembled in the dry riverbed of Ame-no-yasunokawa, the heavenly river. They decided to send another of Amaterasu's sons, Amenohohi-no-kami, to subdue the land. This deity, the *Kōjiki* (15: 21) notes, was the ancestor of the Izumo rulers and an untrustworthy emissary. The *Engishiki*, in contrast, sees him as someone sent to prepare the eventual subjugation of the land. In any case, he descended to the Central Land of Reed Plains but began to curry favor with Ōkuninushi and did not return for three years.

The Heavenly Deities Subdue the Land:
Second Attempt, with Pheasant

Once again Takamimusubi and Amaterasu-ō-mikami assembled the eight million deities and asked for advice. This time they decided to send the *kami* Ame-no-wakahiko. To ensure he was better prepared, they gave him a magical bow and arrows. This attempt was not any more successful than the first. Like his predecessor, Ame-no-wakahiko was seduced by the earthly deities, courting and marrying Ōkuninushi's daughter Shitateru-hime. Possibly by doing so he hoped to become Ōkuninushi's heir. In any case, the *Kōjiki* reports he planned on keeping the land for himself. After eight years with no results, the heavenly deities started worrying again, and they once again convened a meeting. They sent the pheasant to question Ame-no-wakahiko. The *kami* shot the pheasant to death with the bow and arrow he had received with his commission. The arrow passed through the pheasant, then rebounded all the way up to heaven, to the dry riverbed where Takamimusubi-no-kami and Amaterasu-ō-mikami were still in conference. Takamimusubi-no-kami recognized the arrow and, showing it to the assembled deities, said a spell: "If this arrow has been used against evil *kami*, then let Ame-no-wakahiko be safe from it; if he be treacherous, let it slay him!" and he thrust it down the way it had come. The arrow hit Ame-no-wakahiko in the chest, and he died. His wife's laments were so loud they were heard in heaven, and Ame-no-wakahiko's parents and siblings knew he was dead and made a funeral house. Houses in which people died, or those associated with death, were polluted and were therefore, if at all possible, erected for the purpose, then torn down again. One consequence of this custom, prevalent in pre-

Nara Japan, was the constant movement of the Yamato capital, which occurred whenever a reigning monarch died. This was observed until the foundation of Nara in the sixth century C.E.

The Heavenly Deities Subdue the Land: Third Time Lucky

Once again the heavenly deities conferred, deciding to send Takemikazuchi-no-kami (a powerful warrior deity). Accompanied by Amenotoribune-no-kami (bird-boat deity, who may have been merely his transport) or by Futsunushi-no-kami (another sword deity, this time mentioned in the *Nihonshōki* version), he descended to Inaba beach in Izumo. Unsheathing his sword, he showed his credentials by planting the sword hilt on the crest of a wave, then sitting on the point nonchalantly.

He then inquired of Ōkuninushi what were his intentions with regard to the land, which was the possession of Amaterasu's descendants. Ōkuninushi asked to confer with his son Kotoshironushi. When the younger deity returned from his hunting trip, he heard Takemikazuchi-no-kami's claims, then counseled his father to heed the heavenly deities. With magical gestures, he made himself invisible and retired to a grove to become an invisible *kami*.

"Now will you submit?" asked Takemikazuchi-no-kami.

"I've got another son," replied Ōkuninushi. "He must be asked too."

The son, Takeminakata, arrived carrying a large boulder on his fingertips. He challenged Takemikazuchi to a wrestling bout. As the rebellious son seized Takemikazuchi's arm, the heavenly deity changed it to an icicle. Takeminakata tried again; this time the arm was changed to a sword blade. Takeminakata retired in panic. Now it was Takemikazuchi's turn. He grasped his opponent's arm, crushing it like a reed. Takeminakata ran away, with Takemikazuchi in hot pursuit. The fight ended on the banks of Lake Suwa (in modern Nagano). When Takeminakata was about to be killed, he pleaded for his life, vowing he would settle there, at Lake Suwa, and would yield the land, as his father had, to the heavenly deities. The shrine of Suwa stands there, on the spot, to this day.

Takemikazuchi returned to Ōkuninushi to demand once again whether the latter was satisfied: His sons had agreed to submit. Ōkuninushi admitted that they were in agreement but added a rider: He would have a palace built in Izumo, on Tagishi Beach. It would be a magnificent palace, rooted in the earth and roofed at the height of heaven. There would be a bridge there, over the Heavenly River, by which means Ōkuninushi could come and go. The Heavenly Bird-Boat would also be put at his disposal for the same reason. Special foods from the sea, cooked by fire lit from a fire drill and served on special clay plates, would be offered. And Kotoshironushi would be "the vanguard and the rearguard" of the deities, to ensure that no rebellion took place. He himself, Ōkuninushi, though yielding the material possessions (that is, the land), would retain dominion over the invisible (the realm of the divine, the religious, and the magical). And so it came to pass. To this day the magnificent shrine of Izumo Taisha stands in Izumo. Special offerings are made, and the fire still is lit with a fire drill. (A fire drill is one of the many types of fire-making implements used by premodern people to light a fire at will—an important skill for any person or people without modern conveniences. It consists of a bowlike implement whose string is wrapped around a length of hard wood. This "arrow" of hard wood is inserted into a board of soft wood surrounded by some tinder or punk. By drawing the bow rapidly back and forth, sufficient heat can be generated by friction, which lights the tinder.) This illustrates the magical nature of Ōkuninushi: The ability to make fire would have been, in a traditional society, a highly magical act.

The Heavenly Grandson Descends to Take Possession of the Central Land of the Reed Plains

The time had come to settle the land, and Takamimusubi-no-kami and Amaterasu commanded her son Ame-no-oshi-homimi-no-mikoto to get on with it. He demurred, as he had before, and suggested that his newborn son, product of his union with Takamimusubi-no-kami's daughter, should be sent instead. The two grandparents agreed, and the heavenly grandson, Ninigi-no-mikoto, was dispatched to the land. As he was about to leave, a fearsome glowing apparition appeared at the heavenly crossroads. The heavenly deities sent the crafty and decisive Ame-no-uzume to inquire who the interfering deity was. He identified himself as Sarutahiko-no-kami, an earthly deity. He had a ferocious aspect: An inner fire made his mouth, posterior, and eyes glow cherry-red. He was over seven feet tall, and his nose was seven hands (about eighty-five centimeters) long. However, convinced by Ame-no-uzume, he consented to serve as a guide to the heavenly grandson. Amaterasu and Takamimusubi-no-kami ordered five other deities, including Ame-no-uzume, to accompany their grandson and serve as his subordinates and counselors. Eventually they became the ancestors of the most important Yamato clans. Amaterasu also gave her grandson the *magatama* beads and mirror that had been used to lure her from her cave, and the sword Kusanagi she had received from her brother, Susano-wo. She then ordered a number of other deities to serve him in various ritual and managerial capacities. The heavenly grandson descended through the multiple layers of heaven to Mount Takachio in Himuka (in modern Kyushu), where he built his palace.

Having built his palace, he courted Kōnōhanasakuya-hime, daughter of Oya-matsumi-no-kami, a mountain deity. In addition to Kōnōhanasakuya-hime (Flower-blossom princess), the father also gave the bridegroom his older daughter, the ugly Iwanaga-hime (Long-rock princess). He returned the ugly sister, and her ashamed father said: "I gave my two daughters to the divine grandson to ensure his life would last as long as the rocks, and as flourishing as the blossoms of the trees. He has rejected Long-rock princess, and therefore his prosperity and life shall be as evanescent as the blossoming of the trees." And indeed, from that day on, the emperors have never lived very long.

After they had spent no more than one night together, Kōnōhanasakuya-hime became pregnant. Her husband accused her of infidelity with one of the earth deities, for, after all, how could she have become pregnant after only one night of marriage? She proved her innocence by setting fire to the parturition house, from which she and the baby emerged unscathed. The child was named Hoderi-no-mikoto, and after him were born Hosuseri-no-mikoto and Ho-ori-no-mikoto, also known as Amatsuhiko-Hikohohodemi-no-mikoto.

Ho-ori Loses His Brother's Fish-Hook

Hoderi, Ninigi's oldest son, was a fisherman, whereas Ho-ori, the last born, was a hunter. Each had a luck fetish—an object that ensured success in their enterprise—a fishhook and hunting implements, respectively. Ho-ori badgered his brother to exchange fetishes, which the elder brother finally consented to. But Ho-ori was such a poor fisherman that not only did he not catch a single fish, he even lost the fishhook fetish. When the time came to return the fetishes to their original owners, Ho-ori could not come up with the goods, and even a gift of five hundred fishhooks made from the fragments of his sword would not mollify his older brother.

Eventually, pressed by his brother, Ho-ori received some advice from a passer-by. Making a bamboo coracle, he set out to sea, where he found the fish-scaled palace of Owatatsumi-no-kami, *kami* of the sea. There he hid himself in the branches of a tree overlooking the palace wall and awaited the coming of the sea-king's daughter. A maid out to draw water from the well saw him reflected in her pitcher and offered him a drink. Drawing a jewel he wore around his neck, he moistened it with his saliva and dropped it into the water vessel, whereupon it stuck. The servant showed it to her mistress, Toyotama-hime, and the princess went out to see the handsome young man her handmaiden had described. They immediately fell in love and became man and wife. Introduced to his son-in-law, Owatatsumi-no-kami immediately recognized Ho-ori as

Ninigi's son. He blessed the wedding, giving the customary trousseau of one hundred tables laden with gifts.

After living with his wife for three years, Ho-ori became homesick. He explained his circumstances to his father-in-law. Owatatsumi promptly summoned all the fishes and asked if any had found the lost fishhook. A bream had something lodged in his throat, which proved to be the missing article. Owatatsumi instructed the young man in a spell that would bring bad luck to the hook's user.

He then instructed the young man to build his rice paddies at a different elevation from his brother's: "If he builds them high, you build them low; if he builds low, you build high. Since I am the lord of the waters, if he builds high, I will deprive his fields of water; if he builds low, I will flood them."

In addition, Owatatsumi gave Ho-ori two jewels, one that would raise the tides, the other that would lower them. Should Hoderi attack, Ho-ori could use the tide-raising jewel to drown him. Should the brother be penitent, then Ho-ori could lower the tides and give his brother his life. He then sent a crocodile to carry Ho-ori in one day to his old home. There he did as instructed by Owatatsumi. His brother became poorer and more desperate, eventually attacking Ho-ori, who countered with the tide-raising jewel. When Hoderi pleaded with his brother, Ho-ori used the other jewel to save him. And so it went, until Hoderi vowed to serve his brother.

Toyotama-hime emerged from the sea to join her husband and give birth to their first child. They built a parturition hut on the beach, and she instructed her husband not to observe her as she gave birth. Curious, he secretly watched and saw his wife turn into a giant crocodile as she experienced the birth-pangs. Ashamed that she had been seen in her animal state, Toyotama-hime returned to the sea, leaving her child with its father. Though she was angry at her husband for disobeying her request, she sent her younger sister, Tamayori-hime, to nurse the child. Ho-ori then dwelt in his palace of Takachiho for five hundred years.

Jimmu Tenno, the First Emperor

The son of Ho-ori and Toyotama-hime eventually married his aunt, Tamayori-hime. They had four sons. When they came into adulthood, the youngest, Kamu-Yamatoihare-hiko-no-mikoto, suggested to the eldest, Itsuse-no-mikoto, that they should leave the palace of Takachiho their great-grandfather had built in Himuka in Kyushu, and travel to establish imperial rule. They traveled peacefully for the most part, resting from time to time for lengthy periods in halls they built along the way, or were entertained by the local inhabitants. At Shirakata, however, they were ambushed by Nagasunehiko of Toumi, a local ruler. Itsuse-no-mikoto was wounded. The two princes nonetheless defeated their enemies and traveled on to the land of Kii, where Itsuse died of his wounds.

Kamu-Yamatoihare-hiko-no-mikoto and his entourage traveled to Kumano in Kii, where a mysterious force affected them and they all fell asleep. A man from Kumano named Takakuraji came to Kamu-Yamatoihare-hiko-no-mikoto, the future emperor, bringing him a sword. In a dream, Takakuraji had seen the two heavenly deities Amaterasu-ō-mikami and Takamimusubi discussing the difficulties their descendant was experiencing. They ordered Takemikazuchi-no-kami (the deity who had subdued Ōkuninushi and his sons) to descend and help. He suggested they send down his sword through a hole in the roof of Takaku-raji's storehouse and alert the owner to pass the gift along. "Indeed," concluded Takakuraji, "when I woke this morning, I found the sword and hastened to present it to you." As soon as the sword was brought to him, all of the unruly deities of the Kumano mountains, who were responsible for the spell that had put the emperor and his men to sleep, were vanquished.

Takamimusubi then sent a giant crow to lead his descendant to safety. Kamu-Yamatoihare-hiko-no-mikoto journeyed on, meeting many local deities who greeted him with respect, until he reached a place called Uda. At Uda were two chiefs of the Ukashi people, Elder-brother and Younger-brother. When the crow came to ask whether the heavenly deities' descendant would be received, Elder-brother Ukashi shot at the messenger with a humming arrow (intended to produce fear in the victim). He then built a trap inside a festival hall constructed to welcome his guests. But his younger brother disapproved, and he came and disclosed the trap to the intended victim. Thereupon Elder-brother Ukashi was driven before Kamu-Yamatoihare-hiko-no-mikoto's forces into the hall and was caught by his own trap and hacked to bits by his intended victims. They also composed a satirical song:

> On the high place of Uda
> We set a bird net.
> We waited,
> But no birds were caught.
> Instead, a fine whale
> Fell into our net.

Kamu-Yamatoihare-hiko-no-mikoto then traveled on to Osaka, where eighty men of the Tsuchigumo lived in a traditional pit dwelling. He invited them to a feast with his men acting as servitors, one man standing behind each guest. At a signal, the eighty servants drew their swords and killed the eighty heroes of Osaka. Finally, after subduing many other tribes, Kamu-Yamatoihare-hiko-no-mikoto built himself a palace called Kashihara at Unebi and assumed his reign-name, Jimmu Tenno, as first emperor of Japan.

Yamato-takeru, the Hero of Yamato

Several generations of emperors passed. Emperor Keikō had two sons, Ousu-no-mikoto and Wousu-no-mikoto. "Large Mortar" and "Little Mortar" were apparently twins. Their father, as was the custom at the time, had had to carry around a rice-pounding mortar while his wife was in labor, and he was somewhat annoyed at the length of time the birth took, hence the names. Ousu-no-mikoto, the elder brother, failed to join the emperor for the morning or evening meals (at that time, the Japanese ate only two main meals a day). Some time before, Ousu-no-mikoto had been commissioned by his father to bring him two sisters, famed for their beauty, to be his wives. The son took the two for himself, substituting two other women, so he was in bad odor with his father in any case.

The emperor asked his second son, Wousu, to teach his older brother some manners.

Five days passed and the older brother still did not appear.

"Why hasn't your brother come? Have you warned him about his behavior?" the emperor asked his second son.

"I have," replied the stripling calmly.

"How did you warn him?"

"I caught him in the morning, when he went to the outhouse. I crushed him, then tore off his arms and legs, wrapping them in a mat and throwing them away."

The emperor was not unnaturally terrified at this display of savagery and strength, and dispatched his son to the west, where dwelt two rebellious men, Kumasō-takeru (Heroes of Kumasō) the Elder and the Younger, telling Wousu to kill them. Equipped only with a set of women's clothing supplied by his aunt, the High Priestess of Amaterasu-ō-mikami at Ise, and his small-sword, Wousu set off.

When he arrived at the Kumasō domain, he found they were about to celebrate the construction of a new pit dwelling. Guards surrounded the new construction. The young lad waited for the feast, then combed his hair over in the way of young girls and dressed in his prescient aunt's gift. With these he sneaked in with the local women. The Heroes of Kumasō were very much taken by this fresh and unknown maiden and had "her" sit between them during the feast.

When the drinking and excitement had allayed their caution, our hero drew his short sword from his bosom and stabbed the Elder Hero of Kumasō to death. The Younger Kumasō-takeru jumped up to flee, but was caught by the prince at the foot of the ladder leading up from the pit. There the attacker grabbed his victim and stabbed him clear through the body from behind.

"Don't remove the sword!" cried the Kumasō-takeru..

The young prince assented.

"Who are you?" asked the Younger Kumasō-takeru.

"I'm the son of emperor Keikō, who rules all these islands. He sent me to pacify you disrespectful Kumasō."

"We are the bravest men in the West, and you have killed us," said the Younger Kumasō-takeru. "I therefore bestow upon you the title we bore. You will be known henceforth as Yamato-takeru, Hero of the Yamato."

When Kumasō-takeru had had his say, the prince, now known by his new name, withdrew the sword, slicing his victim like a ripe melon. On his way back, he subdued all the local mountain and river deities.

Yamato-takeru's father must have been less than reassured by his savage offspring's return, and the next we hear of him, he was dispatched to kill Izumo-takeru, another local hero. Yamato-takeru prepared an imitation sword of wood, which he wore instead of a real one. Then he entered the land of Izumo, pretending friendship with his intended victim. One day the two heroes went to bathe in the Hii River. Yamato-takeru emerged first from the water and cried "Let us exchange swords!" The other agreed, taking Yamato-takeru's fake sheathed sword and thrusting it through his sash. Then Yamato-takeru said, "Let's practice fencing." Yamato-takeru then drew his borrowed blade and killed his hapless victim. Never at loss for words, he then mocked the other in a poem:

> The hero of Izumo,
> Land of the heavy cloud banks.
> Wears a sword,
> Vine sheathed
> But alas, without a blade.

He then returned to report to his father.

The emperor was not anxious to keep his rather intemperate son at home, so he sent him on another mission, this time to subdue the East. The emperor also gave his son a single attendant and a magical spear. On his way, Yamato-takeru stopped once again with his aunt, the high priestess of the shrine to Amaterasu-ō-mikami at Ise. He complained to his aunt that his father wanted to get rid of him, sending him to subdue a country without any troops. His aunt, helpful as ever, gave him the sword Kusanagi, which had been the gift of Susano-wo, and a bag.

"Should there be a problem," she said, "Open the bag."

On his way he met a maiden, Miyazu-hime, in Owari, and promised to marry her on his return. He then proceeded to the East and subdued the tribes there. Eventually he reached Sagamu. The king of that land (taking a page from Yamato-takeru's own book) pretended friendship, but said:

"Near here is a plain. In the middle of it is a pond, where lives a rebellious and unruly deity."

When the hero went to check on the pond, the king set fire to the grass on the plain. Yamato-takeru looked into the bag he had been given and found fire-making flints. He mowed down the grass around him with his sword (justifying the sword's name of "Grass-cutter") then set a counterfire. He then killed the king and all his clan, burning them in their houses, and called the place Yakitsu (Burning ford). Never at a loss for words, he was making a pun: *yaki* can also mean "roast".

On his way back home, he had to cross the sea straits at Hashirimitsu. But the deity of the crossing stirred up the waves, and the boat was about to sink. Yamato-takeru's consort, Otōtachibana-hime, sacrificed herself to the waves, piling sedge mats, skin mats, and silk mats one on the other, then laying them and herself as offering on the waves. The boat proceeded on its way, and the princess sank into the waves. Only her comb was washed ashore. At the pass of Ashigara, as Yamato-takeru was eating his rations, the deity of the pass assumed the form of a white deer. Yamato-takeru took a piece of wild garlic he was eating and struck the deer, killing it. At the top of the pass he remembered his wife, and sighing, named the land he had pacified Azuma ("My wife"). After pacifying more lands on his way, he returned to Owari and married Miyazu-hime, whom he had courted on his way to the East. Leaving his bride at her house and entrusting her with his sword Kusanagi, he went to subdue the deity of Mt. Ibuki. Without a sword, he decided to take on the deity with his bare hands. On his way he met a giant boar, which was the deity in disguise. "This must be the deity's messenger, sent to distract me," he said to himself, and proceeded up the mountain. But the deity caused a hailstorm that struck Yamato-takeru and dazed him, so he had to come down off the mountain, mortally ill. He walked from there, progressively getting worse (and composing poems about his condition, in the best heroic tradition) until, at Nōbo, he died.

As his wives and children (presumably the story compresses several years of the hero's life, during which he married several times, became emperor, and fathered children) assembled to construct his tomb, the spirit of the hero was transformed into a giant white bird, which flew away. It finally alighted near the shore at Shiki, where his tomb was built and is called the White Bird Tomb.

The Empress Jingū Subdues Korea, and the *Kami* Hachiman Is Born

Years later, with imperial rule established, Emperor Chūai was playing his zither when his empress, Okinagatarashi-hime, known as Jingū, became possessed and uttered the following prophecy: "There is a land to the west, abounding with treasures of gold, silver, and jewels. I give you this country."

The emperor was suspicious, dismissing the words as those of a deceiving *kami.* In any case, he was preparing for an expedition to subdue the Kumasō of the South. He therefore replied, "When one climbs a mountain and looks westward, one sees only the sea."

The enraged *kami* then said (through the empress), "*You* will not rule this promised land." And, indeed, the emperor soon died. After a lengthy process of exorcism and searching out sins throughout the country, the empress prophesied again, giving the same instructions, with one rider: "The child in your womb will rule that land." The *kami* giving these instructions were Sokojutsu-no-ō, Nakajutsu-no-ō, and Uwajutsu-no-ō, children of Izanagi and lords of the sea. The now-pregnant Empress Jingū then assembled a fleet and army, made offerings to the *kami,* and was borne by the good winds across the sea to the land of Shiragi (the kingdom of Silla in Korea), whose king became a vassal offering annual tribute. The king was designated a royal stable-groom. Though not a high rank, this was not a mark of shame: It was definite acknowledgment of the king of Shiragi's position at court, and in effect, a royal honor (he didn't have to feed or curry the horses with his own hands!). The king of Kudara also became a vassal, and his lands became property of the Japanese throne. Meanwhile the empress delayed the birth of her son by tying rocks to the waist of her skirt.

When she returned to Japan, her child, named Ōjin, was born in a place called Umi. At Matsura in Tsukushi she ate a meal on the banks of the river. Using grains of rice for bait, she fished from some rocks for *ayu* (a small river fish). This was during the fourth month, and since then, only women can catch the *ayu* on that month using the traditional method taught by Jingū.

Upon her return, Empress Jingū was faced by a rebellion of two of Emperor Chūai's children by another wife. The imperial forces used a ruse, saying that the baby emperor was dead. When the rebels came to inspect the funeral ship bearing the supposed body, the loyalist army attacked, chasing the rebels to Yamashiro. The loyalist general then used another ruse, announcing that the empress had died. The rebels again believed the story and unstrung their bows. The loyalists attacked again, and the rebels were defeated, whereupon they jumped into the waters of Lake Biwa and drowned.

Ōjin reigned as emperor for fifty-two years. His mother, Jingū, lived for one hundred. He had many children from several wives and extended the domain of the empire. While thus engaged, however, he was also a man of culture. He ensured that his sons and other men of his court were diligent in their studies. During his reign, many Korean immigrants—craftsmen, traders, and scholars—settled in his domains. As a consequence, he was deified with his mother as Hachiman, the *kami* of both war and culture.

THE AGE OF HEROES

The subsequent mythological age was an age of heroes. Though the doings of the Imperial family were noted in great detail in the *Kōjiki* and the *Nihonshōki*, they turned from the mythical to the mundane: the murders, squabbles, loves, and children of assorted emperors and empresses. Many of these details may be factual and, indeed, can be traced through documents and artifacts of the time.

In parallel, however, and recorded not in the "official" accounts of the emperors' reigns and chronicles, myths began emerging about individuals—mainly men but also some women—who performed acts of heroism and strength. Some of these are enhancements of real historical events, seen through a mythical lens. Many of the earlier heroes were continuing the work of "pacifying" the countryside started by Ninigi-no-mikoto and were working under the authority, claimed or real, of the emperor. Later heroes, such as Yoshitsune, were warriors through and through. Their loyalty was to their clan and lord, or to themselves alone. And, as we get to later myths, more and more Buddhist elements are inserted, until the Shintō elements we saw in the creation and pacification tales—myths about how things came to be, myths about the *kami*, myths that gave charters to various families or clans—tend to disappear.

Historically, the Age of Heroes corresponds to the Heian (794–1185) and Kamakura (1185–1333) periods of Japanese history. A multitude of heroic myths emerge from this age: Tawara Toda, the archer hero and ally of the dragon king; En-no-Gyōja, the ascetic wizard and subduer of demons; and Kōbō Daishi, the Shingon saint, are all products of the Heian period. In each case the hero is a real historical figure to whom a mythical dimension has been added. The warrior heroes such as Tawara Toda and Raikō act in the name of the emperor, subduing rebels and bandits, many of them monstrous in appetite and appearance. The saints and wizards are all busy extending the rule of law (the emperor's) and the realm of the Law (the Buddha's). If the previous mythical period was one of creation and then conquest, this period is one of consolidation and civilization of a fractious hinterland. Two important myths arose from this period: the heroic tale of Yoshitsune, the perfect warrior; and the *kamikaze* divine wind sent by the *kami* Hachiman in the battle against the invading Mongol-Chinese armies of Kubilai Khan (1274, 1281).

The heroes are generally a rough lot. Like Yamato-takeru, they triumph by a combination of guile and force, using treachery and disguise when necessary. One important feature to remember is that they often operated with a retinue of retainers, sometimes one loyal servant, sometimes more. Many of these retainers, such as Musashibō Benkei and Kintarō, became more popular than their masters.

Tawara Toda, the Archer

Among the early heroes was Fujiwara Hidesato. Nicknamed Tawara Toda (Lord Rice Bale) for his ability to lift a rice bale (60 kg, or 132 lb.) in either hand, Tawara Toda was the foremost archer of his time. When a local ruler in the Kantō area (in what is today Chiba prefecture), Taira no Masakado by name, rebelled against imperial authority, Tawara Toda went to inspect the rebel, trying to decide whether to support him. He found Masakado eating dinner and agreed to share his meal. As they ate, Toda noticed that Masakado was absently picking up grains of rice he had spilled onto his robes and popping them into his mouth. At that he decided that Masakado was a mean man, unlikely to be generous to his supporters, and he promptly joined the imperial forces and brought about the defeat of Masakado.

Tawara Toda went on to other adventures. His most famous involved meeting Ryūjin, the dragon *kami.* As the hero was about to cross a bridge on Lake Biwa, he found his way blocked by a serpent. He stepped carefully over the animal, which turned into a dragon. The dragon informed the hero that he was Ryūjin, and that his kingdom was being plagued by a giant centipede. Tawara Toda accompanied the dragon back to his realm, where he confronted and attacked the centipede. His first arrows were shot accurately, but to no effect. He mastered his resources, wetted his last arrow with his own saliva, and with the arrow thus magicked, shot the centipede to death. The inexhaustible sack of rice he received from the grateful dragon may also have brought about his nickname.

Raikō and His Band of Heroes

Minamoto-no-Yorimitsu was a famous archer during the reign of Emperor Murakami. Nicknamed Raikō, he is credited with ridding the land of many robbers and rebels (the terms being almost synonymous in Japan at that period) and extending the rule of the emperor throughout the land. Raikō is at one and the same time an extension of the imperial will, following in the footsteps of Jimmu Tenno and a figure of the sort that was extremely important for later Japanese myth: the head of a group of heroes, rather than a lone hand. The myths about Raikō, which can be found in various localities throughout Japan, have a distinctly local flavor, associating topographic features with the imperial will, and thus associating wide-flung areas of the empire with imperial rule.

Woman Heroes

Though Japanese culture has, at least since the injection of Chinese culture, been intensely male-oriented, Japanese myths contain a number of instances of female heroes. Amaterasu and Empress Jingū have already been discussed, and they belong properly to the pre-sinicized era. However, even during the aristocratic and medieval periods there were a few instances of female warriors.

Of them the one who is most famous in Japanese myth is Tomoe Gozen, the wife of Kido Hidesato, one of the Minamoto generals. There is no evidence of her existence beyond the legend, which tells of her military prowess (she led a troop of some three thousand defending against Taira attacks). Several other female heroes are also recorded, including some strong women, able to lift rice bales or fight with tree boles.

What is common to all these myths is their tragic overtones: In almost all cases, Tomoe Gozen included, the woman ends up either being killed or being made the property of an eventual victor. In that sense these stories are part of the myths that tell of things-as-they-should-be. Strong as a woman is, she is after all a woman and therefore must play second fiddle (or concubine) to a successful man.

Benkei and Yoshitsune

This story starts, oddly enough, with the servant, not the master. Benkei was a *sōhei*, one of the armed monk-soldiers who defended their monasteries (in his case, Enryakuji, of the Tendai sect, on Mt. Hiei). The *sōhei* of Mt. Hiei—which is clearly visible from today's Kyoto, weather and pollution permitting—were in the habit of descending on the imperial court whenever their monasteries did not receive what they considered their due in respect or handouts, and the monasteries and temples were not fighting among themselves. Benkei was a powerful man of violent temper. He wore black-lacquered armor, which made him instantly recognizable. On one occasion, Benkei stole the giant bell of the Miidera temple over the mountains on the shores of Lake Biwa, east of the capital, and carried it home on his shoulders. Japanese temple bells tend to be large items. The one at Miidera is almost the height of a man. Prevailed upon by his abbot to return it, he contemptuously gave the bell a kick, and it bounced back to its place of origin.

At one stage, unable to find a rival to test his mettle, Benkei set up shop in the middle of one of Heian-kyō's major bridges. He had made a vow, he said, to have armor forged of the swords of one thousand warriors. He therefore challenged every passer-by who carried one to a duel, the sword to be forfeit to the winner. One day a handsome youth tried to cross the bridge. He was made up in the proper manner for a young *bushi* (warrior) who had not yet undergone the adulthood ceremony, and he was playing a flute. Because he also carried a sword, Benkei challenged him. The young man, Ushiwakamaru (Young Bull) by name, nimbly outfought his gigantic opponent, defending himself with little but his flute and folding fan. Benkei was so impressed by his foe that he vowed to serve Ushiwakamaru for the rest of his life.

Ushiwakamaru himself, better known by his adult name, Yoshitsune, was the younger son of the Minamoto clan chief who had lost his head to the Taira. He had only been saved by the quick wits and sheer grit of his mother, who had married her Taira captor. Ushiwakamaru had been sent to serve as a novice in a temple on Mt. Kurama, north of the capital. His elder brother, Yoritomo, by now an adult, was in hiding in eastern Japan. At Kurama, Yoshitsune (not, apparently, religiously inclined) was wont to wander the woods, where he made friends with a *dai tengu*, a wild forest spirit. The *tengu* had instructed the young man in the art of fencing, and by the time he had left Mt. Kurama to come to the capital, he was already the best-trained fencer in Japan.

When Yoritomo raised the flag of rebellion against the Taira, Ushiwakamaru, now bearing his adult name Yoshitsune, became one of his generals. Numerous military victories are ascribed to him, the greatest being the final defeat of the Taira at Dan-no-Ura. But his fame endures, and myths about him emerged, because of his brother's attempts to kill him. Yoritomo, always highly suspicious of his subordinates, became convinced that Yoshitsune intended to supplant him. In a series of campaigns Yoritomo forced Yoshitsune to flee, finally catching and burning Yoshitsune to death along with his castle and retainers. Japanese myth claims that Yoshitsune actually escaped, establishing himself as a Mongol warrior named Temujin, and giving birth to the Mongol dynasty of Genghis Khan. Throughout his exploits, he had the loyal Benkei at his side. Once, while they were crossing a frontier barrier at San no Kuchi, Yoshitsune, who had a "Wanted" notice out for him, had to disguise himself as a servant, and Benkei posed as his master. To complete the ruse, Yoshitsune required that Benkei beat him in front of the barrier commander. So moved was the commander by Benkei's obvious distress at having to beat his "servant" that he let them through.

The greatest myth of the Age of Heroes, however, relates to the nature of Japan rather than to any particular individual. The thirteenth-century invasion of Japan by Mongol fleets provided plenty of examples of individual heroism. However, the event is remembered more vividly because of the phenomenon of the *kamikaze,* the divine wind that the *kami* blew up to defend the Japanese nation. This, the climactic myth of the age of heroes, found expression during World War II as young Japanese men sacrificed themselves in a vain attempt to stop a modern invasion. The myth of the modern *kamikaze* relates modern Japan directly to its mythical past. It lives on, in a sense, in the new Yasukan, the memorial hall to Japan's fallen soldiers at the Yasukuni shrine in Kudanshita, Tokyo. And while many individual Japanese credit neither the medieval *kamikaze* nor the modern ones as a divine event, the power of the myth is evident in the numbers of modern visitors and the economics of building and maintaining the hall.

BUDDHIST MYTHS

Buddhist myths are substantially different from those of Shintō origin. Virtually all of the Buddhist-related myths have to do with the establishment of the Buddhist Law in one way or another. They are also, with the exception of myths regarding Shakyamuni, rarely sequential. They can be divided into two rather broad categories. The first contains the myths of Indian and Chinese origin that deal with the establishment of Buddhism. They do not refer directly (or even indirectly, by and large) to Japan. Though retold in Japan, they are in effect Buddhist myths from which the Japanese have made a selection to bolster the choice of particular Buddhist venerated figures: Buddhas and boddhisattvas, gods and sages.

The second broad category contains myths associated either with specific Japanese Buddhist sages, such as Kōbō Daishi, or local stories—of miracles, piety, ghosts, and demons—that have been elaborated into Buddhist morality tales.

The Life of Shakyamuni and the Formation of Buddhism

The details of Shakyamuni's life—his conception, birth, upbringing, and notably his life as religious teacher—have been central to much Buddhist literature. Many of these tales have been transported to Japan. Significantly, some of the myths have provided mythological foundations for figures in the mix of Shintō and Buddhism that prevailed in Japan until the Meiji era (late nineteenth century). For example, *dakini*, a class of female anthropophagous demons in Hindu mythology, has been translated into the myth of the goddess Dakini in Japan, who because she flies on a white fox has been associated with Inari as the *honji* (Buddhist aspect of a Shintō deity).

The thrust of the Shakyamuni myths in Japan has been the ability of the Law, and of the Buddha to bend evil, in the form of demons, to his will. This is accomplished not by violence but by persuasion. Significantly, in Japanese myth, there are few evil beings. Mischievous, disobedient, and fractious, yes; but the concept of evil (in the Christian sense) does not emerge coherently in the mythology.

There are also a number of myths, such as the retrieval of the Law by Ryūgo (Nagarjuna, a major figure in early Buddhism) from an iron tower in Southern India, which connect the life of Shakyamuni with the establishment of Buddhism in Japan: Ryūgo, for example, is seen as the sage-founder of the Mahayana form of Buddhism, which is the forerunner of all Japanese Buddhist sects.

The Arrival of Buddhism in Japan

The second thrust of Buddhist myths in Japan concerns myths associated with the establishment of Buddhism in Japan. Since Buddhism arrived from so many sources, there have been a great number of such myths as well. These myths mostly tell of how, through struggle and perseverance and the timely intervention of one or another of the Buddhist gods, the Law arrived in Japan, sometimes in the form of a blazing jewel, or of a scroll of writings. Intermediate stages exist as well, as for instance the hugely popular series of myths that deal with the foundation of Zen in China by Daruma. No myth links Daruma directly with Japan, and yet the figure has been immensely popular in art and folk representation.

A second popular figure is that of Kōbō Daishi. Perhaps his personal popularity (the sect he founded in Japan, Shingon, has always appealed more to the aristocracy) is due to the fact that he was uninvolved, until fairly late in life, with the court in Heian-kyō. As a consequence, he is very much seen as a popular figure by commoners. The eighty-eight-stage pilgrimage that he founded in

Shikoku and the worship of Konpira that he established are still very much alive in people's consciousness. Many people still do the famous pilgrimage route, but large portions are by bus and train, which sort of spoils much of the earlier magic. Much of the pilgrimage route is now covered in concrete and asphalt, victim of Japan's continued urbanization. Other myths, about founders such as En-no-Gyōja, or even about monks and abbots, followers of the Buddha, and so on, also fit into this category, though they may have no "historical" progression.

Morality Tales

The final set of myths derived from Buddhism are more in the nature of morality tales or homilies. Collections of these tales, which demonstrated the virtues of adhering to Buddhist precepts, were published frequently from the Kamakura period onward. Some of them have become extremely famous: One example is the legend of Dojōji, in which a young woman smitten by a handsome priest tries to seduce him, and when the love affair fails, as inevitably it would, she is transformed into a ravening dragon (this has become a staple of Kabuki drama).

Unlike the Shintō myths, the Buddhist myths tend to be either highly personalized or punctuated, rather than chronological. Myths about the Buddha Shakyamuni are the most coherent, as are myths about individuals in Japanese history. The morality tales seem to be embedded in Japanese history (there is often a specific historical referent, for example, "In the days of Emperor Kimmu . . ."), but certainly upon examination, the historical referent is rarely significant for the myth, and it may well have been some later addition intended to provide veracity and authenticity.

MYTHICAL SPACES

Like members of many other cultures, Japanese define themselves in terms of a conceptual, or mythical, time and space. The structure of these concepts in Japanese thinking is complicated by two issues. First is one we have already discussed: the varied sources—native Japanese, Chinese and Indian imports, and Western science—from which they are drawn.

The second is, paradoxically, the nature of Japanese language and writing, which allows and encourages puns, plays on words, and "deliberate" warping of meaning by jumping from one mode of communication, for example common speech, to another mode, writing *kanji*, to make a pun or elicit a meaning. The intention of word play and puns is not all facetious or humorous. It helps people embed their experience in some common ground, to share experiences and non-material ideas, and it creates a shared set of concepts, unique to those who share the same language.

The creation of mythical times and spaces in Japanese myth is therefore the intersection of a number of factors, not all of them mythical in nature. Landscape features, antique and forgotten rituals and practices, political events, and human attempts to organize their experiences in a meaningful way create the mythical reality.

Perhaps the most significant issue regarding mythical space, which is true to all of the myths and myth complexes discussed here, is the relationship between the cosmos and the deities. In Buddhism and Shintō (unlike the Judeo-Christian system), the deities are part of the world. Even though they have a great deal of power and freedom to act as they will, even when they are, as in Jōdō Shinshū and Nichiren-shū, monotheistic deities, they are still limited by the cosmic rules that surround them. They cannot, on a whim or for any reason, change the basic cosmological rules that are fundamental to the universe. The effect of works, good or ill, on human destiny, and the nature of human beings are things with which the deity, no matter how compassionate or interested in salvation, must work.

Buddhist Spaces

The spaces of Buddhist cosmology are at one and the same time symbolic representations of the moral and theological themes that Buddhism preaches (largely for the adept, the priest, and the religious expert) and very real parts of the cosmos that one might, and possibly will, visit at some time (for the main body of believers). In rough terms, the cosmos can contain within itself any number of universes, all proceeding from past to future. At the same time, the universe is divided into several realms. What connects these realms is the symbolic/topographical feature called Mt. Meru (Sumeru in Sanskrit).

Called Sumi in Japanese, Mt. Meru is the mythical and physical representation of the universe in Buddhist thought. The roots of this mountain lie in hell, where the souls of those who have done evil in their life suffer torment until they expiate their sins or acknowledge the mercy of Buddha (depending on Buddhist sect). On its flanks toil those who are on the path, the way to achieve Buddhahood. The upper slopes contain the domains of the various Buddhist deities, with their armies, attendants, subordinates, and servants: a giant host of hosts. At the peak are the paradises of the various directions (two, that of the West and that of the East, feature heavily in Japanese cosmology), and at the peak is the Realm of Formlessness, where those who have attained nirvana can be found.

Hell is a contradictory concept in Buddhism. Punishment for sins in life should, in theory, occur in the process of rebirth. Nonetheless, Jigoku has a very real mythical existence. Like Dante's version, there is a hell to fit every crime. Monsters and *oni* (demons), many borrowed from Indian or Chinese cosmology, torment the denizens with fire, ice, and instruments of torture. The number and kind of *loggia*, to follow Dante's terminology, depend, once again, on which Buddhist sect is doing the defining. The one common major feature of hell is the dry riverbed that runs through, or beside, it. In this foggy plain are the souls of innocents such as aborted children, who have noone to assist them in their climb to better realms. Before hell also flows Shozukawa, the hell river, which only the souls of the dead, stripped of their possessions by the Shozuka-no-baba (the hell hag), can pass.

The universe of the living is effectively limitless. Japanese Buddhist cosmology recognizes that though Japan is the most important of all locations, there are myriad worlds without end encompassed within the universe.

The myriad realms of the deities lie above, arrayed in a variety of locations and systems. Supreme over all these, and responsible for the defense of Mt. Meru (that is, of the entire Buddhist Law that Meru represents), are the four Tenno. Each marshals his own particular gifts; for example, Bishamon, guardian of the North, is also the guardian of earthly treasure. Each also marshals his own host of followers and soldiers who defend that particular direction.

Above these, toward the ultimate peak, are the paradises of the various Buddhas, the peak itself being occupied by ___ Buddha (fill in the blank according to your sect).

The schematic described here is just that: a schematic. Its details vary considerably, and none of it appears as a full description in any myth. Rather it is an abstract drawn from the many viewpoints that express the entity called Buddhism. Certainly the motif of the mountain is very powerful in Buddhist thought. In Japan it has been reinforced by the native predilection for mountains and mountain deities, and may well have been one of the reasons Buddhism found such easy acceptance in Japan.

Shintō Spaces

Shintō cosmology and topography are far simpler than Buddhism's. The definition of the various realms of the cosmos is also far more clearly delineated, with actual geographical features framing much of the mythical topography.

The realm of the heavenly *kami*, Takamagahara (Plain of Heaven), overarches the realm of the earth. Within heaven lie the halls of the various gods, though we have a description of only one: that of Amaterasu-ō-mikami. It has specialized halls for the usual domestic tasks—weaving is mentioned—as well as paddy fields and dikes. Running through heaven is a riverbed. The river itself has been dammed upstream so that the *kami* have a wide assembly place (necessary in a system that rules by consensus, as the Japanese still do, and where the participants number eight million). The river runs from a range of high mountains. Heaven is bounded on its earthly side by a shallow stream: This is where Amaterasu confronts her wayward brother.

Two significant features in heaven are its exits. There is the Heavenly Floating Bridge, often identified with the Milky Way, which joins heaven to earth, and from which the earth was created. There is also a major crossroads, of which one road leads to heaven, the other to earth: This is where Sarutahiko awaited the descent of the heavenly grandson.

The earth is composed of several parts. The first is the sea, which appears boundless. It preceded the land, which was drawn from it "like the shoot of a reed." The land itself is composed of islands, some formed originally from the drops that coalesced on the tip of Izanagi's jeweled spear, others born of the intercourse between Izanagi and his mate, Izanami. The main component of these islands are the ones that make up the Japanese archipelago. The topography here is that familiar to us from modern Japan, though the names have changed and many places are identified very doubtfully. Certainly the plains and mountains of Yamato (in the modern Kansai area); the Yoshino mountains on the Kii peninsula (southeast of Yamato); Lake Biwa, which borders Yamato to the east; Izumo to the northwest; and the Seto Sea and island of Kyushu to the south are all identified and play a part in the myths. The Korean Peninsula features as well, especially two of the three major Korean polities of the time, Silla and Paekche.

The domain of the sea god, variously Owatatsumi-no-kami or Ryūjin, is like the earth except that the denizens are fish rather than humans. In former times, until Ho-ori's disagreement with his wife, the domains of the sea and the land were one expanse. Now they are separate parts of the earth. Other parts of the earth are reachable through caves or fissures in the earth's crust. Perhaps the most important is an undefined realm across the sea. This is the homeland of such *marebito* (visiting deities) as Sukunabikona, the magician dwarf god who helps Ōkuninushi complete the construction of the land started by Izanagi. There is some reason to suggest, argues Ouwehand, that this land, sometimes identified (following a Chinese legend) as the Isles of the Blessed, is in reality the final realm of myth: the Land of Yōmi.

The Land of Yōmi exists underground. It is a damp and dark place, devoid of light and color. We have no clear topography of the place. The dead, judging by the description in the *Kōjiki* and the *Nihonshōki*, exist in halls as they do in life. Their torment, if such there is, consists of being separated from their former lives and particularly from their loved ones and friends. No other torments are in evidence, nor is the land of Yōmi a place of punishment. Yōmi is merely a place of utter pollution from which no one returns.

Chronology: Historical and Mythical

Time Period	Key Historical Events	Myth or mythical period	Dates
		Age of Creation	
		Emergence of the *kami*. The creation of the islands of Japan.	
Evidence of preceramic culture	Shell mounds		9000 B.C.E.
Jōmon	Pottery culture; pit housing; large villages.		ca. 7000–250 B.C.E.
	The birth, life, and miracles of the Buddha in India.		565(?)–486
		Ōkuninushi. The Subjugation of the land by the heavenly deities. The Izumo myths of Susano-wo??	
		Mythical date of the accession of Jimmu Tenno.	660 B.C.E.
		Age of Emperors	
Yayoi culture			ca. 250 B.C.E.–300 C.E.
Yamato Period			300 B.C.E.(?)/300 C.E.(?)–645
		Yamato-takeru.	

	Japanese trade colonies in Korea	Empress Jingū invades Korea.	ca. 2nd century B.C.E. (or more likely, 366 C.E.)
Kofun Period	Construction of *kofun* monumental tombs. Expansion of Yamato state.		400 C.E.–593
	Introduction of Buddhism from Korea.		552 or 538
	King of Paekche sends image of Miroku-butsu to Emperor Kimmei.		545
	Regency of Shōtoku Taishi.		593–622
	Seventeen-article rescript.		604
	First embassy to China.		607
		Oracle of Miwa declares Buddhist priests are to perform funeral rites.	616
	Taika Reform. Chinese-influenced administrative revolution, the entire government being remodeled on the plan of the Chinese bureaucracy. Head of Yamato clan declared sovereign son-of-heaven on Chinese model.		645
		En-no-Gyōja performs miracles. Foundation of Shugendō.	634–701
Nara Period	Nara becomes first fixed capital.		710–784
	Dedication of the Great Buddha statue (Daibutsu) of Tōdaiji in Nara.		752
	Life of Kōbō Daishi. Establishment of 88-stage pilgrimage on Shikoku.	Miracles performed by the Daishi.	774–835

	Ryōbu-Shintō accepted as proper doctrine.		ca. 700–800
Heian Period	Capital established at Heian-kyō (modern Kyoto).		794–1185
	Introduction of Tendai sect.		805
	Introduction of Shingon sect.		806
	Twelfth and last embassy to China.		838

Age of Heroes

	Fudō statue brought to Kantō.	Raikō and his four vassals. Tawara Toda kills Taira-no-Masakado.	940
	Heiji conflict; military supremacy gained by Taira clan.	Tomoe Gozen Hachimantarō, etc.	1159–1160
	Founding of the Jōdō (Pure Land) sect by Shōnin (1133–1212). Jōdō-Shinshu sect founded by Shinran		1175
	Gempei War between the Minamoto and the Taira.	Minamoto-no Yoshitsune and Benkei.	1180–1185
Kamakura Period			1185–1333
	Title of shogun granted to Yoritomo.		1192
	Mongol invasions.	Nichiren-shōnin's miracles.	1274, 1281
Ashikaga (or Muromachi) Period			1338–1573
Sengoku (Civil War) Period			ca. 1480–1568
	Portuguese arrive at Tanegashima; introduce Western firearms		1542 or 1543

Azuchi-Momoyama (or Shokuhō) Period			1568–1600
	Occupation of Kyoto by warlord Oda Nobunaga.		1568
	Nobunaga assassinated.		1582
	Osaka Castle built by Toyōtōmi Hideyoshi		1586
	Hideyoshi supreme in Japan.		1590
	Hideyoshi's invasion of Korea.		1592
	Death of Hideyoshi and withdrawal of troops from Korea.		1598
	Victory of Tokugawa Ieyasu at the Battle of Sekigahara.		1600
Tokugawa (or Edo) Period	Assumption of power by Tokugawa clan. Capital moved to Edo. Era of secluded and peaceful country.		1600–1868
	Title of shogun acquired by Ieyasu.		1603

Modern Age

Meiji Period	Formal restoration of Imperial rule and end of shoguns. Japan starts to modernize. Imperial capital established at Tokyo (formerly Edo).	Consolidation of the myth of Japan.	1868–1912
	Sino-Japanese War Japan defeats China.	"Triumph of Japanese spirit."	1894–1895
	Russo-Japanese War. First defeat of a European power by a non-European.		1904–1905
	Annexation of Korea.		1910

Taishō Period		1912–1926
Shōwa Period		1926–1990
	Outbreak of war with China.	1937
	Attack on Pearl Harbor, start of Pacific War of World War II.	1941
	Kamikaze attacks. Surrender of Japan.	1945
Heisei Period	Death of Shōwa Emperor (Hirohito). Succession by his son.	1991–

3

DEITIES, THEMES, AND CONCEPTS

AE-OINA KAMUI (AINU)

A "teacher" *kamui* and culture hero who taught humans the domestic arts. Armed with a magical and irresistible spear of mugwort (*Artemisia vulgaris*, a bitter aromatic herb), Ae-oina Kamui fought many battles on behalf of humankind. Instructed by Kamui Fuchi, the *kamui* of the hearth, he taught weaving and other domestic tasks to Ainu women. He is depicted as wreathed in mist or smoke. When this parts briefly, he is seen to be skirted by flames from his feet to his belt, wearing a coat of elm-bark fiber, its hem aflame, and a girt with a flame-tipped sword-sheath. The flames indicate his strongly virtuous character and his association with Kamui Fuchi.

There are a number of myths of his origin, due most probably to regional differences among Ainu tribes: Some say he was born of the elm tree, or fathered by the sun or by thunder, or even by Pakoro Kamui, the deity of pestilence and smallpox.

In the myths of some Ainu areas, Ae-oina Kamui is identified with Okikurmi, the culture hero and magician. He/they are often referred to as *Ainurakkur*, meaning the father of the Ainu. He is at the same time a savior and a dangerous *kamui*. In one myth, he kills a magical giant char with his spear of mugwort, saving humanity from famine. In another myth he fights a famine crone, who has built fish traps to block the salmon from the people. He breaks all her fish traps, then releases herds of deer and schools of fish from the snow on his snowshoes. And another myth recounts how he forces the sister of the owl deity, Chikap Kamui, to marry him after defeating Chikap Kamui in battle.

Ae-oina Kamui/Okikurmi is credited with teaching humans the important basics of being Ainu (i.e., human). Philippi summarizes these teachings as (1) ritual activities appropriate for men and for women; (2) handicraft techniques specific to men (carving) and women (needlework); (3) fishing, hunting, and gathering techniques; (4) architecture; (5) medicine; (6) dispute settlement (that is, law); and (7) entertainment and singing.

Ae-oina Kamui finally returned to heaven, or, in some epics, left for another country, in disgust at the depraved ways of the Ainu. With his departure started the long decline of the Ainu. Thus the Ainu equate their subjugation by the Japanese in terms of the departure of their culture hero.

See also Kamui Fuchi; Okikurmi.

References and further reading:

Munro, Neil Gordon. 1962. *Ainu Creed and Cult.* London: Routledge and Kegan Paul; London and New York: K. Paul International, distributed by Columbia University Press, 1995.

Philippi, Donald L., trans. 1979. *Songs of Gods, Songs of Humans: The Epic Tradition of the Ainu.* Princeton: Princeton University Press.

AIZEN-MYŌ-Ō

Deity of love and sex, worshiped by prostitutes, landlords, singers, and musicians. One of the Myō-ō (heavenly kings). Despite his ferocious appearance he is considered to be beneficial to humankind. Originally he was a deity of the Shingon and Tendai esoteric schools and represented love and desire for enlightenment and union with the Buddha. With time, desire was interpreted as carnal desire as well, and Aizen became patron of the "Floating World": the evanescent world of the entertainer and prostitute, which, though decried incessantly in Buddhist thought and literature, was deeply embedded into actual life.

Aizen is portrayed as having a red body and face, and six hands. These hold a bell, a five-pointed *kongō* (a double-ended weapon representing diamond and thunderbolt; see *Weapons*), an arrow, a bow, and a lotus bud. He has three eyes, one set vertically in the middle of his forehead, and his erect hair is topped by a *shishi* (q.v.), lion's head. His expression is ferocious and angry. He represents passions conquered, and subjugation of oneself, and one's external enemies through self-control.

During the second Mongol attack on Japan (1281) Aizen Myō-ō was invoked. He shot an arrow from his bow, which precipitated a tempest—the *kamikaze*—which sank the Mongol fleet.

In addition to being the patron of entertainers, Aizen is also worshipped as patron of dyers and cloth sellers. The reason is a play on words between Aizen and *aizome* (dyeing with indigo). He is worshiped as such in the Nichiō-ji temple in Tokyo.

See also Animals: shishi; *Kamikaze;* Weapons.

References and further reading:

Frank, Bernard. 1991. *Le pantheon bouddhique au Japon.* Paris: Collections d'Emile Guimet. Reunion des musees nationaux.

AJISHIKITAKAHIKONE-NO-KAMI

One of the many thunder deities. The son of Ōkuninushi, he is the tutelary deity of Kamo province. He was a friend of Ame-no-wakahiko, who had been dispatched by the heavenly deities to subdue the land. After Ame-no-wakahiko had been killed for rebelling against the heavenly *kami*'s orders, Ajishikitakahikone-no-kami arrived at the obsequies, but was mistaken by the dead deity's parents for their son. Ajishikitakahikone, enraged at being confused with a polluting corpse, drew his sword and destroyed the funerary house, then left in high dudgeon.

He is often portrayed as a baby (no doubt due to his outburst at the funeral) who, unable to sleep, is carried by his mother up and down a ladder in order to lull him to sleep. The sound of growing thunder is the result of his being pulled up and down the ladder. The same myth is told, of course, of the other thunder deities as well.

See also Ame-no-wakahiko; Swords; Takemikazuchi-no-kami; Thunder Deities.
References and further reading:
Aston, William G., trans. 1956. *Nihongi.* London: Allen and Unwin.
Philippi, Donald, trans. and ed. 1968. *Kōjiki.* Tokyo: Tokyo University Press.

AMA-NO-UZUME

The *kami* who enticed Amaterasu-ō-mikami from her cave by dancing a lewd dance. Ama-no-uzume is one of the most active deities in Shintō mythology. One of the most aggressive, powerful, and crafty of the deities, she features in many of the world foundation myths.

When the sun goddess, incensed by the behavior of her brother, hid herself in a cave, it was Ama-no-uzume-no-mikoto who enticed her out. She bound up her sleeves and hair with sacred vines and carried a fan of *sasa* leaves (a grass similar to bamboo). Overturning a bucket, she stamped and danced upon it, then becoming possessed, she danced a lewd dance, exposing her breasts and genitals, causing the audience of worried *kami* to laugh out loud, thus enticing the solar deity from her hiding place.

When Ninigi-no-mikoto was ready to descend from the Plain of Heaven to the Central Land of the Reed Plains, his way was blocked at the Eightfold Cross-roads by Sarutahiko-no-kami, an earth *kami*. Ama-no-uzume—considered a woman of great character and force—was dispatched by Amaterasu-ō-mikami and Takamimusubi-no-kami to demand explanations and subdue him as necessary, which she promptly did. As a consequence, she became one of Ninigi's advisers and companions in the descent to the land. As she had been the first to recognize Sarutahiko, Ninigi-no-mikoto commanded her to accompany Sarutahiko home when the latter's work as guide to the Central Land of the Reed Plains was done. Subsequently she became the ancestress of an important imperial clan and assumed the name of her protégé, Sarutahiko. It is possible, and some people hold, that they became man and wife. The accounts of her are a testimony to her determination and ruthlessness: Incensed by the sea cucumber's refusal to support the heavenly grandson, she promptly slit its mouth with her dagger, so that it is silent to this day.

She is sometimes worshiped as patroness of performers and dancers. She also appears as Otafuku or Okame: a full-cheeked, plump peasant woman laughing happily, whose name Otafuku means "large breasts." As such she is considered by some to be the *kami* of mirth, and she is accompanied by her husband, the peasant Hyottoko, who is identified with Sarutahiko. Both of these deities are addressed fervently during the November festival of *Tori-no-ichi* (Cock market), when merchants buy pictures or masks of the pair, together with wide bamboo rakes "to rake in fortune."

> ***See also*** Amaterasu-ō-mikami; Animals: sea cucumber; Ninigi-no-mikoto; Sarutahiko.
> ***References and further reading:***
> Aston, William G., trans. 1956. *Nihongi*. London: Allen and Unwin.
> Joly, Henri L. 1967. *Legend in Japanese Art*. Tokyo: Charles E. Tuttle Co.
> Philippi, Donald, trans. and ed. 1968. *Kōjiki*. Tokyo: Tokyo University Press.

AMATERASU-Ō-MIKAMI

Sun deity ancestress of Japan's imperial house and dominant heavenly *kami* of Japan. Amaterasu is the penultimate child of Izanagi and Izanami of the second, successful mating of the two founder deities. Having been born and assuming her place, she was offered an extreme insult by her brother, the wayward deity Susano-wo. After a suspicious meeting when he came to take leave of her (he was to rule over the underworld), she indulgently allowed him to live in the Realm of the Heavenly Deities. He reciprocated by polluting her fields with abominable acts, then throwing the flayed carcass of a horse onto her palace while she and her attendants were weaving. As a consequence, Amaterasu-ō-mikami withdrew into a cave, taking the light of the sun with her and rolling a great rock before the entrance. The deities, after assembling, managed to lure her from her cave. This was accomplished by Ama-no-uzume, who, dancing lasciviously, made the gods laugh. Intrigued by the levity, Amaterasu, peering from the cave, was entranced by the jewels the *kami* had hung in a tree. She asked why all the hilarity and was told that there was another deity in heaven fairer than she. She was then shown a mirror, which reflected her own face. As she peered into the mirror, Amano-tachikara-ō-no-kami, the strongman deity of heaven, pulled her from the cave. As a consequence, the mirror and jewels became part of her regalia.

Her grandson, Ninigi-no-mikoto, was ordered to descend and take possession of the Central Land of the Reed Plains, which he accomplished at her instructions after receiving a sword from her hands. She assisted him in the conquest of the Central Land of the Reed Plains by sending allies and assistants.

Amaterasu is the *primus-inter-pares* of the Shintō pantheon. It is particularly remarkable that she is neither male nor the first born of her parents. This is notable coming from a society in which women's positions have been secondary, and in which primogeniture is a feature. The discrepancy may be accounted for by the fact that the ancient Japanese, before the infiltration of Chinese ideas (aggressively male and hierarchical) allotted positions of religio-political power to women. Many of the myths in the *Nihonshōki* and the *Kōjiki* indicate that women occupied a prominent position in ancient Japanese thinking. On the other hand, there is also indication, both from the two mythological records and from other sources, that rulership was often dual: a younger and an older brother, or, as is the case in the Yamato myth, a female shamaness and a male ruler. The latter was ritually subordinate and his prestige was lower, but probably had a great deal of political power, as is the case of Amaterasu's male counterpart, Takamimusubi-no-kami. However, she is by no means a passive female deity. When Susano-wo ascended to heaven, she, apparently concerned about his motives, not only armed and armored herself but actually performed *shiki*, the earth-pounding ritual performed by archaic warriors before battle (and still performed today by sumo wrestlers before a match). Her strength (or perhaps her determination, far more important in the Japanese scheme of things) is attested to by the fact that her legs sank into the earth to her knees at each stamp.

Under the *honji-suijaku* theory, Amaterasu was considered an avatar of Dainichi Nyōrai, Buddha of the sun. For Nichiren she represented the true Japanese aspect of the solar Buddha.

Amaterasu-ō-mikami's main shrine is at Ise. It is rebuilt every twenty years of plain wood from a nearby sacred grove. Branch shrines are found throughout Japan. She is considered the ancestress of the imperial house, and thus by extension of the Japanese people, whose houses constitute cadet houses to the emperor's.

See also Ama-no-uzume; Izanagi and Izanami; Susano-wo; *Dōzoku-shin.*
References and further reading:
Aston, William G., trans. 1956. *Nihongi*. London: Allen and Unwin.
Nakamura, Kyoko Motomochi. 1983. "The Significance of Amaterasu in Japanese Religious History." In *The Book of the Goddess, Past and Present*, pp. 176–189. New York: Crossroad.
Philippi, Donald, trans. and ed. 1968. *Kōjiki*. Tokyo: Tokyo University Press.

AMENOMINAKANUSHI-NO-KAMI

The first *kami* to come into existence out of nothing. He is considered by some to be the original *kami* of heaven and earth, though this is a matter of interpretation. Immediately upon his appearance, and after doing what he had come to do, he (one assumes it was a male) became a "hidden" *kami*, that is, one who does not take a part in subsequent affairs.

References and further reading:
Aston, William G., trans. 1956. *Nihongi.* London: Allen and Unwin.
Philippi, Donald, trans. and ed. 1968. *Kōjiki.* Tokyo: Tokyo University Press.
Sasaki, Kiyoshi. 2000. "Amenominakanushi no Kami in Late Tokugawa Period Kokugaku." Tokyo: Institute for Japanese Culture and Classics, Kokugakuin University. http://www.kokugakuin.ac.jp/ijcc/wp/cpjr/kami/sasaki.html# para0060.

AME-NO-UZUME
See Ama-no-uzume.

AME-NO-WAKAHIKO
The second of the deities dispatched by the heavenly deities to subdue the Central Land of the Reed Plains. He was armed with the heavenly deer-slaying bow and the heavenly arrows. He descended to the land and took as his wife Shitateru-hime, Ōkuninushi's daughter. He plotted to gain control of the land for himself and resided there for eight years.

The senior deities, Amaterasu-ō-mikami and Takamimusubi-no-kami, convened all the deities and sent the pheasant to inquire why Ame-no-wakahiko had not returned. Advised by a wise woman who heard the pheasant's queries, he shot the bird with one of his heavenly arrows. It rebounded from the pheasant's body up to heaven, coming to rest by Amaterasu and Takamimusubi. After showing the arrow to the rest of the heavenly deities, Takamimusubi bespelled the weapon to kill Ame-no-wakahiko if his arrow had been shot with evil intent; otherwise it would do no harm. He then thrust it down the way it had come. Ame-no-wakahiko was killed instantly as the arrow pierced his breast.

The myth gives rise to a traditional Japanese saying about the returning arrow, implying something similar to "Evil to him whom evil thinks." The myth is partly an elaboration on the common human motif of "third time lucky," with Ame-no-wakahiko being the unsuccessful second try. At the same time, it is probably also a mythicization of the various attempts made by the Yamato state to impose its rule over the neighboring nation states.

See also Amaterasu-ō-mikami; Animals: pheasant; Takamimusubi-no-kami.
References and further reading:
Aston, William G., trans. 1956. *Nihongi.* London: Allen and Unwin.
Philippi, Donald, trans. and ed. 1968. *Kōjiki.* Tokyo: Tokyo University Press.

AMIDA NYŌRAI

The merciful Buddha of the Pure Land. The conceptualizations of Amida have always been very vague in Japanese myth. Like many other Buddhas and bodhisattvas, Amida appears in myths, if at all, as influencing the protagonist or as a figure of appeal, but never as an active protagonist himself. Nonetheless, the presence of Amida is a very powerful one in Japanese myth, and a great many other religious figures appear either as his avatar or representing him in one way or another.

Amida is portrayed as a seated, contemplative Buddha. He is often shown accompanied by the boddhisattvas Kannon and Seishi-bosatsu. The origins of Amida may well be found in the figure of Ahura Mazda, the Persian-Zoroastrian god of light. Certainly Joly, at least, argues that the great similarities in both characteristics and ritual addresses to Amida make it all but certain that this figure represents a transfer into Buddhism of elements of Zoroastrian worship. One thing that lends supposition to this idea is that Amida has no existence in any of the original Buddhist sutras. The belief in Amida is a product of the expansion of the Chinese empire under the T'ang, when contact was established on a regular basis with Persia and its ideas.

Though Amida is a background figure in Japanese mythology, he is of primary importance in Japanese religion. A major figure in esoteric Buddhism, belief in Amida was promulgated by Hōnen, who sought an "easier path" to salvation than that advocated by earlier Buddhist schools. Because Amida is infinitely merciful, this requires little more than a repetition of the *nembutsu* formula *"Namu Amida Butsu"* (Hail Buddha Amida). Amida is all-hearing, and a repetition of this formula ensures the repeater entrance into Jōdō, the Pure Land of paradise. The Buddha Amida is venerated as the main deity of the Jōdō and Jōdō-Shinshu sects. His main characteristics are love and benevolence. Thus the way to salvation is dependent simply upon repeating the *nembutsu* (in Jōdō), or by absolute belief and trust in the deity (Jōdō-Shinshu).

See also Kannon; Seishi-bosatsu.
References and further reading:

Eliot, Sir Charles Norton Edgcumbe. 1959. *Japanese Buddhism.* London: Routledge and Kegan Paul.

Frank, Bernard. 1991. *Le pantheon bouddhique au Japon.* Paris: Collections d'Emile Guimet. Reunion des musees nationaux.

Getty, Alice. 1988. *The Gods of Northern Buddhism.* New York: Dover Publications.

Joly, Henri L. 1967. *Legend in Japanese Art.* Tokyo: Charles E. Tuttle Co.

ANIMALS

As in most traditional societies, animals play a part in many myths. Some of these myths are of the explanatory type, others have to do with aid to deities and

Group of tanuki figures wearing leaf hats and drumming on their distended bellies.
(C. Rennie/ArkReligion.com)

heroes, and still others are somewhat more puzzling. Certain animals have been traditionally associated with particular deities, which may or may not be evidence of totemism (the association of humans with animal ancestors) in archaic Japan. Doves are traditionally associated with Hachiman, the war deity. Inari's messenger and companion is a fox. The *kunitsu kami* (earth deities) seemed especially able to present themselves in the shape of animals: Yamato-takeru encountered two of them, and the second brought about his death.

Three animals in particular attracted the Japanese imagination and are dealt with separately: the rabbit or hare, the fox, and the badger. All of these animals, (particularly the fox) were considered to be powerful and magical. The other animals described in this section occur as monsters or as saviors or servants in various myths. Some are purely mythical whereas others are based on second- or third-hand reports that Japanese heard of animals in "foreign parts." Some of these animals are briefly described here.

Centipede

Centipedes were impure, polluted animals associated with the dead. Thus Susano-wo, when he entertained his descendant Ōkuninushi when the latter had married Susano-wo's daughter, had centipedes in his hair instead of lice.

A giant centipede was harassing the kingdom of Ryujin, the dragon king, under Lake Biwa. The hero Tawara Toda was enlisted to aid the beleaguered monarch. He shot three arrows at the giant monster, whose body length covered a mountain, finally overcoming the beast with his last arrow.

Crocodile

Though not living in Japanese waters, crocodiles may have been known to the early Japanese from Buddhist sources; from China, where they live in the Yangtze River; or from reports of marine crocodiles. A row of crocodiles allowed the rabbit of Inaba to leave its island in the myth of Okuninushi and his eighty brothers. Another crocodile, chosen from an assembly of the beasts, helped Ho-ori-no-kami return to confront his brother during the dispute over the lost fishhook.

Crow

Crows were generally birds of good omen. The giant eight-lengths crow Yata-garasu was sent by the heavenly deities to guide the future first emperor Jimmu Tenno, on his way from Kumano to Yamato. In another form, some *tengu* have the form of crows.

The Ainu recognized two types of crow. One was despised, and the subject of myths that showed how stupid and bad tempered he was; the other was respected and considered a good omen. In the early days, the sun was threatened by a monster, which swallowed it. The earth became dark, and there was no warmth. Pashkuru Kamui, the crow, flew at the monster and pecked ferociously at its tongue. In panic, the monster regurgitated its prey, bringing back the light and warmth. On another occasion, when the first Ainu were starving, the crow guided them to a stranded whale, whose flesh saved the humans. As a result, the crow is honored as a friend of humankind.

Elephant

In Japanese iconography the elephant is a tusked, fanged, mythical beast. It appears in both Buddhist and Shintō iconography.

In Buddhism, the elephant represents the historical Buddha. Some of the Japanese ideas derive from Buddhist *jataka* tales (which tell of the Buddha's life and activities, sometimes in fabulous detail). Fugen-bosatsu, a major boddhisattva, rides a white elephant with blazing red eyes or face and six tusks that represents the reincarnation of Shakyamuni before he became the Buddha. Fugen appears to those who meditate upon the sutras.

The Japanese had not seen elephants until the sixteenth century, so representations of elephants tend to be elaborated by the fancy of the artist. In Shintō, the elephant is portrayed, along with other fabulous beasts such as leopards and dragons, on the beams of Shintō shrines. The association may derive from the *makatsugyō*, an Indian water monster, part elephant, part crocodile, part dolphin, which also represented the river Ganges. Arriving in Japan, the idea was translated into a clawed, tusked-and-fanged short-trunked finial of roof and ceiling beams. Presumably because of its watery associations, the elephant serves to protect wooden structures against fire and to bring about the rain.

Kirin

A mythical animal, symbol of purity. Somewhat akin to the European unicorn, the *kirin* only appears to those who are pure at heart. It is reputed to run across the clouds. A creature of Chinese origin, the *kirin* features in art and iconography, much less in actual myth texts.

Pheasant

Nakime the pheasant was dispatched to inquire of the dilatory Ame-no-wakahiko why he had not returned to Takamagahara to report on his doings in the Central Land of the Reed Plains.

Rabbit

A sly, clever creature not unlike B'rer Rabbit of the United States. The rabbit of Inaba tricked the sea crocodiles into lining up between the island of Oki and Cape Kēta, where he wanted to go, by promising to count the size of the crocodile family. Skipping over their backs, he could not resist gloating at his cleverness and was seized by the last in line, getting away only after being skinned. Grateful for Ōkuninushi's healing advice, he prophesied that Ōkuninushi would successfully wed the princess Ōkuninushi and his brothers were competing for.

Sea Cucumber

A type of echinoderm (a soft, spiny sea creature) that is popular as a snack with liquor, the sea cucumber was the only one of the fish that, by its silence, refused to serve the offspring of the heavenly deities (i.e., Ninigi-no-mikoto). As a consequence, Ama-no-uzume, one of Ninigi's companions, slit its mouth with a dagger, giving it its current shape and causing it to lose its voice.

Shishi

A mythical "lion" of Chinese tradition, imported into Japan. They have large bulging eyes, curly bushy tails, and a playful temperament. Monju-bosatsu rides a *shishi*. *Shishi* are generally impervious to magic, and Japanese legend has it that though very protective of their cubs, *shishi* throw each cub over a cliff to test its vitality and toughness. The most significant feature of the *shishi* is their protective nature, and they are thus invoked as playful and nonthreatening protectors of children.

Spider

Spiders occur in a number of myths, notably in the tale of Raikō. The Tsuchigumo harassed Yamato in the time of Jimmu Tenno and was vanquished by smoking the spider in its den. Several other myths tell of maleficent, often giant spiders that needed to be vanquished by heroes.

Tanuki

Usually translated as "badger," this is an animal—*Nyctereutes procyonides*—related to the raccoon. It is reputed to be sly and mischievous, with magical powers. It is depicted with a pot belly and enlarged scrotum, on either of which it might play as on a drum. *Tanuki* sometimes disguises himself as an itinerant monk and begs at the wayside or steals the belongings of passers-by. In one famous story, the *tanuki* disguised itself as a kettle, only to be filled with water and boiled, leading to a desperate escape.

Toad

A magical animal mentioned in both *Nihonshōki* and *Kōjiki* in the Sukun-abikona myth. The toad, according to ancient belief, was considered a great traveler and had been everywhere. The toad is either an accomplice or a messenger of Kuyebiko, the scarecrow deity, who knows everything. Gama-sennin, the toad sage, carries a three-legged toad with him, though perhaps not the same as the scarecrow's. The animal's warty skin and apparent immunity to most predators, as well as its apparent longevity, made it an element in the Daoist pharmacopoeia of longevity, an idea that apparently entered Japanese culture as well.

Turtle

The *minogame* (mythical turtle) is usually represented as having a luxuriant bushy tail. It is one of the animals of the four directions (tiger, dragon, phoenix, and turtle) imported from China. It is reputed to live a thousand years. It is thus emblematic of longevity.

Zodiacal Animals (*Jūnishi*)

Like many other mythological and religious phenomena, Japanese mythology has imported the idea of the zodiac from a Chinese origin. Each zodiacal animal is associated with a particular year, as well as month. The idea of *yaku-doshi* (momentous years) is still very prevalent in Japan and has social implications that are quite significant. The twelve zodiacal animals are combined with the cycle of five elements (fire, water, earth, metal, air) to produce a sixty-year cycle. A well-known example of the effects of *yakudoshi* is that of girl children born in the year of horse-fire. Believed to be destined to become widows, few men will marry them. As a consequence, the Japanese birthrate in those years is far lower than in previous or subsequent years, as many couples avoid having a child for fear the baby would be a girl, and thus unmarriageable.

> ***See also*** Ama-no-uzume; Fugen-bosatsu; Hachiman; Inari; Jimmu Tenno; Tawara Toda; Takamimusubi; Ninigi-no-mikoto.
> ***References and further reading:***
> Joly, Henri L. 1967. *Legend in Japanese Art.* Tokyo: Charles E. Tuttle Co.

APASAM KAMUI (AINU)

The spirit of the threshold. An important Ainu *kamui*, Apasam Kamui is the protector of the passage from the wild outside to the tame inside of Ainu culture. Though Apasam is not considered one of the "major" deities of the Ainu pantheon (that is, unlike Kamui Fuchi, Apasam Kamui is not honored or called on at many rituals), Apasam is nonetheless the *kamui* called upon whenever changes of state are occurring. The most important, perhaps, is requests for Apasam to protect women during difficult labor, and to protect people from such angry *kamui* as the dreaded smallpox *kamui*, Pakoro Kamui. Apasam is often conceived of as a dual *kamui*, either a male and female couple or a dual entity, perhaps similar in concept to the Roman Janus.

For the Ainu, living as they did in close contact with nature, the delineation of boundaries was crucial both materially and intellectually. Each settlement of Ainu controlled a *kotan*, a domain from which they drew their living and that they were able and willing to defend. Yet the very nature of the society demanded that they cross the boundaries between one *ramat* and another, as the salmon and the deer and bears moved about. Unsurprisingly, therefore, they needed a figure that could oversee these passages and enable them to be carried out fearlessly and without trouble. The same was true of their households; the difference they saw between themselves as civilized beings, and their neighbors—the Japanese and the Okhotskians—who they viewed as uncivilized, had a lot to do with their pursuits within the house (carving, weaving, wine-making) and the contrast with the wild outside where such cultured activities were not pursued. Apasam Kamui exemplified all of these differences and the transitions between them.

See also Kamui Fuchi

References and further reading:

Etter, Carl. 1949. *Ainu Folklore: Traditions and Culture of the Vanishing Aborigines of Japan.* Chicago: Wilcox and Follett Co.

Munro, Neil Gordon. 1962. *Ainu Creed and Cult.* London: Routledge and Kegan Paul; London and New York: K. Paul International, distributed by Columbia University Press, 1995.

ASSEMBLY OF THE GODS

In many of Japan's myths, the *kami* assemble together to debate or deal with crises or with the normal management of their affairs. Thus one assembly was called to deal with the events surrounding Amaterasu-ō-mikami's retirement into the cave after Susano-wo's outrages. Other assemblies were called to deal with the matters surrounding the subjugation of the Central Land of the Reed Plains. The assemblies recorded in the *Kōjiki* note that these take place in the dry riverbed of the Heavenly River. In Heian and later Japan, dry riverbeds were usually the major open spaces available for city dwellers to meet, have fairs, and performances of dance and *sarugaku* (the predecessor to classical Nōh theater). Thus it was fitting that the *kami* would have assembled in a similar manner, particularly considering that there were eight million of them. Most of the recorded assemblies were convened by Takamimusubi-no-kami and Amaterasu-ō-mikami.

The *kami* also assemble annually at Izumo on the tenth month, to discuss what has happened across the land as well as the behavior of its denizens. The one exception to the gathering is Ebisu, who is deaf to the summons. During this month, prayers to the deities and most festivals are suspended, the exception being the festival for the *kami* of war, Hachiman.

The idea that important decisions should be reached by consultation and consensus is a cornerstone of Japanese sociopolitical thinking. Even today, well-managed Japanese companies take care to consult even the most junior employees affected by a policy decision. Though often obeyed more in form than in substance, the idea is nonetheless an important concept in Japanese culture. The idea that the *kami*, responsible for celestial management, would settle their affairs in what amounts to a public meeting does not strike the Japanese as out of the ordinary, but rather as good managerial practice.

> **See also** Amaterasu-ō-mikami; Ebisu; Hachiman; Takamimusubi-no-kami.
> **References and further reading:**
> Ballon, R. J. 1990. "Decision Making in Japanese Industry." Tokyo: Sophia University Business Series 132.
> Philippi, Donald, trans. and ed. 1968. *Kōjiki.* Tokyo: Tokyo University Press.
> Rohlen, Thomas P. 1974. *For Harmony and Strength: Japanese White Collar Organization in Anthropological Perspective.* Berkeley: University of California Press.

ATAGO-GONGEN

The guardian deity of Mt. Atago, north of Kyoto, protective deity of fire and of protection from conflagration. Like many *gongen,* Atago-gongen is largely a Shugendō deity. Mt. Atago, which guards the northwest approaches to the imperial capital of Heian-kyō (now Kyoto), was the haunt of *tengu* (goblins), particularly a very powerful one named Tarōbō. During the reign of Emperor Monmu (701–704), the sages En-no-Gyōja, founder of the Shugendō syncretic sect, and Taichō, founder of the Hakusan Shugendō monastery, were ordered to clear the mountain of the goblins. Tarōbō surrendered to the two sages and promised to become the protector of the mountain and to mount a vigil against fire. As a consequence, he is often viewed as the guardian of Jizō, or an avatar of this boddhisattva, who is appealed to for protection for children against being burned by the hearth.

Atago-gongen, mounted on a horse and carrying the symbols usually carried by Jizō (the ringed staff and the desire-canceling jewel), is titled Shogun Jizō. On his white horse he flanks Kannon on one side, mirrored on the other by Bishamon. During the Heian period, when the famous general Tamuramaro subdued the Ezo (the Ainu) in northern Japan, he dreamed that his patron, Kannon, appeared to him promising her aid and that of her generals, Bishamon and Jizō. As a consequence Jizō, in his form as Atago-gongen, still overlooks and protects the ancient capital.

See also Bishamon; En-no-Gyōja; Jizō; Kannon; *Tengu.*

BAKEMONO

A general word for ghosts and other night walkers worthy of fear. See Ghosts.

BATTABARA-BOSATSU

The tutelary venerable of the bath in Zen monasteries. Battabara was an Indian monk who attained enlightenment in the bath. He was entering the bath with seven other monks when he suddenly, being between pure and impure (one foot in the water, one outside), experienced enlightenment. Battabara thus became the patron of bathing, and his figure (or a board with his name), usually carrying the stick used to stir the warm water, is kept in every bathroom in Zen monasteries.

The myth of Battabara illustrates two concerns of the Zen school. First, enlightenment can come to any individual at any time. Second, bathing is intrinsic to the Japanese lifestyle, and to religion in general, because it indicates the ability to free oneself from pollution (and thus, in Zen thinking, from the illusions of this world). Like all *bosatsu,* Battabara can lead the individual to enlightenment in this life.

References and further reading:
Frank, Bernard. 1991. *Le pantheon bouddhique au Japon.* Paris: Collections d'Emile Guimet. Reunion des musees nationaux.

BENKEI

Monk-soldier during the period of the Gempei war (1180–1185) and devoted companion of Ushiwakamaru/Yoshitsune. Benkei was born to the daughter of a blacksmith near Shingū. His mother ate iron and may have been a descendant of Dōjō-hōshi. His father was either a *yamabushi* or a priest, or perhaps the thunder deity. Benkei's mother was pregnant in a miraculous manner for three years and three months. He was born with a full head of hair that reached his knees and a full set of teeth.

In his grandfather's smithy he hammered the anvil into the ground and collected firewood by the treeload. In his youth he was called Oniwaka (Young demon) for his pranks and ferocity. On one occasion when challenged, he held aloft a large rock to crush his challenger: The rock can still be seen today.

Temple bell (Courtesy of the author)

Because of his wildness and perhaps his huge appetite, he was made a novice at Enryakuji temple on Mt. Hiei (thus his familiar surname—Musashibō, or "Priest Musashi"), where he studied to be a *yamabushi.* Eventually he became a *sōhei,* one of the monk-soldiers of the temple. Originally a position for less intelligent and devout monks, the *sōhei* had become threats to order in the capital by the eleventh century. Benkei was eight feet tall and had the strength of a hundred men. Annoyed by the monks of Miidera (traditional rivals of Enryakuji) on the shores of Lake Biwa east of Hiei and the capital, he carried away the massive bell of Miidera temple and placed it at his own monastery on Mt. Hiei, overlooking the capital from the northeast. When the bell refused to toll, only uttering "I want to return to Miidera" when struck, the hero gave it a kick that rolled it down the mountain and back to the gates of Miidera. His price for returning the bell (he agreed to return it only after the intercession of his abbot) was a satisfactory meal. His depredation emptied the temple's larder and cellar. The cauldron from which he ate can still be seen in Miidera today: He was not, apparently, a dainty eater, and the marks of Benkei's teeth are on the cauldron still.

As a *sōhei* he needed weapons and armor, and his way of equipping himself was as eccentric as the rest of his life. For weapons he carried, in addition to his sword, a quiver of tools: *masakari* (broad ax); *kumade* (rake), *nagihama* (sickle-weapon), *hizuchi* (wooden mallet), *nokogiri* (saw), *tetsubō* (iron staff), and *sasumata* (half-moon spear). These were the weapons of the common man, not the bred warrior, and Benkei is often known as "Nanadogu Benkei" (Benkei of the Seven Tools). He also ordered himself a special suit of armor to fit his gigantic frame. The armorer told him it would take one thousand swords to make the suit, and these he vowed to collect. For this purpose he stationed himself at one end of the Gōju Bridge in Kyoto, challenging all comers to surrender their swords or fight. He was on the point of adding the last sword to the collection when he challenged a young boy, Ushiwakamaru, and was promptly defeated. Benkei then became the young man's devoted retainer.

Benkei's devotion to his master—whose full name became Minamoto-no-Yoshitsune—was extreme. He is epitomized as both a loyal retainer and as wild genius tamed by craft. In the most famous episode attributed to him, he helped his disguised master pass for a low-ranking monk by beating him at a barrier at Ataka (in modern Ishikawa prefecture) guarded by men loyal to Minamoto-no-Yoritomo, Yoshitsune's brother and nemesis. The conflict between the respect for a lord and the need to humiliate the lord and save his life became an enduring theme in Japanese literature and art. One charming story attributed to him has it that while writing a draft of a letter Yoshitsune wanted to send to his brother, Benkei was disturbed by the sound of crickets. Furious, he shouted out loud "Silence!" and since then, the environs of the Manpukuji temple in Koshigoe (near Kamakura) have been free of the sound of the insects. Benkei was finally killed defending his master's castle against Yoritomo's forces.

Benkei is usually depicted wearing black armor under a priest's coif. He is thus often known by his priestly name, Musashibō Benkei. In some depictions he wears the hexagonal pillbox hat of the *yamabushi* and is seen carrying his seven implements on his back. And he is just as often shown following a youthful, almost childish looking Ushiwakamaru. Benkei is barely mentioned in the *Heike Monogatari*, one of the main sources about the Gempei war and its aftermath. His life is more extensively documented (and possibly fabricated) in the *Gikeiki* (translated by McCullough as *Yoshitsune* [1966]), written two centuries later. The popular appeal of this figure was so strong that whatever his origins, his stature grew to that of one of the best-known Japanese mythical heroic figures.

See also Dōjō-hōshi; Taira; Yoshitsune.

References and further reading:

Brandon, James R., and Tamako Niwa, adapters. 1966. *Kabuki Plays*. New York: S. French.

Kitagawa, Hiroshi, and Bruce T. Tsuchida, trans. 1977. *The Tale of Heike (Heike Monogatari)*. Tokyo: University of Tokyo Press.

McCullough, Helen Craig, trans. 1988. *The Tale of the Heike*. Stanford: Stanford University Press.

———. 1966. *Yoshitsune: A Fifteenth-Century Japanese Chronicle* (Gikeiki). Stanford: Stanford University Press.
Ouwehand, Cornelius. 1964. *Namazu-e and Their Themes: An Interpretative Approach to Some Aspects of Japanese Religion.* Leiden, the Netherlands: E. J. Brill.
Sieffert, Rene. 1995. *Histoire de Benkei.* Paris: P.O.F.

BENZAITEN

Often called "Benten," she is the only female member of the Shichi Fukujin. She is depicted riding on a dragon and playing a Chinese lute (pipa, or *biwa* in Japanese). Benzaiten is the deity of love and of feminine accomplishments and also the boddhisattva of entertainers.

Benzaiten is the personification of the river that flows from Mt. Meru, where, according to some traditions, the Buddha has his abode. Her name means "the deity of talent and eloquence." She is identified as a river *kami* and as the sea goddess as well. The famous "floating" shrine of Itsukushima, built on in the shores of the Seto Inland Sea near Hiroshima, is dedicated to her.

She is often pictured accompanied by a small white snake with a woman's head, called Ugajin, the name of an important fertility *kami.*

See also Mountains; Shichi Fukujin; Ugajin.
References and further reading:
Joly, Henri L. 1967. *Legend in Japanese Art.* Tokyo: Charles E. Tuttle Co.

BIMBOGAMI

The god of poverty. Bimbogami's attentions will lead to poverty and misery, and people in some locations in Japan will carry out personal rituals to avert the god's gaze. His attendant is the Death Watch beetle (*Anobium notatum*), a small black insect that infests rotted wood and old wooden houses, whose clicking betrays the presence of the *kami.* Bimbogami is black, and he is the shadow of Fuku-no-kami, the *kami* of wealth.

Until the latter half of the twentieth century, poverty was a very real threat for most Japanese. The average person could do little to stave off poverty, sometimes due to the exactions of landlords, sometimes to absence of work or famine. Poverty and the *kami* of poverty could not be avoided or propitiated. One could only hope that it would pass one by. There are thus no shrines or temples to Bimbogami.

References and further reading:
Joly, Henri L. 1967. *Legend in Japanese Art.* Tokyo: Charles E. Tuttle Co.

BINZURU-SONJA

One of the Buddha's first disciples (*rakan*) who fell from grace and is usually not allowed into the hallowed company. Some say he came from a long line of physicians. He was unfortunately addicted to drink, and the Buddha had to warn him several times against his weakness.

In one version of his myth, the Buddha was asked by a wealthy merchant for help. The merchant and his household had been plagued by demons. Being busy, the Buddha sent one of his senior disciples, Binzuru, to attend to the matter. Binzuru carried out the exorcism, and the evil was banished. The grateful merchant then prepared a feast for the disciple. After many entreaties by his host, Binzuru finally succumbed to an offer of a small cup of wine. Not able to stop, he soon drank too much, and the evil demons were released. The Buddha was very annoyed and dismissed Binzuru from his company. Binzuru, still the devoted disciple, would stand outside the hall where the Buddha lectured, to follow the lesson. When the Buddha was about to die, he summoned Binzuru and told the former disciple that he was aware of his devotion and he was therefore forgiven, but that Binzuru could never enter nirvana: He was bound to serve the people forever.

In another version of the myth, the first disciples, sixteen in number, were meditating. Binzuru (who seems to have been a more earthy figure than most), commented casually on the beauty of a passing maiden. As a consequence he was banished from the fellowship of the disciples. Forgiven on the Buddha's deathbed, he was nonetheless condemned to minister to those unable to attain enlightenment rather than enter nirvana.

Statues of Binzuru are commonly found outside temple buildings. They may be painted red or made of red wood. (For those who prefer the drink story, many people experience a flush when drinking alcohol, and a red face in Japan signifies someone given to drink.) All the statues of Binzuru are polished and shiny from the hands of believers. One rubs the saint's body at the spot of one's own pain, and the affliction goes away.

The myth of Binzuru is part of the vast body of myth and belief that anchors Japanese Buddhism to the here and now. Although the esoteric and soteriological elements of Buddhism are not concerned with bodily afflictions and illness, this is clearly a concern of anyone living in the world. As a consequence, many myths attach to particularly "mundane" or merciful figures to help ease personal affliction. Kannon, Jizō, and the saint Kōbō Daishi are examples, along with Binzuru, of Buddhist figures whose main attraction for the average Japanese person is the help they give in the mundane world. Binzuru is at one extreme of these figures: a popular, nonsaintly figure nonetheless attached deeply to Buddhism. At the other end of the continuum is Kannon, a divine figure attached directly to the Buddha's mercy. The Daishi is somewhere in-between.

See also Jizō; Jūrokurakan; Kannon; Kōbō Daishi.

References and further reading:
Frank, Bernard. 1991. *Le pantheon bouddhique au Japon.* Paris: Collections
    d'Emile Guimet. Reunion des musées nationaux.
Statler, Oliver. 1984. *Japanese Pilgrimage.* London: Picador.

BISHAMON-TEN

One of the Shichi Fukujin (seven gods of good fortune), Bishamon-ten is depicted
as an armored warrior in the Chinese style, carrying a Chinese halberd. In his other
hand he carries a small pagoda—the traditional repository for scrolls of the Buddhist canon (the sutra). Bishamon is the protector of Buddhist Law, and consequently, the god of happiness: By his protection people can find happiness and
avoid misfortune. Bishamon-ten's miniature pagoda, or reliquary, has five superimposed parts representing the elements of the universe. It also represents the iron
tower from which Ryūgo (Nagarjuna) received the secret scrolls of the Law. He is
master of the northern direction and as such, traditionally, the dispenser of
largesse and good fortune (which accounts for his membership in the Shichi Fukujin), because the North was supposed to be the land of treasures guarded by spirits.

Bishamon-ten is also a member of the Shi Tenno, the four heavenly protec-
tors/emperors. Therefore, in his own character, Bishamon-ten is viewed as protector in times of war. In his persona as protector of the Law, he aided Shōtoku
Taishi in his war to establish Buddhism at the imperial court. The famous war-
lord Uesugi Kenshin (1530–1578) was consecrated to Bishamon-ten, and one of
his banners always bore the first syllable of that deity's name.

See also Ryūju; Shichi Fukujin, Shi Tenno; Shōtoku Taishi; *Takarabune.*
References and further reading:
Joly, Henri L. 1967. *Legend in Japanese Art.* Tokyo: Charles E. Tuttle Co.
Eliot, Sir Charles Norton Edgcumbe. 1959. *Japanese Buddhism.* London: Routledge
    and Kegan Paul.

CENTRAL LAND OF THE REED PLAINS

A name used in archaic writing for Japan. *See* Toyoashihara-no-chiaki-no-
nagaioaki-no-mizuho-no-kuni.

CHIKAP KAMUI (AINU)

The owl deity, and also the master of the domain, Kotankor Kamui. *See*
Kotankor Kamui.

CHIMATA-NO-KAMI

God of crossroads, highways, and footpaths, represented by a phallus. Chi-
mata–no-kami is the child of Izanagi-no-mikoto, born of the trousers (hence, presumably, his phallic identity) Izanagi threw down when he started his

purification after his visit to the underworld. Originally perhaps a phallic deity of fertility and joining, his phallic symbol was placed at crossroads. Even today such phalluses (some very large) of wood or stone can be found in small rural shrines. In some well-known *onsen* (hot spring spas) Chimata-no-kami is erected, and men with sexual problems, as well as women wishing for children, will come to stroke the phallus and ameliorate their condition. Chimata-no-kami is one of the aspects of Dosōjin.

See also Dosōjin; Izanagi and Izanami.
References and further reading:
Philippi, Donald, trans. and ed. 1968. *Kōjiki.* Tokyo: Tokyo University Press.

CHISEIKORO KAMUI (AINU)

The Ainu god of the house. He resides in the northeast corner of the house, where the household treasures—swords, robes, lacquered boxes, and tubs of Japanese manufacture—are stored. Together with Kamui Fuchi, the hearth goddess, he protects the house. He is often said to be her husband.

The relationship between Chiseikoro and Kamui Fuchi exemplifies the domestic relationships among the Ainu. Although the husband was dominant in some areas, it was also clear from this and other mythical relationships that in the domestic sphere, the woman was dominant. And clearly, Chiseikoro is responsible for treasures that were the domain of men: imported and trade articles.

See also Kamui Fuchi.
References and further reading:
Munro, Neil Gordon. 1962. *Ainu Creed and Cult.* London: Routledge and Kegan Paul; London and New York: K. Paul International, distributed by Columbia University Press, 1995.

CHŪJŌ-HIME

"Guard-general princess" is the Japanese Cinderella, and a paragon of the virtue of filial devotion. Born, according to the story, on the eighteenth day of the eighth month of the eighteenth year of emperor Shōmu's reign (747), she was the daughter of an imperial minister and his wife, a royal princess. Childless, they appealed to Kannon and were granted a daughter in exchange for the life of one of the parents. At the age of three (some say five), therefore, the young girl's mother died. Her father subsequently remarried. The stepmother hated the girl and ordered her taken into the mountains and killed. She was saved from death and brought home to her father. Disappointed, however, by the vanity of the world, she entered a monastery, where she meditated upon Buddha Amida, praying for the reincarnation of her mother in the Pure Land of the West. Years of austerity followed, during which she became a "living Buddha." As she was at the end of a period of austerity, Amida Butsu appeared to her in the form of a nun, and, in response to her prayers, wove a cloth of five colors in one night, depicting the Bunki mandala, which shows the cosmography of the Pure Land. The mandala covered the entire wall of the room she was in (a considerable feat, considering that looms of the day were much smaller than the width of a room).

Chūjo-hime represents one of the most familiar and well-loved of the Buddhist miracle stories. Many of those were promulgated and told throughout Japan as examples of Buddhist principles and of the power of Buddhism. The myth is so attractive to Japanese because it contains major elements of Japanese ideology: filial piety, austerity in search of an ideal, and the mercy of the Buddha.

> **See also** Amida Nyōrai; Kannon.
> **References and further reading:**
> Glassman, Hank. "Chujo-hime, Convents, and Women's Salvation."
>   http://www.columbia.edu/cu/ealac/imjs/programs/1998-fall/Abstracts/
>   glassman.html.

CHŪSHINGURA

The *Chūshingura* (Treasury of Loyal Retainers) tells the tale of the forty-seven retainers of the lord of Akō who were loyal beyond death. In the early eighteenth century, the young and inexperienced Lord Asano Naganori of Akō drew his sword in the shogun's palace after being mortally insulted by Lord Kira Yoshinaka, a shogunal retainer and master of ceremonies. Because of this, Asano was sentenced to death. Forty-seven of his retainers swore to avenge their lord's death on the man who had caused the incident, even though the shogunal government had forbidden their official request for a blood feud. For three years they pretended to obey the government's ruling and acted as *rōnin* (masterless warriors), while secretly making preparations. In early 1703 they made their way to the villain's home in Edo (now Tokyo), attacked the premises, and placed Lord Kira's severed head on the grave of their lord.

The shogunate government wished to execute them as common criminals, but due to public pressure, which was excited by the conspirators' self-sacrifice, allowed them to commit *sepukku* (ritual disembowelment) instead. Several plays, including *Chūshingura*, were written about this event, which is reenacted every year in November, though the costumed retainers now travel on the subway from the location of Lord Kira's villa in Shinagawa (where the murder took place) to the graves of the loyal band in the Sengakuji temple.

The *Chūshingura* myth is one of the most popularly influential in Japan. It reinforced and dramatized the ideas of self-sacrificing loyalty that were the basis for the Japanese view of themselves as capable of utmost loyalty. The plays were as popular among the elite as among the common people and when staged today still evoke the Japan of warrior virtues. The *Chūshingura* embodied the virtues of *bushidō*, the Warrior's Way, which was formulated during the Edo-period peacetime. It provided some of the underpinnings of the blind ferocity and loyalty exalted by the Imperial Japanese Army during the lengthy years of the Pacific War (circa 1936 to 1945, and including World War II).

The story of the forty-seven *rōnin* is one of three major national myths of Japan (the other two being the *kamikaze* and the divine antecedents of the imperial house). It defined for Japanese civil society since the eighteenth century what being Japanese was: self-sacrificing, loyal to one's superiors beyond the grave, and capable of limitless sacrifice. Whatever the facts of the story (some historians argue that the original quarrel was Asano's fault, not Kira's), the drama was incontestable. It was felt not only by the warrior class who governed Japan but also, and no less, by the townspeople, who were already becoming a significant cultural factor. The idea of loyalty became so deeply ingrained that it was easily exploited by Imperial Army recruiters and modern industrial concerns alike. That the myth is based on actual events, and that these events can be verified by anyone wishing to see the graves of the protagonists, makes it even more powerful and imposing.

See also Divine Descent; *Kamikaze.*

References and further reading:

Shioya, Sakae. 1956. *Chūshingura: An Exposition: Illustrated with Hiroshige's Coloured Plates.* 2d ed. Tokyo: Hokuseido Press.

Takeda, Izumo, Miyoshi Shoraku, and Namiki Senryu. 1971. *Chushingura, the Treasury of Loyal Retainers: A Puppet Play.* Translated by Donald Keene. New York: Columbia University Press.

Tucker, John Allen. 1999. "Rethinking the Akō Rōnin Debate: The Religious Significance of *Chūshin Gishi.*" *Japanese Journal of Religious Studies* 26(1–2): 1–38.

DAIGENSHURI-BOSATSU

Zen protector of monasteries and Buddhist Law, and protector of seafarers. Tradition has it that he was one of the sons of Asoka, an Indian emperor of the Mauryan dynasty who was a strong supporter of Buddhism. Reborn a magistrate on the southern coast of old China, he was noted for his piety and justice to the day he died.

In one story, Dōgen, the founder of the Sōtō Zen sect, had traveled to China, staying for four years and studying the principles of sudden enlightenment. On the final night of his stay, he was busy copying a rare manuscript given him for the purpose by his teacher. Daigenshuri's spirit appeared to Dōgen and aided the sage's efforts, supplying him with illumination throughout the night.

As Dōgen returned home across the stormy China Sea, Daigenshuri—who had boarded the ship unknown to the sage—calmed the storms and insured that the Zen idea would reach the shores of Japan safely. Daigenshuri is thus portrayed in the dress of a Chinese magistrate, with a tall hat, symbol of his rank. One of his hands is shading his eyes, indicating his dual responsibility as guardian of the Law and as a navigator at sea.

References and further reading:
Joly, Henri L. 1967. *Legend in Japanese Art.* Tokyo: Charles E. Tuttle Co.

DAIKOKU

God of wealth, and one of the Shichi Fukujin (seven gods of good fortune), he is Ebisu's father. Normally depicted as a jolly man with lucky fat earlobes, he wears a soft squashed hat and flourishes a wooden mallet. Every blow of the mallet brings forth a shower of oval-shaped *ryō* (gold coins). Daikoku wears voluminous court trousers, and he is perched upon two or three bales of rice. Daikoku is so wealthy and happy that he is unconcerned by the rats that accompany him and gnaw into the bales: There is bound to be more grain. The presence of the rats also implies the lesson that one should always work to preserve one's riches, otherwise they will be carried away by misfortune. Daikoku is particularly worshiped by farmers and, as the god of wealth, by merchants. His image in the form of plaques or sometimes small figurines can be found in many shops throughout Japan. He is sometimes identified with Ōkuninushi, the *kami* of Izumo and the Lord of the Land, because one way of writing his name is "Great land," the same as Ōkuni(nushi).

Daikoku is one of the most powerful and enigmatic of Japanese *kami*. His name also can be written as "Great black," and he is identified with the Indian Buddhist deity Mahakala, the dark lord. His transformation from Mahakala and his association with Ōkuninushi tie him to magic and necromancy. And though this association has declined in importance since the Edo period, Daikoku's importance is indicated by the fact that the main pillar of a traditional house is still called *daikokubashira* (daikoku pillar) to this day. Notwithstanding Daikoku's power, he is still most commonly known as a rather jolly member of the Shichi Fukujin and the father and associate of Ebisu.

See also Ebisu; Ōkuninushi; Shichi Fukujin; Takarabune.
References and further reading:
Joly, Henri L. 1967. *Legend in Japanese Art.* Tokyo: Charles E. Tuttle Co.
Frank, Bernard. 1991. *Le pantheon bouddhique au Japon.* Paris: Collections
    d'Emile Guimet. Reunion des musees nationaux.

DAINICHI NYŌRAI

Buddha represented as the sun. Dainichi is the Japanese translation of the Sanskrit *Maha-Vairocana* (Great Illumination), the central emanation of the universe. Dainichi is often represented as seated at the heart of a red lotus with eight petals, representing the fount of all things. He is viewed in Shingon thought as the center of wisdom and mercy and the main (sometimes, sole) universal deity.

Dainichi is often identified in Ryōbu ("both sects," that is, Buddhist and Shintō syncretism) with Amaterasu-ō-mikami. He represents the ultimate reality of the world. He is often depicted holding a double-headed, three-pronged lightning bolt—a *kongo*—which emphasizes his role in sudden enlightenment.

See also Amaterasu-ō-mikami; Weapons.
References and further reading:
Joly, Henri L. 1967. *Legend in Japanese Art.* Tokyo: Charles E. Tuttle Co.

DAITOKU MYŌ-Ō (-BOSATSU)

One of the heavenly kings, he is the defier of death. He carries weapons of war, including a lightning-hilted sword and a spear. His face is contorted with concentration, and he, like many of the other Myō-ō, is surrounded by flames. His face and body are blue, and he may be represented with any number of faces and arms. He rides a bull or buffalo—the symbol of perseverance against resistance—and in some areas of Japan was worshiped primarily by owners of draft animals, whose patron he was. He is sometimes identified with Monju-bosatsu.

See also Monju-bosatsu.
References and further reading:
Joly, Henri L. 1967. *Legend in Japanese Art.* Tokyo: Charles E. Tuttle Co.

DAKINITEN

A Buddhist deity who is often conflated with Inari. Dakiniten is the Japanese transformation of a type of female Indian demon called *dakini,* attendants of Kali, goddess of death, and bearers of her blood cup. They were converted to Buddhism by Dainichi Nyōrai. In Japan, the demon type became changed to a single person: Dakiniten. She is usually depicted sitting on a flying white fox. Her face is white. She is the patroness of magical spells, and there are special spells said in her name to promote success. The flying fox on which she rides originated in India, and this relationship creates her association with Inari, as either his assistant or as an avatar, she being the *honju* (universal deity), he being the *suijaku* (Japanese manifestation). She carried a flaming jewel (the sign of Inari) in her left hand. She is sometimes, though rarely, identified as Sae-no-kami.

See also Dosōjin (Sae-no-kami); Fox; Inari.
References and further reading:
Smyers, Karen. 1999. *The Fox and the Jewel.* Honolulu: University of Hawaii Press.

A doll of Daruma, Zen founder, peering out from an offering tray (Courtesy of the author)

DARUMA

The Japanese rendition of the name Boddhidarma, a Buddhist sage who brought a form of Buddhism to South China and became the founding saint of Zen Buddhism. Most of the myths surrounding Daruma are of Chinese origin and in Chinese settings. Daruma arrived in China in a mysterious way, in response to the need to teach the Buddhist Law. He founded the Shōrinji temple (Shaolin in Chinese) and gathered many students. In his pondering upon the Law, he decided that the way to salvation was through meditation. As a result, he spent nine years meditating facing a wall, in which time his legs withered to stumps. Finally, falling asleep just before reaching enlightenment, he ripped off his eyelids in a rage and threw them away. Where they landed grew a magical bush, whose leaves could be brewed into a liquid that would banish sleepiness. This bush became known as *cha* (tea) and is drunk to this day as a refreshing antidote to sleep.

Daruma noticed that his disciples were having difficulty in maintaining the immobility and concentration required in order to complete their enlightenment. As a consequence, he formulated a series of body and arm exercises, including jumps and kicks, and taught his disciples how to practice martial moves as an aid to concentration. This was the beginning of the various *kenpo* (fist art) styles that evolved into unarmed combat we know today.

Finally, once the monastery and his teachings were well established, Daruma stepped onto a reed, which bore him across the sea to the West, back to his homeland in India.

Daruma is usually depicted wearing red robes (in reference to the saffron robes of Buddhist monks), one drape of the cloth held over his head like a hood, and barefoot. He is bald, with a beard and fierce staring eyes. He is often depicted in the form of a round-bottomed doll that when pushed over immediately rights itself. He is, in effect, the patron saint of determination and self-discipline. Before undertaking an effortful commitment, many Japanese will acquire a Daruma doll with blanks for eyes, then paint in one eye. The second eye is painted in only when the commitment has been accomplished. Collections of seven such small dolls can be bought, with reference to the idea that even Daruma is reputed to have failed six times before succeeding in the seventh try in reaching enlightenment.

> *References and further reading:*
> Joly, Henri L. 1967. *Legend in Japanese Art.* Tokyo: Charles E. Tuttle Co.

DATSUEBA

A skeletal figure who denudes the dead of their clothing as they cross the Shozukawa River at the entrance to the world of the dead. Datsueba (Naked Old Man) strips the dead of whatever clothes they were buried in, whether rich or poor, and hangs them on the branches of a leafless tree. Datsueba is thin, all his bones showing and his cheeks sunken. His denuding of the passers to the land of the dead is said to make perfectly clear to them that they have finally left the land of the living, never to return. In some versions he is called, or has a female counterpart, the Shozuka-no-baba.

> *See also* Shozuka-no-baba; Underworld.
> *References and further reading:*
> Frank, Bernard. 1991. *Le pantheon bouddhique au Japon.* Paris: Collections
> d'Emile Guimet. Reunion des musees nationaux.

DIVINATION

Divination was, and in some places still is, an important aspect of Japanese belief. Many of the deities mentioned in the myths practiced divination. The *kami* Hitokotonushi (One Word Master) could be applied to for terse answers to questions put to him. Kotoshironushi, one of Ōkuninushi's sons, was another important divination *kami.* In many other instances in the *Kōjiki* and *Nihonshōki,* actions and results are determined by divination, which the *kami* themselves practice. The two most notable instances are the divinatory contest between Amaterasu-ō-mikami and her brother Susano-wo to determine whether Susano-wo intended to usurp his sister's position, and the Empress Jingū's divinatory trance that precipitated her invasion of Korea. Several deities could be applied to to divine the answers to specific questions, and the practice was so widespread that few major decisions were reached without reference to divination. A special bureau existed in the imperial government responsible for nothing else than divination and interpretation. To this day a number of shrines and temples hold lengthy divination rituals, some lasting for over twelve hours. Divinatory rituals such as that can involve the use of a boiling cauldron, the use of patterns made by evergreen leaves, trance, usually by *miko* (temple maidens), dreams, contests, and so on.

The heavy use of divination is not surprising considering the difficulties of life in premodern Japan. Hunger and famine were always around the corner, and life was not safe from human or nonhuman afflictions—disease, earthquakes, fire. Unsurprisingly, many of these disasters were personified: hunger (Hidarugami), poverty (Bimbogami), earthquake (Namazu), fire (Kagutsuchi-no-kami). The process of personification is not random or whimsical. It allows humans a means, however fanciful or technically weak, to affect and deflect the calamities. This is particularly the case because, as noted elsewhere in this volume, the moral position the Japanese adopted was that of a family. Impersonal fire can, and will, burn without control. But fire personified as a deity is a reasonable *person*, and, moreover, a member of one's family however many times removed, and may be, therefore, propitiated. The major problem with all deities, as Guthrie (1980) notes, is that one needs a means of communicating with them. Divination is one such means, and it includes within itself the understanding that the communication will be uncertain and often even vague. None of the oracles mentioned in the myths provide direct, clear answers. Like all communication, the responses are often unspecified and elliptical and sometimes are disregarded by recipients. Even the *kami* themselves are prone to divination, perhaps for the same reason: There are so many of them that no single *kami* is able to act without, in some way, receiving input from others. The Assembly of the Gods can perhaps be seen in this light: a form of divining the *kami* (in the sense of the immanent power, rather than the personified deities) will.

> ***See also*** Amaterasu-ō-mikami; Assembly of the Gods; Bimbogami; Hidarugami; Hitokotonushi; Kagutsuchi-no-kami; Namazu; Susano-wo.
> ***References and further reading:***
> Guthrie, Steward. 1980. "A Cognitive Theory of Religion." *Current Anthropology* 21(2): 181–204.

DIVINE DESCENT

One of the three most powerful myths of Japan as a nation (the other two being the *kamikaze* and loyalty exemplified in the *Chūshingura*). The myth of the descent of the heavenly grandson, Ninigi-no-mikoto, to rulership provides a direct connection between the divine and the Japanese people. Combined with the concept of *dōzoku* (extended household relationship), this implies two things: that individual Japanese are directly related to the divine, and that the political system of emperorship is divinely sanctioned.

The turning point of Japanese society, following this myth, is the descent of Ninigi-no-mikoto from heaven to assume his rulership, following the mandate of his heavenly grandparents. Everything else in Japanese polity flows from this one event. The myth is clearly one that was reinforced, and perhaps engendered, by the ruling class of the Yamato state, and reinforced by the Japanese empire. And, though all Japanese know this myth, not all subscribe to it, nor do all see it as the foundation charter of the state. Nonetheless, political philosophers, as well as nationalist-inclined religious and political figures, tend to take this myth seriously as a political and national charter.

Since the end of World War II and the abolition of the formal relationship between religion and the state in Japan, the myth is no longer as central as the pre–World War II government wished it to be. It is, however, still an extremely powerful viewpoint among many Japanese.

See also Chūshingura; Divine Rulership; *Kamikaze*; Ninigi-no-mikoto.
References and further reading:
Aston, William G., trans. 1956. *Nihongi*. London: Allen and Unwin.
Dale, Peter N. 1986. *The Myth of Japanese Uniqueness*. New York: St. Martin's Press.
Philippi, Donald, trans. and ed. 1968. *Kōjiki*. Tokyo: Tokyo University Press.

DIVINE RULERSHIP

Divine rulership was attributed to the line of emperors descended from Amaterasu-ō-mikami. However, establishing the rulership of the land was a long process. Masakatsu-no-mikoto was ordered to go down and assume rule, but he declined the honor in favor of his newborn son, Ninigi-no-mikoto, who set forth a program of pacification that ended only many generations later. Ninigi-no-mikoto's grandsons spread out from Ninigi's palace in eastern Kyushu and pacified all tribes on their way, eventually establishing the divine kingdom in Yamato. All the emperors of Japan, male and female, from that day to the current emperor, Heisei, are of this lineage.

For ancient Japanese—and no less for modern ones, at least up to World War II—the divine authority of the emperor was unquestioned. The genealogy was sanctified and was tremendously important both to the position of the emperor and to the entire Japanese political system. In a very short time (relatively speaking) after the establishment of the Yamato state, the emperors lost their political clout. First it was to the Fujiwara family (and, in fact, the Fujiwara family and their cadet branches are as much the imperial house in Japan as any other, except that because they contributed the *female* side, this is discounted), then to the shogun of the Minamoto *bakufu*, then to the Hōjō regents (claiming to be another offshoot of the Fujiwara!), other shogunal branches, and strongmen. Whomever the ruler was, the emperor, a descendant of the heavenly *kami*, continued to reign. Notwithstanding a few political hiccups after the Kamakura shogunate ended, the imperial line has not attempted to rule since. Having been politically displaced did nothing to lower the prestige and reverence with which the emperor was held. In practice, the government that held the person of the emperor was the legitimate government, and with a few very archaic exceptions, such as Taira no Masakado, there have been no attempts to dismiss the imperial family. At the heart of the reasoning was the fact that the imperial lineage was *demonstrably* (at least, in myth) the direct link between the heavenly *kami* and humanity. Unlike European or Chinese ideas of divine rulership, divinity was not conferred upon the ruling emperor by the gods or by merit so much as a very real, unquestioned part of his very person.

See also Amaterasu-ō-mikami; Divine Descent; Jimmu Tenno; Ninigi-no-mikoto.
References and further reading:
Aston, William G., trans. 1956. *Nihongi.* London: Allen and Unwin.
Philippi, Donald, trans. and ed. 1968. *Kōjiki.* Tokyo: Tokyo University Press.

DŌJŌ-HŌSHI

A child endowed by the thunder deity with supernormal strength. One day, the story tells, a man was working his fields when the thunder *kami* fell to ground. The farmer, who had been leaning on his iron hoe (iron is considered a sovereign defense against snakes and thunder), wanted to strike the fallen (and presumably terrifying) apparition. The thunder *kami* then promised, in exchange for his life, a wondrous child.

The farmer returned home, and some time later his wife conceived and then gave birth to a boy. He was born with a snake around his head (the thunder deities are strongly associated with snakes; see, for example, the myth of Izanami in the underworld). The boy was troublesome, uprooting trees in his play, or drinking the village well dry. Eventually he became a novice to a temple, where he was a diligent student but also strong enough to save the temple in times of trouble. Many of his descendants, including women, were as strong as he was. It is said that among his descendants was Benkei's mother.

There are a number of Japanese myths in which a strange boy appears to a man or a couple and grows up with the strength of many men, or sometimes other powers. The Dōjō-hōshi myth is repeated in numerous variants across Japan. Many of these strong-men are described as giants, or as demigod heroes who formed the hills and rivers of the landscape. Some such heroes include the giants Sakata-no-kintoki and Musashibō Benkei.

See also Benkei; Kintoki; Raiden; Snakes; Thunder Deities.
References and further reading:
Ouwehand, Cornelius. 1964. *Namazu-e and Their Themes: An Interpretative Approach to Some Aspects of Japanese Religion.* Leiden, the Netherlands: E. J. Brill.

DOSŌJIN

Deity of crossroads and of fecundity. Dosōjin is often represented by a wooden or stone phallus, and offerings of wooden phalloi are made at Dosōjin shrines. Dosōjin is often referred to as Sae-no-kami, and it is possible that at some time in the past the functions or nature of these deities might have been different. He is also identified with Chimata-no-kami, born of Izanagi's trousers.

Dosōjin, deity of the crossroads and fecundity, worshipped by offerings of phalluses in a small rural shrine. (Courtesy of the author)

Sarutahiko, who helped in pacifying the Central Land of the Reed Plains, was deified and worshiped as Dosōjin. Dosōjin in his character as Sae-no-kami is also seen (as is the scarecrow deity) as the repository of knowledge about the world. These two functions—prosperity and knowledge—were clearly related in Japanese thinking (as elsewhere, for example, in Greek mythology) by the association with crossroads: This is where both goods and articles would be exchanged; and with the phallus representing fecundity. Unsurprisingly, many other deities are associated with this complex as well, for example, Dakiniten, who is seen as a deity of plenty, and also of knowledge, or perhaps better, information.

See also Chimata-no-kami; Sarutahiko.
References and further reading:
Czaja, Michael. 1974. *Gods of Myth and Stone: Phallicism in Japanese Folk Religion.* New York and Tokyo: Weatherhill.

DŌZOKU-SHIN

The *kami* of an extended family cluster. Families in some areas of Japan, particularly the Northeast and mountain areas where land was scarce, would organize themselves into family clusters. These consisted of a main house—the *honke*—and several branch houses originating either from the main house or from other branch houses, called *bunke*. The houses' relations were hierarchical, each one owing obligations directly or indirectly to the *honke*. These obligations were financial, political, and, most important, ritual. Each branch house was obligated to support, in worship and offerings, the shrine of the main house. The *kami* worshiped by the main house thus became the *dōzoku-shin* of the entire cluster.

Often the *dōzoku-shin* was viewed as the ancestor of the main house, and thus of all members of the branch houses as well. *Dōzoku* that have the dragon-*kami* Ryujin as their deity often accept that the dragon-*kami* or a magical snake was the ancestor (sometimes ancestress) and founder of the main house.

In a broader context, the Japanese people as a whole constitute a *dōzoku.* The Imperial House is the *honke,* and all other Japanese households are *bunke* related and differentiated by their closeness to the imperial house. The *dōzoku-shin* in this case would be Amaterasu-ō-mikami, tutelary deity and ancestress of the imperial household.

See also Amaterasu-ō-mikami; Divine Descent; Divine Rulership; Ryūjin.
References and further reading:
Shimizu, A. 1987. "Ie and Dōzoku—Family and Descent in Japan." *Current Anthropology* 28: 85–90.

EARTHLY *KAMI* (*KUNITSU-KAMI*)

Deities who inhabited and ruled the earth before the descent of the heavenly grandson. The vast category of *kunitsu-kami* is usually opposed to the concept of *amatsu-kami* (heavenly kami). Many of the myths of the *Nihonshōki* and of the *Kōjiki* have to do with the struggle between the heavenly and earthly *kami*. The earthly *kami* do not in any sense represent evil, merely opposition to the divine way of things, and to the domination of the heavenly *kami*. There is no single myth that explains the presence of the earthly *kami*, though one could argue (as do some mythical exegeses) that the earthly *kami* are simply those *kami* born of Izanami and Izanagi's labors and who were not "assigned" to heaven.

In many cases, earthly *kami* accept the domination of the heavenly *kami* with good grace and proper humility, offering their daughters as wives and being appointed rulers of their locales. This happens often in the myth of the heavenly grandson, as well as Susano-wo, who is both heaven-born and an earthly *kami* by his expulsion from heaven. In other cases (Takeminakata-no-kami, Ōkunishushi's son, is one major example) they resisted, only to be defeated more or less spectacularly by the hero of the hour, be it Takemikazuchi or Yamato-takeru.

The primary earthly *kami* is Ōkuninushi, as indicated by his name (Master of the Land), his activities (creation of the land), and his importance during the subjugation. Another figure is Oyamatsumi, who gave his daughter to Susano-wo to wed. The name may simply be a generic title for any mountain *kami*, as it appears several times in the *Kōjiki* in different contexts.

In a broader interpretative sense, the earthly *kami* serve two functions. On the one hand they (or at least, some of them) may have been local clan deities that were subdued by the Yamato in their march to imperial greatness. In another sense, they also represent the personification of the land itself: a recounting of the process whereby the Yamato overcame not only the peoples living in particular places in Japan but also the locale itself, absorbing it into the empire. The presence of inferior earthly *kami* also bolstered the Japanese court's view of itself, as masters of the peasants around them who worked for the aristocratic manors. The aristocrats often saw themselves as the authors and genitors of civilization and culture, which they brought to the inferiors under their control, thus the necessary subordination of those who worked the earth, as well as, symbolically, the earth itself.

See also Divine Rulership; Ōkuninushi, Oyamatsumi, Susano-wo; Takemikazuchi; Takeminakata; Yamato-takeru.

References and further reading:
Aston, William G., trans. 1956. *Nihongi*. London: Allen and Unwin.
Philippi, Donald, trans. and ed. 1968. *Kōjiki*. Tokyo: Tokyo University Press.

EBISU

Kami of luck and good fortune, patron of fishermen, and a member of the Shichi Fukujin. Ebisu is often depicted in concert with his father, Daikoku. He wears traditional Heian period clothes and brimless black hat, is usually holding a fishing rod, and holds a large red *tai* (sea bream) under his arm or slung over his shoulder. Ebisu is a *marebito* (a "visiting" deity, whom one does well to treat with respect). Fishermen, particularly along the shores of the Seto Inland Sea, often catch him in their nets as he floats from place to place. If the trawl is hauled in, he transforms himself into a curiously shaped stone. The crew possessing such a stone, if it is worshiped and given proper offerings of drink and fish, will have fortunate catches. Ebisu is one of the *rusugami* (caretaker *kami*) who keep an eye on the land while the gods are having their annual assembly at Ōkuninushi's palace in Izumo. He does not heed the summons for the assembly because he is deaf, or pretends to be. He therefore invented the practice of clapping hands and ringing a bell at a shrine to attract the attention of the *kami*. This is still practiced today by every visitor to a shrine. The *kami*, particularly Takamimusubi-no-kami, are very suspicious of Ebisu's absences, and they test Ebisu's hearing from time to time, which is why he doesn't always answer petitioners.

As the *kami* of good fortune, Ebisu aids merchants in finding and accumulating wealth. He is also sometimes identified with Sukunabikona, another *marebito*, or with Kotoshironushi-no-kami. Like many *marebito*, he sometimes appears as a wandering traveler who if treated hospitably will provide good fortune. He is also sometimes identified with the god Hiruko, who has neither arms nor legs. In the Ryukyus, Hiruko goes to live in the palace of the dragon-king of the sea, returning at adulthood to become god of fishermen and of commerce (Ebisu). Ebisu is sometimes identified with whales, because like Sukunabikona and Ebisu, they come during a season bringing bounty, then depart again to the depths of the sea.

The fish he holds—a *tai*, one of the most palatable fish in Japan's seas—is homonymous with *medetai* (congratulations). It is a staple of Japanese weddings and other major celebrations that invoke good fortune.

The figure of Ebisu is extremely enigmatic, as evidenced by the number of other *kami* he is associated with. Of all the Shichi Fukujin—his most popularly recognized identity—he is the most elusive and ungraspable. He is at one and the same time friendly and threatening, available to the common man and extremely elusive. If anything, he is the antidote, or opposition, to many of the things the *kami* stand for. Not of any one place, he is at all places, and always a wanderer.

> **See also** Daikoku; Hiruko; Kotoshironushi-no-kami; *Marebito*; *Rusugami*; Shichi Fukujin; Sukunabikona.

Ebisu, one of the seven gods of good fortune, holding a fish. (Courtesy of the author)

References and further reading:
Joly, Henri L. 1967. *Legend in Japanese Art.* Tokyo: Charles E. Tuttle Co.
Naumann, Nelly. 1974. "Whale and Fish Cult in Japan: A Basic Feature of Ebisu Worship." *Asian Folklore Studies* 33: 1–15.
Sakurada, Katsunori. 1980 (1963). "The Ebisu-Gami in a Fishing Village." In *Studies in Japanese Folklore,* edited by R. Dorson. New York: Arno Press, pp. 122–132.

EMMA-Ō

King of the dead and their judge. He appears in the robes of a Chinese magistrate, carrying a *shaku* (a thin, flat board about one foot long that was used by court officials to rest scrolls they were reading on, and became a symbol of rank and authority) and wearing a crown or bonnet on which appears the character "king." He has a fierce expression with a red face and protruding canine teeth, but like Jizō, with whom he is sometimes identified, he cares for those under his care. He is merciful, and one can also appeal to him for help from disease. Emma-ō is a Buddhist figure of Chinese antecedents. Because both he and Susano-wo are rulers of the underworld, they are identified as one and the same.

See also Jizō; Susano-wo; Underworld.

References and further reading:
Joly, Henri L. 1967. *Legend in Japanese Art.* Tokyo: Charles E. Tuttle Co.

EN-NO-GYŌJA

Mythical founder of the Shugendō order of syncretic practice in the seventh century and a powerful wizard. Also known as En-no-Ozunu and En-no-Ubasoku (an *ubasoku* is an unordained monk). He is supposed to have lived between 634 and 701, but there is no evidence of his existence aside from later writings. According to myth he lived as a hermit in the mountains of Katsuragi, on the border between the provinces of Kii and Yamato, where he meditated and practiced magic. He was able to coerce demons to do his bidding in mountains and water. He revered Buddhism and used the power of its spells to produce his magic.

He was powerful enough to call several deities and *oni* to him, commanding them to build a bridge between Mt. Katsuragi and Mt. Kimpu. The oracle deity Hitokotonushi-no-kami slandered the sage, saying he was plotting to usurp the emperor. En-no-Gyōja (En the Ascetic) was exiled, and he withdrew into the mountains to meditate. There he practiced the magical formula of Kojaku-ō, the peacock king, which allowed him eventually to subdue and control Hitokotonushi. Due to his magic, the ascetic was able to fly and even reach heaven itself. He was accompanied by two demons he had subdued, and under their master's direction they built bridges for pilgrims in the mountains. Among other feats, he is the Johnny Appleseed of Japan: He planted ten thousand cherry trees on Mt. Yoshino, and their blossoms may be enjoyed by visitors today.

On a visit to Shikoku he found a valley ravaged by a fiery serpent. Using his powers, he subdued the serpent and bound it to the earth. This magic lasted for over a century, until it had to be renewed by Kōbō Daishi.

En-no-Gyōja is revered by the *yamabushi* (mountain ascetics, also called *kebōzu*, "hairy priests," because they did not shave their heads as other Buddhist priests and monks do) as the founder of their order. The story of the sage's control of the oracle deity may be an explanatory myth for the activities of the *yamabushi* as diviners, twined with a story that emphasizes the superiority of Buddhist over native Shintō practices. For many Japanese throughout history, the importance of Buddhism was that it offered magical solution to daily distress and fears. The *yamabushi*—esoteric practitioners whose rituals were based largely on Shingon—were often the only visible religious presence in remote mountain villages. Their adherence to the teachings of this remote mythical leader gave the *yamabushi* a strong claim to practice magic and supernatural powers.

See also Hitokotonushi; Kōbō Daishi; Kojaku-ō.

References and further reading:

Earhart, H. Byron. 1970. *A Religious Study of the Mount Haguro Sect of Shugendo.* Tokyo: Sophia University Monumenta Nipponica.

Nakamura, Kyoko Motomuchi. 1997. *Miraculous Stories from the Japanese Buddhist Tradition: The Nihon Ryoki of the Monk Kyokai.* New ed. Richmond, VA: Curzon Press.

Statler, Oliver. 1984. *Japanese Pilgrimage.* London: Picador.

FII NU KANG (RYUKYUAN)

The deity of the hearth. In the very diffuse system of Ryukyuan beliefs is generally considered a female and the point of access to the world of the *kang* (deities). Fii Nu Kang is probably the most frequently addressed of the Ryukyuan *kang*, and there is usually both a household hearth and a communal hearth through which she can be addressed. Very similar to, but far less personified than, the Ainu deity Kamui Fuchi.

The difficulties of lighting and maintaining a fire, and the centrality of the hearth, are not too apparent to modern life. They are, however, critically important to technologically simple people, and many religions have extolled and preserved the sanctity of the hearth. It is not surprising to find that the hearth deity is of paramount importance to both Ainu and Ryukyuans. This importance is overshadowed in complex polities such as the Yamato state by deities who support the Great Tradition and are supported and maintained by the state apparatus.

See also Kamui Fuchi.

References and further reading:
Herbert, Jean, 1980. *La religion d'Okinawa.* Paris: Dervy-Livres. Collection Mystiques et religions. Série B 0397–3050.
Lebra, William P. 1966. *Okinawan Religion: Belief, Ritual, and Social Structure.* Honolulu, University of Hawaii Press.
Sered, Susan Starr. 1999. *Women of the Sacred Groves. Divine Priestesses of Okinawa.* New York and Oxford: Oxford University Press.

FOOD DEITIES

The ability of Japan's traditional societies to maintain a food surplus, and thus ensure freedom from famine, was limited. It is thus unsurprising to find that a number of Japanese deities are recognized as *kami* of food, and that several different myths account for food in human life.

The most important food *kami*, ritually speaking, is Toyoukebime (also Toyouke-ō-mikami and Toyouke-no-kami), or "Plentiful food princess." One of the daughters of Wakamusubi-no-kami, who came into being from the urine of Izanami as she lay dying from giving birth to the fire deity, she is not otherwise mentioned in the myths. However, her main shrine is the *Geigū* (Outer Shrine) at Ise-jingū. The Inner Shrine is the famous shrine to Amaterasu-ō-mikami, Shintō's major shrine, indicating that food was secondary only to the existence of the imperial house.

However, another myth is far more significant for understanding the Japanese approach to food. This is the double myths of Ukemochi-no-kami (from the *Nihonshōki*) and of Ōgetsuhime (from the *Kōjiki*). Both of these myths are similar in outline, though the actors differ. In the *Nihonshōki* version, Ukemochi-no-kami was an earthly deity who was the *kami* of food. Tsukiyomi-no-mikoto, Amaterasu's younger brother, was sent to her as emissary by his sister. Ukemochi-no-kami offered him food that she extracted from her mouth. Insulted by her actions (because the food was polluted by having been in her mouth), Tsukiyomi-no-mikoto kills her, then returns to Amaterasu to report on his actions. Amaterasu banishes him to the night sky but sends to see the corpse. In the corpse various useful items are discovered: in her head, cattle and horses; in her forehead, millet (the most important food grain before the introduction of rice); on her eyebrows, silkworms; in her eyes, panic grass (another food grain); along with rice in her belly, and wheat, soybeans, and red beans in her genitals.

The *Kōjiki* version has different protagonists. In his wanderings on the earth, after having been exiled from heaven, Susano-wo came upon the deity Ōgetsuhime. She gave him shelter and offered him food. This she extracted from her mouth, nose, and rectum. Insulted, he killed her. From her corpse grew various things useful for humankind: silkworms from her head, rice seeds from her eyes, millet from her ears, red beans from her nose, wheat from her genitals, and soybeans from her rectum. There is no mention of Susano-wo's fate after the murder, but we know from the myth of Ōkuninushi that he eventually came to rule in a great hall. Susano-wo has a second connection to food. His daughter Ukanomitama-no-kami, by his second wife, Kamu-ō-ichi-hime, is revered as a food deity. It is possible that the differences between different tellings of the same myth may represent two mythical traditions, that of Yamato and that of some other culture.

Finally there is, of course, Inari. The Inari myth recounts an old man appearing with sheaves of rice over his shoulder. Although this myth is clearly related to food, it is no less an aristocratic rather than a commoner myth: Rice during the Heian period, when Inari worship first became widespread, was a newfangled food, the province of the aristocracy in the capital Heian. It did not become important as a major staple until much later.

The issue of food was crucial for the Japanese as for any agriculturally-based society. However, they also acknowledged the fact that growth implied death, and that the death of the previous season's plants was a necessary part of the next season's crops. It is no less important that the Japanese in these myths were actually dealing with two oppositionary phenomena that they associated culturally. One is the association of food with decay, and thus of life with death. Inevitably, one follows, and is dependent on, the other. Death was highly polluting in Japanese culture, and this aspect of the myth is strongly emphasized in both versions of the food goddess myth. Indeed, the Japanese are perhaps the only culture that identifies foodstuffs with excretion (though perhaps the authors of both versions were exhibiting a hint of a sense of humor in associating beans with the rectum).

Another cultural opposition is in evidence in these two central myths as well. The kitchen, where food was provided for men, was the essential domain of women. And women in archaic Japan could be divine, but they could also be polluted by their association with menstrual and birth blood, a polluting status that was reinforced with the arrival of Chinese culture (where women were *always* subordinate to men) and Buddhism (where women were definitely polluting). The authors of both versions (as well as the myth of Toyouke's origins) seemed to be hinting at the contradiction that pure food for pure men was nonetheless prepared by impure women.

See also Amaterasu-ō-mikami; Inari; Susano-wo; Tsukiyomi-no-mikoto.
References and further reading:
Aston, William G., trans. 1956. *Nihongi.* London: Allen and Unwin.
Philippi, Donald, trans. and ed. 1968. *Kōjiki.* Tokyo: Tokyo University Press.

FOX

Animal that features in many legends, either as messenger to the deity Inari or as a sly magical creature. As messengers of Inari, foxes are protected and their goodwill solicited. As magical animals they are feared and sometimes killed. Foxes are both good and bad omens. As night howlers and haunters of temple gates (near the graveyards, which are on the grounds of Buddhist temples) they were considered bad omens. But white foxes, black foxes, and nine-tailed foxes were considered good omens from the gods.

The fox can give a variety of gifts. A fox marrying a human produces half-fox human offspring with great powers, sagacity, and strength. Or the fox might provide its human spouse with a magical device—a jewel is common—that will, for example, fool tax-assessors into believing the fields are barren. Foxes also reward benefactors and punish transgressors.

Foxes in general, and white foxes in particular, were reputed to be the messengers of Inari, *kami* of wealth and harvest and worldly success. This may be because the rice harvest was associated with the yearly migration of the Yama-no-kami (Mountain deity) from the mountains to the rice fields, where he assumed the title of Ta-no-kami (Rice-paddy deity). Similarly, the fox moves between the wild areas of the mountains and the area of human habitation on the plain. Foxes, particularly the envoys of Inari, were also reputed to carry a ball of fire about with them, with which they could both enchant and be enchanted. Inari shrines are always flanked by statues of foxes, some carrying bags of rice, some carrying jewels, others sheaves of rice. White figurines of foxes are offered at Inari shrines as well. In some shrines it is possible to borrow these images for a time to ensure success in a venture.

Foxes became associated with Inari in the following manner. A pair of old magical foxes lived in the mountains. They were both of unusual appearance: The husband had silvery points on his fur, and the wife had the body of a fox but the head of a deer. They had five progeny, equally strange. One day they went and knelt before the shrine to Inari. They said, "Though we are dumb brutes, we are not without finer feelings, nor without sense, and we desire to serve the shrine in some capacity to do good." As a consequence, they and their brood were made the guardian assistants of Inari, as they remain, appearing in people's dreams and reporting what was going on to the *kami*.

Foxes have magical powers whether associated with Inari or not. In particular they have the ability to transform themselves into people. Travelers at night who are solicited by a beautiful woman are probably being ensorcelled by a fox. The only way to find the truth is to observe whether the lady has a tail—the only part of its anatomy the animal is unable to transform.

One of the most common legends concerns the fox wife: a fox, who for one reason or another (usually tragic) assumes the shape of a woman. In one famous

A lively fox guardian before a shrine of Inari. (M. Fairman/ArkReligion.com)

story, the fox spirit follows a drum that had been made of the hide of one of its offspring. In another, Abe no Yasuna saved a fox from hunters. Some time later he courted and married a beautiful young woman named Kuzunohana. She left him after bearing a son, Seimei, who became the famous wizard and astrologer Kamo Yasunari. Yasunari saved the life of the emperor by discovering that an illness was caused by a nine-tailed fox who had disguised herself as human and become the emperor's favorite concubine. The famous hero Yoshitsune had his own encounter with a fox. In the Kabuki play *Yoshitsune senbon zakura,* a fox takes on the guise of Yoshitsune's retainer Tadanobu following the drum made of his parent's skin. He hears the voice of his parents when the drum is struck. When Yoshitsune learns of this, he gives the drum to the fox, who, in return, supplies the hero with magical protection.

A man once met a beautiful woman; they married and had a child. They had a dog who gave birth to a litter at approximately the same time. But when the puppies grew a bit older, they started barking whenever the wife was near. She begged the man to kill them, but he refused. Then one day the wife was startled by a puppy that she had come too close to. The puppy started barking, and she jumped on to the fence and turned back into her natural form of a fox. The husband loved his wife dearly and, vowing never to forget her, begged her to return to sleep with him at night (*kitsune* = "come and sleep" but also "fox"), which she agreed to do.

Far more serious is fox possession. Possessed people bark, eat from dishes on the floor, and are fearful of dogs. They may be successful at the expense of their neighbors, and were thus shunned and attacked in Japan until recently. In some recorded instances whole families were extirpated because they were suspected of being fox-possessed and thus preying upon their neighbors.

The various aspects of the fox—powerful, willful, dangerous, and malicious but also family-oriented and loyal—created an image that was both admired and feared. Foxes are, in effect, a variation on the *marebito* theme of powerful strangers. The fear foxes engendered was projected upon successful families in farming villages in a form of envy transference: One was expected to rejoice at a neighbor's fortune, yet at the same time, one was envious. Thus accusations of being foxes, often leveled against wealthy families, served in small, close-knit Japanese hamlets as a way of expressing envy and jealousy in a form that was mythically and socially acceptable.

See also Inari; *Marebito*; Yoshitsune.
References and further reading:
Goff, Janet. 1997. "Foxes in Japanese Culture: Beautiful or Beastly?" *Japan Quarterly* 44 (2): 66–71.

Nozaki, Kiyoshi. 1961. *Kitsune: Japan's Fox of Mystery, Romance and Humor.* Tokyo: Hokuseido Press.

Smits, Ivo. 1996. "An Early Anthropologist? Oe no Masafusa's 'A Record of Fox Spirits.'" In *Religion in Japan: Arrows to Heaven and Earth,* edited by Peter F. Kornicki and I. J. McMullen. Cambridge: Cambridge University Press, pp. 78–89.

Smyers, Karen. 2000. *The Fox and the Jewel.* Honolulu: University of Hawaii Press.

FU-DAISHI

The protector of libraries and collections. Fu Xi (497–569) was a learned abbot and philosopher in Liang, a Chinese kingdom of the period of the Six Dynasties. He invented a rotating vertical table that allowed storage and display, and the honoring, of the entire Buddhist canon, the *Daizōkyō.* As a consequence, he and his two sons, Fujō and Fuken, who usually flank his image, are considered guardians of libraries.

Many ecclesiastical libraries in Japan show these three figures. Fu-daishi himself is usually shown seated on a broad Chinese chair, his two sons as smaller figures standing on either side. The sons are portrayed often as laughing monks, like Hōtei. However, one is shown with his mouth open (saying *om,* the first syllable), and the other's mouth is closed (saying *hum,* the last syllable), indicating their role—like the *koma-inu* and the Ni-ō—as guardians of the Law from beginning to end. Fu-daishi is popularly known as *warai Botoke,* the laughing Buddha, an image also popular in the West.

See also Koma-inu; Ni-ō.
References and further reading:
Joly, Henri L. 1967. *Legend in Japanese Art.* Tokyo: Charles E. Tuttle Co.

FUDŌ MYŌ-Ō

One of the most popular deities in Japan, and the most commonly depicted of the heavenly kings, Fudō, whose name means "Immovable," represents resolute and immovable determination. Fudō is the supreme barrier against evil and subduer of forces hostile to the Buddhist Law. He is the direct envoy of Dainichi Nyōrai and is his avatar. Fudō is portrayed carrying a sword and a rope to bind evildoers. His body is usually black or blue. His eyes are staring, and his facial expression is fierce. He is also often portrayed as having two long fangs projecting from his mouth. Fudō stands or sits cross-legged on a rock, signifying his immobility and steadfastness, and is surrounded by flames. Fudō is always accompanied by two young servitors; on his left is Kongara-dōji ("What is it about?" boy), who carries a lotus flower and stem signifying the Law, and on his right is Seitaka-dōji (Gangling youth), whose one hand shields his eyes while the other holds a gourd, signifying the cosmos or the emptiness of life.

Fudō Myō-ō surrounded by flames (Courtesy of the author)

Fudō grants strength to withstand all perils and to overcome tribulations. *Gyōja* (Shugendō ascetics) would invoke Fudō's name before engaging in austerities such as standing under waterfalls, walking across coals, or climbing sword-blade ladders. He is also invoked during the *goma* fire ceremonies in Shugendō practice and in the Tendai and the Shingon esoteric schools of Buddhism. He is the most active of all avatars of the Buddha.

Fudō, paradoxically for his association with fire, is also the deity of waterfalls. This comes about because of his title as "the Immovable." Shugendō ascetics would appeal to him to aid them during periods of meditation under freezing mountain waterfalls, to keep them still and unmoving under the cold and pressure of the water.

Fudō's main shrine is at Narita City (near Tokyo's international airport). The image enshrined there was made in China. The sage Kōbō Daishi was told in a dream that it wanted to travel to Japan, and when he returned home he brought it with him. It was deposited at Takao-zan, a mountain temple about 40 miles from the fishing village of Edo (now modern Tokyo). During the Masakado rebellion, the statue was brought close to the rebel headquarters, and a fire ritual was performed before it for three days, as consequence of which the rebel was defeated. The statue indicated it wished to stay in the neighborhood to continue to subdue evil. The emperor had lots cast for the site of a sumptuous temple, and Narita won. The temple houses a sword donated by Emperor Shujaku, which banishes insanity and evils of possession by foxes.

See also Kōbō Daishi.

References and further reading:
Eliot, Sir Charles Norton Edgcumbe. 1959. *Japanese Buddhism.* London: Routledge and Kegan Paul.

Frank, Bernard. 1991. *Le pantheon bouddhique au Japon.* Paris: Collections d'Emile Guimet. Reunion des musees nationaux.

Macgovern, William Montgomery. 1922. *An Introduction to Mahâyâna Buddhism, with Especial Reference to Chinese and Japanese Phases.* London: Kegan Paul and Co.

FUGEN-BOSATSU

The boddhisattva of good practice. He is represented riding on one of the elephants that support the world (a borrowing from Indian cosmology). Fugen represents the virtue embodied in the world, including all the buddhas and boddhisattvas of all the multiple universes. He carries a fly-whisk, a symbol of majesty and rule. Often a companion of Monju-bosatsu, they flank images of the Buddha Shakyamuni, the historical Buddha. Fugen appears to those who meditate upon the sutras, riding his six-tusked elephant. This elephant is the incarnated nature of the Buddha, who first appeared on earth in his incarnation of a six-tusked elephant.

Fujin, the wind god, carrying the sack of winds. (Suzuki Kiitsu/The Bridgeman Art Library/Getty Images)

See also Animals: elephant; Monju-bosatsu; Shakyamuni.
References and further reading:
Frank, Bernard. 1991. *Le pantheon bouddhique au Japon.* Paris: Collections
d'Emile Guimet. Reunion des musees nationaux.
Joly, Henri L. 1967. *Legend in Japanese Art.* Tokyo: Charles E. Tuttle Co.

FUJIN

The wind god. He has a demon's staring, horned, and fanged head, and claws on his hands and feet. He grasps a bag from whose open mouth issue the winds. He is sometimes shown as companion to Raijin (Raiden) the thunder deity.

Winds were, of course, of great importance to the Japanese. They brought the monsoon rains upon which much agriculture depended, but they were also present in the form of typhoons, dangerous winds that could flatten towns and spread fires.

See also Raiden.
References and further reading:
Joly, Henri L. 1967. *Legend in Japanese Art.* Tokyo: Charles E. Tuttle Co.
Okuda, Kensaku, ed. 1970. *Japan's Ancient Sculpture.* Tokyo: Mainichi
    Newspapers.

FUKUROKUJU

Member of the Shichi Fukujin, he represents longevity, wisdom, and occasionally, carnal pleasure. He is represented as a small-statured man, almost a dwarf, whose bald, hair-fringed head is sometimes the length of his body. He is dressed in Chinese robes and is reputedly the avatar of a Chinese philosopher. The shape of his head evokes the image of a phallus, and he is often displayed in the form of a traditional *harigata* (dildo), or as a statue of that shape. This may either be a result of the original shape of his head or because of the Chinese association of longevity and Daoist wisdom with sex and the principles of yin and yang (female and male). His image can thus often be found, together with another of the Shichi Fukujin, Jurojin—with whom he is often confused—in Japan's red-light districts. He is sometimes accompanied by a stag, a symbol of longevity. Fukurokuju is usually portrayed as a jolly, fun-loving deity, more at home in the company of Ebisu and Hōtei than the other more dour of the Shichi Fukujin.

See also Ebisu; Hōtei; Jurojin; Shichi Fukujin.
References and further reading:
Joly, Henri L. 1967. *Legend in Japanese Art.* Tokyo: Charles E. Tuttle Co.

FUTSUNUSHI-NO-KAMI

A sword or warrior *kami* dispatched with Takemikazuchi to subdue the Central Land of the Reed Plains (as told in the *Nihonshōki*). He is one of the *kami* in the composite Kasuga Daimyōjin deity. He is the main deity worshiped at the Katori shrine as a martial and protective deity. A famous sword-fighting school—the Katori Shinden-ryu—is named for him. He is appealed to for protection, success in the martial arts, and guidance at sea. In the Kasuga shrine, Futsunushi is worshiped as an avatar of Yakushi Nyōrai.

See also Kasuga Daimyōjin; Ōkuninushi; Takemikazuchi.
References and further reading:
Aston, William G., trans. 1956. *Nihongi.* London: Allen and Unwin.

GAKI
See Ghosts.

GAMA-SENNIN

"Toad sage," also known as Kosensei. An elderly man with a warty hairless skin, he is said to live forever, able to change himself into a toad. He is one of the immortal sages, of Chinese Daoist origin, who are associated with longevity and medicine. Gama-sennin's constant companion is a three-legged toad, whom he often carries on his hand or back. He is also the creator and manufacturer of magical pills, and whomsoever manages to secure them is able to extend his lifetime. Gama-sennin himself sheds his skin like a toad, and thus renews himself as necessary.

The adoption of the immortals concept from Daoist origins was done unsystematically in Japan, and without much of the philosophical-popular basis that formed the origin of these ideas in China. Gama-sennin is one of the most popular of these figures, often depicted in carvings and drawings.

See also Sages.
References and further reading:
Joly, Henri L. 1967. *Legend in Japanese Art.* Tokyo: Charles E. Tuttle Co.

GEKKA-Ō

Buddhist name of deity of marriage. *See* Musubi-no-kami, p. 298.

GHOSTS

Yūrei are a name given to a number of mythological phenomena that can be subsumed under the English term *ghosts.* Many of these stories fall under the category of legend or entertaining story rather than myth. However, they contain some mythical elements that are important.

Yūrei stories can be grouped into a number of categories. One of the most important mythical elements is the idea of *gaki,* or hungry ghosts. In Japanese social thought, individuals were members of a household, or *ie,* before their birth, during their lives, and after death. The dead were expected to be maintained—by worship, offering, and remembrance—by their descendants. When this was not done, the ghost would become dangerous, preying on the living and bringing afflictions such as maladies. The idea perhaps originated in China, but it fit well into the Japanese conceptions of the role of the family.

Ghosts of defeated armies and warriors occupy a prominent place in mythology. There are a number of myths related to the calamitous defeat of the Taira clan at Dan-no-Ura (1185). A well-known story tells of Hoichi, a *biwa* (lute) player. Traditionally, lute playing was an occupation reserved for the blind, and Hoichi was no exception. One night he was approached by a samurai in full armor. The soldier informed the musician that he was the retainer of a visiting daimyō who wanted his presence to be kept secret, and who wished to hear a recitation of the *Heike Monogatari,* the story of the defeat of the Taira. After playing for some nights to the august company, he was questioned by the abbot at the temple where he was staying. The abbot had him followed, and he was eventually found playing by himself in the rain at the memorial stone to the drowned infant emperor Antoku. Other fallen warriors are often reported to appear under specific circumstances or places associated with their death.

A second major theme of interest is the "ghost mother" who cares for her child even after death. A woman who visited a sweet shop, purchasing a special kind of local candy, was observed clandestinely by the shop owner, then followed to a gravesite in which her baby was found against the dead body, sucking contentedly on the sweet. Similar stories are to be found throughout Japan.

A third theme is that of malevolent ghosts. Sea ghosts follows ships or fishermen, demanding the use of a pail. If they are not provided with a pail without a bottom, they fill the boat with water. The ghosts of those who have died on high mountains or mountain passes may seek to entice passers-by to their deaths, or kill them outright. Temples (and their associated graveyards) are often the sites of ghostly apparitions, whether as warnings or by vengeful ghosts.

Defeated armies aside, most of these stories highlight the fears and anxieties common to the Japanese. The "ghost mother" myth illustrates in one setting the intense emotional relationship between Japanese and their mothers that has been documented by recent psychological and sociological studies, and female obligations to protect and nurture even beyond the grave. The uncertainty of sailor's lives and the risks they run are alluded to in the stories of ghosts enticing crews to their deaths. And the specter of starvation and want has haunted the Japanese countrypeople until fairly recently.

For the Ainu, ghosts were an expression of the evil side of a deceased person. These *tukap* may appear in the dreams, either to convey a message from the deceased or to bring a message from Kamui Fuchi, or some other important *kamui*. As a result of such an apparition, the person's *ramat,* or spirit, may undertake a journey. If the *ramat* loses its way or cannot return for some reason—such as the sleeper's sudden waking—then the person may die.

Ghost stories and legend are mythological in two senses: First, they constitute explanatory tales for *local* communities, that is, they are part of the Little Traditions rather than the imperial or national myth corpus. Second, in some instances, for example, the myths related to the defeated Taira clan, ghost stories constitute "cultured myths" used to evoke mood and feeling, rather than specific explanatory tales. They are related to the imperial and national myths in that they evoke concepts of self-sacrifice and loyalty to one's superiors even beyond death.

See also Kamui Fuchi; Taira.

References and further reading:
Iwasaka, Michiko and Barre Toelken. 1994. *Ghosts and the Japanese: Cultural Experience in Japanese Death.* Logan: Utah State University Press.
Smith, Robert J. 1974. *Ancestor Worship in Contemporary Japan.* Palo Alto: Stanford University Press.

GONGEN

A general term for syncretic deities who are protectors of mountains or important areas. There are a number of such *gongen,* the title usually preceded by the locale name. The one exception is the deification of Tokugawa Ieyasu (1543–1616), founder and first shogun of the Tokugawa dynasty, often simply called "Gongen-sama" (Sir Gongen).

Gongen are expressions of the *honji-suijaku* concept, by which Shintō deities and Buddhist ones were seen as the same. Thus the local deities of mountains at specific localities in Japan were "Buddhiscized" and received the title *gongen.* In formal terms they are the avatars of named boddhisattvas.

See also Atago-gongen; Zaō-gongen.

References and further reading:
Grapard, Allan. 1992. *The Protocol of the Gods: A Study of the Kasuga Cult in Japanese History.* Berkeley: University of California Press.

GO-SHINTAI

Representation of the *kami* in Shintō worship. Every Shintō shrine houses an object associated with the *kami.* These objects are extremely varied. In fishing villages, odd-shaped stones caught in fishermen's nets are assumed to be the *go-shintai* of the *kami* Ebisu and are enshrined either in the boat itself or in a small shrine on the shore. Objects associated with the *kami*—bows and stirrups, both associated with war for the *kami* Hachiman; writing brushes in Tenjin shrines; statues of Inari—may be enshrined too. Some *go-shintai* are actual statues of figures dressed in court robes or, in the case of Inari, the deity's fox messenger. *Go-shintai* are surrounded both metaphorically and actually with layers of secrecy. They are ensconced in containers that are rarely opened (never, in the case of the imperial household regalia at Ise and some others), which are often wrapped in several layers of cloth and paper. Opening such a container, when it is done, is part of a lengthy ritual. The three most important *go-shintai* in Japan are the three items of the imperial regalia.

See also Hachiman, Imperial Regalia; Inari.

References and further reading:
Ashkenazi, Michael. 1993. *Matsuri: The Festivals of a Japanese Town.* Honolulu: University of Hawaii Press.
Aston, William George. 1905. *Shinto: The Way of the Gods.* London: Longmans, Green, and Co.

Ono, Sokyo. 1962. *Shinto: The Kami Way*. Rutland, VT: Charles E. Tuttle.
Ross, Floyd Hiatt. 1965. *Shinto: The Way of Japan*. Boston: Beacon Press.

GOZU-TENNO

The emperor Gozu, ox-headed deity of the underworld in Buddhist mythology.
He is the deity of disease and plague and is therefore invoked for protection
against the calamities he brings. He is similar to other mythological figures such
as the Ainu Kenash Unarabe, invoked because of fear and their power to do
harm. Gozu-tenno is often identified with Susano-wo, who was banished to rule
the underworld by his father, Izanagi.

> *See also* Kenash Unarabe; Susano-wo.
> *References and further reading:*
> Joly, Henri L. 1967. *Legend in Japanese Art*. Tokyo: Charles E. Tuttle Co.

GUT LENGTH

Modern myth prevalent in the last decades of the twentieth century. Japanese
people are said to have longer gut length due to a historical diet that was primarily vegetarian. This is supposedly a distinguishing feature of the Japanese, and
indicates their physical as well as mental uniqueness, and difference from the
rest of humankind.

The myth was first formally stated as such in the 1980s by Hata Tsutomu,
then the Japanese agricultural minister. Though part of an economic-political
defensive move (Hata was arguing against importation of American beef, claiming that Japanese, being largely vegetarians historically, had a longer gut and
therefore could not digest beef), it was firmly believed by many Japanese, and
often repeated colloquially.

> *See also* Japanese Uniqueness.
> *References and further reading:*
> Dale, Peter N. 1986. *The Myth of Japanese Uniqueness*. New York: St. Martin's
> Press.

HACHIDAI RYŪ-Ō

Eight dragon kings. Originally the *naga* or snake spirits of Indian belief, these
became the dragon kings in China, from whence they arrived in Japan. The eight
dragon kings rule dragon- and snake-kind, and are personified in the form of
Ryūjin, the dragon *kami*. They reside under the ocean or in large lakes, and their
abode is a magical palace surrounded by gardens. The dragon kings are not all-
powerful. Their magic resides in a ball, or pearl, whose virtue is that it controls
desires. They are also vulnerable to other powerful entities, as the story of
Tawara Toda indicates. Generally benevolent, one or another of these dragon

kings (they are undifferentiated) play a part in many Japanese myths. Urashimatarō stayed with the dragon king, as did some of the culture heroes, notably Tawara Toda, who saved the dragon king's kingdom.

See also Ryūjin; Tawara Toda.

References and further reading:

Joly, Henri L. 1967. *Legend in Japanese Art.* Tokyo: Charles E. Tuttle Co.

Ouwehand, Cornelius. 1964. *Namazu-e and Their Themes: An Interpretative Approach to Some Aspects of Japanese Religion.* Leiden, the Netherlands: E. J. Brill.

Visser, Marinus Willem de. 1913. *The Dragon in China and Japan.* Amsterdam: J. Müller; Wiesbaden: M. Sändig, 1969.

HACHIMAN

"Eight banners," one of the major deities of the Shintō pantheon, Hachiman is associated with the activities of war and culture. As a Buddhist deity he is worshiped as a *daibosatsu* (great Buddha) and protector of Buddhist temples. *Go-shintai* in Hachiman shrines are generally either a bow or a stirrup, referring to the classical mounted archer, and more rarely a writing brush, referring to his nature as deity of culture and learning. Doves are his messengers. Appealed to during the Mongol invasions of Japan, Hachiman sent the *kamikaze* (divine wind) to sink the combined Mongol-Chinese-Korean fleet.

In the second century C.E. Empress Jingū, following a vision from the *kami*, engaged in a campaign of conquest in Korea. Pregnant by her deceased husband and fearful that childbirth would slow down the campaign, she wrapped herself with tight bandages and tied a stone weight to her belly, thus managing to carry the baby for three years in the field. Her son, the emperor Ōjin to-be, was born once the campaign was over. Jingū had dreamed that if her son was born after the campaign was won, he would be a deity, and the child was born with a mark resembling a bow guard on his forearm, thus confirming his wondrous origin. In the sixth or seventh century, the mother-and-son combination were identified together as the deity Hachiman.

Ōjin, the fifteenth emperor of Japan according to the *Kōjiki*, invited Korean and Chinese scholars to educate his son and courtiers in the ways of the world. As a consequence Hachiman is the patron god of writing and culture, as well as war, divination, and protection.

References and further reading:

Joly, Henri L. 1967. *Legend in Japanese Art.* Tokyo: Charles E. Tuttle Co.

HACHIMANTARŌ

See Heroes.

HASHINAU-UK KAMUI (AINU)

Hunting goddess in Ainu mythology. She protects hunters, often appearing to a good hunter to show him the best place to find game. She is also the deity of the full catch for fishermen. Of great assistance to humankind, she was born of the base-plate of the fire-drill. Some say she is a relative of Shiramba Kamui, others that she is sister to Kamui Fuchi, goddess of the hearth. She is also called Isosange Mat (Bringing-down-game woman), and appears as a small bird to show hunters the location of their prey. In her person as Kamui Paseguru (Potent person), she is represented by the aconite plant, with which the Ainu would poison their arrows for the hunt.

For the Ainu, who subsisted largely on gathering, fishing, and hunting, Hashinau-uk Kamui is obviously of great importance. She may be invoked as an aid in childbearing and is often described as having an infant on her back.

> *See also* Kamui Fuchi; Shiramba Kamui.
> ***References and further reading:***

Ainu Mukei Bunka Densho Hozonkai. 1983. *Hitobito no Monogatari* (Fables of men). Sapporo: Ainu Mukei Bunka Densho Hozonkai, Showa 58 (1983), English and Japanese.

Munro, Neil Gordon. 1962. *Ainu Creed and Cult.* London: Routledge and Kegan Paul; London and New York: K. Paul International, distributed by Columbia University Press, 1995.

Ohnuki-Tierney, Emiko. 1969. *Sakhalin Ainu Folklore.* Washington, DC: American Anthropological Association. Anthropological Studies 2.

HEAVENLY FLOATING BRIDGE

The vantage point between heaven and the formless waters from whence Izanagi, stirring with his jeweled spear, stirred the waters. As a consequence, the liquid formed clumps, and drops of water falling from the tip of the spear formed the islands, bringing about the creation of the Central Land of the Reed Plains. The Heavenly Floating Bridge is sometimes equated with the Milky Way, though that celestial phenomenon is more usually interpreted as the Heavenly River. The bridge joins the heavenly and earthly realms, though its precise nature is undisclosed.

> *See also* Izanagi and Izanami.
> ***References and further reading:***

Aston, William G., trans. 1956. *Nihongi.* London: Allen and Unwin.

Philippi, Donald, trans. and ed. 1968. *Kōjiki.* Tokyo: Tokyo University Press.

HEROES

Like most other mythologies, Japanese mythology includes a list of heroes. Most of these heroes were samurai of note, whose reputation may have been enhanced with the retelling. They are largely characterized by the concept of loyalty—to one another or, more important, to their superior—which is their driving characteristic. Many of the heroic myths are structurally similar. Two themes predominate. One is the struggle against hopeless odds and eventual defeat. The other is the statement, in action, of principles that have become almost a byword for Japanese culture: the virtues of group action, loyalty, and honor. The heroes depicted here, and in separate entries, such as Benkei, Kintoki, and Yoshitsune, are not by the standards of the modern world necessarily wholly admirable. Many are avaricious, and some are vicious and disruptive. But to the people of the Japanese Middle Ages they displayed precisely the qualities of bravery and dedication that were the hallmark of the age. This entry provides a number of exemplary heroes. The list is by no means exhaustive, and only a few of the most notable heroes are mentioned.

Hachimantarō (original name: Minamoto-no-Yoshiie) was born in 1042 (d. 1103). On the eve of his birth his father had dreamed he was handed a sword by the *kami* Hachiman, deity of war, and he thus nicknamed the boy Hachimantarō (Young Hachiman). A famous archer, warrior, and general, Hachimantarō was capable of sending an arrow through three armored men. He was also the main force in subduing the Ezo of northern Honshu. While warring during a period of severe drought, he shot an arrow into a rock and brought forth clear water for his troops. On one occasion crossing a river during a storm, he threw his armor overboard, which not only calmed the river but dammed its flow to this day. He was so well known as an archer that when the emperor fell ill, the mere twanging of Hachimantarō's bowstring was sufficient to scare away the *oni* that was the source of the malady.

Minamoto-no-Tametomo, Hachimantarō's grandson, was seven feet tall, and his left arm was longer than his right, making him a great archer like his grandfather. He carried an eight-foot-long bow, and his arrows were five feet long. He boasted about his prowess and in one incident challenged two bowmen to shoot arrows at him. He caught the missiles in his hands. He was very violent as a boy, and like another hero, Yamato-takeru, was sent away, in his case to the isle of Kyushu, which he subjugated in two years. He became a follower of Emperor Go Shirakawa and during the Hōgen Insurrection (1156: fighting between Taira and Minamoto that brought about the end of the Heian era) killed two warriors with a single arrow. The victorious Taira exiled him to Oshima after severing the muscles of his arm. Nonetheless, he remained a formidable archer, and when men were sent to kill him, he sank the leading boat with one arrow. Subsequently he committed suicide rather than fall into his enemies' hands. In some legends it is said that he escaped his assassins to the Ryukyu Islands, founding the ruling house there.

Tomoe Gozen, a great beauty, became the concubine of Yoshinaka, a hero of the Taira, after her father's defeat. She killed a number of men during the fight, on one occasion turning aside a tree trunk one warrior aimed at her head. She was captured and then became the concubine of another of the victors.

Watanabe-no-Tsuna, one of Raikō's retainers, spent the night in front of the Rashōmon gate of Heian, which was reputed to be the location of the last *oni* in Japan (Watanabe's master, Raikō, having cleared the rest out). The *oni* Ibarakidōji, who had been one of the retainers of Shutendōji, whom Raikō and his retainers had killed in an earlier adventure, attacked after midnight. Watanabe cut off the *oni*'s arm in the struggle, but the demon escaped into the night. The hero secreted the gruesome relic in a box. Years later an elderly woman begged to see the arm, and when the box was opened, she changed into an *oni*, took the arm, and escaped. When Raikō fell ill, a monster thought to kill him, but Raikō cut off the monster's tongue. Watanabe followed the bloody trail the monster had left. Deep in a mountain cave he found a giant spider, six feet high, its legs covered with sword-hard bristles. Using a pine tree as a club, he battered the spider to death.

Minamoto-no-Yorimasa, a descendant of Raikō's, killed the *nuye* (a chimera with the head of a monkey, claws like a tiger, and a tail that ended with a serpent's head) that had afflicted the emperor with illness, shooting in the dark with his bow. He committed suicide after the defeat of his candidate for the emperorship, and his spirit was transformed into fireflies because he burned with spite and greed during his life.

One of the most significant heroic figures for the modern era was Kusunoki Masashige. A famous warrior at the end of the Kamakura period, he was a partisan of Emperor Godaigo and a first-class guerrilla leader. During Godaigo's attempt to reestablish imperial rule on the wane of the Kamakura shogunate, Kusunoki was one of his main supporters. He died in a futile battle at Minatogawa (near modern Kobe), obedient to the emperor's command, and against his own better strategic judgment. He was mythicized by the Shōwa war government as the perfect example of self-sacrifice and obedience to the emperor. As a consequence, he was made into an inspiration for the *kamikaze* corps of the imperial airforce and navy at the end of World War II.

The character of most of the heroes of Japanese myth is, at least, ambiguous. They are prepared to use all means, fair and foul, to attain their goal. Most of them are graced by physical prowess, and many of them come to tragic ends. Two other features identify the heroes of the period (historically speaking, most of them, perhaps with the exception of Yamato-takeru, operate during the Heian and Gempei periods). Quite often they are members of assemblages of heroes, such as Raikō's band. And they operate with the imprimatur of, or claim to be supporting, the emperor. Nonetheless, as is made clear from their actions, they are individualists, even egoists, reaching for their own goals. This is particularly true in the case of Tawara Toda, who explicitly dithers between choosing to side with the emperor or with the usurper Masakado. Finally, just as the heroes of the archaic periods, the descendants of the heavenly grandson, bring about topographical features and names, so too do the heroes of this era, albeit in a much reduced scale. In this period, the islands of Japan have emerged as places with well-known and clearly identifiable features, and the heroes lend their names (and strengths) to the creation of local and national myths.

See also Benkei; *Kamikaze;* Kintoki; Raikō; Tawara Toda; Yamato-takeru; Yoshitsune.

References and further reading:
Joly, Henri L. 1967. *Legend in Japanese Art.* Tokyo: Charles E. Tuttle Co.
McCullough, Helen Craig. 1959. *The Taiheiki.* New York: Columbia University Press.
———. 1988. *The Tale of the Heike.* Stanford: Stanford University Press.
Rabinovitch, Judith N. 1986. *Shōmonki: The Story of Masakado's Rebellion.* Monumenta Nipponica Monograph 58. Tokyo: Sophia University Press.
Sato, Hiroaki. 1995. *Legends of the Samurai.* Woodstock, NY: Overlook Press.

HIDARUGAMI

The spirit of hunger. This is an evil spirit or ghost that can inflict itself on travelers in remote locations. When possessed by such an apparition, the individual becomes faint, often losing consciousness, which can be restored only with difficulty by applying *mochi* (pounded rice cake) or some other ritually special foodstuff. Untreated, the victim will die. Hidarugami is often interpreted as a form of ghost of someone who died a lonely death on some moor or mountain pass. Attacks of Hidarugami can be avoided by carrying a morsel of rice or *mochi,* or by reciting *nembutsu* or some other distracting prayer.

The prevalence of Hidarugami stories, which are found throughout Japan, is an indication of the very real problems of hunger and starvation that threatened most of the rural population of Japan in premodern times. Like most premodern people, Japan's population has gone through recurrent periods of famine because of crop failure or greedy landlords. The specter of Hidarugami is thus a personification of a very real and immediate problem for this population. The problem was particularly severe for those individuals who had no support group—travelers and pilgrims. The cure for Hidarugami is one that, under the circumstances, was almost guaranteed to work.

See also Amida Nyōrai; Ghosts.
References and further reading:
Iwasaka, Michiko, and Barre Toelken. 1994. *Ghosts and the Japanese: Cultural Experience in Japanese Death.* Logan: Utah State University Press.

HIDESATO FUJIWARA
See Tawara Toda.

HIKOHOHODEMI
See Ho-ori-no-mikoto.

HI-NO-KAGUTSUCHI
See Kagutsuchi-no-kami.

HIRUKO
The leech child, first born of Izanami and Izanagi. In the *Kōjiki* Hiruko is portrayed as a failure. He was born after his mother had erred in addressing Izanagi before he addressed her. Hiruko, born without arms or legs (thus one interpretation of his name, leech child) was placed in a boat of reeds and floated away. Hiruko is nonetheless a powerful deity. He is identified with Ebisu, another *marebito* or wandering deity: In one myth, Hiruko's boat brought him eventually to the palace of the dragon king of the sea, from whence he returns at odd times as the deity of fishermen and is called Ebisu.

Another interpretation of the same myth depends on another reading of the name: sun child. In this version the limbless Hiruko is actually the recurring phenomenon of the sun, which is another form of *marebito*, visiting humans with blessings on a regular schedule.

Though they seem at odds, the two versions are closer than one might think. One of the major themes of Japanese mythology is the dualistic relationship between purity and pollution, and between life and death. The association of femininity with pollution and death (as exemplified in the visit of Izanagi to his wife in the underworld) is one of those paradoxes. The association of purity and pollution exemplified in the oppositional interpretation of Hiruko's name may well be another case in point: Ancient writers may well have been at pains to point out that purity springs from pollution, and that the two are not so far apart as might be thought.

> *See also* Ebisu; Izanagi and Izanami.
> ***References and further reading:***
> Aston, William G., trans. 1956. *Nihongi.* London: Allen and Unwin.
> Philippi, Donald, trans. and ed. 1968. *Kōjiki.* Tokyo: Tokyo University Press.
> Ouwehand, Cornelius. 1964. *Namazu-e and Their Themes: An Interpretative Approach to Some Aspects of Japanese Religion.* Leiden, the Netherlands: E. J. Brill.

HITOKOTONUSHI-NO-KAMI

The "One-word deity" of Mt. Kaduraki. One day Emperor Yūryaku was ascending Mt. Kaduraki with his retainers. They were dressed in uniforms of blue attached with red cords. As they ascended, they spied another group of people dressed in the same way. The parties approached one another. The emperor understandably demanded to know the identity of these people, who by their dress seemed to be claiming kingship in opposition to himself.

The opposing party mirrored the emperor's demands.

The emperor and his men fitted arrows to their bows. The emperor then said, "Tell us your names, before we discharge our arrows" (the code of conduct for warriors was to identify themselves individually before engaging in combat).

"Since I have been asked first," retorted the leader of the other group, "I shall tell you that I am the One-Word-Master deity of Kaduraki!"

The emperor promptly apologized, saying he did not realize the *kami* manifested himself in this form, and he and his attendants stripped and offered their clothes to the deity. The deity accepted the gifts and accompanied the emperor to the base of the mountain.

Hitokotonushi is a *kami* often invoked for divination. His responses were in the form of a single word, which could determine the fate of the individual. Later Shugendō tradition has it that the *kami* accused En-no-Gyōja falsely of plotting to usurp the throne and was subsequently subdued by the sage and made to do the sage's bidding.

See also Divination; En-no-Gyōja.
References and further reading:
Nakamura, Kyoko Motomuchi. 1997. *Miraculous Stories from the Japanese Buddhist Tradition: The Nihon Ryoki of the Monk Kyokai.* New ed. Richmond, VA: Curzon Press.
Philippi, Donald, trans. and ed. 1968. *Kōjiki.* Tokyo: Tokyo University Press.

HODERI-NO-MIKOTO

Eldest son of Ninigi-no-mikoto and Kōnōhanasakuya-hime. His father suspected Hoderi was not his natural son, as his mother announced she was pregnant after one night with her husband. As a consequence, Hoderi was born in the midst of the flames his mother set in the birthing house to prove he was of divine origin.

As an adult, Hoderi the fisherman quarreled with his brother, Ho-ori-no-mikoto, after the younger brother lost his brother's fishhook. Persecuting his younger brother, Hoderi came to grief when Ho-ori allied with Owatatsumi-no-kami, deity of the sea, and received the tide-raising and tide-lowering jewels.

See also Ho-ori-no-mikoto; Kōnōhanasakuya-hime; Ninigi-no-mikoto.

References and further reading:
Aston, William G., trans. 1956. *Nihongi.* London: Allen and Unwin.
Philippi, Donald, trans. and ed. 1968. *Kōjiki.* Tokyo: Tokyo University Press.

HO-ORI-NO-MIKOTO (HIKOHOHODEMI)

One of the children of Ninigi-no-mikoto and Kōnōhanasakuya-hime, and the grandfather of Jimmu-Tenno, first emperor of Japan. He was nicknamed Yamasachi-no-hiko (Mountain luck prince) and Hikohohodemi. His brother Hoderi-no-mikoto was a master fisherman, and one day they agreed to exchange lucks. But when Ho-ori tried fishing he was unable to catch a single fish, and lost the luck—the fishhook—in the bargain. Hoderi insisted on the return of his luck, but Ho-ori was unable to comply. Even breaking his sword and making a gift of five hundred fishhooks from it did not mollify his brother. He then offered a thousand hooks, to no avail, as his brother insisted on the original hook.

Ho-ori escaped to the palace of Owatatsumi-no-kami, lord of the sea. He climbed a tall tree near the palace and was seen by Toyotama-hime-no-mikoto, the sea deity's daughter. They fell in love. Owatatsumi-no-kami, recognizing Ho-ori and knowing his parentage, entertained him royally, and the two lovers were married. After three years in the palace, Ho-ori pined for home and told his father-in-law the reason for his exile. The sea deity summoned all the fish and found the hook in the throat of the sea bream. He returned the hook to Ho-ori and taught him a curse to put on it. Owatatsumi-no-kami also gave his son-in-law the tide-raising and tide-lowering jewels, with which he could destroy his brother's rice fields by denying them water or inundating them, as necessary.

One was chosen from among the assembly of crocodiles to take Ho-ori home and to report on his safe arrival within one day. Using the devices given by his father-in-law, Ho-ori soon triumphed over his brother, causing him to drown, and then saving him by using the jewels. As a result, Hoderi became his obedient servant.

Toyotama-hime-no-mikoto joined her husband to give birth to their child on dry land. She begged him not to observe her during the birth, but he did so nonetheless. As she gave birth, she changed back to her natural form as a giant crocodile. Ashamed of having been seen, she abandoned the baby to its father and returned to the sea, but sent her younger sister, Tamayori-hime, to nurse the child.

A number of universal themes intertwine in this myth. They include the younger-brother/older-brother envy competition (see, for example, Jacob and Esau in Genesis), the palace of the dragon king under the sea (see, for example, the myth of Urashimatarō), the Melusine myth of the silkie mother who returns to the sea when she is seen bathing, and the Japanese fascination with jewels as items of power. As is not unusual in Japanese mythical perspective, it is the *younger* brother who is the winner of the contest, humbling his elder brother: another universal theme. This particular myth also marks the end of the divine era in the classical texts (*Kōjiki* and *Nihonshōki*). From this point on, much of the myth concentrates on the doings of humans rather than of divinities: The next myth has to do with Jimmu Tenno, who, for all his divine ancestry and the help he receives from the deities, is a human rather than a deity himself. The theme of closing off the direct path between humans and divinities is also evident in another element: When Toyotama-hime returns to the sea, she also closes off the easy passageway to the undersea world her father rules. And though it is still possible to reach the other worlds—Tokoyo, the dragon king's realm under the sea, Yōmi—the passage is no longer a matter of fast travel along a road. From this point onward the three major realms—the earth, the sea, and the heavens—are separate domains.

> ***See also*** Hoderi-no-mikoto; Jimmu Tenno; Ninigi-no-mikoto; Owatatsumi-no-kami.
> ***References and further reading:***
> Aston, William G., trans. 1956. *Nihongi*. London: Allen and Unwin.
> Philippi, Donald, trans. and ed. 1968. *Kōjiki*. Tokyo: Tokyo University Press.

HŌTEI

One of the Shichi Fukujin (seven gods of good fortune) and an incarnation of Amida Nyōrai and of Miroku-bosatsu. Hōtei is depicted as a fat, jolly, bald priest with fat pendant lucky ears. He may be surrounded, or climbed on, by laughing and playing children. His most important asset is the sack (*hōtei*) from which he takes his name. It is full of treasures that he dispenses, Santa Claus–like, to deserving children. He also carries a large rigid Chinese fan, with which he can waft happiness onto those surrounding him.

Hōtei is one of the most popular of the Shichi Fukujin and of all the deities. His identification in popular imagination with Amida may be related to the fact that unlike Ebisu, for example, he does not demand much but is more concerned with giving.

> ***See also*** Amida Nyōrai; Miroku-bosatsu; Shichi Fukujin.
> ***References and further reading:***
> Joly, Henri L. 1967. *Legend in Japanese Art*. Tokyo: Charles E. Tuttle Co.

HOTOKE

The general term for Buddha. This is used in two rather different senses, indicated throughout this text by upper or lowercase first letter.

Immediately after their passing, and for several years after that, the deceased are termed *hotoke* by most Japanese. The period is informal and varies from one household to another, but it can usually be considered the length of time until the individual is no longer recognized or remembered personally by members of the household. During this stage, the *hotoke* has an intense personal interest in the doings of members of the household, is likely to return during the annual *O-bon* (equivalent to All Souls Day) in midsummer, and is remembered in rituals and even in casual conversation. Once this period of several years, even decades, has passed, the individual becomes merged in the far more featureless mass of the household's *kami*, who are remembered collectively rather than as individuals. *Hotoke* who are not treated properly—that is, presented with gifts of food, incense, prayers, or sutra readings—by their families or a temple may become *gakki* (hungry ghosts) or some other form of *akuma* and will plague people or locations.

The Buddha (without personal qualification) is *Hotoke*—in other words, *not* referring to a specific named Buddha but to the concept of "a Buddha." The concept encompasses the idea of a benevolent, caring being who can be appealed to for help, including salvation or material assistance.

See also Ghosts.

References and further reading:
Smith, Robert J. 1974. *Ancestor Worship in Contemporary Japan.* Palo Alto, CA: Stanford University Press.

IDA-TEN

The titular deity of the meal in some Zen sects. He is portrayed in full armor and carrying a sword. He is supposed to have had a violent temper, and is thus also a warrior deity: He is a guardian king of the south. After the Buddha had entered nirvana, a swift-footed demon stole one of the teeth of the cadaver and escaped at great speed. Ida-ten, one of the master's disciples, saw the theft. He pursued immediately, bounding over mountains and across rivers, until he finally trapped the thief and retrieved the relic. The Japanese expression *Ida-ten hashiri* (to run like the wind) derives from that story.

Ida-ten is mentioned in the premeal prayers at Sōtō Zen temples. He presides over the meals as protector of nourishment, but also as a warning about combating and controlling the appetites.

References and further reading:
Joly, Henri L. 1967. *Legend in Japanese Art.* Tokyo: Charles E. Tuttle Co.

IMPERIAL REGALIA

The three treasures of the Japanese imperial household—sword, mirror, and jewels. The sword is reputed to be the weapon granted by Amaterasu-ō-mikami to the imperial grandson, Ninigi-no-mikoto, with orders to pacify the Central Land of the Reed Plains and establish the Yamato/Japanese nation. Mirrors had been associated with the sun goddess as the device that induced her to exit the cave she was hiding in. They were used in premodern Japan to represent the spirit, or *mitama*. Metal mirrors are displayed prominently in most shrines today, representing the spirit of the shrine's *kami*. Comma-shaped jade or carnelian jewels have served as indications of royalty in the Korean peninsula since well before the establishment of the Japanese state, and were thus presumably adopted by the Japanese from their more developed neighbors.

Each of the items is associated with a color—red for the sword, white for the mirror, and green for the jewels—which have implications of power, purity, and growth. These colors appear, alone or in combinations, in numerous symbolic elements, such as the trefoil that marks certain shrines, banner colors, and even formal correspondences.

> ***See also*** Amaterasu-ō-mikami; Jewels; Mirror; Ninigi-no-mikoto; Stones; Swords.
> ***References and further reading:***
> Aston, William G., trans. 1956. *Nihongi*. London: Allen and Unwin.
> Philippi, Donald, trans. and ed. 1968. *Kōjiki*. Tokyo: Tokyo University Press.

INARI

Kami of rice, prosperity, and plenty. One of the most popular deities, Inari is most often depicted accompanied by his messenger, the fox. His symbol is a flaming jewel. Inari shrines are instantly recognizable by their asymmetrical red-painted *torii* gates, red-lacquered walls, and statues of foxes. Such shrines are commonly found throughout Japan's rural areas and in many places in towns as well.

Inari's major shrine is at Fushimi Inari, near Kyoto, where he has been worshiped since the Heian period. One of Inari's cognomens is Ukanomitama-no-kami, roughly meaning "The deity of nourishment," though Ukanomitama may be an earlier female version of the food deity and is mentioned in the *Kōjiki* as a daughter of Susano-wo. His usual name, Inari, refers to *ine* (the rice seedling) and may be read as "Rice carrier."

In the eighth century a man by the name of Irogu used a rice cake for target practice. His arrow pierced the cake, which changed into a white bird and flew away. Irogu chased the white bird to the top of Mt. Fushimi. There he found rice growing (in Japanese, *ine-nari*), and started the worship of the *kami*. At first a purely local agricultural deity, Inari's fortunes rose when he was appointed the guardian deity of Tōji temple, then run by Kōbō Daishi, who had just been appointed the emperor's priest. It rose again when the emperor fell ill, and it was only by granting Inari high court rank that the emperor's illness was cured.

In Buddhism, Inari is referred to as Inari Daimyōjin. In a previous life, both

An Inari shrine guarded by a fox figure dressed in a red bib for good fortune. (Courtesy of the author)

Inari and Kōbō Daishi, the great Buddhist saint and founder of the Shingon sect, were disciples of the Buddha. They pledged that in a future life they would be reborn in the Eastern Lands, Kōbō Daishi to spread the word of the Buddha, and Inari to protect the sacred teachings (a story similar to that told of the Ni-ō). One day, while staying at an inn, the disciple now reborn as Kōbō Daishi met an unusually tall and vigorous old man carrying sheaves of rice on his shoulder. The saint invited the old man to come and visit him, and indeed, several years later, when Kōbō Daishi's first monastery at Tōji was established, the old man appeared at its southern (fortunate) gate, carrying more sheaves of rice and accompanied by his family. The saint then granted the man/*kami* the land that was to become the Fushimi Inari shrine.

The close association between Buddhism and the Inari cult lasted until 1873, the year the separation of Buddhism and Shintō was formally ordered by the government (Fushimi Inari shrine was served by Buddhist priests of the Shingon sect until that time). It is still common in rural areas to find an Inari shrine served by a priest from Tendai or Shingon.

With the rapid rise of commercialism and wealth in the Edo period, partic- ularly in the merchant towns, Inari assumed an added function as the *kami* of merchant wealth and prosperity. Later, during the Meiji period and extending into the modern period, he has become the *kami* of industry and finance. In modern Japan his shrines are to be found at the corners of market streets and on the tops of skyscrapers in the financial districts of Japanese cities.

Inari's fox is provided for in each shrine by a small round opening cut in the base of the wall. The opening is to allow the fox, the *kami* messenger and informant, to come and go unimpeded. Those who wish to solicit the deity's goodwill, often leave offerings of *inari-zushi*, cooked rice in a fried tofu wrapping soaked in sweet rice liquor. The fox, who is very fond of this sweetmeat, is expected to provide the *kami* with only good news about the supplicant.

Inari belongs neither to the heavenly nor to the earthly *kami*. His late inclusion in the pantheon is due, perhaps, to his importation from unknown Chinese sources, or to the mutation of an earlier food deity such as Ukanomitama under Buddhist auspices. A syncretic deity, he may be portrayed in his Buddhist version as an elderly man, or in the Shintō version as a man in court robes riding a fox. Often Inari is portrayed carrying a large key, which signifies the richness of the granaries he controls.

Inari is concerned with all worldly success. He is known as Manzoku Inari (Fulfillment Inari) and as Susshe Inari (Success Inari). He is sometimes identified with Dakiniten, particularly among warriors who adopted him as their household deity (*yashikigami*), since they are both depicted riding on a white fox, carrying the wish-fulfilling jewel in one hand and a sheaf of rice in the other.

> ***See also*** Dakiniten; Food Deities; Fox; Kōbō Daishi; Ni-ō; Ōgetsuhime; Ukemochi-no-kami.
> ***References and further reading:***
> Smyers, Karen. 1999. *The Fox and the Jewel.* Honolulu: University of Hawaii Press.

IZANAGI AND IZANAMI

The male and female creator *kami*. The last two of the many deities that emerged from chaos, Izanagi (He-who-invites) and his female counterpart Izanami (She-who-invites) were summoned by the first-formed *kami* to create the world out of chaos and rule it. They were given the jeweled spear Ama-no-Nuboko to accomplish their task. Standing on the Heavenly Floating Bridge, they gazed at the formlessness below, puzzled about the procedure. Eventually Izanagi suggested they try stirring the "fragrant moisture" below the bridge with the spear. Pulling the spear up, a drop fell from the tip and coalesced into the island of Onogoro, to which the two descended. There they decided to make

Amaterasu, Shinto goddess of the Sun. (Victoria & Albert Museum, London/Art Resource, NY)

their abode. They built their house, the Eight Measure Palace, around a central pillar, the Heavenly August Pillar. Deciding to populate the land, Izanagi turned to the left and walked round the pillar, while Izanami turned right and did the same. Rounding the pillar, they met each other coming in opposite directions. Izanami could not contain herself and called out "Oh, what a comely youth!" Izanagi, delighted, replied "Oh, what a comely maiden!" but added that it was inappropriate that a woman should make her greeting before the man. Still confused as to their further actions, they were instructed in the act of generation by two wagtails. Izanami soon bore her husband a child, but because she had spoken first, the child Hiruko was ugly, as boneless and limbless as a leech. Putting the child disgustedly into a boat constructed of reeds, they tried again, but once again produced a monster.

Thereupon the two deities ascended via the Bridge of Heaven and requested advice. The older gods informed them that the problem was that Izanami, the woman, had greeted her male counterpart first against the rule of nature. Chastened, the two returned to earth. Once again they circled the pillar, he to his right, she to her left. This time, though, Izanagi greeted his consort first, saying "What a delightful maiden!" to which she replied appropriately. Their mating was fruitful. Izanami gave birth to the islands of Awaji, Shikoku, Oki, Kyushu, Tsushima, and, finally, Honshu, the largest. They named the land Oyashima-kuni, the Land of Eight Great Islands. After that, Izanami gave birth in quick succession to the other minor islands that surround the main ones, and to the main *kami* of sea and harbor, of wind, trees, mountains, and so on.

The happy occasion was interrupted by the birth of the *kami* of fire, Kagutsuchi-no-kami, whose fiery body seared his mother during birth. Izanagi made utmost efforts to resuscitate his wife but ultimately failed. As she died, various *kami* issued forth from her limbs. Her death, the corruption of her body, and the sorrow it engendered were the first experienced in the newly created world. Thus ended the divine creation of Japan.

The tears Izanagi shed at the death of his wife brought forth further deities. Angered by the sight of the newly born fire *kami* who had been the cause of Izanami's death, Izanagi drew his sword and decapitated the infant. The blood coalescing on the sword brought forth eight martial *kami*, including the important Takemikazuchi-no-kami and his peer, Futsunushi-no-kami. Eight more fierce *kami* of mountains and iron emerged from the infant's body and limbs.

After a lengthy period of mourning, Izanagi determined to go down to Yōmi, the land of the dead, to rescue his wife. After long travel down precipitous places, he spied a large mansion, which he thought must be his destination. The front gate of the mansion was guarded by demons, and Izanagi sneaked around to an unguarded back entrance. Inside the castle he spied his wife and called her name. They greeted one another lovingly, and Izanagi entreated his wife to come back with him, so that they could complete the act of creation imposed on them by the elder *kami*. Izanami replied that though she would like to obey him, her return was impossible because she had eaten food while in Yōmi.

Izanagi begged her to reconsider, and she finally agreed to go into the mansion and ask the deities of the place whether there was any way for her to return. In the meantime, she cautioned her husband to not by any means look into the interior of the mansion. He agreed to the condition, but after waiting for a full day, he was seized by a sudden foreboding. Snapping one of the teeth of his hair comb, he lit it for a torch and stole into the building. There, to his horror, he found Izanami's dead body. She had appeared to him in her original form as his beautiful wife, but now she appeared as a rotting corpse. Eight snake-formed thunder *kami* had been born from the corpse and were still attached to the remains. Revolted by the horrible sight, Izanagi dropped his torch and fled. The sound of the falling torch awoke Izanami, and she vowed to take revenge for his faithlessness. At her word, the hag of Yōmi and the thunder deities pursued the frightened widower.

Izanagi delayed the hag, first by throwing down his headdress, which became a bunch of grapes that she picked and ate; then by tossing down his second comb, which became bamboo shoots, which the hag ate as well. Izanami then sent the eight thunder deities with a thousand and five-hundred warriors after him. He warded them off as he ran by backslashing with his sword. He then reached the pass of Yomotsu Hirazaka, where a tree with three peaches was growing. Ambushing his pursuers, he forced them back with the peaches (presumably because they represented life, as opposed to death—a Chinese idea originally). Acknowledging his debt to the fruit, he declared them divine and gave them the position of protecting the people of the Central Land of the Reed Plains.

Finally, Izanami herself took up the pursuit. Izanagi then rolled a huge rock to block the pass of Yōmi. Izanagi and Izanami then stood at either side of the rock and took their leave, Izanami vowing that she would kill a thousand of the folk of the Central Land of the Reed Plains every day to avenge herself. To this Izanagi retorted that he would set up one thousand and five-hundred parturition houses, and thus more than make up by births what had been decimated by death. From that time on Izanami has been known as the Yomotsu-ō-kami (Great deity of Yōmi). The entrance to Yōmi, still blocked by the rock called Blocking-Great-Deity-of-the-Door-of-Yōmi, is at Ifuya Pass in the land of Izumo.

Izanagi realized that he had been polluted by his visit to the land of the dead. He went to a small river-mouth near Tachibana in Himuka on the island of Tsukushi (Kyushu) to purify himself. From the clothes he shed were born more *kami*, and as he washed in the river, fourteen *kami*, first of pollution, and subsequently of purification, were born of the ablutions.

The last three children were born as Izanagi washed his left eye, his right eye, and finally his nose. To the first of these, Amaterasu-ō-mikami, he gave the necklace of jewels he wore, charging her to be the ruler of Takamagahara (the plain of high heaven). He charged the boy child born of his right eye, Tsukiyomi-no-mikoto, with responsibility for the night. The child born last, of his nose, called Susano-wo, he charged with responsibility for the sea. Susano-wo, instead of assuming his responsibilities, wept and complained, demanding to go to Yōmi to see his mother. Furious, Izanagi banished him from his post to join Izanami in Yōmi. Thereupon Izanagi retired to live in Taga in Afumi.

Most scholars agree that the myth of Izanagi and Izanami does not constitute a creation myth in the Biblical sense: Neither humans nor animals or vegetation are brought forth. Instead, what is mentioned is the name of political divisions (the names of islands and provinces) with which the Yamato scribes would have been familiar. Once these have been established, they are populated by deities. People, plants, and animals are givens. The importance of this myth rests on its political underpinnings: How is rule established, and by whom? The founder (rather than "creator") pair are present to provide an unassailable argument about the relationship of the Yamato court to the heavens, on the one hand, and to the land, on the other. Considering the later mythical description of dominating the land, the Yamato needed all their force and cunning, as well as compelling arguments, to ensure that the polities they were dominating stayed dominated. As we know from archaeology and political record, this was not a given thing, nor was it easily attained or, once attained, maintained. It is not therefore surprising that a great deal of effort, and mythical space, went into a detailed account of which areas were being claimed.

A second important theme is related to the first. The importance of women—politically and socially—in early Japan became badly eroded as the Japanese came under Confucian Chinese influence. In the Confucian system (as well as in Buddhism) there was no question about the subordination of women. All three native cultures in the Japanese islands, in contrast, have actual (in the Okinawan case) or relic (in the Japanese and Ainu case) ideas that assume greater interdependence between men and women, and far more political equality. The indications of female inferiority—the explanation for Hiruko's formless birth, and Izanami's relegation to the polluted land of the dead—seem to be indications of more male-oriented influences, Chinese or otherwise. This in turn relates to the tension between pure and impure, which is the foundation of Shintō religious ideas. Pure food emerges from impure dirt. Pure men must associate with impure women. Death and corruption give rise to green shoots and new life. All three of these themes are interrelated and mixed in this particular myth. Political changes in the Yamato state aside (by the time the mythological texts were written, women rulers no longer reigned), these ideological tensions between life and death, purity and pollution, and men and women were to become the substrate for much of Japan's ideology in the following centuries. It is therefore significant that the major deities mentioned—Amaterasu, Tsukiyomi, Susano-wo, Takemikazuchi, Ukemochi—are born without contact with a mother's sexual parts, thus in the male-dominated view preserving their purity and *kami* (in the adjectival sense).

Finally, the elder deities who preceded the founding pair are largely—Takamimusubi is the exception—passive. Once they have arrived (and perhaps symbolize, as some scholars argue, the act of creation of the universe and its principles) they no longer feature in the myths. It is the active deities brought about by Izanagi and Izanami's union (even after her death, the deities born are considered hers as much as his) that have active parts, and become "worshiped" as opposed to "hidden" deities in subsequent myths.

Like the Yamato-takeru and Ōkuninushi myths, the myth of Izanagi and Izanami has echoes across the Eurasian continent. Many of the specific themes (visit to the underworld, founding goddess to death goddess, throwing out three items to prevent pursuit) are to be seen in European myths as well. Other themes—founding brother-sister couple, birth of deities from body parts—can be found throughout Southeast Asia. These similarities may have to do with population diffusion, or they may be the result of the existence of universal archetypes in human thinking: a mythical version of "great minds think alike."

See also Amaterasu-ō-mikami; Assembly of the Gods; Heavenly Floating Bridge; Hiruko; Kagutsuchi-no-kami; Susano-wo; Takamimusubi-no-kami; Thunder Deities; Tsukiyomi-no-mikoto; Underworld.

References and further reading:
Aston, William G., trans. 1956. *Nihongi.* London: Allen and Unwin.
Davis, S. Hadland. 1913. *Myths and Legends of Japan.* London: George Harrap. Facsimile edition 1992, New York: Dover Publications. *Annotated Collection of Legends, Folktales, and Myths.*
Katō, Genchi. 1908. "The Ancient Shinto Deity Ame-No-Minaka-Nushi-No-Kami Seen in the Light of to-Day." *Transactions of the Asiatic Society of Japan* 36: 139–162.
Namahira, Emiko. 1977. "An Analysis of 'Hare' and 'Kegare' in Japanese Rites of Passage." *Minzokugakku Kenkyu* 40: 350–368.
Philippi, Donald, trans. and ed. 1968. *Kōjiki.* Tokyo: Tokyo University Press.
Sasaki, Kiyoshi. 2000. "Amenominakanushi no Kami in Late Tokugawa Period Kokugaku." Tokyo: Institute for Japanese Culture and Classics, Kokugakuin University. http://www.kokugakuin.ac.jp.

IZUMO

Izumo is an area on the Japan Sea side of Honshu Island (approximately modern Shimane Prefecture) to the west and north of Yamato, and an archaic polity that was the Yamato state's most serious rival for dominance. Izumo features in the original foundation myth a number of times. Besides being politically important, it was also the home to both Susano-wo and his descendant Ōkuninushi, leader of the earthly kami. When the heavenly grandson and his heirs assumed control over the central Land of the Reed Plains, it was at Izumo, more than anywhere else, that their rule was contested, and eventually acknowledged, by Ōkuninushi and his sons.

Extrapolating from what is said in the *Kōjiki* and the *Nihonshōki*, it is likely that Izumo was an independent nation-state or polity, one of the many that the Chinese recorded as controlling the Japanese islands. This conclusion is also supported by recent archaeological finds.

It seems likely that Izumo challenged the supremacy of the Yamato state in the Nara area to its southeast. The Yamato, using a combination of threats, military action, astute diplomacy, magical spells, and cooptation, managed to subdue the Izumo and then attach them as subordinate allies to the nascent Yamato empire. All of this took place sometime around the second or third century C.E., though Japanese traditional dating makes this about the fifth century B.C.E.

There are two aspects of Izumo that need to be considered in parallel: the

Izumo polity and its opposition to the Yamato, on the one hand, and its mythical significance on the other.

As a polity the Izumo were (apparently) less centralized than their Yamato neighbors. In effect, they represent perhaps a pattern of the original archaic Japanese political system unmodified by contacts with the more advanced Koreans and Chinese. They were, however, a powerful external force. Their resistance, judging solely from the mythical texts, must have lasted for several generations at least. The degree of ritual autonomy they managed to maintain was unprecedented. To this day Izumo Taisha, the shrine dedicated to Ōkuninushi, is the most powerful independent shrine in Japan. Izumo retained a great deal of autonomy in the form of its worship as well as in its architecture and internal organization. It is likely that within the accommodation to the Yamato state, the Izumo people, or their leaders, insisted on a privileged position for their tutelary kami.

As a mythical place, Izumo is the connection and entry point between the three realms of Heaven, Earth, and the Underworld, including Tokoyo-no-kuni, the mysterious land. Certain caves in Izumo were said to lead directly to Tokoyo-no-kuni. Izumo's direct connection to heaven is also recounted in the myths. Ōkuninushi's agreement with Takemikazuchi specifies that he has use of a heavenly boat to take him up and down to heaven. And it is at Ōkuninushi's hall, in Izumo Taisha, that the kami gather from all over Japan in the tenth month for the assembly of the Gods.

Izumo's connection with wizardry and the underworld are evident throughout the myths about it. They arose, perhaps, because the Yamato, in common with other societies, assigned to their most powerful opponents the label of wizards and necromancers, or else because Izumo rituals were indeed concerned with material efficacy, or perhaps simply because the Yamato needed an identifiable place for the starting place of many of their myths about the underworld.

See also Izanagi and Izanami; Ōkuninushi; Susano-wo; Underworld; Yamato-takeru
References and further reading:
Aoki, Michiko Yamaguchi. 1974. *Ancient Myths and Early History of Japan: A Cultural Foundation.* New York: Exposition Press.
———, trans. 1971. *Izumo Fudoki.* Tokyo: Sophia University Press.
Aston, William G., trans. 1956. *Nihongi.* London: Allen and Unwin.
Philippi, Donald, trans. and ed. 1968. *Kōjiki.* Tokyo: Tokyo University Press.

JAPANESE UNIQUENESS

A prevalent modern myth claiming that the Japanese people, or their culture, are unique. The myth has a complex history. Like in many other cultures, some intellectuals have made extensive claims to Japanese primacy and cultural uniqueness and supremacy. In the early eighteenth century Motoori Norinaga was already claiming that one reason it was self-evident that Japan was unique was the extraordinary quality of Japanese rice.

The creation of a self-laudatory myth of Japanese uniqueness, often called *Nihonjin-ron* (Japanese logic), may well be the creation of Japanese intellectuals and bureaucrats in the late nineteenth and early twentieth centuries, argue many scholars. Certainly the expressions of *Nihonjin-ron* in daily life tend to emerge from the musings of Japanese intellectuals, then are accepted as true by many other Japanese (and, of course, denied or ignored by many others). In one early expression of Japanese uniqueness a Japanese anthropologist argued that the uniqueness of the Japanese was due to the fact the Japanese genome had been isolated from the rest of Asia for millennia, and that it therefore developed in unique directions. A later interpretation argued that the uniqueness was the result of the mainly vegetarian diet of the Japanese, creating a unique temperament and intracultural understanding between Japanese. In a later development of this myth, circa the mid-1990s, it was argued that as a consequence of a diet that eschewed meat, Japanese intestines were longer than those of other people, proving their physical uniqueness. The physical difference argument is also evident in the myth attaching intellectual and particularly emotional qualities to blood type. The Japanese, it argues, are largely and almost homogeneously type AB, which predisposes them to particular qualities of empathy and internal unity.

All of these myths tend to have two implicit, and often explicit, similarities: (1) The myth, however expressed in detail, argues that the Japanese are an unusually homogenous people (in culture, physical characteristics, social abilities, empathy, etc.); and (2) the myth supports the argument that the Japanese cannot be understood by people from other cultures. Among other features cited are the uniqueness of the Japanese language (conveniently ignoring its similarities to Korean), the "nonexplicit" or indirectness of the language (that is, many grammatical elements, such as personal particles, or subject, can be omitted in a sentence), and the ability of the Japanese, consequently, to communicate effectively without words or by using limited vocabulary.

The prevalence of these myths is hard to assess, though some scholars such as Befu and Oguma have done a great deal of work on the subject. Like other myths discussed here, this modern myth is one that some Japanese adopt explicitly, some reject, and the majority of the population are content to have available in their inventory of myths that can be appealed to at need.

References and further reading:
Befu, Harumi. 2001. *Hegemony of Homogeneity: An Anthropoligical Analysis of Nihonjin-ron.* Japanese Society Series. Melbourne: Trans Pacific Press.
Dale, Peter N. 1986. *The Myth of Japanese Uniqueness.* New York: St. Martin's Press.
Oguma Eiji. 2002. *The Genealogy of Japanese Self-images.* Translated by David Askew. Melbourne: Trans Pacific Press.

JEWELS

Tama (jewels) play a prominent part in Japanese mythology. They are significant symbolic elements for both Shintō and Buddhist myths. In Shintō, the jewel is usually, but not always, a *magatama* or comma-shaped jewel of jade or carnelian. These comma-shaped beads, with a hole in the "head," have been found in many graves in Japan and Korea. Jewels first appear in Shintō mythology in Amaterasu's divination/trial-by-combat confrontation with her errant brother, Susano-wo. On that occasion, he chewed on the jewels she had woven into her hair to keep them in separate bunches. The jewels in this case were clearly symbols of chieftainship for archaic Japanese. From his actions emerged several deities. A similar string of jewels was used to draw Amaterasu from her cave after Susano-wo's later outrages. The tide-raising and tide-lowering jewels, owned presumptively by Owatatsumi, *kami* of the sea, feature in a number of myths, most notably that of Ho-ori and his fight with his brother Hoderi. Many of the weapons described in the Shintō myths were jeweled: the spear with which the land was created by stirring the seas is one, and Susano-wo's jeweled sword is another. Jewels are often elaborated into the Shintō triskelion of three *magatama* jewels, their heads to the center. One exception to the comma-shaped jewel is the flaming jewel that represents Inari, *kami* of wealth and rice. In this case the jewel is round, sitting at the base of a flame that surrounds and protects it. Inari's foxes are closely associated with these flaming jewels, representing (depending on the particular interpretation) either the *kami*'s *mitama* or the deity's Buddha nature.

In Buddhist myths jewels are associated with a number of deities. Jizō carries a jewel, as do some of the other Buddhist deities. They are the symbol of purity, sometimes of nirvana, and will dispel evil. Jizō often carries a jewel that dispels evil, while his counterpart, Kokuzō, carries the jewel of existence. Other jewels carried by Buddhist deities—Kannon often carries one—will satisfy desires and bring about good fortune and happiness.

Perhaps the most important jewel in Buddhism, though not generally referred to as such, is the diamond. The hardness and brilliance of this stone was well known to the Indians, and the early Buddhists viewed the diamond as emblematic of enlightenment and the role of the Buddhist Law: illumination, essentially unchangeable. One of the major Buddhist sutras, the *Taizōkyō* or Diamond Sutra, has become extremely popular in Japan. "Diamond" has been equated in Buddhist thought with thunder/lightning, and as a consequence a great many Buddhist deities, particularly the more militant ones, carry a weapon, the *kongō*, representing both thunder/lightning and the diamond.

Dragons, both the Shintō and the Buddhist varieties, are associated with jewels, usually in a round shape, an idea probably derived from Chinese Daoism. Thus Owatatsumi, *kami* of the sea (often represented in the form of a dragon), Ryūjin, and other dragon deities are represented, or appear, in myths carrying or giving jewels.

The Shichi Fukujin are often represented carrying, sometimes juggling, with a jewel as part of the cargo of the Takarabune. They too are demonstrating the association of jewels with well-being and prosperity, and the hopes that these will endure.

The enduring qualities of jewels such as jade, ruby, pearl, carnelian, and diamond, and their importance in the luxury economy of the court, meant that they implied great wealth, fortune, and magical properties. In terms of their mythical importance, however, the term jewel (the Chinese ideogram is an object in the possession of a king) represented majesty and power. Their hardness and brilliance represent the very essence of stones: hard, durable and natural. It is not surprising that they play an important role in Japanese mythology. Perhaps more than any other material item in ancient Japan, jewels were associated with good things, both material and spiritual.

> ***See also*** Amaterasu; Ho-ori-no-mikoto; Inari; Jizō; Kannon; Kokuzō; Owatatsumi;
> Ryūjin; Shichi Fukujin; Stones; Swords; Weapons.
> ***References and further reading:***
> Joly, Henri L. 1967. *Legend in Japanese Art.* Tokyo: Charles E. Tuttle Co.
> Smyers, Karen. 1999. *The Fox and the Jewel.* Honolulu: University of Hawaii
> Press.

JIGOKU
See Underworld.

JIMMU TENNO
First emperor of Japan, great-grandson of Ninigi-no-mikoto, and great-great-grandson of Amaterasu-ō-mikami. He was the last son of Amatsuhiko-no-mikoto, the son of Ho-ori-no-mikoto from his marriage to the daughter of Owatatsumi, the *kami* of the sea.

From their father's palace in Takachiho, Jimmu Tenno (he was named at the time Kamu-Yamatoihare-hiko-no-mikoto) and his eldest brother traveled east to establish their peaceful governance over the land.

The two brothers traveled leisurely eastward, building palaces and staying in some places for several years at a time. At Hayasuhi, Kamu-Yamatoihare-hiko-no-mikoto met an earthly *kami* (that is, not one of those who had descended from Takamagahara, the heavenly realm, with Ninigi-no-mikoto) fishing from a tortoise's back. This deity, Sawonetsuhiko, agreed to act as guide on the sea lanes.

At Shirakata the brothers were ambushed by a certain Nagasunehiko of Toumi. Kamu-Yamatoihare-hiko-no-mikoto's brother was wounded by an arrow and died later of the wound.

At Kumano, Kamu-Yamatoihare-hiko-no-mikoto and his troops fell asleep, ensorcelled by the deities of Kumano in the shape of a bear. A person of Kumano called Takakuraji presented a sword to the sleeping hero, and he and his troops promptly woke up and vanquished the unruly deities of Kumano. The sword had been sent on the orders of Amaterasu-ō-mikami by Takemikazuchi-no-kami, and was named Futsu-no-Mitama.

From Kumano, the hero was guided by a giant crow sent by the heavenly deities, meeting and accepting as his retainers many earthly deities. A man of Uda, Yeukashi, attempted to ambush the hero but was frustrated. Yeukashi then prepared a trap in the hall he built, but his design was frustrated by his younger brother, Otoukashi, who disclosed the plot to Kamu-Yamatoihare-hiko-no-mikoto. Yeukashi was driven into his own trap and was killed. Subsequently, in the process of pacification, the eighty strong men of the pit dwelling of Osaka were killed at a feast. Finally, the hero assumed his reign name, Jimmu Tenno, and built a palace at Kashihara in Yamato and ruled from there.

The exploits of Jimmu Tenno, with their detailed place names and the names of his supporters and opponents, seem to be a mythical retelling of an actual historical event or process: the gradual conquest by a people or state called Yamato of other states and nations in central Japan. In this view, starting in Kyushu (the "west" of the myth, though actually southwards), the Yamato migrated (or conquered) over a period of years across the Sea of Japan to the Kii Peninsula, and from there, past the area that is now Osaka to the area around modern Nara, where they established the Yamato kingdom. Clearly, of course, the myth, which indicates that certain supporters were ancestors of important early Japanese clans, was written or recorded as a sort of imperial charter, justifying and explaining both place names and social and political relationships with the imperial house. It took several centuries from the establishment of the Yamato court in central Japan for the imperial system to spread throughout the

Japanese islands. In the process, the ancient place names and origins have been lost. Some of the elements repeated in the myth clearly indicate archaic origins: rituals, marital customs (several of the protagonists marry their female relatives in what in modern Japanese society would be considered an act of incest), and dwellings (there are, for example, remains of pit dwellings that have been uncovered by archaeologists).

> ***See also*** Amaterasu-ō-mikami; Animals: crow; Ninigi-no-mikoto; Swords; Takemikazuchi-no-kami; Yamato.
> ***References and further reading:***
> Aston, William G., trans. 1956. *Nihongi.* London: Allen and Unwin.
> Davis, S. Hadland. 1913. *Myths and Legends of Japan.* London: George Harrap. (Facsimile edition 1992, New York: Dover Publications.) Annotated collection of legends, folktales, and myths.
> Philippi, Donald, trans. and ed. 1968. *Kōjiki.* Tokyo: Tokyo University Press.

JINUSHIGAMI

"Landlord *kami*," that is, the *kami* who is the tutelary deity of a particular area. Ōkuninushi is the *jinushigami* of the Izumo area. Other *kami* of various titles and importance may be the *jinushigami* of a particular grove, shrine precincts, or household.

The association of a particular *kami* to an area is a common phenomenon. *Jinushigami* may be of lower rank in the Great Tradition scheme of things, but they are the *kami* actually worshiped most frequently, particularly in rural locations, where they may be Yama-no-kami or Ta-no-kami as well, and where their goodwill is important for daily survival.

In a broader context, many of the *kunitsu kami* (earthly *kami*) that joined the heavenly *kami* to pacify the earth were in effect *jinushigami.* The Ainu have their own master of the land in the form of the giant owl, Chikap Kamui, who is responsible for and keeps an eye on each of the clan domains. The local *kang* in Ryukyuan culture fulfill a similar function.

> ***See also*** Chikap Kamui; Earthly *Kami* (*Kunitsu kami*); Jimmu Tenno.
> ***References and further reading:***
> Stefansson, Halldor. 1985. "Earth Gods in Morimachi." *Japanese Journal of Religious Studies* 12 (4): 277–298.
> Toshimasa, Hirano. 1980. "Aruga Kizaemon: The Household, the Ancestors, and the Tutelary Deities." *Japanese Journal of Religious Studies* 7 (2–3):144–166.

JIZŌ

A boddhisattva, one of whose particular concerns is the roadways, and thus by extension, lost children. Together with Kannon, he is the most popular boddhisattva in Japan. Jizō is portrayed as a child-featured Buddhist monk, his head shaven. His task is to ensure compassion on earth during the three-thousand-year era between the death/accession to nirvana of Shakyamuni Buddha, and the arrival of Miroku, the Buddha of the future. Jizō comforts those in pain or distress, succors captives, and assists all those in need. He is the guardian of the roads in the Buddhist pantheon, and his statues are present along roadsides in many parts of Japan. His particular concern is the souls of children, including those of aborted embryos and those who died in childbirth. He finds them wandering on the banks of a stony waterless riverbed in Jigoku (hell), assists them in the construction of the piles of stones that are their penance, and conducts them to the Pure Land. He is often twinned with Kokūzō-bosatsu. Because of his role as protector of those in distress on earth, and his connection to the underworld, he is also sometimes identified with Dōsōjin or Sae-no-kami, the *kami* of the crossroads. Statues of Jizō were therefore often erected along lonely mountain passes or on particularly difficult roads. Jizō statues often appear in groups of six, as Roku Jizō, because as a bodhisattva he took the vow to function simultaneously on all six states of transient existence.

Jizō is one of the most popular of all Buddhist deities. He often holds the Desire Banishing Jewel in his left hand, and a staff tipped with rings in his right. The sound of this staff (still used by priests in many temples) banishes evil and brings about rejoicing. It also lets his lost charges know he is around. Statues of Jizō are often dressed by distressed parents with the red cap and bib that are emblematic of childhood. Visitors will often pile up stones before a Jizō to help in alleviating the children's penance. Jizō's protection is also assured against fire. Children living in open-hearthed homes (as most Japanese houses were in the past) were constantly exposed to burning themselves, and thus Jizō was appealed to to counter this. As a consequence, he is also associated with Atago-gongen, deity of protection against fire.

Though principally a gentle saint, his identification with Atago-gongen means that like many other deities, he has another side: He is also a martial deity known as Shogun Jizō (General Jizō). As such he is a patron of warriors; most notably, of Shōtoku Taishi and Hachimantarō.

> **See also** Atago-gongen; Dōsōjin; Heroes: Hachimantarō; Kokūzō-bosatsu; Pure Land; Shakyamuni; Shōtoku Taishi.
>
> **References and further reading:**
> Dykstra, Yoshiko Kurata. 1978. "Jizo, the Most Merciful: Tales from Jizo Bosatsu Reigenki." *Monumenta Nipponica* 33 (2): 179–200.
> Eliot, Sir Charles Norton Edgcumbe. 1959. *Japanese Buddhism.* London: Routledge and Kegan Paul.

Frank, Bernard. 1991. *Le pantheon bouddhique au Japon.* Paris: Collections d'Emile Guimet. Reunion des musees nationaux.
Getty, Alice. 1988. *The Gods of Northern Buddhism.* New York: Dover Publications.

JUICHIMEN-KANNON

See Kannon.

JUROJIN

The god of longevity of the Shichi Fukujin, he is portrayed as a thin old man in the dress of a scholar, accompanied by a deer and a crane, symbols of longevity and felicity. He leans on a staff to which is attached a scroll carrying the secret of everlasting life. He is often confused with his peer, Fukurokuju, but unlike that bald jolly dwarf, he has a serious expression at all times.

> *See also* Fukurokuju; Shichi Fukujin.
> *References and further reading:*
> Joly, Henri L. 1967. *Legend in Japanese Art.* Tokyo: Charles E. Tuttle Co.

JŪROKURAKAN

The sixteen arhat, or Buddhist saints, who by their asceticism are perfect examples of the monastic way of life. The *rakan* are predecessors or disciples of the Buddha, openers of the way for the Buddhist Law. They are represented as emaciated men in poses of meditation. They include Binzuru-sonja (the venerable Binzuru), Ragora-sonja, Ingada-sonja, Chudahandaka-sonja, and others. The names of others vary from one tradition or temple to another.

The *rakan* appear, usually, in the iconography of Zen monasteries and temples, where their presence serves as a model to be emulated by the monks and meditators. The exception, Binzuru, is placed outside the hall, because he broke either the vow of chastity or of sobriety and is thus not allowed in the august company.

> *See also* Binzuru-sonja.
> *References and further reading:*
> Frank, Bernard. 1991. *Le pantheon bouddhique au Japon.* Paris: Collections d'Emile Guimet. Reunion des musees nationaux.
> Joly, Henri L. 1967. *Legend in Japanese Art.* Tokyo: Charles E. Tuttle Co.

KAGUTSUCHI-NO-KAMI

Kami of fire. He was the cause of his mother Izanami's death, burning her genitals as he was born. His father, Izanagi, beset by grief for his wife, decapitated the newborn. From his blood, which dripped off his father's sword, emerged eight powerful and violent sword *kami*, and from his dead body emerged eight deities of volcanoes and rocks.

Fire was an obvious problem for people who lived in houses made of wood and straw: a good servant, a terrible master. In Edo, the Tokugawa capital (from 1616; today's Tokyo), fires were so common they were known as "the flowers of Edo." Some scholars argue that the birth of fire, and particularly the emergence from fire of mountains (volcanoes), iron, and swords, was a metaphor for the establishment of the new social and material forms generated by Yayoi culture.

The birth of fire marked the end of the creation of the world and the start of death. Nonetheless, Izanami only accuses fire of being rather capricious and hard-hearted in causing her death. In the *Engishiki*, from which the latter part of the myth comes, she hides herself from Izanagi in her death throes. Then she bears several children: Mizuhame-no-mikoto (a water *kami*), the clay princess, the gourd, and the water reed, instructing them to pacify Kagutsuchi if he became violent. The water, the gourd to transport it, and wet clay and reeds to smother fire were traditional fire-fighting equipment. In many places in Japan today there is a midwinter ritual of placing reed and evergreen bundles in the eaves to control fires.

> *See also* Izanagi and Izanami; Mizuhame-no-mikoto.
> ***References and further reading:***
> Aston, William G., trans. 1956. *Nihongi*. London: Allen and Unwin.
> Bock, Felicia G. trans. 1970. *Engi-shiki: procedures of the Engi era.*
> ———. 1985. *Classical Learning and Taoist Practices in Early Japan, With a Translation of Books XVI and XX of the Engi-Shiki*. ASU Center for Asian Studies (Occasional Paper No. 17).
> Philippi, Donald, trans. and ed. 1968. *Kōjiki*. Tokyo: Tokyo University Press.

KAMADO-GAMI

The stove, or kitchen, *kami*. Instructions for worshiping this *kami* were issued in an imperial rescript mentioned in the *Kōjiki*. It seems this was an after-the-fact recognition by the imperial court of what amounts to a Little Tradition. Kamado-gami oversees the activities in the house and may report, perhaps via the *jinushigami*, on the activities of members of the household. All these reports, and the resulting rewards and punishments, are discussed at the Assembly of Gods in the tenth (lunar, traditional calendar) month at Izumo.

For individuals (in contrast to the state) the Kamado-gami would have been all-important. Relics of that importance can be found in Ryukyuan and Ainu culture, where Fii-nu-kang and Kamui Fuchi are the central deities for most activities. In mythology the Kamado-gami would have been far overshadowed by heroic tales and the activities of the heavenly deities, but that does not detract from his (or her) central importance for daily life.

See also Assembly of the Gods; Fii-nu-kang; Jinushigami; Kamui Fuchi.
References and further reading:
Philippi, Donald, trans. and ed. 1968. *Kōjiki.* Tokyo: Tokyo University Press.

KAMI

A spiritual power or deity. The concept, under different names (*kamui* in Ainu, *kang* in Ryukyuan), is pervasive throughout Japanese mythology. At its basis, it refers to the numinous power that is spread unevenly throughout the world. Potent, pure, and essentially nonpersonalized, *kami* may mean power and may be dissipated or aggregated, according to human (or divine) actions. Pollution repels *kami*, whereas purity attracts it. Actions and objects that have this purity may attract *kami* or imbue *kami* on their own.

Personalized deities are called *kami* as well. The term *kami* is used as a title appended to the names of certain deities, thus Amaterasu-ō-mikami. The Japanese *kami* tend to be highly personalized, sometimes having distinct and identifiable personae and preferences. There are also numerous unnamed and attributeless deities. The totality of *kami* is expected to be too numerous to count and is referred to as *yaoyorozu-no-kamigami* (the eight million various *kami*). Deities associated particularly with the state cult and national Shintō are usually carefully defined, named, and provided with ranks and titles. Other *kami* (particularly those worshiped exclusively in smaller communities) are far less carefully delineated.

A similar situation exists for the Ainu *kamui*. Some, like the hearth goddess Kamui Fuchi, are carefully delineated, others less well so. The Ainu do not appear to have a general category such as *yaoyorozu-no-kamigami*. Ainu *kamui* tend to have very specific associations, such as the *kamui* of the undertow.

The reverse is true for Ryukyuan *kang* (the term varies between isles and island clusters in the archipelago). Although *kang* are viewed in almost all cases as individual beings, similar in form to humans, they are rarely provided with particular attributes, dress, or activities to distinguish them. They are, in fact, rarely well defined, and quite often almost incidental to the rituals Ryukyuans perform. With some few exceptions, most of which may better be described as "culture heroes" rather than worshiped deities, they are not associated with particular myths beyond "they are the ancestors/*kang* of our group (lineage or hamlet)."

See also Amaterasu-ō-mikami; Kamui Fuchi; *Yaoyorozu no kamigami.*

References and further reading:

Aston, William George. 1905. *Shinto: The Way of the Gods.* London: Longmans, Green, and Co.

Guthrie, Steward. 1980. "A Cognitive Theory of Religion." *Current Anthropology* 21 (2): 181–204.

Havens, Norman, trans. 1998. *Kami.* Tokyo: Institute for Japanese Culture and Classics, Kokugakuin University.

Herbert, Jean. 1980. *La religion d'Okinawa.* Paris: Dervy-Livres. Collection Mystiques et religions. Série B 0397–3050.

Lebra, William P. 1966. *Okinawan Religion: Belief, Ritual, and Social Structure.* Honolulu: University of Hawaii Press.

Munro, Neil Gordon. 1962. *Ainu Creed and Cult.* London: Routledge and Kegan Paul; London and New York: K. Paul International, distributed by Columbia University Press, 1995.

Ohnuki-Tierney, Emiko. 1969. *Sakhalin Ainu Folklore.* Washington, DC: American Anthropological Association. Anthropological Studies 2.

Ono, Sokyo. 1962. *Shinto: The Kami Way.* Rutland, VT: Charles E. Tuttle.

Robinson, James C. 1969. *Okinawa: A People and Their Gods.* Rutland, VT: Charles E. Tuttle.

Ross, Floyd Hiatt. 1965. *Shinto: The Way of Japan.* Boston: Beacon Press.

Sasaki, Kiyoshi. 2000. "Amenominakanushi no Kami in Late Tokugawa Period Kokugaku." Tokyo: Institute for Japanese Culture and Classics, Kokugakuin University. http://www.kokugakuin.ac.jp/ijcc/wp/cpjr/kami/sasaki.html#para0060.

Sered, Susan Starr. 1999. *Women of the Sacred Groves: Divine Priestesses of Okinawa.* New York and Oxford: Oxford University Press.

Vance, Timothy J. 1983. "The Etymology of Kami." *Japanese Journal of Religious Studies* 10 (4): 277–288.

Wehmeyer, Ann, trans. 1997. *Kojiki-den (Motoori Norinaga), Book 1.* Ithaca, NY: Cornell University East Asia Series, Number 87.

KAMIKAZE

"Divine wind." In 1274 and again in 1281, when Japan was invaded by Korean-Mongol fleets, the invading fleets were destroyed by typhoons—the divine wind—sent by Hachiman, the deity of war whose aid had been appealed to by the numerically inferior Japanese forces. The divine wind was viewed as the ultimate defense of Japan by Shintō scholars and laity alike. The *kamikaze* is one of the three central Japanese myths. (The other two are the myth of imperial descent from the heavenly *kami,* and the myth of *bushido,* particularly as exemplified by the forty-seven *rōnin.*)

For the Japanese of the thirteenth century, the threatened Mongol invasion was, historically and politically, a major watershed. It was the first time the entire military might of Japan had had to be mobilized for defense of the nation. Until then, even foreign wars were little more than squabbles that involved one

Group of young kamikaze pilots poses before leaving for action. (Hulton Archive/Getty Images)

or another faction within Japan—essentially domestic affairs. With the Mongol invasion Japan became exposed to international politics at a personal and national level as never before. That the Japanese forces won two consecutive victories against numerically and materially superior foes was something most Japanese appreciated. That the victory was the consequence of almost improbable nonhuman factors made it a miracle. In the years between the first and the second invasion the entire nation became aware—through the distribution of sutras that were to be read by individuals and in temples, through the preaching of priests, particularly those like Nichiren who were highly nationalistic—that some miracle was to be expected. When the miracle actually happened, skeptics were quickly converted. The idea that the *kami* or Buddhas were protecting Japan became a very personal one.

Thus, in the final months of World War II, the name was revived for suicide pilots and submariners (about four thousand of them actually carried out attacks) sent out in unsuccessful attempts to stop the U.S. fleet. Once again, the nation was under severe threat. Once again, the authorities, secular as well as religious, made very clear that the Japanese were defending themselves against insurmountable odds. And once again, the only salvation that could be expected would come from the only two sources that had demonstrably, in the past, done such an office: the self-sacrifice and fighting spirit of the Japanese warrior, and intervention by the *kami*/Buddhas. Using suicide bombers by air and by sea was less a *technical* response to lack of weaponry than an attempt to recreate the self-sacrifice of the original period of the *kamikaze.* Japan's leaders *knew* the *kamikaze* pilots would not stop the American fleets. But they were also part of the Japanese myth that said, roughly, that if the Japanese warrior would do his part and sacrifice his life in the doing, then the *kami* would do theirs. This time, of course, the myth failed to live up to its billing.

The appearance of the *kamikaze* is significant in two senses: the construction of pan-Japanese nationalism during the feudal period, and the extension of the idea of direct relationship between the *kami* and the imperial household to all of the Japanese nation. The concept has had its ups and downs and has been constantly manipulated by the powers-that-be in Japan. Nonetheless, even in the start of the twenty-first century it is a fundamental idea held to by many Japanese.

> ***See also*** *Chūshingura;* Divine Descent; Hachiman; Heroes.
> ***References and further reading:***
> Barker, A. J. 1971. *Suicide Weapon.* London: Pan/Ballantine.
> Nagatsuka, Ryuji. 1972. *I Was a Kamikaze: The Knights of the Divine Wind.*
>   Translated by Nina Rootes. London: Abelard-Schuman.
> Warner, Denis, Peggy Warner, and Sadao Seno. 1982. *The Sacred Warriors: Japan's*
>   *Suicide Legions.* Cincinnati, OH: Van Nostrand Reinhold Company.

KAMIMUSUBI

The third deity to come into existence at the beginning of the world at Takamagahara. Kamimusubi is one of the three "single *kami*," that is, without a counterpart or genitor. However, this deity is later identified as the parent of Sukunabikona. It also seems from the context, as well as from the actions ascribed to this deity, that Kamimusubi is female, because in the *Nihonshōki* Takamimusubi-no-mikoto (who came into being just before Kamimusubi), a male deity, is identified as Sukunabikona's parent as well.

Also known as Kamimusubi-Mioya-no-mikoto (Generative great parent deity: the "great parent" title is usually accorded to females), Kamimusubi is the one who took the various foodstuffs born from the murdered food deity, Ōgetsuhime, and gave them to humankind. Later she restored Ōkuninushi to life, after he had been killed for the first time by his brothers. He obviously had a soft spot for her because she is mentioned in the song that concludes his agreement with Takemikazuchi-no-kami: Takamagahara is mentioned principally as her/his abode.

At a more mundane level it is certainly possible that Kamimusubi may have been an important deity for the Izumo, as well as for the Yamato. This is one of the many points of similarity between the two polities that helped in their amalgamation.

>*See also* Ogetsuhime; Okuninushi; Sukunabikona; Takamagahara; Takamimusubi; Takemikazuchi.
>
>*References and further reading:*
>Aston, William G., trans. 1956. *Nihongi.* London: Allen and Unwin.
>Philippi, Donald, trans. and ed. 1968. *Kōjiki.* Tokyo: Tokyo University Press.

KAMUI
See Kami.

KAMUI FUCHI (AINU)
Hearth deity. One of the most important deities for the Ainu, Kamui Fuchi was significant in her own right, as well as an access point to the world of the gods. Her full name is Apemerukoyan-mat Unamerukoyan-mat (Rising Fire Sparks Woman Rising Cinder Sparks Woman). Together with Shiramba Kamui she is "owner of the world." The hearth at the center of each Ainu house was her abode, and it also served as the gateway through which the *kamui* and people could communicate.

In the most common myth, Kamui Fuchi descended from the heavens, accompanied by Kanna Kamui, *kamui* of thunder and lightning, in his guise as a fiery snake. Another tale has it that she was born from an elm tree that had been impregnated by Kandakoro Kamui (the Prime Originator *kamui*). In another myth, she was born of the fire drill, together with her sister Hashinau-uk Kamui, *kamui* of the chase.

The hearth, her abode, also serves as the abode of the dead, and ancestors are actually known as "those-dwelling-in-the-hearth." Because the Ainu believe in transmigration, it is the holding place from which new souls are assigned to bodies in the act of human procreation. As a consequence, the hearth must be kept pure; nothing is allowed to contaminate it. At night Kamui Fuchi retires to rest as the coals are covered with ashes, but the fire itself must never be extinguished. So important is her position that Kamui Fuchi never leaves her house. Instead, she deputizes other *kamui* to act for her in the mundane world. When a woman gives birth (and there is consequent fear of pollution from blood), a new fire is laid for the occasion, at the other end of the house, near the birth site, and another *kamui* deputizes for the hearth goddess.

Kamui Fuchi was the goddess who instructed Ainu women in the making of *kut* (sacred girdles), and for this and other gifts she taught humankind, she is styled Iresu Kamui (People Teacher). Among her servants and deputies (since she cannot leave the hearth) are Mintarakoro Kamui, guardian of the precincts, and Rukoro Kamui, guardian of the privy. Like other *kamui* she lives a perfectly mundane life. In one myth, her husband was seduced away by Waka-ush-Kamui, deity of the sea. The insulted goddess challenges her rival, and the two women engage in a sorcerous duel, from which Kamui Fuchi emerges the winner. She returns to her house, and her shamefaced husband finally returns as well, bearing indemnity gifts.

The varied roles of Kamui Fuchi, and most notably her role as guardian of access to the realm of the *kamui,* make her one of the most powerful in the Ainu cosmology. She is, in effect, the major contact point with any domestic ritual. Unsurprisingly, she is also considered the judge of human domestic affairs: Those who pollute in her presence, or do not maintain proper relationships within the household, incur her wrath. In a society heavily dependent on the benefit of fire and the hearth, fear of her punishment would have been a potent element of social control. Moreover, though she was served by men, her ties to women insured some balance between the sexes, at least inasmuch as familial and household affairs were concerned. Her myths demonstrate the relative independence and power that women assumed in Ainu society. Her name "Fuchi" may well have survived into Japanese in the form "Fuji," thus Mt. Fuji, a live volcano.

>*See also* Hashinau-uk Kamui; Kandakoro Kamui; Shiramba Kamui; Waka-ush-kamui.

>**References and further reading:**

>Etter, Carl. 1949. *Ainu Folklore: Traditions and Culture of the Vanishing Aborigines of Japan.* Chicago: Wilcox and Follett Co.

>Munro, Neil Gordon. 1962. *Ainu Creed and Cult.* London: Routledge and Kegan Paul; London and New York: K. Paul International, distributed by Columbia University Press, 1995.

KANDAKORO KAMUI (AINU)

"Possessor of the sky." Ainu god who is the prime originator. From his abode in the heavens, he deputized Moshirikara Kamui to prepare the world for the inhabitation of men. Though a powerful deity, Kandakoro is by no means a supreme being. His mythical presence is necessary to cause the emergence of the world, but he plays a very small part in future developments. Instead his role is more of mediator and general overseer, somewhat like Chikap Kamui, owner of the land (and, in a sense, the Japanese Ōkuninushi).

Like a great many people unafflicted by capitalism, the Ainu were keenly aware of the fact that the land could not be "owned." It could be utilized for a period of time, and then passed into someone else's usufruct. The various "owner" *kamui* are, in this sense, an appreciation and understanding of the temporary nature of possession against the enduring nature of the land itself: a moral (and sensibly ecological) imperative to preserve the land.

See also Chikap Kamui; Ōkuninushi.

References and further reading:

Etter, Carl. 1949. *Ainu Folklore; Traditions and Culture of the Vanishing Aborigines of Japan.* Chicago: Wilcox and Follett Co.

Munro, Neil Gordon. 1962. *Ainu Creed and Cult.* London: Routledge and Kegan Paul; London and New York: K. Paul International, distributed by Columbia University Press, 1995.

Ohnuki-Tierney, Emiko. 1969. *Sakhalin Ainu Folklore.* Washington, DC: American Anthropological Association. Anthropological Studies 2.

KANG

See Kami.

KANNON (KANZEON-BOSATSU)

A compassionate boddhisattva, Kannon (Chinese: *Guanyin*; Sanskrit: *Avalokiteshvara*) is often represented as a companion or avatar of Amida Nyōrai, the Buddha of the Pure Land. One of the most popular representations of the boddhisatvas, Kannon represents the essence of compassion. As such, she may serve as an intermediary to Amida, the Buddha of the Far West. In her original form as the Indian Buddhist saint Avalokiteshvara, Kannon was a male disciple of the Buddha. Imported as part of Buddhist theology into China, the Indian male saint became a female boddhisattva.

Following Chinese belief, she is the compassionate deity of mercy and is sometimes portrayed as carrying a child, because of her particular mercy for children and the helpless, though she is not a mother herself.

She is represented in a variety of ways. Among them are Jūichimen Kannon, showing her with eleven faces, representing her eternal vigil in assisting people; Batto Kannon, with a miniature horse head as her hair ornament (In this form she is the patroness of carters and horse copers, as well as a protector from smallpox); and Niorin, wherein she is portrayed with four arms, one supporting her cheek, and considered patroness of fishermen. She sometimes carries the wish-granting wheel or the Vase of the Waters of Life, which she sprinkles about her with a lotus bud. Both of these items have esoteric significance as representing the Buddhist Law, but for most people it is sufficient that she carries the possibility of restoring and continuing life.

The most famous temples of Kannon in Japan are the one in Asakusa, a working-class district of Tokyo, and the remarkable Sanjusangendō (33,333

18-mile-high goddess Kannon on turtle, Nagasaki, Japan. (Chris Rennie/Robert Harding World Imagery/Getty Images)

Kannon hall) in Kyoto, a long gallery with tier upon tier of thousand-handed Kannon. Worshipers, largely women, come to these temples to pray for kinfolk and children. The number 33 is sacred to Kannon, and she appears in thirty-three different manifestations. A major pilgrimage route of thirty-three Kannon temples stretches from the Pacific Ocean side of Japan in Kumano, through Kyoto, to the Japan Sea. There are numerous temples and shrines to Kannon throughout Japan, both in Buddhist and Shintō form.

Kannon is, unsurprisingly, one of the most beloved figures of Japanese mythology and belief. She is the representation of pure mercy, and the major female figure in the mythology. In a sense, she is the epitome of the contradiction embedded within Buddhism: the difficulty in reconciling mercy and salvation to others with the nature of Buddhahood, which is beyond desire or action.

See also Amida Nyōrai; Jizō.

References and further reading:

Dykstra, Yoshiko Kurata. 1986. *The Konjaku Tales: Indian Section (Tenjiku-Hen), Part 1/Part 2 from a Medieval Japanese Collection.* Osaka: Kansai University of Foreign Studies.

Eliot, Sir Charles Norton Edgcumbe. 1959. *Japanese Buddhism.* London: Routledge and Kegan Paul.

Frank, Bernard. 1991. *Le pantheon bouddhique au Japon.* Paris: Collections d'Emile Guimet. Reunion des musees nationaux.

Getty, Alice. 1988. *The Gods of Northern Buddhism.* New York: Dover Publications.

Joly, Henri L. 1967. *Legend in Japanese Art.* Tokyo: Charles E. Tuttle Co.

Kobayashi, Sakae. 1992. *Religious Ideas of the Japanese Under the Influence of Asian Mythology.* Nishinomiya: Kansei Gakuin University.

Matsunaga. Alicia. 1974/1996. *Foundations of Japanese Buddhism.* Los Angeles: Buddhist Books International.

Sjoquist, Douglas P. 1999. "Identifying Buddhist Images in Japanese Painting and Sculpture." *Education About Asia* 4 (3); http://www.aasianst.org/.

KAPPA

A water creature reputed to seduce people into rivers or ponds, then drown them. The *kappa* has the body of a monkey and a tortoiselike shell covering its torso. On the top of its head the *kappa* has a depression that is filled with water. On land this may be covered by a metal cap. This depression allows the creature to live on land unless someone causes the *kappa* to spill the water, whereupon it becomes helpless. This can be done by tripping it, or by bowing. The *kappa* is extremely polite and will always bow back, spilling the fluid and rendering itself helpless.

Kappa are very licentious, and they attract young women and children to the water side, whereupon they seize their victims and pull them down to drown. They also torment horses, sometimes by eviscerating them through the anus.

Kappa are experts at *aiki-jutsu* and other bone-locking and wrestling techniques, and are reputed to have taught these skills to humankind: One retainer of Toyotomi Hideyoshi's, Rokusuke by name, was reputed to have overcome a *kappa* (presumably by the politeness route) and as a consequence became an unbeatable wrestler. It is this ability that allows *kappa* to control their victims. *Kappa* are also experts at bone setting, and those wishing to practice as bone setters and doctors sometimes solicit the *kappa*'s aid. One way of bribing a *kappa* is by offering a cucumber or other cucurbit, of which the creature is reputedly fond. Kappa are often portrayed riding on a cucumber or a squash, and a type of rolled sushi with a cucumber inside is called a *kappa-maki.*

Some authors suggest that *kappa* represent in conventional form some of the tragedies of human life in preindustrial Japan—babies that have been aborted or killed as a means of population control, and possibly the mothers of unwanted children who have drowned themselves in grief. This supposition is strengthened by the *kappa*'s appearance: babyish and thin, the water-depression perhaps representing the infant's fontanel.

References and further reading:
Jolivet, Muriel. 2000. "Ema: Representations of Infanticide and Abortion." In *Consumption and Material Culture in Contemporary Japan,* edited by M. Ashkenazi and J. Clammer. London: Kegan Paul International, pp. 79–96.

KASUGA DAIMYŌJIN

The "Great bright deity of Kasuga": a syncretic deity and the protector of the Nara temple and shrine complex. The Kashima Daimyōjin is syncretic in two ways: The deity is a composite of five deities, and each of the five deities is a pair of Shintō *kami* and Buddhist deity. The main deity is Takemikazuchi, the thunder *kami,* who is seen as a *gongen* of Fukukensaku Kannon. The others are Futsunushi-no-mikoto (Yakushi Nyōrai), Amenokoyane (Jizō), Himegami (Jūichimen Kannon), and Ame-no-oshikumone-no-mikoto (Monju-bosatsu).

Originally supported by the Fujiwara family, who virtually ran Japan as they controlled the emperor, the Kasuga Daimyōjin was promoted as a protector of the area of what had become Yamato province (the area of Nara and the new capital, Heian).

The importance of the Kasuga deity is that such "combined" deities were to become a major model for all Japanese deities to some extent or other, where deities are combined, almost indifferently, according to political, economic, and social exigency, in popular belief and worship.

See also Gongen; Jizō; Kannon; Monju; Takemikazuchi.

References and further reading:
Grapard, Allan G. 1992. *The Protocol of the Gods: A Study of the Kasuga Cult in Japanese History.* Berkeley: University of California Press.
Tyler, Royall. 1990. *The Miracles of the Kasuga Deity.* New York: Columbia University Press.

KAWA-NO-KAMI

God of rivers. Larger rivers have their own gods, but all waterways are under Kawa-no-kami's authority. When rivers flooded in archaic times, the gods were sometimes appeased with human sacrifices. The introduction of Buddhism meant the end of this practice. Instead, dolls made of straw or flowers were substituted and offered to the Kawa-no-kami. This custom is still extant today in some areas of Japan.

References and further reading:
Sadler, A.W. 1970. "Of Talismans and Shadow Bodies—Annual Purification Rites at a Tokyo Shrine." *Contemporary Religions in Japan* 11: 181–222.

KENASH UNARABE (AINU)

A blood-sucking female monster dwelling in swamps. Kenash Unarabe will often assume the guise of Hash-uk Kamui, deity of the hunt, to lure hunters away and lead them through the swamps until they tire, whereupon she drinks their blood. She will conceal her face with long tresses, by which she may be distinguished from Hash-uk Kamui. Kenash Unarabe, together with a variety of diseases and poisonous and unhealthy waters, emerged from the decomposing remains of the tools the gods used in their making of the earth.

Kenash Unarabe's fondness for blood makes her, paradoxically, important to the Ainu. She is invoked during rituals for a birthing mother, and for menstruating women, to come and remove the pollution, her reward being drinking the flowing blood. For Ainu as for many other people, blood was an important and powerful mystical element. This is particularly true of the polluting aspect of childbirth and menstruation. Unsurprisingly, as in this case, very powerful mythical figures are invoked in order to deal with the pollution. Kenash Unarabe's origin in association with polluting and diseased matter means that invoking her addresses these problems with a very powerful counterforce, but one that is potentially malevolent, uncontrollable, uncertain, and therefore threatening.

See also Hashinau-uk Kamui.

References and further reading:
Munro, Neil Gordon. 1962. *Ainu Creed and Cult.* London: Routledge and Kegan Paul; London and New York: K. Paul International, distributed by Columbia University Press, 1995.

KIM-UN KAMUI (AINU)

The bear god. Also known as Metotush Kamui and as Nuparikor Kamui (Mountain God). An Ainu myth recounts how one day a beautiful young woman went with her baby on her back to collect forest bulbs. While washing them in a river, she started singing a song, and her sweet voice attracted a bear. Frightened, she abandoned her baby and her clothes and ran away. The bear was disappointed that the beautiful singer had stopped her music, but, investigating the pile of clothes, found the baby. He cared for the baby for several days, feeding it from his saliva, which he dropped into the baby's mouth.

The men of the village came to the place, and discovered the baby alive and healthy. They were immediately convinced that the bear was Kim-un Kamui, followed its tracks, and shot it dead. They then arranged a feast of the bear's meat, raised the bear's head on a stand offering it wine and *inau*, and by doing so, freed its *ramat* to return to heaven.

One day the bear god went to visit a friend, leaving his beloved wife and their baby behind. He lost track of time until the crow came to tell him that his wife had gone down to the village of the humans and had not returned. The bear rushed to his house and, picking up the little one, followed his wife. The fox tried to ensorcel him, and two men shot arrows at him, but he continued on his way unharmed. He followed the men to the village, where he was greeted by Kamui Paseguru (the aconite poison goddess), who invited him to come and visit Kamui Fuchi, the hearth goddess. While they were speaking thus, the fox continued his enscorcellment. Kamui Paseguru then leapt upon Kim-un Kamui, and he lost consciousness. When he awoke he was high in the branches of a tree. Below him lay the body of an old bear, and a young cub played nearby. The men returned and captured the bear cub. They then worshiped the dead bear, putting up *inau*, who protected the meat from predators and demons. The meat was taken down to the village, where the bear god was offered wine, *inau*, and dumplings made of millet. He also found his wife sitting by the hearth. They feasted for several days with Kamui Fuchi, the hearth goddess, then went back to their home laden with gifts. They threw a feast for the other *kamui*, and when their young cub later came back, also laden with gifts of wine and *inau*, another feast.

Bears were not necessarily so benevolent, and another *kamui yukar* tells of how a bear maiden of evil disposition (an *ararush*) went down to a human village and killed a woman. Chastised by Kamui Fuchi, she restored the woman to life. She was then entertained by the villagers, and, leaving her earthly covering, returned to the land of the *kamui* bearing the usual gifts of wine and *inau*, and told her kinfolk of human generosity. The humans feasted on her discarded mundane form.

The bear is a significant figure in Ainu mythology and is the focus of a major cult and ritual. Villages that could do so would, in traditional times, capture a bear cub alive. It was fed and treated almost as a family member for a year, and then, during the bear ceremony, was shot to death with arrows. Its skull was added to the skull repository, and its flesh was eaten to free its *ramat* (spirit) to return to Kim-un Kamui's home in the sky. For the Ainu, killing and eating the bear was not an act of ingratitude or cruelty: Rather, they were releasing the bear spirit to return to its natural place, bearing tales of their piety and good manners. The central ritual of Ainu life—the raising, then killing of a bear cub—was explained in this myth as an act of the reciprocal relationship between the *kamui* and humans.

> *See also* Hash-Inau-uk Kamui; Kamui Fuchi.
> *References and further reading:*
> Ainu Mukei Bunka Densho Hozonkai. 1983. *Hitobito no Monogatari* (Fables of men). Sapporo: Ainu Mukei Bunka Densho Hozonkai, Showa 58 (1983), English and Japanese.
> Batchelor, John. 1971. *Ainu Life and Lore: Echoes of a Departing Race*. Tokyo, Kyobunkwan, and New York: Johnson Reprint Corp.
> Kayano, Shigeru. 1985. *The Romance of the Bear God: Ainu Folktales (Eibun Ainu minwashu)*. Tokyo: Taishukan Publishing Co.
> Munro, Neil Gordon. 1962. *Ainu Creed and Cult*. London: Routledge and Kegan Paul; London and New York: K. Paul International, distributed by Columbia University Press, 1995.
> Philippi, Donald L., trans. 1979. *Songs of Gods, Songs of Humans: The Epic Tradition of the Ainu*. Princeton: Princeton University Press.

KINASHUT KAMUI (AINU)

The snake deity. Generally friendly and helpful to humans, he controls the worst behavior of snakes. Snake spirits trouble people with eye disease, paralysis, and other ills, and Kinashut Kamui, if appealed to, is able to evict these evil spirits from their victim. Kinashut Kamui is the brother of Nusakoro Kamui (though they are sometimes regarded as one). He protects communities against other evils, most notably typhoid.

> *See also* Nusakoro Kamui.
> *References and further reading:*
> Munro, Neil Gordon. 1962. *Ainu Creed and Cult*. London: Routledge and Kegan Paul; London and New York: K. Paul International, distributed by Columbia University Press, 1995.

KINTOKI (ALSO KINTARŌ)

A giant hero, one of the four Shi Tenno who were Raikō's (Minamoto-no-Yorimitsu's) retainers and loyal attendants. His name means "Golden boy" due to the brilliant red color of his skin. He was born (or fostered) to a *yama-uba* at Mt. Ashigeru. He grew up wrestling with, beating, and making friends with the wild animals and *tengu*. His inseparable tools were his *masakari* (broad ax) and his giant saké bowl. He participated in Raikō's adventures until the latter's death, then returned to wander, wild and naked, on Mt. Ashigeru. His saké bowl and ax perhaps indicate his origin as a wild being, possessor of the elixir of life embodied in saké.

Kintarō is one of the most endearing figures in Japanese mythology. His picture, usually in the form of a prepubescent child wearing only a chest protector (a sort of apron Japanese children wore instead of clothes in premodern times) and frequently accompanied by a bear, can be found on saké bottles, insurance companies' logos, toys, and almost everywhere else. In the very rigid atmosphere of Japanese society he represented for most Japanese the freedom and strength to be oneself, even in the extremes of drunkenness. In the most common image he is portrayed uprooting a tree so that he and his companion—a bear he had wrestled into submission—could cross a gorge on their way to his home.

See also Raikō; *Yama-uba.*

References and further reading:

Ouwehand, Cornelius. 1964. *Namazu-e and Their Themes: An Interpretative Approach to Some Aspects of Japanese Religion.* Leiden, the Netherlands: E. J. Brill.

Sato, Hiroaki. 1995. *Legends of the Samurai.* Woodstock, NY: Overlook Press.

KISHIMŌJIN

One of the most popular of Buddhist deities, she is the protector of infants. Originally an Indian demon named Hāriti, she sustained her five hundred offspring with the bodies of children she caught. The Buddha trapped her youngest and favorite offspring under his begging bowl. He relented when she promised to abandon her anthropophagous practices, whereupon, regretting her previous existence, she devoted herself to the protection of infants. In return, the Buddha promised that offerings would be made for her sustenance in all his monasteries. In an alternative telling of the myth, she and her assistant *rakasha* (demons) reported to the Buddha and expressed their desire to protect all infants born under the Law.

Kishimōjin is represented as a woman carrying an infant in one arm. In her other hand she holds a branch and fruit of the pomegranate: a fruit that because of its many seeds represents fecundity in the Asian mainland as it does in Europe. The blood-red seeds of the pomegranate are said in Japan to represent the human flesh Kishimōjin used to consume as an ogress. As a consequence, many Japanese will refuse to eat pomegranates because they say the fruit tastes of human flesh. The image of Kishimōjin with the infant in her hands is similar to the image of Kannon in a like stance, and thus, perhaps, the idea of both of them as patronesses of childbirth took over, in Japanese Buddhist thinking, from the image of Koyasu-gami, the deity of childbirth, who is identified with Kōnōhanasakuya-hime.

See also Kannon; Kōnōhanasakuya-hime.
References and further reading:
Frank, Bernard. 1991. *Le pantheon bouddhique au Japon.* Paris: Collections d'Emile Guimet. Reunion des musees nationaux.

KŌBŌ DAISHI

Saint, miracle worker, and founder of the Shingon Buddhist sect. To Kōbō Daishi are attributed a vast array of miracles and wonders. He established the worship of Konpira-daigongen in Kompira-san on Shikoku Island and founded the temple complex on Kōya-san. The facts of his life are dramatic enough, even without the mythical dimension.

Born in 774 in Shikoku to a family that had been exiled from Heian, the capital, he assumed the name Kukai as a Buddhist priest. He died in 835, after predicting the day of his death and painting in the eyes of his own portrait. He was posthumously given the name Kōbō Daishi (Great teacher of spreading the law), a special title, in 921 by the imperial court.

His brilliance as a child was such that he was soon ordained as a monk, assuming the name Kukai (air-sea), and sent to the capital to study. There he was selected to accompany one of the infrequent, tedious, long, and dangerous imperial missions to China. Of the fleet of three ships, only two made it. The one bearing the ambassador and Kukai lost its way and was sequestered by a suspicious regional Chinese governor. Kukai's eloquence won the governor over, and the mission was sent on to Xian, the capital. The young priest dipped into many forms of Buddhism, finally settling on the Quen-yen esoteric form, to be known in Japan as Shingon. The patriarch Hui-ko of the Chinese Quen-yen sect declared the young Japanese to be his chosen successor and ordered him to return to Japan to spread the true word. He returned to Japan but was unable to expound his theories because of political events at the capital, Heian-kyō. Eventually he established the headquarters of the Shingon sect in Heian, moving the main temple and monasteries to Mt. Kōya. He established Japan's longest and most famous pilgrimage route, the eighty-eight temple circuit of Shikoku (about one thousand miles in length).

Kōbō Daishi is credited with one of the greatest Japanese inventions of all: the *kana* syllabaries. Each of the two sets (*hiragana* used for verb endings and grammatical particles; *katakana* used for foreign words, but originally intended to allow women to write) has forty-seven symbols. There are also two modifying marks that allow hardening a consonant. He wrote the syllables down in the form of a poem, called "Iroha," in which each of the syllables appears, but only once:

I-ro-ha-ni-ho-he-to
Chi-ri-nu-ru-wo
Wa-ka-yo-ta-re-so
Tsu-ne-na-ra-mu
U-(w)i-no-o-ku-ya-ma
Ke-fu-ko-e-te
A-sa-ki-yu-me-mi-shi
(W)e-hi-mo-se-su-n
(Colors are fragrant
But they fade away.
In this world of ours none lasts forever.
Today cross the high mountain of life's illusions,
And there will be no more shallow dreaming,
No more drunkenness. [Nelson 1974])
(Note: wi and we are no longer used in modern Japanese.)

The miraculous life of the Daishi started while he was still a boy. A loner and mystic since childhood, he soon was the subject of his first miracle. At the age of seven, the boy who was to become Kōbō Daishi climbed a mountain near his home. Reaching the peak, he threw himself off, crying, "If I am destined to serve the Law, let me be saved, otherwise let me die." A company of *arhats* then appeared and brought the boy safely to the ground. Later, when he assumed his priestly name Kukai, the morning star flew into his mouth as he was doing austerities, proclaiming him a saint.

The Daishi was, among other talents, a sculptor of note. He has carved statues of the boddhisattva Kokuzō (his special patron) and Shakyamuni into living trees, which can still be seen today. In one case he used a sick farmer's sickle to carve an image of himself, and so cured the man. In another, he carved a statue of Yakushi out of a living trunk using nothing but his fingernails. He is said to have carved a special statue in three of the four ancient provinces of Shikoku (Awa, Iyo, Tosa), where the eighty-eight-stage pilgrimage associated with his name and his birthplace are located. The fourth province, Sanuki, did not benefit from a statue because the pilgrimage path through it was easy, and its government was welcoming to pilgrims: Presumably, a statue was not required to keep an eye on them. Two of those statues (the one in Iyo, and the one in Tosa) still exist, whereas the Awa statue has been lost.

While still searching for his way in life, he came upon a young woman who, while living in a mountain hut, wove cloth for her living. She gave him some cloth and told him that she was the daughter of a court official who had had to flee the capital because of involvement in a plot. Kannon had appeared to her mother in a dream and warned her of imminent arrest, and the pregnant woman had escaped to the mountains, where she gave birth to the baby girl. Moved by the story, the saint started carving a statue of Kannon-bosatsu. When the statue was finished, a cloud descended and the girl was revealed as Kannon-bosatsu herself. Kōbō Daishi installed the statue he had carved on the summit and built a temple: Kirihata-ji (Cut-cloth temple), which is there to this day.

The Daishi, as he is known, accompanies every pilgrim on the pilgrimage route he established around the island of Shikoku. Women on pilgrimage are under the Daishi's protection, and in numerous myths, he intervenes to help women deliver safely. He also cares for children born on pilgrimage, supplying their needs if necessary if their parents die.

The Daishi's care extends to the pilgrims' material needs as well. There are still a number of places in Japan, on the pilgrimage route and off, where the Daishi brought forth good water for the people to drink. While walking in Awa the saint was thirsty and could find no stream. Eventually he smelled a wonderful fragrance. He prayed, and pure fresh water welled up from the bottom of the earth and filled a handy depression. In the depression he saw a wonderful bright rock, which he carved into a statue of Yakushi. It became too dark to work, so the moon obliged and the night became as day with the moonlight until the saint had finished his carving.

As did most miracle workers, Kōbō Daishi dispelled demons and pests wherever he went. Some of his exorcisms repeated and strengthened those performed by En-no-Gyōja a century before the Daishi. There are no foxes on Shikoku, and people there are immune to fox magic. That is because the Daishi expelled all the foxes for their tricks, which he feared would distract the pilgrims. While traveling in the mountains of Shikoku, near the pilgrimage route he later established, the Daishi came to a valley that was being ravaged by a fiery snake. The snake had been subdued a century earlier by En-no-Gyōja, but had since revived. The saint called on his patron, the boddhisattva Kokuzō, who bound the snake firmly and extinguished its fire for all time. At another time, the Daishi came to Muroto, a cape jutting out of Shikoku Island, which is, among other things, a setting off point for explorers searching for the route to the fabulous land of Tokoyo-no-kuni. He found the people of the place plagued by demons who lived in a huge camphor tree on top of the mountain. The saint abolished these monsters and carved his own image on the trunk of the tree. Eventually, when he returned from China, he returned to Cape Muroto, cut down the tree, and used the wood to build a monastery, one of those on the pilgrimage route. The statue is still kept there, shown only once a year on the saint's death day.

Several of the miracles performed by the Daishi relate to fish. At the place that was to become a large pilgrimage site, the saint met a merchant leading a pack horse loaded with dried and salted mackerel. The saint asked for a fish, but the merchant refused. After a while, the merchant's pack horse suddenly stumbled and fell ill. The man, having heard that a holy man was on pilgrimage in the area, ran back and begged the Daishi for help. The saint gave the man his begging bowl and bade him fill it with seawater. Uttering a spell, the saint had the man give the water to his horse, which recovered at once. The amazed merchant offered the saint a fish. The saint took the fish, waded into the sea, and, after a prayer, loosed the salted fish into the waters. The revived animal promptly swam away. The merchant then became a monk and built a chapel, which became known as Saba Daishi (Mackerel Daishi).

A similar myth is told around Mt. Koya. A woman was roasting small *ayu* (sweetfish) on skewers over a fire. The saint begged for one. He carefully took it off the spit, put it in the water, murmured a prayer, and the fish swam away. To this day the fish in the river that flows by Mt. Koya have three small spots on their head and body: the mark of the skewer. Another time he was crossing a riverbed when the sharp shell of a river clam cut his foot. He touched the offending clam with his staff, and since then, the shellfish in that river have smooth shells.

When the Daishi's days were numbered, he could see his death day clearly. One of his disciples, an imperial prince, painted the saint's portrait. The Daishi admired the portrait, then painted in one final detail: the eyes. The following day his body was still. His disciples placed him in a tomb on Mt. Koya. Some time later, the emperor had a dream in which the saint requested a new robe: As the Daishi personally accompanied each pilgrim who walked the eighty-eight stations of the pilgrimage on Shikoku, his own had become quite tattered. The emperor hastily dispatched an official to Mt. Koya. The tomb was opened in the presence of the abbot. The saint appeared wreathed in mist and smoke. The official and the abbot were the only ones who could see the saint clearly, but an acolyte, whose hand had been placed on the saint's knee, was left with a sweet-smelling hand for the rest of his life. The Daishi was barbered and dressed in the new robe by the abbot. He then informed the emperor that he had taken a vow not to die but to await the coming of Miroku, the future Buddha, and gave signs from which it was possible to calculate that Miroku would arrive 5,670,000,300 years into the future. The three hundred represented the years since the saint's death.

The case of Kōbō Daishi illustrates how myth in Japan ties together the world of the divine and of the mundane. That Kōbō Daishi lived as a real man is beyond dispute. From material evidence that still exists, it is also clear that he was an exceptional man: gifted artist, architect (he laid out the Shingon headquarters on Mt. Kōya), scholar, and consummate politician. The variety and extent of myths about him are elaborations of his actual deeds, and quite often the activities of other Buddhist figures in areas such as Yoshino (where Mt. Kōya is located) and Shikoku are attributed to him.

In effect the mythologization of the Daishi is a morality tale, Buddhist style: from a relatively humble beginning, he achieved greatness, even divinity, by constant and unremitting endeavor. He ties together a large number of different threads that are significant for Japanese culture. Three are notable in this volume. First is the theme, already mentioned above, of the transformation of a common man into divinity. The Buddhas, says the myth, are concerned. They *do* help the common man, and the common man *can* become a Buddha himself. The second theme is the (Shintō) theme of the unity of the Japanese nation. The Daishi is an inhabitant of both common people's houses and those of emperors and aristocrats. He associates with them all on the basis of personal relationship, unmediated by ritual or pomp. A third theme is the theme of art, or perhaps more accurately, style. Shingon recognizes that Buddhahood can be attained through art. For the Daishi, doing things elegantly was as much a way of attaining enlightenment as following any precept: Aesthetics is close to godliness. It is, in fact, godliness.

The influence and fame of the Daishi are so great that even the miracles associated with other holy figures are generally attributed to him. For example, the myth about Saba Daishi was originally attributed to another saintly figure: Gyōgi. Even the invention of the syllabary attributed to the Daishi may not be historically accurate. Nonetheless, he is such a towering cultural figure that he overshadows everyone else in Japanese thought.

See also En-no-Gyōja; Kokuzō-bosatsu; Konpira; Miroku-bosatsu; Yakushi Nyōrai.
References and further reading:
Hakeda, Yoshito S. 1972. *Kukai*. New York: Columbia University Press.
Nelson, Andrew N. 1974. *Japanese-English Character Dictionary* (2d ed.). Rutland and Tokyo: Charles E. Tuttle.
Statler, Oliver. 1984. *Japanese Pilgrimage*. London: Picador.

KOJAKU MYŌ-Ō

The peacock king. One of the four divine kings protecting the sacred Buddhist Mt. Meru from each of the sides, Kojaku rides a peacock, emblematic of fire and the sun, and opposed to water. Snakes, sometimes identified with dragons, are emblematic of water, but also of poison. Thus Kojaku is the protector against poison and other things that menace the body or the spirit. For that purpose,

Kojaku (or the peacock) can provide a spell against poison. Kojaku may be represented with several arms. In one hand he carries a peacock feather, in another a stem of millet indicating fecundity. Other hands may carry a lotus blossom (the foundations of the Buddhist Law) and a fruit of good fortune.

See also Snakes.
References and further reading:
Frank, Bernard. 1991. *Le pantheon bouddhique au Japon.* Paris: Collections d'Emile Guimet. Reunion des musees nationaux.
Joly, Henri L. 1967. *Legend in Japanese Art.* Tokyo: Charles E. Tuttle Co.

KŌJIN
See Sanbo Kōjin.

KOKKA SHINTŌ
National Shintō was a government attempt during the Meiji, Taishō, and early Shōwa periods (1868–1945) to establish Shintō as the driving ideology and religion of the Japanese state. The roots of this ideology lay in the Mito school of National Learning, an eighteenth-century reaction to the Buddha-ization of the Tokugawa shogunate. In National Learning thought, Japan was the land of the *kami,* and the Japanese people were members of an all-encompassing *dōzoku* whose "main house" was that of Amaterasu-ō-mikami, and her heir and representative on Earth, the Japanese emperor.

In 1873 the Meiji government of the time dictated the separation of Buddhist and Shintō places of worship. Deities that had been worshiped in dual forms (Ryōbu) as Buddhist and Shintō deities were now required to be worshiped separately. Over a period of several decades, Shintō shrines were "rationalized"—assigned rank and income—within a comprehensive state system. Shintō priests were trained and forbidden to use Buddhist forms of ritual. And a system that placed the emperor as a divinity was established formally, along with a process of ranking all *kami.*

Aspects of Kokka Shintō were opposed or supported in varying degrees in different parts of the country. The general rankings of *kami* that have emerged today are often the result of the Kokka Shintō system, which was abolished as a branch of government with the Allied Occupation's Shintō Directive of 1945.

Kokka Shintō is an extreme case of the adoption of a series of myths, told by different voices at different periods, into a unified, formalized, official creed. It sustained the Japanese government through several decades, and the "official" mythology it espoused was at the basis of much of the behavior and actions of the Japanese in the decades leading up to and during World War II. One of the benefits conveyed by the Occupation period was the decoupling of government from religion in the Shintō Directive of 1945. From our point of view, the benefit is the freeing of Japanese myth-making from the shackles of formal government approval, allowing the existence and recreation of multiple myth versions and a multitude of different myth styles and voices.

See also Amaterasu-ō-mikami.

References and further reading:

Hardacre, Helen. 1989. *Shinto and the State: 1868–1988.* Princeton: Princeton University Press.

Havens, Norman, trans. 1998. *Kami.* Tokyo: Institute for Japanese Culture and Classics, Kokugakuin University.

Kitagawa, Joseph M. 1987. *On Understanding Japanese Religion.* Princeton: Princeton University Press.

KOKŪZŌ-BOSATSU

The boddhisattva of space and of potential. He carries the magical jewel of existence, and in his right hand, a sword of happiness, which represents the bounty of the heavens. Sometimes his right hand is portrayed as being in the position signifying giving. Kokūzō dispenses good luck and wisdom to the body and to the spirit. Invoking his name, one can be assured of the preservation and retention of memory, and thus he is also the boddhisattva of ascetic practice, where long repetitive formulae need to be repeated again and again. By repeating his name, one can retain the entire corpus of the Buddhist Law. Children aged thirteen appeal to Kokūzō for intelligence, and they may receive talismans on April 13 (the day dedicated to Kokūzō) to enhance their intelligence. In his association with the bounty of heaven, Kokūzō is represented by the rain, and by a dragon who brings rain. He is also associated with the planet Venus, which is his celestial manifestation. He was the protective patron of Kōbō Daishi, the founder of Shingon and Japan's foremost Buddhist saint.

See also Jewels; Kōbō Daishi.

References and further reading:

Statler, Oliver. 1984. *Japanese Pilgrimage.* London: Picador.

Visser, Marinus Willem de. 1931. *The Bodhisattva Kokuzō in China and Japan.* Amsterdam: Verhandelingen der Koninklijke Akademie van Wetenschappen. Afdeeling Letterkunde. Nieuwe Reeks.

KOMA-INU

"Korean dogs." They protect most shrine and many temple entrances from the entrance of evil. One male and one female sit on either side of the entrance. They originate from similar lion figures in China, and probably have even earlier antecedents in India. In their protective function they serve for Shintō shrines a

Guardian koma-inu from a shrine (Courtesy of the author)

similar function to that of the Ni-ō guardians at the entrance to Buddhist temples. The Chinese originals were fanciful renditions of Indian traditions of an animal that did not exist in China. The Japanese copies of these, with even less familiarity with the zoological original, were even more fanciful and subsequently labeled "dogs." Because the idea was transmitted from China via Korea, they became Korean dogs.

In most cases, the pair, representing a male (his mouth is open, and he emits the primal first sound, *yo* [Sansk. *om*]) and a female (her mouth is closed, and she emits the final sound, *in* [Sansk. *hum*]) also represent Chinese ideas of the complementarity and opposition between *yang* (male) and *yin* (female) universal principles. The female is often accompanied by her cubs.

These two guardians, with their semicomical pop-eyed expressions, are often confused with *Kara-shishi*, the lion of the lion dance and a favorite image of later (Edo-period) art. The *koma inu*, like the *shishi*, are reputed to be fierce in protecting their young with absolute devotion, and are thus appropriate guardians for shrines.

See also Animals: lions.
References and further reading:
Joly, Henri L. 1967. *Legend in Japanese Art.* Tokyo: Charles E. Tuttle Co.

KONGŌ

The diamond weapon. It represents the *Taizōkyō* (Diamond Sutra), one of the main sutras of Buddhism, the sagacity of which pierces all evil. A great many Buddhist deities carry the *kongō*. It is usually shaped in the form of a short handle with rectangular or hexagonal spikes like chisels sticking out of either end. Those can have one, three, or five prongs. It is used as a symbolic implement, made of bronze, in Tendai and Shingon rituals.

The *kongō* brings together three elements of esoteric and exoteric Buddhism, as it represents thunder, diamond, and a weapon all at once. In esoteric Buddhism—Shingon and Zen—the possibility of sudden illumination was a main feature. The power of the Buddhist Law to pierce, suddenly and forcefully, through ignorance and illusions was a crucial concept, repeated often in iconography, and therefore attached regularly to the character of numerous deities.

Thunder/lightning also stood for pure, immutable truth that could not be obscured, and was thus represented by diamond, the hardest substance known, brilliant with an inner light, and having manifold reflections, just as the Buddha is reflected in all creatures. Many Buddhist thinkers and sects conceived of themselves as fighting an unending battle against ignorance, illusion, and death. The *kongō* in this guise is the perfect weapon that illuminates and shatters illusions.

See also Ni-ō; Shi Tenno; Weapons.
References and further reading:
Frank, Bernard. 1991. *Le pantheon bouddhique au Japon.* Paris: Collections d'Emile Guimet. Reunion des musees nationaux.
Okuda, Kensaku, ed. 1970. *Japan's Ancient Sculpture.* Tokyo: Mainichi Newspapers.

KŌNŌHANASAKUYA-HIME

Daughter of Oyamatsumi-no-kami, a mountain deity; also Ninigi-no-mikoto's wife, and mother to the quarreling deities Hoderi and Ho-ori. Oyamatsumi gave his two daughters, Iwanaga-hime (Long-rock princess—also a play on "long life") and Kōnōhanasakuya-hime (Flower-blossom princess) as wives to Ninigi-no-mikoto after he descended to earth at Himuka. Ninigi returned the older sister, claiming she was ugly. Her ashamed father said, "I gave my two daughters to the divine grandson to ensure his life would last as long as the rocks, and as flourishing as the blossoms of the trees. He has rejected Long-rock princess, and therefore his prosperity and life shall be as evanescent as the blossoming of the trees." From that day on, says the *Kōjiki*'s author, emperors' lives have been short-lived.

Kōnōhanasakuya-hime became pregnant after only one night with her new husband. The suspicious heavenly grandson accused her of infidelity with one of the earth deities, for, after all, how she could have become pregnant after only one night of marriage? Incensed, she set fire to the parturition house, from which she and the baby Hoderi-no-mikoto emerged unscathed. In consequence, she is also identified with Koyasu-gami, the *kami* of easy childbirth (*Ko-yasu* can also be read as "Child-easy"), who in Buddhism was identified with Kishimōjin, because she gave birth safely in the middle of flames and adversity.

Blood, like death, was a major pollutant to the Japanese. In archaic times, a woman would give birth in a special menstruation hut (not an uncommon feature of many simple societies), which would be torn down or burnt after the birth, so as not to pollute the home. A similar house would be built in case of expected death, and for the funeral obsequies, as the story of Amenowakahiko's funeral shows. Kōnōhanasakuya-hime proved her innocence by burning down the parturition house while she was still inside. In doing so, she also became patroness of easy childbirth.

The legend of Kōnōhanasakuya-hime and her husband and sons is a significant one because it marks the nexus of a number of themes. Most significantly, it marks the passage of heavenly descent from deities to mortals (albeit heroic ones). In marrying an earthly deity, the heavenly grandson was assuming some of the qualities of mortals, and, indeed, becoming mortal himself. For the writers of the early compendia and their audiences, this was a necessary step in explaining the mortality of the emperors and the imperial line, who were divine by descent but, nonetheless, subject to mortal frailty, as much of the later parts of both *Kōjiki* and *Nihonshōki* attest. Emperors (and thus the commonality as well) die because of a fatal choice made by Ninigi-no-mikoto, the link between the heavenly deities and the imperial line. Death had been introduced earlier, by Izanami, but Ninigi's choice explains why *all* men, even those who are divinities like the heavenly grandson's descendants, would die in time. The exploits of Kōnōhanasakuya-hime's sons continue this theme, as the boundaries between men, however heroic, and the *kami* are defined and structured.

Kōnōhanasakuya-hime is worshiped as the deity of Mt. Fuji, often under her Buddhist-derived name, Sengen.

> *See also* Hoderi-no-mikoto; Ho-ori-no-mikoto; Kishimōjin; Ninigi-no-mikoto; Sengen.
> *References and further reading:*
> Aston, William G., trans. 1956. *Nihongi.* London: Allen and Unwin.
> Philippi, Donald, trans. and ed. 1968. *Kōjiki.* Tokyo: Tokyo University Press.

KONPIRA-DAIGONGEN

The guardian deity of the Inland Sea (between Shikoku, Kyushu, and Honshu). Thus he is patron of navigators, of fishermen, and of trade, which were important for the region. He is also known as Zōsusan (Standing on an elephant's head, for the shape of the mountain on which his main shrine, Kotohira-gu, stands) and Konpira-ryū-ō (Konpira king of dragons). In Shintō, Konpira has been known as Kotohira since the Meiji restoration. He is one thousand *shaku* (feet) long and has a thousand heads and a thousand arms.

Konpira is one of the major protective deities, and the complex of shrines and temples on Konpira-san, in modern Kagawa (northern Shikoku), is a major pilgrimage site established by Kōbō Daishi.

> *See also* Kōbō Daishi; Kokutai Shintō.
> *References and further reading:*
> Statler, Oliver. 1984. *Japanese Pilgrimage.* London: Picador.

KŌSHIN

See Sarutahiko-no-ō-kami.

KOTANKOR KAMUI (AINU)

The Ainu land, or domain (*kotan*), deity. He is also called Chikap Kamui (owl deity) because he is represented as a great owl. The owl was considered to be the watcher, or master, of the local domain. He ensured that proper rituals were carried out and that, in general, humans and *kamui* behaved themselves in his domain.

Famine struck the land, and wishing to send a message to heaven to inquire about the cause, Kotankor Kamui asked Crow to be a messenger. The instructions and message he gave were rather lengthy. On the third day of the recitation, Crow dozed off, and Kotankor Kamui killed him in anger. Once again the deity asked for a messenger, and this time the Mountain Jay responded. On the fourth day of the recitation, the new messenger dozed off and was killed in turn. Dipper Bird finally appeared and with great respect listened for six days and six nights to the message, then flew off to the heavens.

The messenger returned with the news that the game deity and the fish deity had stopped sending their gifts to humans because the humans had become contemptuous of the gifts received, and did not treat them properly. Kotankor Kamui then taught the humans how to kill fish properly with a fish maul, and, after killing a deer, how to offer their heads some *inau*. The fish and the deer (spirits) therefore come home rejoicing, and the humans do not fear famine.

Kotankor Kamui was considered a dispenser of wealth and success, and in some areas his eyes were said to drop tears of gold or silver.

The hondo crow (*Corvinus coronoides*) and the mountain jay were despised by the Ainu. The Siberian dipper (*Cinculus palasii*) on the other hand was considered a harbinger of good fortune. This myth both serves as an explanatory myth for the relationship with these animals and reemphasizes to the Ainu listeners the importance of making proper offerings, and of the proper ritual behavior that, because of the uncertainties of their lives, tried to ensure their survival.

See also Chikap Kamui.
References and further reading:
Philippi, Donald L., trans. 1979. *Songs of Gods, Songs of Humans: The Epic Tradition of the Ainu.* Princeton: Princeton University Press.

KOTOSHIRONUSHI-NO-KAMI

Son of Ōkuninushi, he is a *kami* of oracular pronouncements. His full name, Yahe-Kotoshironushi, means something like "Eightfold-word master," indicating that his pronouncements were valuable and penetratingly deep. He counseled his father to submit to the rule of the heavenly deities. He is invoked for oracular pronouncements in some shrines to this day.

When the heavenly deities sent Takemikazuchi-no-kami to pave the way for the arrival of the heavenly grandson, he accosted Ōkuninushi with the heavenly deities' demands. The earthly *kami* wished to consult with his two sons. Kotoshironushi agreed to submit to the heavenly deities. However, he clapped his hands magically, caused a green thicket to grow, and became a "hidden" kami.

His withdrawal was not total, however, because his father insisted that he become "vanguard and rearguard" to the heavenly *kami*. In view of his name, this presumably meant that like the scarecrow deity Kuyebiko, the oracular Hitokotonushi, and others, he was an oracular deity whose pronouncements could direct even the paths of the heavenly deities. However, as a hidden *kami* he no longer took part in the activities of the world, reserving his intervention to the provision of divinatory utterances.

> *See also* Divination; Hitokotonushi; Kuyebiko; Ōkuninushi; Takemikazuchi.
> *References and further reading:*
> Philippi, Donald, trans. and ed. 1968. *Kōjiki*. Tokyo: Tokyo University Press.

KOYASU-GAMI

Female deity of childbirth conflated with Kōnōhanasakuya-hime and with Kishimōjin. *See* Kōnōhanasakuya-hime; Kishimōjin.

KUMO

See Animals: spider.

KUNITSU-KAMI

See Earthly *kami*.

KURAOKAMI-NO-KAMI

One of the *kami* that came into being from the blood of Kagutsuchi-no-kami, the fire god killed by Izanagi. Later evidence from the *Manyoshu* (a collection of poems from the Heian era and before) indicates that Kuraokami was a dragon deity responsible for rainfall. He may be identified with Okami-no-kami, a deity who was the father of two princesses who married the descendants of Susano-wo and Ōkuninushi.

> *See also* Ryūjin.
> *References and further reading:*
> Philippi, Donald, trans. and ed. 1968. *Kōjiki*. Tokyo: Tokyo University Press.

KUYEBIKO

The scarecrow deity, who enlightened Ōkuninushi about the parentage and nature of the dwarf *kami* Sukunabikona. This deity, although he is unable to walk, knows all there is to know under the heavens. Kuyebiko may have emerged principally as a *kami* of the rice paddy; however, he is one of the large number of divinatory *kami* who assist both *kami* and humans in their affairs but are otherwise hidden or passive in heavenly and earthly affairs.

> *See also* Divination; Ōkuninushi; Sukunabikona.

References and further reading:
Philippi, Donald, trans. and ed. 1968. *Kōjiki.* Tokyo: Tokyo University Press.

MAREBITO

Visiting deities. Mysterious visitors, often from across the seas or deep in the mountains, are a staple of many Japanese local myths. These strangers, if treated kindly, fed, and entertained, are likely to emerge as donors of important foundation gifts. Sukunabikona, the dwarf *kami* who assisted in the creation of the land, is one such *marebito.* Another is Ebisu, who in his personification as patron of fishermen is worshiped as a visiting deity. The ancestors who return to visit the household during the *bon* season in midsummer are *marebito* as well. In all cases, great importance is to be placed on treating these powerful beings with respect, offering them food, and, after they have visited for a while, sending them back to their original homes across the sea or in the mountains.

The idea of visiting deities is a reflection of the lives the peasantry led throughout much of Japan's history and prehistory. Isolated by mountain barriers in small, steep river valleys, many farmers and other producers had little, if any, contact with the outside world. Outside visitors were therefore regarded with a mixture of suspicion (an outsider could be a threat, a robber, or a tax gatherer) mingled with respect (outsiders were often powerful and dangerous) and a touch of hope (visiting doctors and *kebozu* were often the only providers of news, medicine, and emotional palliatives). Moreover, for the peasants the changes of seasons were personalized in the form of the complementary Ta-no-kami/Yama-no-kami deities. The Ta-no-kami's visits in the spring were solicited and eased because it was the Ta-no-kami who provided food in the fields. It was thus crucial to maintain an attitude of correctness in dealing with strangers who might be tempted otherwise to harm one.

The myth of the visiting stranger with hidden powers emerges in the twentieth century as well. One of the longest-running television series in Japan has been *Mito Komon,* which tells the story of a retired elderly daimyō (lord) who travels incognito throughout Japan in the eighteenth century, dispensing justice, rewards, and punishments. Japan's dealings with foreigners can be viewed as an extension of the *marebito* myth. Foreign specialists in nineteenth-century Japan were brought to dispense gifts—western science and technology—and after having been feasted and laden with gifts, were sent back to their homeland. Until a decade ago, many Japanese would have been horrified at the idea of foreigners settling permanently in Japan. Many corporations now practice the *marabito* myth in similar ways, bringing in specialists for brief periods of time, feasting them royally, then sending them back home after extracting gifts of information and knowledge. Whether this is a conscious use of the *marebito* myth or an unconscious echoing of a traditional cultural practice is difficult to determine.

See also Ebisu; Sukunabikona; Underworld; *Yama-uba.*

References and further reading:

Hori, Ichiro. 1968. *Folk Religion in Japan.* Chicago: Chicago University Press.

Jones, Hazel J. 1980. *Live Machines: Hired Foreigners and Meiji Japan.* Tenterden: Paul Norbury Publications.

Sakurada, Katsunori. 1980 (1963). "The Ebisu-Gami in a Fishing Village." In *Studies in Japanese Folklore,* edited by R. Dorson. New York: Arno Press, pp. 122–132.

Yoshida, Teigo. 1981. "The Stranger as God: The Place of the Outsider in Japanese Folk Religion." *Ethnology* 20 (2): 87–99.

MARISHI-TEN

One of the seven sages who have been placed into the sky as the stars of the Great Dipper. Marishi-ten himself is the embodiment of the rays of light that precede the sunrise, in other words, the harbinger of Dainichi Nyōrai. Marishi-ten, who is sometimes portrayed as male, sometimes as female, is also a patron of warriors. S/he is portrayed riding on a wild boar, and sometimes is portrayed as having three heads, one of them a pig's face. The wild boar represents audacious advance without fear, a desirable quality for a warrior. Marishi-ten is armored, has six hands, and is armed with a sword, trident, and bow and arrow. In particular s/he is patron god of archers. The grave of the forty-seven *rōnin* of the *Chūshingura* in Sengaku-ji temple in Tokyo is watched over by a figure of Marishi-ten. S/he was originally the Hindu warrior-god Indra, becoming a Buddhist figure of protection soon after the emergence of Buddhism as an organized religion.

See also Chūshingura; Dainichi Nyōrai.

References and further reading:

Frank, Bernard. 1991. *Le pantheon bouddhique au Japon.* Paris: Collections d'Emile Guimet. Reunion des musees nationaux.

MIROKU-BOSATSU

The boddhisattva of the future (Sanskrit: *Maitreya*). The future Buddha is to rise as the savior once the time is ripe. In this view, Shakyamuni, the historical Buddha, was one of a long chain of Buddhas extending through past ages. Having brought the way of enlightenment to humankind, he departed to his own nirvana. In some Buddhist schools, however, this posed a problem of salvation in later ages. The coming of the boddhisattva Miroku solves this problem by promising the possibility of salvation in the future. The figure of Miroku in Japanese thought is close to that of a messiah in European thought, promising the possibility of salvation in this world, as opposed, for example, to Amida, who promises salvation in the Pure Land in the afterlife.

Miroku is popularly associated with the figure of Hōtei, one of the Shichi Fukujin. He is thus represented as an obese laughing monk with pendant ear lobes, carrying an enormous sack from which he dispenses gifts.

See also Amida Nyōrai; Hōtei; Shichi Fukujin.

References and further reading:

Frank, Bernard. 1991. *Le pantheon bouddhique au Japon.* Paris: Collections d'Emile Guimet. Reunion des musees nationaux.

Getty, Alice. 1988. *The Gods of Northern Buddhism.* New York: Dover Publications.

Joly, Henri L. 1967. *Legend in Japanese Art.* Tokyo: Charles E. Tuttle Co.

MIRROR

The *kagami* (traditional mirror) was a metal disk—usually of bronze or silver—with a high polish. The mirror first appears as the device by which Amaterasu-ō-mikami was lured from her cave. Mirrors were used in divination as well as in sorcery, and in one myth a court nobleman threw his mirror overboard as a sacrifice to the deities during a storm that threatened to capsize his ship, indicating how precious these objects were.

A mirror forms part of the Japanese imperial regalia, representing the *mitama* (spirit) of the deity. Its ritual color is white, and many shrines are decorated with streamers of this color.

"Magical" mirrors are still in existence. Made of bronze, they will reflect an image of Kannon carved into the *back* of the object. They were considered of great merit and high value because they reflected the mercy of Kannon's existence. The incision of the image on the *back* of the bronze mirror produces concoidal blemishes, invisible to the eye, on the polished *front* of the mirror. When bright light is reflected off the polished surface, these invisible blemishes cause a ghostly image in the reflection. This can be quite startling and satisfyingly mysterious even if the viewer *does* know the secret.

See also Jewels; Kannon; Swords.

References and further reading:

Aston, William George. 1905. *Shinto: The Way of the Gods.* London: Longmans, Green, and Co.

Herbert, Jean. 1967. *Shinto—at the Fountain Head of Japan.* London: George Allen and Unwin Ltd.

MIYAZU-HIME

One of Yamato-takeru's wives. On his trip to subdue the East he passed by her house in Owari and promised to marry her. He left the sword Kusanagi in her keeping before attempting to capture the *kami* of Mt. Ibuki, where he was mortally wounded.

> *See also* Swords; Yamato-takeru.
> *References and further reading:*
> Aston, William G., trans. 1956. *Nihongi.* London: Allen and Unwin.
> Philippi, Donald, trans. and ed. 1968. *Kōjiki.* Tokyo: Tokyo University Press.

MIZUHAME-NO-MIKOTO

A water *kami*, last-born deity of Izanami, the creatrix. Distressed for humans after giving birth to the fire god, Kagutsuchi-no-kami, she felt mercy for humankind and so gave birth to four more offspring: Mizuhame, the clay princess, the gourd, and the water reed. These would pacify the fire god if he became rambunctious and evil hearted.

> *See also* Izanami and Izanagi; Kagutsuchi-no-kami.
> *References and further reading:*
> Bock, Felicia Gressitt, trans. and intro. 1970. *Engi-shiki: Procedures of the Engi Era, Books I-V.* Tokyo: Sophia University. Monumenta Nipponica Monographs.

MONJU-BOSATSU

The boddhisattva of sagacity and of the word. Words and thought are both particularly powerful concepts in Buddhist thought. He is the guardian of the words that make up the Buddhist canon. As such, he is particularly well disposed toward those engaged in the effort of study, and temples to Monju-bosatsu (e.g., in Yamadera in Yamagata prefecture) are often visited by those taking university entrance exams. Thus he may be identified with Tenjin, the *kami* of scholarship. He is also associated with the more severe-looking Daitoku-bosatsu.

Monju-bosatsu is often pictured as a young infant carrying in his left hand a scroll and in his right an upright naked sword, with which one can defeat the passions that interfere with studies. He rides a *shishi* lion, a symbol of majesty and rule and the icon of protectiveness toward the young. The *shishi*, like Monju, loves and protects its young but also tests them severely.

> *See also* Animals: *shishi*; Daitoku Myō-ō (-bosatsu); Tenjin.
> *References and further reading:*
> Frank, Bernard. 1991. *Le pantheon bouddhique au Japon.* Paris: Collections d'Emile Guimet. Reunion des musees nationaux.
> Getty, Alice. 1988. *The Gods of Northern Buddhism.* New York: Dover Publications.
> Joly, Henri L. 1967. *Legend in Japanese Art.* Tokyo: Charles E. Tuttle Co.

MOSHIRIKARA KAMUI (AINU)

Creator and preparer of the earth for human habitation. Commissioned by Kandakoro Kamui, he built the features of the land and the sea. Like Kandakoro, Moshirikara plays little part in later myths. Once the world has been established, there is no great need for this creative principle.

> *See also* Kandakoro Kamui.
> *References and further reading:*
> Munro, Neil Gordon. 1962. *Ainu Creed and Cult.* London: Routledge and Kegan
>   Paul; London and New York: K. Paul International, distributed by Columbia
>   University Press, 1995.

MOUNTAINS

Mountains and rivers were the most important elements in the mythological landscape, and both mythical and real mountains feature heavily in Japanese myths.

For archaic Japanese, mountains were sacred. Not only were they the abode of gods, but they were the personification of gods as well. Most such famous mountains, whether the majestic sole peak of Mt. Fuji or the lower hill formations that became mountains in popular imagination, were forbidden places. When a shrine was erected to a deity in that mountain, the mountain was generally put off limits, and the shrine was erected at its base. Gradually some of those rules were relaxed. The feeling that mountains were sacred and the abode of the gods received a reinforcement from Buddhism, for which Mt. Meru was a physical embodiment of Buddhist Law.

In Shintō, two of the most prominent features of Takamagahara, the home of the heavenly deities, are two mountains ranges, one that produces iron, the other that produces ritual resources: Both ritual and iron were the source of majesty and rule in archaic Japan. Other mountains feature prominently in myths as the abodes of deities, both heavenly and earthly. Mt. Fuji is the embodiment and home to a female *kami*, Kōnōhanasakuya-hime, also known as Sengen. Other deities, some named, others unnamed, lived in or on mountains, which they sometimes defended with zeal, as the story of Yamato-takeru's death at Mt. Ibuki shows.

For Buddhism there was only one major mythical mountain—Mt. Meru (Sumeru. Shumisen in Japanese)—all other mountains were emblematic of that one prominence. This was not only a mythical *place* but, more important, a symbolic representation of the cosmos as a whole, of the place of humans, gods, and Buddhas within it. Its flanks were guarded by armies of gods and demons commanded by four generals (the Shi Tenno) who conveyed blessings and defended the approaches of the mountain with equal zeal. And at its peak resided the Buddhas,

Mt. Fuji, personification of Sengen, seen from afar. (A. Tovy/ArkReligion.com)

each in his own paradise. The mountain could be climbed by those individuals determined and bold enough, and, of course, possessing a pure heart. Thus Mt. Meru represented the individual's struggle, passing through layers of reality and experience, to become a Buddha. The image of pilgrimage *up* a mountain was thus an essential element in the practice of Buddhism. When Buddhism was imported into Japan, this particular element was completely in tune with Japanese native attitudes. Many sacred mountains thus became sites of pilgrimage as people followed both Buddhist and Shintō devotions, or mixed them into Ryōbu Shintō.

The syncretic beliefs espoused by theologians such as Kōbō Daishi brought mountains into further prominence. A new form of deity was born—*gongen*—deities of particular mountain locations that were protective deities with a mixed Shintō-Buddhist coloring.

See also *Gongen;* Kōnōhanasakuya-hime; Shi Tenno; Shumisen; Takamagahara.
References and further reading:
Blacker, Carmen. 1975. *The Catalpa Bow.* London: George Allen and Unwinn Ltd.

Earhart, H. Byron. 1970. *A Religious Study of the Mount Haguro Sect of Shugendo.* Tokyo: Sophia University Press.

Grapard, Allan. 1982. "Flying Mountains and Walkers of Emptiness: Toward a Definition of Sacred Space in Japanese Religion." *History of Religions* 20: 195–221.

Hori, Ichiro. 1968. *Folk Religion in Japan.* Chicago: Chicago University Press.

MYŌGEN-BOSATSU

The polar star, one of the seven celestial sages of the Big Dipper constellation. He regulates the seasons and the stars. The veneration of Myōgen is highly syncretic. He has characteristics borrowed from Indian, Chinese, and Japanese beliefs as regulator of the heavens in the same way that the emperor is regulator of the earth. Myōgen is perceived as both a Buddhist and a Shintō deity. He is generally portrayed in the form of a youth in armor, resting on a sword, his head surrounded by the nimbus of the seven celestial sages. He rides a peculiar beast composed of an intertwined serpent and turtle. These two represent the world in total, longevity, and health. He is a warrior, and was often appealed to on the eve of battle.

References and further reading:

Frank, Bernard. 1991. *Le pantheon bouddhique au Japon.* Paris: Collections d'Emile Guimet. Reunion des musees nationaux.

NAI-NO-KAMI

Deity of earthquakes. Nai-no-kami is the formal Shintō aspect of the popular personification of earthquakes, Namazu.

See also Namazu.

References and further reading:

Ouwehand, Cornelius. 1964. *Namazu-e and Their Themes: An Interpretative Approach to Some Aspects of Japanese Religion.* Leiden, the Netherlands: E. J. Brill.

NAMAZU

A giant catfish that lives under the earth. When it swims through the bowels of the world, it brings about earthquakes. Takemikazuchi-no-mikoto (Kashima Daimyōjin) drove the *kaname-ishi* stone through the earth to pin the fish's head in place. The top of the stone is still visible at the Kashima shrine in Hitachi (Ibaragi prefecture). It is a rounded rock, 16 inches or so in diameter and projecting 6 inches above the ground, with a concave upper surface, but it goes down deep into the earth. A popular saying is, *"Yurugu tomo yomoya nukeji no kaname-ishi Kashima no kami no aran kagiri wa."* (Even if the earth moves, have no fear, for the Kashima *kami* holds the *kaname-ishi* in place; Ouwehand 1964).

Namazu and the thunder deity are feared, but they also bring material wealth. The myth of the catfish became particularly prevalent during the Edo period when economic conditions threatened the lives of poor people. Namazu was the cause of earthquakes, which, though they caused trouble and grief to all, caused *more* trouble and grief to the rich—who had more to lose—and might bring relief to the poor, who could escape their harsh lives in the periods of anarchy that followed earthquakes. Namazu thus also represented, at least for the poor (of whom there were many), the *yo-naoshi*, the renewal of the world, when everything turns topsy-turvy and the poor shall inherit the gold of the rich. When Kashima Daimyōjin travels to Izumo to attend the annual conference of the gods on the tenth month, Namazu may exploit this absence and cause earthquakes.

The association of Namazu with wealth and with its wandering over the earth in the absence of the other deities had brought about a parallelism, even an identity, between Namazu and the deity Ebisu, who also does not heed the call to the *kami* assembly in Izumo. Though Namazu often appears in a semihuman form, usually one that predicts, or causes, personal misfortune (in which case one needs to appeal to the Kashima *kami* to ensure his expulsion), he *might*, like Ebisu, also provide wealth.

Namazu gives, or at least lends, riches, if one knows how to solicit him, and if one behaves properly: In many places in Japan there are *kuramaya* (cave storehouses) where one can borrow lacquer bowls or other utensils for use, provided they are returned. These are the property of a local deity, often identified with Namazu. But woe if the utensils are not returned: The loan process as well as the good that the utensils bring terminates immediately.

The thunder (Takemikazuchi) and earthquake (Namazu) deities are related and often refer to one another as "colleagues," or members of the same group. Earthquakes are thus thunder that bides its time under the earth, as can be seen from the eight thunder gods who emerged from the body of the dead Izanami. Another earthquake deity, Nai-no-kami, was worshiped beginning in the seventh century and was later identified with Namazu. During the Meiji period, attempts were made to personify Nai-no-kami as a separate Shintō earthquake deity.

See also Ebisu; Takemikazuchi-no-kami; Thunder Deities.

References and further reading:
Joly, Henri L. 1967. *Legend in Japanese Art.* Tokyo: Charles E. Tuttle Co.
Ouwehand, Cornelius. 1964. *Namazu-e and Their Themes: An Interpretative Approach to Some Aspects of Japanese Religion.* Leiden, the Netherlands: E. J. Brill.

NATIONAL SHINTŌ
See Kokka-Shintō.

NIHONJIN-RON
The special unique qualities of the Japanese people. Modern myth.
See Japanese Uniqueness.

NINIGI-NO-MIKOTO
Grandson of Amaterasu-ō-mikami and founder of the imperial house. Ninigi-no-mikoto, known as the heavenly grandson, was charged with assuming rule over the Central Land of the Reed Plains, which under Ōkuninushi's governance had become troubled and disordered. He received the position after his father had abdicated in his favor. Five future clan heads, and several deities, some armed, were assigned as his assistants; they eventually became the *ujigami* (ancestral deities) of several clans. This myth, argue many scholars, may well be an account of the struggle between the Yamato and other nations (and traditions) for control of the Japanese islands.

Ninigi-no-mikoto (his full name is given as Amē-Nigishi-Kuninigishi-Amatsu-hiko-no-ninigi-no-mikoto) was given three items as symbols of his rank and mission and as *shintai* (objects of worship). These were the string of myriad *magatama* jewels, the mirror that drew Amaterasu from her cave, and the sword Kusanagi that Susano-wo had cut from the tail of the eight-headed serpent and given Amaterasu in apology for his sinful acts. In his conquest, Ninigi was guided by Sarutahiko-no-kami, and advised by Ama-no-uzume. He settled in Himuka on the island of Kyushu. Besides the story of his descent from heaven, which constituted a charter for the Yamato ruling house in its conquest of Japan—most notably of its most serious rivals in Izumo—Ninigi features in two other myths concerning his spouse and children, whose significance is that they mark the beginning of the process of separation between the deities and the emperors, their descendants.

Ninigi-no-mikoto met Kōnōhanasakuya-hime and proposed marriage. Her father, the earth-mountain *kami* Oyamatsumi-no-kami, agreed, and sent the bride rich bridal gifts along with Kōnōhanasakuya-hime's ugly older sister as second bride. Ninigi sent the older ugly bride back and was upbraided by his father-in-law, who explained that the elder sister brought longevity and steadfastness, the younger flourishing like blossoms. Because Ninigi had sent the elder back, the lives of the children of the heavenly deities would be brilliant but short. As a consequence, the emperors' lives have generally been short.

The day after the wedding, Kōnōhanasakuya-hime announced she was pregnant. Ninigi suspected the child was not his. To counter that, his wife set the birth-sequestration hut aflame after sealing the entrances. If the child was of divine descent, she announced, it would survive, but if it were the child of an earthly deity, it would perish. The child, Hoderi-no-mikoto, survived the flames.

In these myths the *Kōjiki* and *Nihonshōki* authors were explaining the paradox of the avowed divinity of the emperors and their very clearly human nature. In fact, the latter halves of both books are a record of not-so-glorious lives of a series of emperors, their assignations, plots against them, murders, and other events: a mundane record of petty rulers that could be found in any culture. The authors were in effect saying that *notwithstanding* this evidence of humanity and mortality, the rulers of Japan were descended from a line of deities, and were in fact deities themselves. The combination of the two messages—political superiority and its charter, and the divinity/humanity paradox—were at the basis of the Japanese state, and survived as its political manifesto to World War II and beyond. It is this myth, perhaps more than any other, which allows the Japanese to think of their emperor—and by extension, of the Japanese state and the Japanese people—as a unified, heaven-descended, yet clearly human, group of people.

> **See also** Amaterasu-ō-mikami; Divine Descent; Divine Rulership; Izumo; Kōnōhanasakuya-hime; Ōkuninushi; Oyamatsumi-no-kami; Sarutahiko-no-kami; Yamato.

> **References and further reading:**
> Aston, William G., trans. 1956. *Nihongi.* London: Allen and Unwin.
> Philippi, Donald, trans. and ed. 1968. *Kōjiki.* Tokyo: Tokyo University Press.

NI-Ō

Two giant figures who are protectors of sacred precincts positioned at the entrance to many shrines and temples. They are otherwise known as *Kongō-rikishi* (Thunderbolt strongman), and shown, seminude, muscles bulging, and faces in terrifying rictuses, on either side of a temple's entrance. They are sometimes said to be two demons who became the zealous disciples and self-appointed bodyguards of the Buddha. One displays a hand-gesture signifying pacification of enemies. His mouth is open, uttering the syllable *om* (the first word; the alpha) and named Misshaku (also identified with Aizen Myō-ō). The other, Kongō (identified with Fudō Myō-ō), may hold a *kongō* (thunderbolt weapon), and his mouth is closed as he utters the syllable *hum* (the final word; the omega).

Many centuries ago a certain king's wives bore him sons after word of the Buddha's preaching had reached his ears. The first wife bore a thousand sons, whom the king wished to have attain perfect enlightenment. The second bore only two sons. One of these two vowed to turn the Wheel of the Law for his thousand brothers; the other vowed to protect the first while he worked. The first was Misshaku, the second Kongō. The Ni-ō represent the duality and union

Misshaku, a ferocious temple Ni-ō guardian, in threatening posture (T. Bognar/ArkReligion.com)

of the material and spiritual, and are in reality (say Buddhist believers) a single god known as Misshakukongō who lives on Mt. Meru and can manifest himself in myriad ways. In effect he is the material manifestation of Dainichi Nyōrai.

The Ni-ō are very popular figures. They have the power to protect babies as well as offering protection against thieves. Because they are barefoot, many people offer them oversized straw sandals to protect their feet. *Rikishi*, strongman wrestlers, have been important ritually in Japan since the Nara period. Sacred wrestling bouts were organized during that period and continue to this day in the tradition of Ōzumo (grand sumo). Wrestlers and wrestling are considered sacred activities, and sumo bouts take place in a pavilion considered a Shintō shrine under the auspices of an umpire dressed in clothes similar to a Shintō priest's. As can be seen from the competition between Amaterasu and Susano-wo, wrestling (along with archery) was a means for both divination and trial by combat. In fact the *shiki* leg movements and hand-clapping that are performed by all sumo wrestlers before a bout are echoes of the ritual Amaterasu carried out before her bout with her brother. It is not surprising to see, therefore, that the idea of a wrestler being in some way sacred has permeated Japanese Buddhism as well. In modern Japan some of this feeling still persists at a popular level: *rikishi* (a colloquial term nowadays for sumo wrestlers) are in great demand during *Setsubun* rituals, when *oni* are exorcised from Japanese houses in midwinter.

See also Amaterasu-ō-mikami; *Kongō*; Oni; Susano-wo
References and further reading:
Cuyler, P. L. 1985. *Sumo: From Rite to Sport.* Tokyo: Weatherhill.

NUSAKORO KAMUI (AINU)

The "community-founding" *kamui*, he represents the dead and is sometimes identified with his brother, Kinashut Kamui, the snake deity. As his name indicates, he is the spirit, and possibly the origin, of *nusa* (*inau*), the shaving-tipped wands that represent the *kamui* in any ritual. He is assisted by Yushkep Kamui, the spider. Nusakoro Kamui is sometimes said to be a female deity. In either case, one of the major responsibilities of this deity is to preserve the row of *inau* arranged in a sort of fence outside the house. This is where the *kamui* came to talk and gossip.

Nusa played an important role in the ritual lives of the Ainu, and like almost all important objects it was deified. Nusakoro Kamui is a messenger to the gods, expressing the Ainu people's admiration and reverence, and carrying to the gods the people's gifts of wine, lacquer boxes, and other riches. In practice, different *inau* were carved to represent/serve as messengers to individual gods. Perhaps more than any other god except Kamui Fuchi, Nusakoro Kamui represents the very strong interdependence between the Ainu and their gods and surroundings.

See also Kinashut Kamui; Kamui Fuchi; Yushkep Kamui.
References and further reading:
Munro, Neil Gordon. 1962. *Ainu Creed and Cult.* London: Routledge and Kegan Paul; London and New York: K. Paul International, distributed by Columbia University Press, 1995.
Ohnuki-Tierney, Emiko. 1974. *The Ainu of the Northwest Coast of Southern Sakhalin.* New York: Holt, Rinehart, and Winston.
Philippi, Donald L., trans. 1979. *Songs of Gods, Songs of Humans: The Epic Tradition of the Ainu.* Princeton: Princeton University Press.

ŌGETSUHIME
See Food Deities.

OKAMUTSUMI-NO-MIKOTO

A *kami* responsible for protection of humankind from painful suffering and pressing troubles. When Izanagi was pursued by Izanami in the underworld, he came upon three peaches. The peaches, representing life, helped him ward off the one thousand five hundred warriors and the eight thunder-snake deities sent after him. In gratitude he deified them as Okamutsumi-no-mikoto and bid this *kami* to protect humankind.

The idea of the peaches may well be an intrusion from a scholar with Chinese learning. Certainly the idea of peaches as protectors and bearers of life (as well as the fruit itself) was introduced from China fairly early in the relations between the two cultures. The fruit in this case, as in many others, is apposite. One of the main themes evident in the Izanagi and Izanami theory, as well as in the issue of food—see for example Ukemochi-no-kami—is the seeming contradiction between the purity of food (and of men) on the one hand, and the impurity of dirt (and of women) on the other. The authors of this myth wanted to point out the duality implicit in the relationship between life and death—an idea that is continued as Izanami pursues Izanagi.

See also Izanagi and Izanami; Ukemochi-no-kami; Yōmi.
References and further reading:
Aston, William G., trans. 1956. *Nihongi.* London: Allen and Unwin.
Philippi, Donald, trans. and ed. 1968. *Kōjiki.* Tokyo: Tokyo University Press.

OKIKURMI (AINU)

Ainu culture hero who features in many myths as an extremely pious powerful man who performs all the rituals, or who calls on the *kamui* for assistance for his people. Okikurmi is wise and good, but he has a counterpart, Samai-unkur, the chieftain of a neighboring village, who is stupid, careless, and weak. The acts of the two are often counterpoised, demonstrating the proper reverential way of dealing with the *kamui*. Although Okikurmi performs the right rituals and is always respectful toward the *kamui*, Samai-unkur, either through stupidity or malevolence, often forgets, or does not perform the right rituals, and brings about calamities on his people. Several myths recount how Okikurmi and Samai-unkur went fishing. In one such, they are met by the North Wind goddess, who dances up a storm. Samai-unkur dies, but Okikurmi, knowing the proper magic, procured a magical bow and arrow, and shoots the deity dead. In another, they harpoon a swordfish that drags their boat across the waves for many days and nights. Again, the weak and indecisive Samai-unkur dies, but the hero knows the magic of the harpoon, curses the fish, then lets him go. The sword-fish dies of the curse and is washed upon the beach, where he is eaten by foxes and unclean crows, instead of being treated royally and enjoying the ritual send-off deities-as-prey are entitled to. In contrast, a tree goddess, entreated properly by Okikurmi, allows herself to be made into a boat that conducts many glorious trading voyages to the Japanese. Once old and broken, the boat is dismissed ritually together with the presents she has been instrumental in acquiring.

Okikurmi also features in myths as a lone hero, succeeding either by wit or agility. In one myth, Okikurmi tricked a *sak-somo-ayep* (a dragon, or snake god, who hates the cold; Ainu dragons live in lakes, and their mere stench is sufficient to kill other beings) into going upriver to its source, where there would be a bride waiting for him. The dragon followed the instructions, but instead of finding a fine house and a waiting bride, as was promised, he found himself in a hornets' nest, where he was stung to death. In another, rather similar myth, Okikurmi appears to an *ararush* (evil monster bear) who has been hoarding the fish and the game on his own drying racks. The hero charms the bear with an *inau* and tells him to leave and find a place over the sea where others of the bear's kind are feasting. The *ararush* does so, dying of hunger when he reaches his objective and finds a rocky shore rather than a paradise. Okikurmi breaks the bear's storehouses and drying racks, releasing the game and fish there, thus allowing them to repopulate the rivers and forests and avert an Ainu famine. On another occasion, Okikurmi ambushes the ferocious man-eating *furi* bird. He hides all the people in the forest, walking about on the beach by himself. When the *furi* stoops, Okikurmi dodges, and the *furi* bird buries itself in the sand, its beak impaling the bottom of the earth. The hero then rushes up and beats the monster to death.

The corpus of Okikurmi myths represents the ideal Ainu man: Tough and able to stand privation, he knows magic and is able to overcome even the most powerful opponents by his knowledge or his cleverness. Above all, Okikurmi myths reiterate the fundamental basis of Ainu life: the need to accommodate to nature by using the proper ritual observances.

See also Ae-oina Kamui.

References and further reading:
Philippi, Donald L., trans. 1979. *Songs of Gods, Songs of Humans: The Epic Tradition of the Ainu.* Princeton: Princeton University Press.

ŌKUNINUSHI

"Master of the land," major earthly *kami,* and concurrently the *kami* of magic and medicine. He is referred to by one of four names in addition to his formal one: Onamuji-no-kami (Possessor of the great name or Possessor of the great land), Ashiharahikō-wo-no-kami (Prince of the reed plain), Yachihokō-no-kami (Eight-thousand spears deity), and Utsushikunitama-no-kami (Spirit deity of the mortal world). The names indicate how significant this *kami* is in Japanese mythology.

A sixth-generation descendant of Susano-wo, he was used by his eighty brothers as servant when they set out to woo Yagami-hime, the beauty of Inaba. At Cape Kēta, the eighty brothers found a badly flayed rabbit and played a cruel joke on him, telling him that if he bathed in saltwater, his skin would heal. Ōkuninushi, following his brothers with the baggage, found the suffering rabbit and advised it to bathe in river water and roll in the pollen of river grass to restore its pelt. Yagami-hime refused the eighty brothers and instead married Ōkuninushi, though she abandoned him and their child when he promoted another to chief wife later in the myth.

At Mt. Tema, the eighty brother deities, seeking Ōkuninushi's life, ordered him to ambush a red boar. Heating a large rock to red-hot, they rolled it down the slope. When he caught the rock, thinking it was the boar, Ōkuninushi was burned to death. His mother ascended to heaven and begged Kamimusubi-no-mikoto to revive him. Kisagai-hime and Umugi-hime (both names of shellfish) restored Ōkuninushi to life at her orders by shaving some of their shell and washing him in clear water. His brothers then crushed him to death in a tree, whereupon he was revived once more by his mother. Ōkuninushi fled for advice to Susano-wo. Arriving at Susano-wo's hall he met Suseri-hime, Susano-wo's daughter, and married her. Susano-wo, apparently incensed by Ōkuninushi's breach of manners (the young couple had not solicited the father's permission) or wishing to test the mettle of his new son-in-law, bid him sleep in a room with snakes, then of centipedes and bees. Each time the hero was saved by his new wife. Susano-wo tried burning Ōkuninushi in a field, but he was saved by a mouse. Ōkuninushi then entered Susano-wo's house and was told to comb his father-in-law's hair for lice (a mark of respect and intimacy). Instead of lice he found centipedes (poisonous creatures feared as causes of death). His wife saved him once again, giving him nuts and red clay that he chewed and spat out, causing Susano-wo to believe that Ōkuninushi was biting the centipedes and spitting them out in an act of great filial piety, and an indication of his immunity to poison. When Susano-wo fell asleep, Ōkuninushi tied his father-in-law's hair to the rafters, blocked the door with a boulder, and, taking his new wife on his back, made his escape.

During his escape he stole the life sword, Ikutachi, and the life bow-and-arrows, Ikuyumiya. But when he tried to steal the jeweled heavenly harp, Amēnonōri-gōtō, it brushed against a tree and woke Susano-wo up. The angered victim tried to pursue the fleeing couple, but brought his house down upon himself when his hair pulled down the rafters. Eventually, after being frustrated by his daughter's advice to her husband, Susano-wo gave up at Yomotsu Hiruzaka, the pass from Yōmi to Izumo (where Izanami had been blocked in pursuit much earlier). He bade Ōkuninushi make Suseri-hime his chief wife, subdue his brothers with the stolen weapons, and rule between heaven and earth. This Ōkuninushi did, after which he completed the labor of creating the land, assisted by the dwarf deity Sukunabikona.

Following the construction of his great hall, Ōkuninushi, as his name (Master of the land) implies, ruled the earth until the heavenly deities, concerned about the anarchy of his rule, sent down representatives to rule the earth. The first two attempts failed, and Ōkuninushi enticed the first two representatives, falling victim only to the third, Takemikazuchi-no-kami (in the *Nihonshōki*, accompanied by Futsumitama-no-kami), who bested Ōkuninushi's son in a wrestling match. Ōkuninushi agreed to the takeover, but only after he had been promised a great hall, special foods cooked on a special fire, and access directly to heaven via the heavenly boat. Not mentioned in the formal histories, but accepted by most Japanese, is the fact that the *kami* from all over Japan (with two notable exceptions, Ebisu and Namazu) convene at Izumo Taisha (a shrine on the site of Ōkuninushi's hall, and considered its mundane counterpart) to report on the passed year's events and discuss the fate of the people.

There is some internal evidence to suggest that the story of Ōkuninushi is an alternative myth to the Yamato creation myth. It is conceivable, suggest a number of scholars, that the Yamato state cult of Amaterasu and the Izumo state cult of Ōkuninushi were in competition. The Izumo strategy appears to have been a set of extensive marital alliances with neighboring states, reflected in the Ōkuninushi myth. With the absorption of the Izumo state by the Yamato state to its east, both myths were combined, carefully positioning the Yamato cult deities as sky deities (and thus superior) and the Izumo deities as more subordinate earth deities. This is strongly evident in the myth of the divine rulership of the land.

Ōkuninushi himself remains a powerful figure. Not only did he create the land, completing the work started by Izanagi and Izanami, but he is also a bridge between the dead and the living, having experienced both states. Unsurprisingly, he is able to move freely between the lands of the living and those of the dead, where Susano-wo rules. The parallel of his escape from Susano-wo and Izanagi's escape from Izanami is probably no coincidence. His immunity to poison and his creative powers make him also a deity of magic and wizardry. As a wizard he is able, unlike others, to travel freely between the two domains of the living and the dead and is even able, unlike Izanagi, to retrieve wealth and a wife from the land of the dead. Moreover, the weapons he stole give him the power to both give and deny life, just as his possession of Amēnonōri-gōtō (the jeweled heavenly harp: another item of loot) presumably indicates his control and power over men and deities, a power that was accorded to music in Japan from early times. Even today, most formal shrine rituals include music, which is supposed to call the deities, entertain, and soothe them.

> **See also** Amaterasu-ō-mikami; Animals: rabbit; Divine Rulership; Sukunabikona; Susano-wo; Weapons: bow.
>
> **References and further reading:**
> Aston, William G., trans. 1956. *Nihongi*. London: Allen and Unwin.
> Kubota, Hideki, and Inoue Hiroko. 1995. *Tune of the Yakumo-Goto: Myth and the Japanese Spirit*. Nishinomiya: Yakumo-goto Reminiscence Society.
> Philippi, Donald, trans. and ed. 1968. *Kōjiki*. Tokyo: Tokyo University Press.

ONI

Demons in the Buddhist pantheon. They constitute one of the six orders of life in Buddhist cosmology. They received less dangerous, more amusing character-istics in popular imagination and art when they were brought to Japan. Japanese *oni* are generally pictured as red, green, or blue humanoids, generally naked but for a loincloth. They generally have two short horns (sometimes one) growing from between their unkempt locks of hair. Their hands and feet are clawed, and they often carry a *tetsubō*, a hexagonal club, as a weapon. They serve in Jigoku under Emma-ō to punish wrongdoers who have been sentenced to hell to expi-ate their sins.

They can and do inhabit the mundane earth, and can be expelled on Setsubun (second day, second month) by a ritual still carried out today: beans are thrown at the home with the invocation *Oni wa soto, fuku wa uchi* (Demons out, good luck in), preferably by a strong man, such as a *rikishi* (sumo wrestler). At other times Shōki, a demon-quelling deity, may be called upon to exercise his function and dispel the demons, who hide from him under furniture and in boxes.

Not intrinsically evil, *oni* are wrathful and uncontrolled, may be anthro-pophagous, and bring about calamities to the land. They can, however, be paci-fied using spells or Buddhist incantations, and they can even become

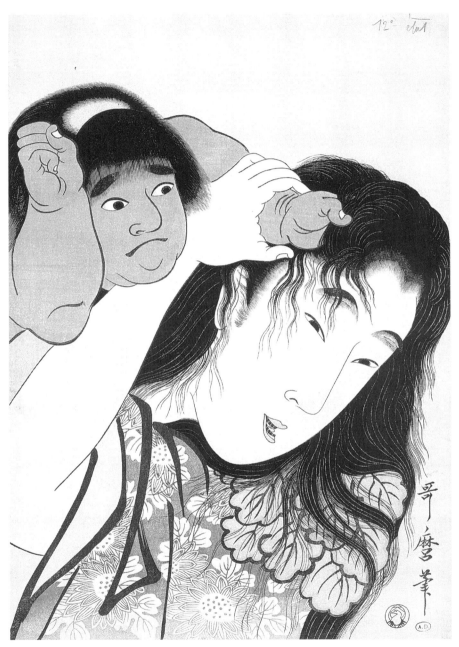

Yamauba and Kintaro, popular Japanese folklore characters, ukiyo-e print, Edo period, late 18th century. (The Art Archive/Bibliothèque des Arts Décoratifs Paris/Gianni Dagli Orti)

boddhisatvas or *kami*. Some become the servants of holy men, such as the two *oni* who served En-no-Gyōja.

In Shintō the active malevolent aspect (*aramitama*) of a deity or human who has been insulted or wronged may be considered an *oni*. Thus Sugawara Michizane is depicted as a demon after his death and while he was dealing out afflictions on Heian-kyō, the capital. It was not until his deification as Tenjin that the afflictions ceased. Kamata argues convincingly that though the word *oni* does not appear in the *Kōjiki*, there are a number of *oni*-like beings, such as Izanami in the underworld; her servant, the hag of the underworld; Susano-wo; and some of the earth *kami*. These all share the duality of wildness and uncontrolled fury. The *Nihonshōki* mentions *oni* in the context of strange dwellers in wild places with odd customs. On this basis, *oni* are beings with strange behavior, often wild and uncontrolled, who dwell in the margins of the world.

Women in particular are potential *oni* because (as the myths tell it) they are given to jealousy. Thus traditional Japanese bridal clothes include a large white headdress called a "jealousy cover" intended to hide the bride's possible demon-horns from the public. Its weight (about 22 pounds) is intended to force the bride's head down and teach her to accept her lot without jealousy.

See also Boddhisattva; Izanami and Izanagi; Ni-ō; Shōki; Susano-wo; Tenjin.
References and further reading:
Joly, Henri L. 1967. *Legend in Japanese Art*. Tokyo: Charles E. Tuttle Co.
Kamata, Toji. 2001. "The Topology of Oni and Kami in Japanese Myth." http://homepage2.nifty.com/moon21/oniB.html.

ORIHIME AND KENGYŪ

Divine lovers separated by parental wrath. Orihime (Weaver princess) was the daughter of the emperor of heaven. She sat daily by the Heavenly River (the Milky Way) weaving cloth that her father dearly loved. After many entreaties to her father, she was allowed to marry Kengyū (Cattle-herder). The marriage was very happy, but in their passion for each other, Orihime neglected her weaving. As a consequence, her wrathful father placed her back in the sky, and she is visible as the star Vega, whereas Kengyū was placed as the star Altair (both among the brightest in the skies), on the opposite side of the Milky Way. They can only meet once a year, on the seventh day of the seventh month. The quarter moon serves as the boat to convey Kengyū to his lover. If Orihime does not attend to her duty, however, the heavenly emperor makes it rain, and they cannot meet, but must pass messages on by a flock of magpies.

The myth is celebrated in Japan as the festival of Tanabata, during which people decorate the streets with giant bamboo fronds hung with colored slips of paper on which poems have been written. The breeze carries the poems' meaning to the intended recipient. Both this myth and its attendant festival were imports from China during the Heian period, though it has been argued that the Chinese myth was superimposed on an earlier native one of the visit of the water *kami* to heaven (i.e., the end of the rainy season). Certainly the concept of "emperor of heaven" (Tien Ta-ti in Chinese) is not originally Japanese. The theme—true love devastated by the demands of duty—is however a favorite one in Japanese romance, whether or not this specific myth is referred to.

References and further reading:

Renshaw, Steve, and Saori Ihara. 1996. "Orihime, Kengyuu, and Tanabata: Adapting Chinese Lore to Native Beliefs and Purposes." *Bulletin for the Philippine Astronomical Society,* 9 (8). Text available 1999, http://www2.gol.com.

ŌTOSHI-NO-KAMI

A *kami* of grain, and one of Susano-wo's children, born in his palace of an alliance with one of his wives, Kamu-ō-ichi-hime, daughter of Oyamatsumi-no-kami. As in the myth of Ukemochi-no-kami, Susano-wo (who is a ruler of the underworld) is tied closely to the concept of food. Food and women represented a paradox to the ancient Japanese in that they were the sources of life, yet, in the dominant ritual conceptions, they were also the sources of, or the derivatives of, pollution.

See also Food Deities; Oyamatsumi; Susano-wo.

References and further reading:

Philippi, Donald, trans. and ed. 1968. *Kōjiki.* Tokyo: Tokyo University Press.

OWATATSUMI-NO-KAMI

The major sea *kami.* One of the children born to Izanagi and Izanami, and also the father-in-law of Ho-ori-no-mikoto, providing the hero with the tide-raising and the tide-lowering jewels. The sea was obviously important to the Japanese, who made a living on its shores. It was a source not only of food but also of trade goods, as this *kami* name indicates (*wata,* meaning "sea," is also is an old word for cotton, which was an early and important import in archaic Japan). Owatatsumi lived in a palace under the sea. He is master of fishes, and his real shape is that of an old dragon (as is the shape of his descendants, as Ho-ori found out).

The location of Owatatsumi's kingdom was often identified with Tokoyo-no-kuni, the mysterious land. There are also clear connections to the land of the dead. Susano-wo was originally slated to become ruler of the sea, but his behavior caused him to be reassigned by his father to the land of the dead. Nonetheless, he is still sometimes identified as ruler of the sea. This conflation of terms may be the result of confused transmission of the mythical tradition, of the mixture of different traditions that existed side-by-side in the Japanese islands during the archaic period, or of a mythical conception that equated the netherworld under, or in, the sea because it claimed so many victims.

See also Ho-ori-no-mikoto; Susano-wo.
References and further reading:
Aston, William G., trans. 1956. *Nihongi.* London: Allen and Unwin.
Philippi, Donald, trans. and ed. 1968. *Kōjiki.* Tokyo: Tokyo University Press.

OYAMATSUMI-NO-KAMI

Mountain god. His daughter Kamu-ō-ichi-hime married Susano-wo after his other daughters were eaten by the eight-headed serpent. Another daughter, Kōnōhanasakuya-hime, mentioned in a subsequent myth, married Ninigi-no-mikoto. Oyamatsumi may have been one of the deities that came into being during the death of the fire deity last-born of Izanagi and is thus Susano-wo's brother as well as father-in-law. From the record in the *Kōjiki* and *Nihonshōki* of their interaction, this seems unlikely. It is possible, therefore, that Oyamatsumi may have been a generic name for *any* mountain *kami.*

See also Izanagi and Izanami; Kōnōhanasakuya-hime; Ninigi-no-mikoto; Susano-wo.
References and further reading:
Aston, William G., trans. 1956. *Nihongi.* London: Allen and Unwin.
Philippi, Donald, trans. and ed. 1968. *Kōjiki.* Tokyo: Tokyo University Press.

OYASHIMA-KUNI

"Great eight islands land." A poetic and traditional name for Japan, derived from the birth of the eight islands to Izanami in her second act of creation. This term is used earlier than Toyoashihara-no-chiaki-no-nagaioaki-no-mizuho-no-kuni (The Land of the plentiful reed plains and the fresh rice-ears), which comes into use in the myth of the heavenly grandson. This may be a mere authorial convention, or it may indicate that there were different sources of these two myths.

See also Izanagi and Izanami; Toyoashihara; Yamato.
References and further reading:
Philippi, Donald, trans. and ed. 1968. *Kōjiki.* Tokyo: Tokyo University Press.

PAUCHI KAMUI (AINU)

An evil spirit that is responsible for psychological disorders. It was born on the Willow-soul River in High Heaven (Pikun Kando) and came down to earth to plague humans. It is also responsible for stomach problems, food poisoning, insanity, and epidemics of frenzied dancing.

For the boreal-forest–dwelling Ainu, madness and stomach ailments were closely linked. Starvation and the ingestion of a number of semipoisonous and hallucinogenic plants brought about similar outbreaks. Japanese officials in Hokkaido in the late nineteenth century reported that a number of villages were wiped out by epidemics of a mysterious "dancing disease" in which the communities starved themselves to death in a dancing frenzy. Whether this was the result of Japanese intrusions and impositions or cases of mass poisoning by some hallucinative substance is not known, but very clearly the Ainu knew, and feared, the emergence of these events.

The pressure of technologically superior cultures on boreal circumpolar societies that occurred in the nineteenth century seem to have brought out similar responses among these people, who largely shared many cultural traits. Thus Pauchi Kamui's effects seem remarkably similar to psychotic afflictions among North American natives such as the *wendigo* syndrome and the Ghost Shirt dance.

Amida Nyōrai (J. Stanley/ArkReligion.com)

References and further reading:

Brightman, Robert A., and David Meyer. 1983. "On Windigo Psychosis." *Current Anthropology* 24 (1): 120–122.

Munro, Neil Gordon. 1962. *Ainu Creed and Cult.* London: Routledge and Kegan Paul; London and New York: K. Paul International, distributed by Columbia University Press, 1995.

PURE LAND

The Pure Land of the West is the paradise of most of the Amidist sects of Buddhism in Japan. There are a number of Pure Lands that appear in Japanese myth, though rarely as coherent places with dimensions and location. The Pure Land of Kannon is located in the south, and many explorers have set forth from Cape Muroto, in Shikoku, in search of it.

Amida's paradise was originally a place where those not yet ready to become Buddhas could spend eons in meditation until they could enter nirvana. In popular myth, however, it became a paradise where all things were good to eat, where the breezes were pleasant and well scented, and where life was a reward for piety and suffering on mundane earth.

See also Amida Nyōrai; Kannon.
References and further reading:
Ouwehand, Cornelius. 1964. *Namazu-e and Their Themes: An Interpretative Approach to Some Aspects of Japanese Religion.* Leiden, the Netherlands: E. J. Brill.
Statler, Oliver. 1984. *Japanese Pilgrimage.* London: Picador.

RAIDEN (ALSO RAIJIN)

One of the many representations of thunder deities. He is represented as a demon-headed being playing upon a series of drums floating in the air around him. He is often accompanied by Fujin, the wind god, whose appearance is similar except that he carries a wind-sack.

Surprisingly, Raiden is reputed to be fond of people's navels, which he will consume unless they are well protected. Many Japanese men to this day will wear a *haramaki*, a cylinder of cloth or wool worn under one's clothing, to protect from Raiden's attentions.

Once a hunter tried to catch Raiden by attaching a human navel to a kite, which he would reel in once the bait was taken. To acquire the bait he killed a woman named O-Chiyo, whom he met in the woods. Raiden saw the corpse and, descending, was struck by O-Chiyo's beauty. He restored her to life by inserting a navel he had been chewing on into her. They married and returned to the sky.

Raiden is also sometimes associated with Tenjin, or Sugawara Michizane, who in his *aramitama* form brought thunder and lightning to Heian after his death in exile.

See also Fujin; Tenjin; Thunder Deities.
References and further reading:
Joly, Henri L. 1967. *Legend in Japanese Art.* Tokyo: Charles E. Tuttle Co.
Ouwehand, Cornelius. 1964. *Namazu-e and Their Themes: An Interpretative Approach to Some Aspects of Japanese Religion.* Leiden, the Netherlands: E. J. Brill.

RAIKŌ

A legendary archer and hero during the reign of Emperor Murakami, who killed numerous demons during his career (948–1021). His original name was Minamoto no Yorimitsu, and though of the *bushi* (warrior) class (that is, not an aristocrat in Heian Japan), he was appointed to several governorships. He was approached in a dream by the daughter of a legendary Chinese archer who declared he was the worthy heir of her father, and who left him a bow and arrows. With his four companions, including the strong man Kintoki, he cleared the land of demons and monsters.

He killed the monstrous Shutendōji, a giant robber who used to feast on human flesh and was a great wine bibber, from whence his name (Chief drunk boy). At night Shutendōji would be transformed into an *oni*. With his band, Raikō set out to kill the ogre. Disguising themselves as *yamabushi*, they carried their weapons and armor in the medicine boxes on their backs. On their way they met a woman who showed them the path to Shutendōji's castle. The Sumiyoshi *kami* gave Raikō a drug to make Shutendōji drunk, a magic golden cap, and silken cords. At the castle they asked for shelter for the night. Shutendōji offered them human flesh, which they pretended to like, and as a consequence, he offered them drink. Raikō offered to make the ogre a potent drink, drugging the wine with the medicine he had received from Sumiyoshi. When the robber had fallen asleep, Shutendōji assumed his real shape as a fanged *oni*. The band armed themselves, bound the ogre with the silken cords, and then cut off his head. The head jumped up and embedded its fangs into Raikō's helmet, but the golden cap saved his life. The headless but still living demon was hacked to pieces by Raikō's retainers.

On another occasion, Raikō and his band killed the *oni* of Mt. Oeyama, who drank human blood instead of wine. In Kaguragaoka they killed the *yama uba* (mountain ogress) dressed in white, with her breasts falling by her knees. She gave way before them, and they forced their way into the underground palace she was guarding. They were enticed into a cave by the vision of a beautiful woman, only to find themselves enmeshed in the cobwebs the magical giant spider had woven. Raikō prayed for assistance to Shōki the demon-queller, and, thrusting with his sword, dispatched the monster. He or one of his retainers, Watanabe no Tsuna, dispatched the shapeshifter bandit Kidōmaru, who could assume the guise of any animal. They spied him in ambush in the form of a bullock and killed him before he could act. Falling ill one day, Raikō was sent some medicine. The medicine made his condition worsen, and, suspecting the messenger, he stabbed him with his sword. One of his retainers followed the blood trail and dispatched the giant spider that had disguised itself as a doctor's assistant.

See also Animals: spider; Heroes; Kintoki; *Oni*; Shōki; *Yama-uba*.
References and further reading:
Joly, Henri L. 1967. *Legend in Japanese Art*. Tokyo: Charles E. Tuttle Co.
Sato, Hiroaki 1995. *Legends of the Samurai*. Woodstock, NY: Overlook Press.

RENGE

The lotus flower, which reproduces in water without being anchored to earth. Therefore it represents the absolute and irreducible truth, as well as the self-engendered nature of the Buddha and the Buddhist Law. More than any object it symbolizes the Buddha as an object/being *sui-generis* requiring no explanation or interpretation. The eight-petalled lotus flower represents the Buddhist Law, and Buddhas are usually represented seated on a lotus flower. Many, such as Kannon, carry a lotus bud in their hands. In the Pure Land of the West, there is a lotus pond. Whenever a Buddhist is born, a new lotus bud floats to the surface. It grows or fades according to the type of life that Buddhist leads.

> *See also* Kannon; Pure Land.
> *References and further reading:*
> Eliot, Sir Charles Norton Edgcumbe. 1959. *Japanese Buddhism.* London: Routledge and Kegan Paul.
> Joly, Henri L. 1967. *Legend in Japanese Art.* Tokyo: Charles E. Tuttle Co.

REPUN KAMUI (AINU)

The killer whale, ruler of the deep sea. As a young boy he was mischievous and unruly, and his sister, who was raising him, punished him for that. They went out to hunt whales, and the sister, after harpooning her own whale, came to the young god's assistance. Finally they filled their house with blubber, staving of famine. In another *kamui yukar,* the young Repun Kamui shot a whale and her young, and generously threw them ashore by a village. He then headed for home. The sea wren came to Repun Kamui with the gossip that the people were cutting up the whale using sickles and axes (that is, they were not showing proper respect for the animal, or for the donor). Repun Kamui laughed this off and returned to his home, saying that the meat now belonged to the humans and they could do as they wished with it.

Sitting in his house, the deity then saw that the sea wren had lied: The humans were cutting the meat up with their sacred swords, dressed in their finest clothes (that is, they were properly respecting the gift from the sea). A winged *inau* then appeared magically in the deity's house, bringing with it a metal goblet of wine, sufficient to fill six tubs, and the grateful prayers of the humans. Organizing a feast, the sea god gave gifts to his fellow deities, thus confirming his eminent status, as well as assuring the humans that the bounty of the sea would keep them from famine.

The mutually dependent relations of humans and *kamui* are well represented in this myth: The humans need food from nature (stranded whales were a major item of food), and the *kamui* need the prayers and offerings of the humans. These offerings increased the social position of the recipient, who would then be inclined to provide more food. Repun Kamui was particularly important for the Ainu because the sea presented opportunities for harvests that were not available on land: from food sources such as stranded whales, from fishing and hunting marine mammals, and from trading expeditions.

References and further reading:

Munro, Neil Gordon. 1962. *Ainu Creed and Cult.* London: Routledge and Kegan Paul; London and New York: K. Paul International, distributed by Columbia University Press, 1995.

Ohnuki-Tierney, Emiko. 1974. *The Ainu of the Northwest Coast of Southern Sakhalin.* New York: Holt, Rinehart, and Winston.

Philippi, Donald L., trans. 1979. *Songs of Gods, Songs of Humans: The Epic Tradition of the Ainu.* Princeton: Princeton University Press.

ROKUJI MYŌ-Ō

One of the heavenly kings. His name means "Six syllables," and he represents the six syllables of the Buddhist creed (*Om ma ne pad me hum*). He has a serene face, often a green body, and carries a curved sword and a trident in two of his six hands. He is the guardian of the foundation of the Buddhist Law.

See also Myō-ō, p. 54.

References and further reading:

Getty, Alice. 1988. *The Gods of Northern Buddhism.* New York: Dover Publications.

Joly, Henri L. 1967. *Legend in Japanese Art.* Tokyo: Charles E. Tuttle Co.

RUSUGAMI

The deities responsible for maintaining the world while the *kami* are in assembly on the tenth month in Izumo. The *rusugami* include the Kamado-gami (kitchen *kami*), Ebisu, and Namazu (the earthquake catfish). Ebisu is usually questioned by the other *kami* (usually the suspicious and aggressive Takemikazuchi) why he did not attend the council but always manages to find some sort of excuse or lie.

In traditional Japanese culture, the practice of leaving a *rusuban* (caretaker) in a house while the family was out was common until fairly recently. Most traditional Japanese houses had no locks, and any burglar could enter simply by lifting the shutters. Polite custom dictates even today that a visitor shout out "Excuse me" to announce his presence. In premodern Japan an individual who did not do so could be attacked with impunity. In this social framework, the absence of the *kami* at Izumo requires a caretaker, because otherwise the social fabric would be threatened by dissolution and anarchy. Excepting Kamado-gami, the *rusugami* are a dissolute lot, which accounts, mythically, for the upsets that occur within Japan, which is supposedly a land ordered by the *kami*.

Protective water-dragons. Detail from a shrine lintel. (Courtesy of the author)

See also Ebisu; Kamado-gami; Namazu.
References and further reading:
Ouwehand, Cornelius. 1964. *Namazu-e and Their Themes: An Interpretative Approach to Some Aspects of Japanese Religion.* Leiden, the Netherlands: E. J. Brill.

RYŪJIN (ALSO RYU-Ō)

The dragon king. Variously portrayed as having a dragon or a giant serpent shape, he is the master of serpents who act as his messengers. Ryūjin appears in dreams, and many people claim to have seen him upon waking. He is variously reported to live in a palace in the sea or in lakes in extinct volcanoes. He carries the tide-raising and tide-lowering jewels.

Ryūjin features in a number of Japanese myths, sometimes as a benevolent ruler or aid to a hero, sometimes as a villain. His palace is generally under the sea, and he is often identified with Owatatsumi-no-kami. As Owatatsumi he aided Ho-ori in warding off the attacks of his brother, Hoderi. An example of the reverse side of his nature concerns a jewel he stole from Kamatari, the founder of the Fujiwara clan, which was retrieved only at the loss of Kamatari's wife, a fisherwoman, who swam down to the dragon's palace, fought him, and rescued the jewel, then drowned. He also stole a bell, which he later gave as a gift to Tawara Toda, who saved Ryūjin's palace from a centipede. The same bell was later stolen by Benkei from the Miidera temple.

The snake can, if treated properly, offer medicines for long life, and Ryūjin can help with one's health. He is often the *ujigami* of Japanese clans.

The bipolar nature of Ryūjin as both protector and fierce and troubling opponent is not surprising. He is associated with the most capricious of all elements, the sea, which, as the Japanese were well aware, brought great benefits and treasures but also caused death and havoc. Moreover, as lord of the serpents, who are associated with thunder and death, and as bringer of rain, he is at the same time a figure of death and life. Ryūjin's good-and-bad nature is a reflection of these realities.

> *See also* Benkei; Ho-ori-no-mikoto; Owatatsumi; Snakes; Tawara Toda; Thunder Deities.
>
> *References and further reading:*
> Aston, William G., trans. 1956. *Nihongi.* London: Allen and Unwin.
> Getty, Alice. 1988. *The Gods of Northern Buddhism.* New York: Dover Publications.
> Philippi, Donald, trans. and ed. 1968. *Kōjiki.* Tokyo: Tokyo University Press.
> Visser, Marinus Willem de. 1913. *The Dragon in China and Japan.* Amsterdam: J. Müller; Wiesbaden: M. Sändig, 1969.

RYŪJU (NAGARJUNA)

One of the disciples of the Buddha Shakyamuni and a patriarch in a line extending from Dainichi Nyōrai to Kōbō Daishi. According to Shingon, he received his secret doctrine (i.e., Shingon's internal doctrine) from the Second Patriarch, Vajrasattva, who lived in an iron tower. It is also said that he received his knowledge from the *nagas* (snake spirits), and particularly from Ryūjin in his palace under the sea. The treatise he wrote on the Buddhist Law is read in order to bring rain, and he is identified with Ryūjin.

> *See also* Kōbō Daishi; Ryūjin; Shaka.
>
> *References and further reading:*
> Getty, Alice. 1988. *The Gods of Northern Buddhism.* New York: Dover Publications.

SAE-NO-KAMI

Kami of the roads. *See* Dosōjin.

SAGES (BUDDHIST AND DAOIST)

Sages are one of the most important classes of "venerated beings" in Buddhist myth. A number of different persons fall into this classification. Collectively, sages are humans (almost all male) whose study of Buddhism, or acts in their lifetimes, were miraculous, exemplary, and erudite. In most cases they are also miracle workers within the area of their activities.

The sages and the stories told about them straddle the border between myth, folklore, and legend. That is to say, the stories about them are not, individually, fundamental to Japanese beliefs or myth. Most Japanese will have come across these myths as part of their childhood stories or as part of their exposure to classical art. The concept of the sage, however, is a compelling and powerful one in Japanese ideology, and in that, the idea constitutes a myth in the sense used here. Sages are fundamentally human. They achieve their mystical powers by effort and internal struggle. Most sages have at least a touch of magical power, but this is not inherent in them. It is the result of effortful study, of continued application and hard work. Sages thus represent the "you-and-me" side of myth. They are very compelling because they point to features of life that are as fundamentally true for Japanese people as are similar myths in other countries. Concentration of mind on achieving one's goal, the need to live within nature, and the quirkiness and ineffable nature of life and being are all expressed by the person of the sage in much the same way as truth-telling and patriotism are represented by George Washington and Nathan Hale.

For convenience's sake I have divided sages in the following discussion into a number of categories. Nonetheless, sages are a mixed lot, and myths about them are sometimes isolates, sometimes part of a broader mythical background. Many of those about whom there are myths in Japan are of Chinese and Indian origin. Sages are particularly important in Zen thinking, and a huge body of tales exists about Zen sages, whose activities serve as examples for future generations of Zen adepts.

The Buddha's Disciples

Many of the Buddha's disciples are named as sages. A number of these sages, such as the *sonja* and the *rakan,* are known not necessarily for the qualities they embodied but for events that supposedly took place during their lifetimes, and which therefore made them fitting intercessionaries in this area. Binzuru-sonja, for example, has become a Buddhist patron of healing because he looked at a young woman during meditation and is therefore placed outside the meditation hall: Common people can therefore approach him without fear of offense, and beg for help. Disciples such as Ryūgo are the founders of Buddhist sects and may well straddle the boundaries between this category (disciples) and the next (saints).

Buddhist Saints

Later Buddhist figures, many of them either founders of schools of Buddhist thought or abbots of famous monasteries and temples, are within this category. The three most venerated such figures in Japan are each a founder of a Buddhist sect or school of thought. Undoubtedly the most well-known and universally venerated is Kūkai, generally known by his posthumous title of Kōbō Daishi. In addition to his historically documented achievements, he is credited with numerous miracles.

A second well-known sage is Boddhidarma, known in Japan as Daruma. Daruma is credited with having established the Zen school in China, at the Shaolin monastery. Most Japanese would be able to recount one or another of the miraculous activities credited to him: the discovery of tea, his indomitable will, or his invention of *gung-fu*. Finally, though only a minority of Japanese are followers of the Nichiren school of Buddhism, Nichiren-shōnin is recognized as a major sage in the Buddhist tradition. He too has miraculous events associated with him, though his fame is perhaps more solidly based on his refusal to compromise with his beliefs. Other well-known sages who fall into this category include the founders of virtually all the Buddhist schools in Japan: Hōnen, Shinran, En-no-Gyōja, and others.

Daoist and Zen Sages

A great many Daoist sages, virtually all of them Chinese, are recognized in Japanese art. Quite often their particular characteristics are noted by Japanese people simply because they are major artistic subjects. In this class can be included *Roshi* (Lao-tse), Gama-sennin, and even Songokku (Stone Monkey), the protagonist and hero of a classical Chinese novel, *Voyage to the West.* These figures are attractive as mythical heroes, even when they do nothing but walk across a bridge, for two reasons. First, the stories are quintessentially human, often amusing, and visually powerful. Second, at a deeper level, they often illustrate points that the various teachings—Daoism and Zen—were trying to make about human nature and about their central cosmological concerns, such as relation to nature and to reality.

> **See also** Binzuru-sonja; Daruma; En-no-Gyōja; Gama-sennin; Kōbō Daishi; Ryūju.
> **References and further reading:**
> Davis, S. Hadland. 1913. *Myths and Legends of Japan.* London: George Harrap. (Facsimile edition 1992, New York: Dover Publications.)

Frank, Bernard. 1991. *Le pantheon bouddhique au Japon.* Paris: Collections d'Emile Guimet. Reunion des musees nationaux.

Joly, Henri L. 1967. *Legend in Japanese Art.* Tokyo: Charles E. Tuttle Co.

Khanna, Anita. 1999. *The Jataka Stories in Japan.* Delhi: B. R. Publishing.

Kurosawa, Kōzō. 1982. "Myths and Tale Literature." *Japanese Journal of Religious Studies* 9 (2–3): 115–125.

Morrell, Robert E. 1982. "Kamakura Accounts of Myōe Shōnin as Popular Religious Hero." *Japanese Journal of Religious Studies* 9 (2–3): 171–198.

Nakamura, Kyoko Motomuchi. 1997. *Miraculous Stories from the Japanese Buddhist Tradition: The Nihon Ryoki of the Monk Kyokai.* New ed. Richmond, VA: Curzon Press. Text at http://campross.crosswinds.net/ books/Miraculous. html.

Statler, Oliver. 1984. *Japanese Pilgrimage.* London: Picador.

SANBŌ-KŌJIN

Deity of fire and of the hearth, and of the kitchen. Identified sometimes with Monju-bosatsu and at other times with Fudō Myō-ō, Sanbō-Kōjin (Three-way rough deity) represents violent forces turned toward the good (the three treasures—the Buddha, the Law, and the community of monks—most important to Buddhism). Sanbō-Kōjin (sometimes called just Kōjin) is a rough and violent deity of uncertain temper. He is the divine expression of fire, controlled and sanctified by use, its destructiveness turned into beneficial paths. He destroys all impurity and all calamity.

A representation of Kōjin is usually placed near the hearth and worshiped scrupulously. He may be represented merely by a *fuda* (memorial tablet) in most households, or by a statue (in Buddhist temples). In such a case he is depicted with a violent contorted face, fangs gleaming, and carrying a bow and arrows, his hair aflame. This makes him the Buddhist equivalent of Kamado-gami.

In some ways Kōjin resembles the Ainu Kamui Fuchi and the Ryukyuan Fii Nu Kang, albeit less powerful than the former. In Japanese myth he has assumed some of the characteristics of the Chinese kitchen god, who supervises the activities of members of the household, reporting on their misdeeds to the village or city god. His association with flames naturally leads to the view that he is an incarnation or aspect of Fudō, who is always surrounded by flames and, like Kōjin, deals with malefactors.

See also Fudō Myō-ō; Fii-nu-kang; Kamado-gami; Kamui Fuchi; Monju-bosatsu.
References and further reading:
Joly, Henri L. 1967. *Legend in Japanese Art.* Tokyo: Charles E. Tuttle Co.

SARUTAHIKO-NO-KAMI

The deity who appeared from the Central Land of the Reed Plains to provide a guide to Ninigi-no-mikoto when he descended to rule the land. His name can be read as "Field-monkey prince." Because the deity appeared at an eightfold cross-roads, he is often viewed as the deity of crossroads; he is worshiped in the form of a phallus as Dosōjin. His initial meeting with the heavenly deities was not auspicious, because he had a fierce aspect and was blocking the roads. He is described as being over seven feet tall, with a nose seven hands long. His mouth and posterior were brightly lit up, and his great mirror-like eyes shone cherry-red from inner flames. He was dissuaded from stopping the heavenly grandson by Ama-no-uzume, who earlier had enticed Amaterasu from her cave.

After helping Ninigi-no-mikoto control the land, he was accompanied on his way home by Ame-no-uzume, who may have married him. In any case, they are both considered the ancestors of an important imperial clan. Sarutahiko subsequently went fishing but got his hand caught in a shell and sank to the bottom of the sea. There he became, or was named for, the different types of seafoam.

As Kōjin (or Kōshin), the *kami* of the roads, he is accompanied by three monkeys: Mizaru, Kikizaru, and Iwazaru—a play on words between *s(z)aru* (monkey) and the formal negative of the verb. Travelers and other people whose livelihood depends on the roads celebrate Iron-Monkey Day in his honor, which occurs every two months at the intersection of the Five Element (pental), Yin-Yang (binary), and Zodiacal (duodenary) calendrical cycles. Many travelers will offer Kōjin little figurines of straw horses to ensure a safe journey.

See also Ame-no-uzume; Dosōjin; Kōshin; Ninigi-no-mikoto.
References and further reading:
Aston, William G., trans. 1956. *Nihongi.* London: Allen and Unwin.
Philippi, Donald, trans. and ed. 1968. *Kōjiki.* Tokyo: Tokyo University Press.

SEISHI-BOSATSU

One of two figures portrayed accompanying Amida-butsu. Seishi is far over-shadowed by the other companion, Kannon.

See also Amida Nyōrai; Kannon.

SENGEN

Kami of the sacred Mt. Fuji. She is also called Fuji-hime (Princess Fuji) and is identified with Kōnōhanasakuya-hime, mother of Hoderi-no-mikoto and Ho-ori-no-mikoto. She is represented wearing a broad hat adorned with wisteria twigs, a play on words between the names of the mountain and the flower that are homonymous in Japanese.

Fuji-san (Mt. Fuji) is the tallest peak in Japan. It forms an almost perfect cone and is clearly visible from a great distance because, as a volcano, it is an iso-late (not part of a mountain chain). The name *Fuji* may be a Japanese pronunci-ation of the Ainu *Fuchi,* and the original deity of the mountain may well have been an Emishi deity of fire. The appearance of the mountain or of Sengen in a dream is an omen of great good fortune.

> *See also* Hoderi-no-mikoto; Ho-ori-no-mikoto; Kamui Fuchi; Kōnōhanasakuya-
> hime.
> **References and further reading:**
> Aston, William G., trans. 1956. *Nihongi*. London: Allen and Unwin.
> Joly, Henri L. 1967. *Legend in Japanese Art*. Tokyo: Charles E. Tuttle Co.
> Philippi, Donald, trans. and ed. 1968. *Kōjiki*. Tokyo: Tokyo University Press.

SHAKA (SHAKYAMUNI, SAGE OF THE SHAKYA CLAN)

The historical Buddha, founder of a revolutionary philosophy in India. Accepting the prevailing metaphysical premise of Hinduism—one's conduct in life determines one's position in rebirth—Shakyamuni, prince and heir of the Shakya kingdom in northern India, reflected on the consequences of this cycle. He concluded that human and other suffering was the result of desires. These desires—for pleasure, for food, for luxuries, for power—were the results of illusions. So long as the individual desired those illusions, he was bound to be reincarnated for more suffering. Shakyamuni's meditations under the bodhi tree eventually suggested a cure for this suffering as well: Cessation of desire through a disciplined life, and search for the truth behind the illusion, could bring about a state of *nibbhana*, lack of desire, or salvation. Realizing this, the individual would become a *buddha* (enlightened one).

Shakyamuni, renamed the Buddha, preached his view of reality, and by the time of his death had established a thriving and growing religio-philosophical sect. This sect grew, after his death, to the major religion on the Indian subcontinent, particularly after its adoption as the state religion by the northern Indian Maurya dynasty. The teachings were transferred by several routes to China, and thence to Japan (in India it subsequently declined and has almost disappeared). Within some Japanese Buddhist schools, Shakyamuni is the Buddha of the current age. Within others, such as Jōdō, he is merely a great saint and teacher.

Numerous myths are told about Shakyamuni: his strength, his compassion, and his wisdom. Most of these are borrowed from Indian sources. For devout Buddhists, the Buddha has thirty-two defining physical marks that set him off from all of humankind. Some, such as the *urna*, or shining ball, in the middle of his forehead, the double-domed skull, and the curling hair, are obvious; others are much less so. The purport of these myths, which originate in India, is to show how unusual Shakyamuni was as a human being. In various other myths he performed awesome austerities, defeated armies of demons, and even challenged Emma-ō (Yama), the Lord of Death.

Many of these tales are told as part of doctrine in some Buddhist sects. They thus constitute myth as defined here. Like Kōbō Daishi, however, many of the myths were originally told about some other hero.

See also Emma-ō; Kōbō Daishi.
References and further reading:
Khanna, Anita. 1999. *The Jataka Stories in Japan.* Delhi: B. R. Publishing.
Komatsu, Chikō. 1989. *The Way to Peace: The Life and Teachings of the Buddha.* Kyoto: Hōzōkan Publishing Co.
Matsunaga, Alicia. 1974/1996. *Foundations of Japanese Buddhism.* Los Angeles: Buddhist Books International.

SHI TENNO

The four heavenly kings who protect the world of Buddhism from evil. Each one is represented by a direction and a color. They also correspond to the four mystic animals (Tortoise, Phoenix, Tiger, and Dragon). To the north is Bishamon-ten (blue). To the west is Komoku-ten (red). To the South is Zōchō-ten (white). To the east is Jikoku-ten (green). Bishamon is also popular as the guardian of the Law and as one of the Shichi Fukujin.

See also Bishamon; Shichi Fukujin.
References and further reading:
Joly, Henri L. 1967. *Legend in Japanese Art.* Tokyo: Charles E. Tuttle Co.

SHICHI FUKUJIN

The seven gods of good fortune. These seven gods, of different origins and associations, are often represented as traveling together in the fabulous Takarabune (Treasure ship). Their representation as a collective along with their ship is most often seen in merchant establishments. Their association in a ship indicates that they are also *marebito* (visiting deities).

The seven are: Benten (goddess of love and the arts), Bishamon (god of protection), Daikoku (god of prosperity), Ebisu (god of good luck), Fukurokuju (longevity and wisdom), Hōtei (good fortune and serenity, generosity), and Jurojin (longevity). Each of these may also appear separately (see relevant entries). As separate deities they have an importance and gravity belied by their amusing representation in the Shichi Fukujin tableau.

Benten carries a lute that signifies her artistic connotations as patroness of the arts. Bishamon is usually depicted holding a miniature pagoda, indicating his role as defender of the Buddhist Law and of preserver of legality in general. He is armed and armored in the Chinese manner. Daikoku is depicted, both in the ship and when appearing in his own person, as sitting on two fat rice bales. The bales are surrounded by mice, because Daikoku's bales are so overflowing he is prepared to allow the rodents to eat their fill as well. He carries in his hand a

Shichi (lion) detail from a shrine lintel (Courtesy of the author)

wooden mallet that when shaken or pounded produces gold coins. On his head he wears a rounded cap of the merchant. Ebisu, with whom Daikoku is most often associated, is considered Daikoku's son. He holds a fishing rod in one hand, and his catch, a large *tai* (sea bream, but homophonous with the word *congratulations*), in the other. He wears commoner clothes from the Heian period. Fukurokuju (also called Fukurokujin) has an elongated hair-fringed head, indication of his wisdom and longevity. Hōtei, one of the most popular of the seven, is depicted as a shaven-headed Buddhist monk, wearing a rumpled robe open at the waist that displays his enormous stomach (the sign of good nature and generosity). He carries, or rests upon, a large sack, from which gifts are dispensed to worthy children. Jurojin is represented with a long white beard and carrying a staff to which is fastened a scroll containing Daoist wisdom. He is always accompanied by a stag, a tortoise, or a crane, all symbols of happy old age.

The *Takarabune* itself is usually drawn as a dragon-prowed Chinese ship. Jurojin's crane often flies overhead, and its sail is often marked with the character for good fortune or with an oval gold coin.

The seven gods and their ship represent one of the strongest streams of Japanese mythology: the ideas and interpretations of the mercantile classes. They represent not so much blind luck as good fortune, particularly for the individual who applies himself. The seven have different origins—Daoism, China, Confucianism, Buddhism, Shintō—and are all associated together in a way that would have made the "official" historians and mythologists of the imperial system blanch. The images are powerful precisely because they appealed (and still do) to the enterprise tinged with fatalism of the merchant, shopkeeper, and urban worker: *Takarabune* representations are probably the most commonly seen religious item in modern Japan.

See also Bishamon; Daikoku; Ebisu; Fukurokuju; Hōtei; Jurojin; *Marebito*

References and further reading:
Czaja, Michael. 1974. *Gods of Myth and Stone: Phallicism in Japanese Folk Religion.* New York and Tokyo: Weatherhill.
Davis, S. Hadland. 1913. *Myths and Legends of Japan.* London: George Harrap. (Facsimile edition 1992 New York: Dover Publications).
Ehrich, Kurt S. 1991. *Shichifukujin: Die Sieben Glücksgötter Japans.* Recklinghausen: Verlag Aurel Bongers.
Joly, Henri L. 1967. *Legend in Japanese Art.* Tokyo: Charles E. Tuttle Co.
Tyler, Royall. 1987. *Japanese Tales.* New York: Pantheon.

SHIRAMBA KAMUI (AINU)

The *kamui* of vegetation, and thus of many household implements and tools, because they are made of wood. He is also present in grains and vegetables. All plants share some of his spirit or essence (*ramat*), and as a consequence, they have some human feelings. For the Ainu, the world surrounding them was alive, and all plants and animals they made use of had *ramat* and needed to be dealt with.

References and further reading:
Batchelor, John. 1971. *Ainu Life and Lore; Echoes of a Departing Race.* Tokyo, Kyobunkwan, New York: Johnson Reprint Corp.
Brett, L. Walker. 2001. *The Conquest of Ainu Lands: Ecology and Culture in Japanese Expansion, 1590–1800.* Berkeley and London: University of California Press.
Etter, Carl. 1949. *Ainu Folklore; Traditions and Culture of the Vanishing Aborigines of Japan.* Chicago: Wilcox and Follett Co.
Munro, Neil Gordon. 1962. *Ainu Creed and Cult.* London: Routledge and Kegan Paul; London and New York: K. Paul International, distributed by Columbia University Press, 1995.

SHŌKI

Demon queller. A figure of protection of Chinese origin, Shōki (Qung Kuei) was a student who had failed the imperial examinations and committed suicide to expiate his shame. The emperor had him buried with honors, and in return, his ghost vowed to rid the world of demons. He is applied to for protection against *oni.*

Shōki is one of the many mythical figures appealed to for dispelling afflictions. As a non-Japanese figure he does not feature in any of the official mythologies. In art his relationship with *oni* is sometimes humorous, with one famous painting depicting an *oni* hiding in Shōki's hat. Another famous *hashira-e* (pillar painting: long narrow paintings intended for hanging against house pillars) depicts only the tip of Shōki's Chinese sword scabbard as he walks away. Behind him, a miserable-looking *oni* wipes his face with relief at having escaped Shōki's wrath.

> **See also** Oni; Sages.
> **References and further reading:**
> Joly, Henri L. 1967. *Legend in Japanese Art.* Tokyo: Charles E. Tuttle Co.

SHŌ-TEN

A Buddhist deity of wealth. Also called Kangi-ten, he is usually worshiped by merchants and portrayed as a man with an elephant's head. He is one of the many deities accepted by Shingon from Indian origins, in this case, the elephant-headed god of wealth, Ganesha.

> **References and further reading:**
> Eliot, Sir Charles Norton Edgcumbe. 1959. *Japanese Buddhism.* London: Routledge and Kegan Paul.
> Frank, Bernard. 1991. *Le pantheon bouddhique au Japon.* Paris: Collections d'Emile Guimet. Reunion des musees nationaux.

SHŌTOKU TAISHI

A real historical figure, protector of Buddhism in its establishment in Japan, and author of Japan's first constitution, the *Jūshichijō-kenpō* (Twelve Article Constitution). Prince Umayado (574–622) was the second son of Emperor Yōmei and became prince regent to Empress Suiko. He was the perfect governor and counselor, ruling wisely throughout his office. His posthumous name, Shōtoku Taishi, means "Prince of Sainted Virtues." Because of his wise and sagacious rule and the concern he gave to the common people, he is sometimes venerated as an avatar of Kannon.

A supporter of Buddhism from his youth, Shōtoku Taishi joined with the Soga clan of the pro-Buddhist party to defeat the Mononobe and Nakatomi (pro-Shintō) conservatives at the battle of Mt. Shigi (in modern Osaka). Once he assumed office, he did his best to ensure the success of the empress's rule, strongly opposing centripetal tendencies among the aristocracy of the Yamato state. He is still venerated as the lawgiver and the founder of the Japanese state. He is reputed to have been a Buddhist scholar of note, having written a Commentary of the Three Sutras at the command of the empress.

Shozuka-no-Baba with offerings for the spirits of the dead (Courtesy of the author)

In mythology, Shōtoku Taishi is depicted both as an avatar of the Buddha and as one who was supported by, and owed his victories to, the boddhisattvas, most notably to Shogun Jizō.

See also Jizō.
References and further reading:
Sansom, Sir George. 1976. *Japan—A Short Cultural History.* Tokyo: Charles E.
    Tuttle Co.

SHOZUKA-NO-BABA
An old hag who lives under the dried-up tree at the bank of the Shozukawa, the river that leads to hell. She deprives the dead of their clothes, which she hangs up on the branches of the tree. This is said to reinforce the idea that they have left their old material life behind them. She has a male counterpart, Datsueba, who may simply be a male variant of the same mythical being.

See also Datsueba; *Jigoku.*
References and further reading:
Frank, Bernard. 1991. *Le pantheon bouddhique au Japon.* Paris: Collections
    d'Emile Guimet. Reunion des musees nationaux.

SHUMISEN (MT. MERU, SUMERU)

The mountain that is the center of the universe in Buddhism. It is guarded on four sides by the Shi Tenno. Thirty-three million gods dwell on its flanks. The paradise of the Buddha is upon its summit. It also represents the arduous and lengthy process a Buddhist must undergo to reach nirvana. Shumisen represents the struggle of individuals and of humanity collectively to become buddhas. A number of mountain pilgrimages in Japan, including Mt. Takao, Mt. Fuji, and the famous pilgrimages of the *yamabushi* at Yoshino and Mt. Haguro, were modeled after the path leading up the flanks of Shumisen.

See also Mountains.
References and further reading:
Earhart, H. Byron. 1970. *A Religious Study of the Mount Haguro Sect of Shugendo.* Tokyo: Sophia University Press.
Getty, Alice. 1988. *The Gods of Northern Buddhism.* New York: Dover Publications.

SNAKES

Snakes feature prominently in Japanese myth, usually in one of three forms: as messengers or avatars of the dragon deity Ryūjin, as shape-changers who entice and threaten people, or as thunder deities. Some other *kami,* such as Ame-no-oshikumone, manifest themselves as snakes.

Many people in Japan today feel that snakes are the messengers of Ryūjin. At least in mythology, snakes and dragons are often conflated, and snakes are considered a minor sort of dragon. Shintō priests and devout laypeople will endeavor to avoid harming snakes or their places of residence.

The best-known myth of the second type is the tale of Dojōji temple. Kiyohime, a maiden, fell in love with Anchin, a young Buddhist priest. For a time he resisted her advances and was true to his vows, but eventually he became entangled and made love to her. His abbot, fearing the worse, identified the source of the youth's listlessness as his illicit amour. The young priest attempted to flee his lover's clutches, only to see her change into a giant serpent, which pursued him. The Dojōji myth has become a staple of *Kabuki* theater, where the lovely maiden is transformed, with the magic of the theater, into a giant monster.

A similar myth to Dojōji is encountered earlier in history. Prince Homuchi-wake, recovering from illness, took Hinaga-hime as a one-night bride (a common practice, as marriage was a fluid affair in Heian Japan). During the night, he discovered she was in reality a serpent and fled the marital bed in panic. Enraged, Hinaga-hime pursued him in a boat. The myth does not tell of the conclusion of the pursuit.

The goddess of Mount Fuji, Konohana sakya hime, traditional figure of the Fuji Asama-jinja temple. (Réunion des Musées Nationaux/Art Resource, NY)

Snakes were associated with lightning and thunder, and thus the snake *kami* were often thunder *kami* as well. There is a strong association in Japanese myth between snakes, death, and thunder. In the creation myth, Izanagi's body in the Land of Yōmi is infested by eight snake deities, who are, at the same time, also thunder deities. Ouwehand argues that the nature and form of snakes reminded the ancient Japanese of the shape of lightning and thus their association with thunder.

See also Dōjō-hōshi; Izanagi and Izanami; Thunder Deities.
References and further reading:
Aston, William G., trans. 1956. *Nihongi.* London: Allen and Unwin.
Brandon, James R., and Tamako Niwa, adapters. 1966. *Kabuki Plays.* New York: S. French.
Ouwehand, Cornelius. 1964. *Namazu-e and Their Themes: An Interpretative Approach to Some Aspects of Japanese Religion.* Leiden, the Netherlands: E. J. Brill.
Philippi, Donald, trans. and ed. 1968. *Kōjiki.* Tokyo: Tokyo University Press.

STONES

Stones feature in a number of Japanese myths. Izanagi rolls a giant rock to protect his escape from his enraged wife in the underworld. The *kaname-ishi* stone pierces through the ground to pin Namazu the catfish in place, because his movements underground cause earthquakes. Ebisu is recognized as a rock caught in the nets of fishermen. The empress Jingū tied rocks to her girdle to delay the birth of her son, the Emperor Ōjin, deified as Hachiman.

In common myths, stones could also be the measure of a man's steadfastness. Many local myths tell of meeting a mysterious stranger in the mountains or on the road, who asks the unwary traveler to hold a stone. The stone grows heavier and heavier, eventually crushing the victim, or, if the victim endures, the visitor (male or female) gives the victim magical powers.

The use of stones as items of worship and reverence is very common in Japan. There is some evidence that the practice was prehistoric in origin. Large and small boulders can still be found throughout the country that have been girdled by *shimenawa* (rice ropes, often of immense girth, decorated with paper streamers, used to indicate sacred precincts). In most cases a local myth explains the significance of the rock. One of the most famous is on the coastline not far from Amaterasu-ō-mikami's main shrine at Ise. There, two rocks—one on the shore, the other in the water—are joined by a sacred rope. They represent an elderly devoted couple who when they died were transformed into rocks.

Stones and rocks of varying sizes are often worshiped as *shintai* (the physical representation/manifestation of a *kami*). It is often sufficient for someone to find a stone under unusual circumstances, or to find a stone of unusual shape,

The Meoto-Iwa, or Wedded Rocks, off the coast of the Shima Peninsula. Legend holds that the spirits of Izanagi and Izanami, Japan's creator gods, are housed in the rocks, which are connected to one another by a straw rope. Lovers often visit the rocks. (Werner Forman/Art Resource, NY)

for it to be made into a *shintai*. The ancient Japanese clearly, and quite naturally, credited unusual stones with great powers and importance.

> **See also** Ebisu; Hachiman; Jewels; Namazu; Takemikazuchi-no-kami; *Yama-uba*.
> **References and further reading:**
> Sakurada, Katsunori. 1980 (1963). "The Ebisu-Gami in a Fishing Village." In *Studies in Japanese Folklore,* edited by R. Dorson. New York: Arno Press, pp. 122–132.

SUIJIN (ALSO MIZU-NO-KAMI)
Kami of water, springs, and sometimes wells. Suijin appears in many guises and most often governs the treatment of springs that provide water for human consumption. Suijin is sometimes conflated with Ryūjin, the dragon *kami* who is also associated with water. Fudō Myō-ō is also sometimes termed Suijin because of his association with the waterfall. In most cases, however, Suijin appears simply as a stone plaque, or even a simple small stone set upright near a spring's emergence.

Suijin expects to be worshiped, or at least noticed. This author, upon leasing a house in northern Japan, was requested by the owner to "honor Suijin occasionally" by placing some saké and flowers on the small stone plaque above a spring on the property.

See also Fudō Myō-ō; Ryūjin.

SUITENGU

One of the sea deities, who is appealed to, to avoid shipwreck. He is shown supported by a tortoise. He is also sometimes considered the deity of luck, because the sailor and fisherman's lot is much dependent upon luck. The name is also a nickname of the child emperor Antoku, who perished at the battle of Dan-no-Ura to the forces of the Minamoto.

References and further reading:
Eliot, Sir Charles Norton Edgcumbe. 1959. *Japanese Buddhism.* London: Routledge and Kegan Paul.

SUKUNABIKONA

A midget deity who assisted Ōkuninushi in completing the creation of the land. Ōkuninushi, after contesting with his father-in-law Susano-wo, got down to finishing the act of creation started by Izanagi and Izanami. At Cape Miwo in Izumo, a midget deity, riding in a boat made of a *kagami* pod (a gourdlike pod from an Ampelopsis vine) and dressed in the skin of a wagtail (a goose in the *Nihonshōki*), appeared to Ōkuninushi and his party. After some inquiries that were met with silence from Sukunabikona, the toad (a member of the party who is a magical animal and has been everywhere) suggested that the scarecrow *kami* Kuyebiko would know the newcomer's identity. Kuyebiko informed them that the midget deity was the child of Kamimusubi-no-kami (according to the *Kōjiki*) who had slipped from her fingers after birth, or of Takamimusubi-no-mikoto (according to the *Nihonshōki*). Sukunabikona joined with Ō-Namuji (Ōkuninushi) to solidify and increase the land. According to the *Nihonshōki*, the two deities then completed the construction of the world and made provisions for curing illness and disease among humans and animals. Included in this were magical spells to dispel calamities of various sorts. Having done so, Sukunabikona returned to his own country, Tokoyo-no-kuni.

Sukunabikona, along with Ōkuninushi, is master of magic and wizardry. Traditionally too, he is associated with the folk figure of Hyottoko, a clownish figure representing the country bumpkin whose twisted-mouthed mask features in many *kagura* (ritual plays).

No less importantly, Sukunabikona is sometimes claimed to be the leech child, Hiruko, and thus, perhaps, is Ebisu as well. In any case, the most important characteristic of Sukunabikona is that he is the *marebito* par excellence. He visits, helps in providing magical gifts and in construction, then departs to his own country. Like other *marebito*—Ebisu and Hiruko in particular—he is both deformed and powerful, setting him apart from the normal run of human (and *kami*) -kind. It is possible that the *marebito* concept is a generalized mythical warning: Be careful of strangers, no matter how odd they look: Treat them well, then send them off.

See also Animals: toad; Ebisu; Hiruko; Kuyebiko; *Marebito*; Okuninushi; Underworld.

References and further reading:
Aston, William G., trans. 1956. *Nihongi.* London: Allen and Unwin.
Philippi, Donald, trans. and ed. 1968. *Kōjiki.* Tokyo: Tokyo University Press.

SUMERU
See Shumisen.

SUMIYOSHI
A *kami* of seafarers and of poetry. Sumiyoshi is a composite deity of Uwazutsu-no-ō, Nakazutsu-no-ō, and Sokozutsu-no-ō (upper sea, middle sea, and lower sea), and provided Empress Jingū with the jewel that allowed her to control the waves in her invasion of Korea. The Sumiyoshi-taisha shrine in Settsu, in modern Osaka, is Sumiyoshi's main shrine, though there are branch shrines throughout the country. It is famous for (among other things) being the site where Prince Genji came to give thanks for attaining marriage with his beloved during the Heian period.

Sumiyoshi is also enshrined at Uji, near Nara, as the *kami* of medicine and healing, carnal lust, and dissipation. Sumiyoshi provided the magic elixir that aided Raikō in subduing the drunkard monster Shutendōji. The relationship between medicine and sexual activity was possibly an import from China, where Daoism laid great emphasis on the relationship between the two. Sumiyoshi's wife-companion in the Uji version is Hashi-hime, deity of lust. It is of course possible, and not unusual, that the Sumiyoshi of Sumiyoshi-Taisha and of Uji are two different deities whose names have become conflated.

There are a number of shrines and temples in Japan dedicated to sexual deities, including a famous temple in Shimoda where Townsend Harris, the first U.S. ambassador to Japan, resided. Harris was given a concubine by the Japanese authorities, whom he subsequently abandoned, and this was elaborated into a myth of unrequited lust in the temple's history. Echoes of this story may have influenced Puccini's *Madame Butterfly.*

Neither the *Kōjiki* nor the *Nihonshōki* are at all reluctant or shy about dis-

Susano'o no Mikoto subduing the eight-headed serpent. (© British Museum/Art Resource, NY)

cussing sex (though many of their translators are: Basil Hall Chamberlain wrote all the suspect events in Latin), or for that matter excretion. Lust and sexual pleasure as a natural consequence of humanity occur in a number of myths, starting with Izanagi and Izanami.

The bimodal importance of Sumiyoshi—as protector and as deity of healing—extends to another aspect of Japanese society. One of the major *yakuza* (organized crime) gangs in Japan is the Sumiyoshi Rengo, whose patron deity is Sumiyoshi as *kami* of healing. The *yakuza* trace the origin of their organization to the itinerant traders of medicines and other goods at fairs during the Edo period, and this gang has adopted the *kami*'s name as its own.

See also Izanagi and Izanami; Raikō.

References and further reading:

Joly, Henri L. 1967. *Legend in Japanese Art.* Tokyo: Charles E. Tuttle Co.

Philippi, Donald, trans. and ed. 1968. *Kōjiki.* Tokyo: Tokyo University Press.

SUSANO-WO

Brother to Amaterasu-ō-mikami, deity of the untamed and the wild storm, and ruler, with his mother, Izanami, of the underworld. He is identified with the Buddhist deity Gozu Tenno, emperor of the underworld and plague carrier, and with Emma-ō, the death king. He is also the founder and major culture hero of the Izumo people. Takehaya-Susano-wo-no-mikoto, to give his full name, is a complex figure, perhaps the most complex in Japanese mythology. In the classical narrative recounted in both *Kōjiki* and *Nihonshōki* he was born after Amaterasu to Izanami. Susano-wo started his career inauspiciously. Born last, he was declared ruler of the sea, but his lamentations for his dead mother, Izanami, brought down the wrath of his father, Izanagi. As a consequence, he was banished to join her in Yōmi, the land of the dead.

Before departing for his new post in the netherworld, Susano-wo went to visit his sister in the High Plain of Heaven. Suspecting his intentions, she awaited him armed and armored on the near side of Amanokawa (the Heavenly River). To assure herself of his good intentions, the two siblings agreed to produce offspring in a form of trial-by-combat. Using the fragments of Susano-wo's sword, Amaterasu produced three female deities. Susano-wo, borrowing her string of jewels, broke them and produced five male deities. They agreed that the females, having been born of Susano-wo's sword, were his offspring, whereas the males, having been born of Amaterasu's jewelry, were hers (the *Nihonshōki*, arguing from the reverse premise, reached the same conclusions), thus Susano-wo declared himself winner of the contest.

Next, the triumphant Susano-wo committed severe acts of pollution: He broke the dykes his sister had built for her rice paddies and threw excrement at his sister's weaving hall, climaxing his activities by flaying a horse and throwing the carcass onto Amaterasu's palace. Amaterasu withdrew into a cave, causing darkness on heaven and on the Central Land of the Reed Plains. The deities of heaven, after the usual assembly and after luring Amaterasu from her cave, promptly banished Susano-wo (this after pulling out his nails and beard and receiving a heavy indemnity fine of one thousand offering trays). While wandering the earth after his banishment, he slew Ōgetsuhime, the deity of food, whom he accused of trying to feed him with polluted substances.

In his wanderings in the Central Land of the Reed Plains, Susano-wo came upon an elderly couple whose daughters, all but one, had been sacrificed to an eight-headed serpent. Susano-wo ordered them to prepare eight barrels of special saké for the serpent. Once the serpent had consumed these and become drunk, Susano-wo emerged from a hiding place, cutting off the serpent's heads. He cut open the serpent's tails and found the great sword Kusanagi, which he gave, as an apology, to his sister. The sword was subsequently passed to Ninigi-no-mikoto when he descended to the Central Land of the Reed Plains. Susano-wo settled in Izumo, and one of his descendants from his marriage to the daughter of the old couple includes Ōkuninushi. Subsequently, he had one of his daughters, Suseri-hime, stolen along with his sword, bow and arrows (that is, the signs of his rule), and his *kōtō* (harp) by Ōkuninushi.

There are several variants to the Susano-wo myth. The *Nihonshōki* recounts in addition to the above that he resided in Kara (Korea) and reached Izumo by stone (or clay) boat, bringing with him the seeds of edible grains and tree saplings that he duly planted. The *Izumo Fudoki* also states that Susano-wo came from Korea but adds that he brought the art of sword forging with him and essentialy, founded the Izumo nation. Local myths still extant in Shimane prefecture (the modern name for the area of Izumo) reinforce the idea that Susano-wo was a great cultural hero, perhaps originating from Korea (Grayson 2002).

Susano-wo is a complex figure because he appears as both villain and hero, and as a figure associating the underworld and the sea. As villain he is an uncontrollable force, something both admired and feared. As hero, he defends against evil. It must not be assumed that Susano-wo is the deity of evil. He is, in fact, a committer of *tsumi*, polluting acts, rather than of evil in the Western or Buddhist sense. These *tsumi* are the result of his uncontrolled nature rather than malevolence. In Japanese terms, it is his *aramitama*, his wild spirit, that predominates. The storm is his element because storms are evidence of blessings (rain and fertility) gone wild and uncontrolled. Shintō traditionally regards death as polluting, and Susano-wo's polluting actions suit him for the role of ruler of the land of the dead. The sea, his original domain, was the location of the Land of Tokoyo, a mysterious land sometimes identified with the underworld, sometimes with the realm of magic.

The deities that emerged from his meeting with his sister are all assigned specific dwelling places in the Central Land of the Reed Plains (that is, Japan). And the record of original Izumo myths recounted above also ensure Susano-wo's place as a significant deity in the process of creating and naming the land. These myths, as well as the myth of Ōkuninushi, his descendant, may well be political myths: a charter for the supremacy of the Yamato royal cult, which incorporated and ordered, in a subsidiary manner, the cults of other, weaker nations during the Yamato period. It is also, however, part of the lengthy statement made in Japanese myth about the relationship between life and death, and about the nature of life: a mixture of regulated, orderly progressions and procedures, and wild, uncontrollable urges and actions.

Susano-wo's character is complicated by his nature as a death god or, at least, as ruler of the underworld. When Ōkuninushi encounters him, he is living in his high hall in Izumo, the entrance to Yōmi, the land of the dead. He has with him the Ikutachi (Life sword), Ikuyumiya (Life bow and arrows) and Amēnonōri-gōtō (Jeweled heavenly harp). His hair is inhabited by centipedes rather than by lice, as a normal person's would. All of these would seem to indicate that Susano-wo is a *taker* of life, as well as the ruler of the dead. But the Japanese wording is such that these instruments have an association with life in general. That they are stolen by Ōkuninushi indicates the ambivalent position of Ōkuninushi as a wizard able to deceive death. The recorders of the myth seem to be indicating their belief in the possibility, if one just knew how (or knew whom), of cheating death.

Like other Japanese myths, the myth of Susano-wo's defeat by his son-in-law has parallels in European mythology. The myth-type of the giant's castle is probably familiar to everyone who has grown up in a Western culture in the form of Jack and the Beanstalk, which has many variants. Given Japanese ambivalence about the underworld, it is not surprising to find the giant's castle in the realm of death, nor to find that the lord of death is also a life giver and creator.

See also Amaterasu; Izanagi and Izanami; Ōkuninushi; Oyamatsumi.

References and further reading:
Aston, William G., trans. 1956. *Nihongi.* London: Allen and Unwin.
Grayson, James H. 2002. "Susa-no-wo: A Culture Hero from Korea." *Japan Forum* 14(3): 465–488.
Philippi, Donald, trans. and ed. 1968. *Kōjiki.* Tokyo: Tokyo University Press.

SWORDS

Swords appear in a number of Japanese myths, and they fulfill an important role as indicators of purity, action, and fortitude. A sword is also part of the regalia of the Japanese imperial house. Swords are represented in one of two forms in mythological iconography. Those depicted from the age of the founding of Japan are generally shown as single-edged straight blades often worn slung from a belt sash. Swords associated with heroes are more often depicted as curved, single-edged, two-hand *tachi* sabers. The former are fabulous in a sense (though some fine examples are still extant), and indicate the claim to antiquity and misty origins of the user and of the sword itself.

When Izanami gave birth to the fire *kami* and was killed by the birth, her husband, Izanagi, drew the sword Ame-no-ō-habari-no-kami (Heavenly wide pointed blade), also called Itsu-no-ō-habari-no-kami (Consecrated wide pointed blade), and killed his son. The blood adhering to the blade, guard, and pommel gave birth to other deities. This sword was a *kami* in its own right. It dammed the waters of the Heavenly River so that the deities could confer in the dry riverbed, as was their custom. When they needed someone to subdue Ōkuninushi, they asked Ame-no-ō-habari to do the job, though he sent his son, Takemikazuchi-no-kami, instead. As the case of the sword Ame-no-ō-habari-no-kami illustrates, swords were considered *kami* in and of themselves.

Susano-wo found the great sword Kusanagi (Grass-cutter) in the tail of the eight-headed and –tailed serpent he slew. Ninigi-no-mikoto was given this same sword by his grandmother, Amaterasu-ō-mikami, to help him in his conquest of the Central Land of the Reed Plains. The sword came into the possession of the hero Yamato-takeru, who, after using it to subdue the people of the East, left it in care of one of his wives in Owari (modern Nagoya), where it is kept today at the Atsuta-jinja shrine. However, some reports attest that the original Kusanagi was thrown overboard by the losing Taira at the sea battle of Dan-no-Ura and was replaced by the sword Hironogoza, forged during the reign of Emperor Sujin. Another of Susano-wo's swords, Ikutachi (Life sword), was stolen by the wizard-deity Ōkuninushi. The sword's name (as well as the character of its bearers) is ambiguous enough to argue that it was a wizardly instrument for conferring, as well as taking, life.

Ajishikitakahikone-no-kami, enraged at being mistaken for his dead friend Ame-no-wakahiko (and thus being compared to a corpse), used the sword Ō-Hakari (Great leaf cutter), also called Kamudo-no-tsurugi (Heavenly way sword), to cut down the funeral house where his friend's corpse was resting.

Takemikazuchi-no-kami's sword, Futsu-no-mitama, was dropped into the storehouse of Takakuraji of Kumano, who was instructed in a dream to hand it to the future first emperor, Jimmu Tenno. This sword, which helped the hero subdue the unruly deities of Kumano, was eventually enshrined as *go-shintai* in the shrine of Iso-no-kami.

The hero Raikō, who cleared Japan of demons and ogres, had a sword, Higekiri (Beard-cutter), with which he dispatched the robber-ogre Shutendōji.

The sword was later loaned to Raikō's attendant, Watanabe no Tsuna, with which he cut off the arm of the Rashōmon *oni*.

The cult of the sword was a prominent part of Japanese belief and myth. Swords, along with bows, were the most important weapon of the gentleman, and there is evidence that the long bow and the sword were the symbols of rule of the emperor in archaic times. The metallurgy of Japanese swords, originally fairly simple, became a sophisticated technology that is hard to duplicate today. Over the centuries the sword underwent two major transformations. The original straight, single-edged blade was used until around the Nara period. These are referred to in the *Kōjiki* as "mallet-headed" swords because the pommel ended in a large, mallet-shaped knob, often heavily decorated—a necessary balance for the long blade (which could measure ten hands, approximately fifty inches). All the blades named in the *Kōjiki* and *Nihonshōki* must have been of this type. Advances in metalworking led to the creation of the composite blade. Made of alternating layers of steel and softer iron, these blades reached their peak during the Gempei wars and soon after. They were short, heavy, curved sabers, called *tachi*, which evolved later, during the Edo period, into the slimmer, longer, two handed *katana*. In mythical terms, the swords that Raikō and other heroes used would have been of the *tachi* type, worn, like the earlier mallet-head swords, slung under the sash with cords.

> **See also** Amaterasu-ō-mikami; Ame-no-wakahiko; Susano-wo; Heroes; Imperial Regalia; Jimmu Tenno; Ninigi-no-mikoto; Raikō; Takemikazuchi-no-kami; Yamato-takeru; Weapons.
>
> **References and further reading:**
> Aston, William G., trans. 1956. *Nihongi*. London: Allen and Unwin.
> Joly, Henri L. and Inada Hogitaro. 1963. *Arai Hakuseki's the Sword Book in Honchō Gunkikō and the Book of Samé Kō Hi Sei Gi of Inaba Tsūriō*. New York: Charles E. Tuttle Co.
> Philippi, Donald, trans. and ed. 1968. *Kōjiki*. Tokyo: Tokyo University Press.

TAIRA

The name of a family, or rather clan, that claimed descent from a branch of the imperial family. The Taira (the Chinese character for their name can be read as *Hei*, and they are thus also known as the Heike or House of Hei), led by Taira no Kiyomori, were called upon by a faction of the nobility in Kyoto to expel the Minamoto from the capital. Their work done, they stayed to control the imperial court. They lost the Gempei wars to the forces of Minamoto no Yoritomo, and were finally defeated decisively at the sea battle of Dan-no-Ura, the straits between Kyushu and western Honshu, by Minamoto no Yoshitsune. The remains of Taira partisans were then hunted down by the victorious Minamoto loyalists.

The story of the rise and, most particularly, fall of the Taira has long excited Japanese romanticism. The Taira were doomed heroes, and their spectacular fall has resounded in art and popular imagination. Thus a particular form of crab found in the Seto Inland Sea is named for them because of the resemblance of the carapace to an armored warrior's face mask: The crabs are said to represent the spirits of dead Taira warriors drowned at Dan-no-Ura. Persistent myths tie various hidden mountain communities of *hinnin* (outcasts) and of *shinobi* (*ninja*) clans to the descendants of Taira partisans hiding from Minamoto retribution.

One of the most famous myths concerning the Taira is the legend of the blind lute player who was called to play before the ghostly court of Taira noblemen as they eternally wait battle.

The popularity of the Taira is related in some ways to the Japanese cultural fondness for fighting in doomed causes. The Taira are always portrayed as more elegant and refined than their Minamoto opponents, doomed from the start to fall to brute strength. A similar enthusiasm is shown for the cause of the Taira's greatest opponent, Minamoto Yoshitsune, who suffered a similar fate to his enemies at the hands of his older brother, the shogun Yoritomo. The popularity of this concept is evidenced by the historical prevalence of lute players, whose repertoire consisted of a recitation of the Taira chronicles and who were to be found throughout Japan until the middle of the twentieth century. A number of Taira-based plays in the Nōh theater exist as well.

See also Benkei; Ghosts; Yoshitsune.

References and further reading:

Kitagawa, Hiroshi, and Bruce T. Tsuchida, trans. 1977. *The Tale of Heike (Heike Monogatari)*. Tokyo: University of Tokyo Press.

McCullough, Helen Craig, trans. 1988. *The Tale of the Heike*. Stanford: Stanford University Press.

———. 1966. *Yoshitsune: A Fifteenth-Century Japanese Chronicle* (Gikeiki). Stanford: Stanford University Press.

TAKAMAGAHARA

The "High Plain of Heaven." The abode of the heavenly deities. It seems, on the basis of the writing in the *Kōjiki* and the *Nihonshōki*, to be not much different than the early Japan the writers were living in. We know that it held at least one palace, that of Amaterasu-ō-mikami, and her rice fields and dikes. The rest of the realm is undifferentiated or, at least, not described, with a few landmarks sketched in. There is the bed of Ame-no-yasu-no-kawa (Heavenly River, also called Amanokawa). Originally the stream ran free, but it was dammed by Ame-no-ō-habari-no-kami, the sword Izanagi carried. The lower, dry riverbed is used by the deities for their assemblies, where they debate matters relating to themselves and the land. There are iron-bearing mountains, the Ame-no-kanayama, and a well, Ame-no-manai, and a further range of mountains, Ame-no-kaguyama, from which divinatory implements can be obtained. We also know that it is separated from the earthly realm by the Heavenly River (Milky Way), spanned perhaps by the Heavenly Floating Bridge, though those two elements are sometimes conflated. At some point there is a meeting of nine ways, where Sarutahiko ambushed the heavenly grandson, though that might be slightly out of the boundaries of Takamagahara itself.

> *See also* Amaterasu-ō-mikami; Ninigi-no-mikoto; Swords.
> *References and further reading:*
> Aston, William G., trans. 1956. *Nihongi.* London: Allen and Unwin.
> Philippi, Donald, trans. and ed. 1968. *Kōjiki.* Tokyo: Tokyo University Press.

TAKAMIMUSUBI-NO-KAMI

The second of the three "invisible" *kami* who came into existence spontaneously at the creation of heaven and earth. Though having no spouse, he nonetheless was the ancestor of a line of *kami*. In the *Nihonshōki* he is the father of Sukunabikona, the midget deity. The same role is assigned to Musubi-no-kami in the *Kōjiki*, which might suggest they are spouses. He is one of the most important deities in heaven, almost the coeval of Amaterasu-ō-mikami. It is he, together with Amaterasu, who convenes the Assembly of the Gods in the dry riverbed of the Heavenly River, whenever that becomes necessary.

He and Amaterasu-ō-mikami convened an assembly of the *kami* when the heavenly *kami* decided to restore control and order to the Central Land of the Reed Plains. He again collaborated with Amaterasu in sending Ame-no-wakahiko to subdue the earth, and when that deity rebelled, sent the pheasant to find out what had happened. After Ame-no-wakahiko killed the messenger pheasant, Takamimusubi-no-kami thrust the arrow back the way it had come and killed Ame-no-wakahiko.

Historically, we know that the Japanese states of the Yayoi and Kofun periods were often ruled by female ruler-shamans. These were usually assisted by a male counterpart who was *ritually* secondary, but *administratively* primary. The same system existed in historical times in Okinawa, where rulership was embodied in a brother-sister rulership, the "king" attending to secular matters, his sister to the divine. It is conceivable that Takamimusubi's and Amaterasu-ō-mikami's mythical positions derive from that archaic system.

> *See also* Amaterasu-ō-mikami; Ame-no-wakahiko; Sukunabikona.
> *References and further reading:*
> Aston, William G., trans. 1956. *Nihongi.* London: Allen and Unwin.
> Philippi, Donald, trans. and ed. 1968. *Kōjiki.* Tokyo: Tokyo University Press.

TAKARABUNE

The treasure ship ridden by the Shichi Fukujin (seven gods of good fortune). It is usually portrayed as a dragon-headed Chinese-style ship with a single mast and sail. The sail is emblazoned with the character reading "good fortune," or an oval, Edo-period *ryō* gold coin. It is often accompanied by a crane above and a turtle below, symbols of longevity and felicity. It sails into port on New Year's Eve, dispensing its treasures. These include the key to the gods' storehouse, a hat of invisibility, an inexhaustible purse, Daikoku's hammer that showers gold coins, a lucky straw raincoat for protection against evil spirits, jewels, assorted boxes or sacks of oval *ryō* gold coins, copper cash, brocade rolls, and other precious items.

See also Animals: turtle; Shichi Fukujin.
References and further reading:
Ehrich, Kurt S. 1991. *Shichifukujin: Die Sieben Glücksgötter Japans.* Recklinghausen, Germany: Verlag Aurel Bongers.
Joly, Henri L. 1967. *Legend in Japanese Art.* Tokyo: Charles E. Tuttle Co.

TAKEMIKAZUCHI-NO-KAMI

A heavenly warrior deity and thunder god, considered son of the heavenly sword Ame-no-ō-habari-no-kami (though he came into being from the blood of the slain Kagutsuchi-no-kami), and the messenger who caused Ōkuninushi and his sons to surrender the Central Land of the Reed Plains to the authority of the heavenly deities. Sent to Izumo, he seated himself on the point of his sword, which he had thrust hilt-first into a wave. He convinced Ōkuninushi and his son Kotoshironushi to submit. The second son, Takeminakata-no-kami, resisted and was defeated in a wrestling match: When he came to seize Takemikazuchi's arm in a wrestling hold, it turned first to an icicle, then to a sword blade. When Takemikazuchi seized Takeminakata-no-kami's, arm, it was crushed like a reed. Later, he sent the sword Futsu-no-mitama to Kamu-Yamato-Iharehiko-no-mikoto (Jimmu Tenno) in Kumano when the emperor had been ensorcelled, to help him continue his subjugation of the land.

Takemikazuchi-no-kami is sometimes regarded as patron of the martial virtues, and by extension, of the martial arts. Some martial arts *dojo* (training halls) in Japan, notably those of *aikido* (a martial art heavily reliant on controlling an opponent's joint movements), may have small shrines dedicated to this deity. One of the reasons, of course, is the *kami*'s steadfastness in accomplishing his tasks. The close attachment to *aikido* derives from the description of Takemikazuchi's defeat of Takeminakata by an arm-hold: an *aikido* hallmark.

In popular myth, Takemikazuchi is important as a thunder god and, even more significantly, as the subduer of Namazu, the giant catfish that causes earthquakes. Takemikazuchi is thus a powerful *aramitama,* or rough spirit. His steadfastness and his earthquake-subduing powers—he drove the *kaname-ishi* (pinning rock) through the catfish to keep it in place—have brought him the title of Kashima Daimyōjin (Great deity of Kashima), and his main shrine is the popular Kashima shrine in Ibaragi prefecture, northeast of Tokyo. Many people still believe that the *kaname-ishi,* which can be viewed today on the grounds of the shrine, is what keeps earthquakes in Japan from being even more severe than they are. He is also a *gongen* as the main deity of the Kasuga complex in Nara, where he is considered the avatar of Fukukensaku Kannon in Ryōbu Shintō. His totem animal is the white deer, though the association between the *kami* and the bodhisattva may be nothing more than the association between the *kami*'s tutelary animal and the deer representing the Deer Park where the Buddha preached.

> **See also** *Gongen;* Kotoshironushi; Namazu; Ōkuninushi; Swords; Takeminakata-no-kami; Thunder Deities; Yamato-takeru.
> **References and further reading:**
> Aston, William G., trans. 1956. *Nihongi.* London: Allen and Unwin.
> Goldsbury, Peter. "Touching the Absolute: Aikido vs. Religion and Philosophy." http://www.aikidojournal.com/articles/ajArticles/_TouchingTheAbsolute.asp.
> Grapard, Allan G. 1992. *The Protocol of the Gods: A Study of the Kasuga Cult in Japanese History.* Berkeley: University of California Press.
> Philippi, Donald, trans. and ed. 1968. *Kōjiki.* Tokyo: Tokyo University Press.
> Ouwehand, Cornelius. 1964. *Namazu-e and Their Themes: An Interpretative Approach to Some Aspects of Japanese Religion.* Leiden, the Netherlands: E. J. Brill.

TAKEMINAKATA-NO-KAMI

One of Ōkuninushi's sons. When the heavenly deities sent Takemikazuchi-no-kami to demand submission, this son refused, but was defeated in a wrestling match with the heavenly emissary. He ran away but was overtaken on the banks of Lake Suwa, where he pleaded for his life. His submission was accepted, and he dwells to this day in the Suwa shrine, where he is worshiped as the deity of Lake Suwa. This myth may be the foundation myth for the shrine, as well as a mythicized account of the surrender of one of the Izumo state's clans to the Yamato Omi clan, who claimed Takemikazuchi as clan ancestor.

Takeminakata-no-kami is sometimes identified with the hunter Koga Saburo, who, persecuted by his brothers, fell into a hole in the earth. He made his way to a wondrous country (or the country of the dragon king, in some versions) where he lived for many years, marrying a princess of that place. He eventually returned, took revenge upon his brothers, and was deified as the deity of Lake Suwa in the name of Takeminakata. This is, of course, a variant of the

Urashimatarō story, and both are related closely to the story of Ho-ori and the daughter of the dragon king. Takeminakata is also identified in the *Nihonshōki* with Amatsumikaboshi, the *kami* of the dawn star (Venus).

> ***See also*** Ho-ori-no-mikoto; Ōkuninushi; Takemikazuchi-no-kami; Ryūjin; Urashimatarō.
> ***References and further reading:***
> Aston, William G., trans. 1956. *Nihongi.* London: Allen and Unwin.
> Philippi, Donald, trans. and ed. 1968. *Kōjiki.* Tokyo: Tokyo University Press.
> Ouwehand, Cornelius. 1964. *Namazu-e and Their Themes: An Interpretative Approach to Some Aspects of Japanese Religion.* Leiden, the Netherlands: E. J. Brill.

TA-NO-KAMI

Kami of the rice fields. The guardian of the paddy, this *kami* is worshiped and invited to enter the paddy rice, to ensure its growth, and to protect the harvest. At the end of the harvest he is sent back to his abode in the mountains, where he is known as Yama-no-kami. Ta-no-kami is sometimes conflated with Inari, also a deity of the harvest and of prosperity generally. However, many Ta-no-kami shrines in the fields lack the special symbols (red torii, fox figures) of Inari shrines, and thus Ta-no-kami (whose responsibilities are for the field, but not, as Inari, for wealth in general) must be considered a separate deity.

> ***See also*** Inari; Yama-no-kami.
> ***References and further reading:***
> Herbert, Jean. 1967. *Shinto—At the Fountain Head of Japan.* London: George Allen and Unwin Ltd.
> Stefansson, Halldor. 1985. "Earth Gods in Morimachi." *Japanese Journal of Religious Studies* 12 (4): 277–298.

TAWARA TODA (TODA HIDESATO, FUJIWARA HIDESATO)

An eleventh-century hero of great strength (his nickname *tawara* means "rice–bale," as he was able to lift a 132-pound bale by himself; for another explanation, see below). In the tenth century, Taira no Masakado, a nobleman from the East, around Edo (now Tokyo) Bay, rebelled against the emperor. Tawara Toda thought of enlisting with him, but when he was granted an audience, the hero saw the rebel prince picking up fallen rice from a mat with his chopsticks. Deciding the rebel was a miser (and presumably unlikely to reward his followers in the way Toda desired), the hero enlisted with the imperial side under a Fujiwara shogun (general). Fearing the hero, Masakado spelled up a hundred images of himself who aped his movements exactly, to act as decoys. The hero crept into the rebel camp at night and felt the wrist of each sleeping Masakado image, finally finding the only one with a pulse and slaying it. The apparitions vanished

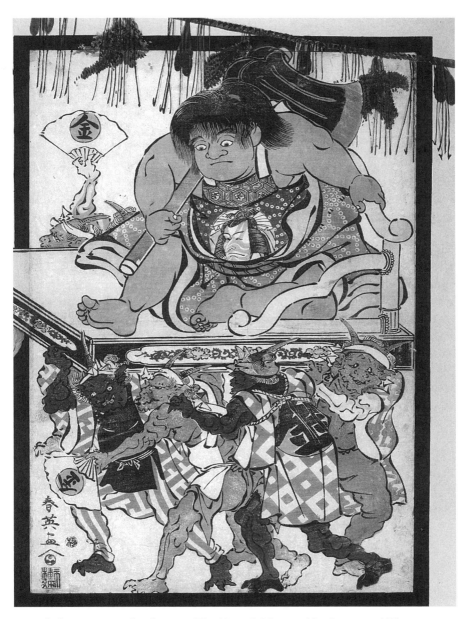

Kintoki borne in state by demons. (The Newark Museum/Art Resource, NY)

with the death of their master. In another version of the story, Toda killed some of Masakado's *kagemusha* (doubles), then started violently insulting Masakado. The rebel prince, unable to bear the insults, replied, and the wily hero killed him with an arrow.

As he was crossing the long bridge of Seta in Omi over an inlet of Lake Biwa, he found a dragon blocking the way. Unconcerned, he passed over the dragon's tail. The dragon identified himself as Ryūjin and said that his domain was being threatened by a giant centipede, longer than a mountain, and that he had been waiting for the passage of a fearless man. The hero slew the centipede with an arrow moistened with his own saliva. In gratitude, Ryūjin gave him a giant bell, which he deposited in Miidera temple—the same bell stolen later by Benkei, which had previously been stolen by Ryūjin himself—along with a magic cauldron that would cook without fire, an inexhaustible roll of brocade, and an inexhaustible bag of rice (hence the hero's nickname).

Tawara Toda represents the protagonists of Japan's heroic age, and his behavior and motivations are closer to the reality of that time than those of many other heroic and romantic heroes described in myths. The samurai ideals familiar from the ideas of *Yamato-damashii* (Japanese spirit) and the *Chūshingura* evolved during the time of national seclusion and peace of the Edo period. The samurai of the Gempei and Civil War period were of a different cut of cloth. Many of them were unabashedly out for what they could get. They were fearless and brave, but they very clearly expected rewards for that bravery and for their actions. Tawara Toda was acting in character in the myth, representing the interests of the *bushi* (warrior) class when it was being established, and before the ideals had modified reality. His characteristics are also the characteristics of the period: strength mixed with guile and a dose of personal magic, as well as help from the deities when necessary (Toda's victory over Masakado is credited, in the Japanese official chronicles, to the statue of Fudō Myō-ō, currently enshrined at Narita, not far from the scene of the action).

See also Animals: centipede; Benkei; *Chūshingura*; Fudō Myō-ō; Ryūjin.
References and further reading:
Joly, Henri L. 1967. *Legend in Japanese Art*. Tokyo: Charles E. Tuttle Co.
Sato, Hiroaki. 1995. *Legends of the Samurai*. Woodstock, NY: Overlook Press.

TENGU

Sometimes benevolent, sometimes malicious mountain sprites. The name is written in Chinese characters as "Celestial dog," and the concept may have been borrowed from China, where comets with long "bushy" tails were considered a form of a heavenly dog. *Tengu* are reputed to be quick to anger and to be experts in sword-making and use. They are associated with mysterious events—sudden laughter, unexplained rock falls, and mysterious voices—that people encounter in the deep mountains. *Tengu* befuddle and confuse people who attract their attention, and they are particularly attracted to ascetics who have retired to mountains to meditate. The *yamabushi* (mountain ascetic) who practiced magical and esoteric rituals in the depths of mountain wilderness contributed to the personification of these spirits and to their appearance in popular imagination.

There are two types of *tengu* described. The *shō-tengu* (little, or minor, *tengu*), also called *karasu-tengu* (crow *tengu*), have the beaks and feathers of crows and their coloration. The more powerful *konoha-tengu* (Tumbling-leaf *tengu*) have bright red human faces, long bulbous noses, wild white hair, and bulging eyes. Both kinds of *tengu* wear the tight leggings and jodhpurlike trousers, colorful surcoats, and small black pillbox hats that are the uniform of the *yamabushi*. They are ruled by an elder, the *dai tengu*, whose white beard falls to his belt.

Tengu are not all malevolent. Properly supplicated and given respect, they may impart some of their legendary skills—stamina, swordsmanship, magical amulets or spells, and knowledge of the mountains—to the proper person. Famous *tengu* include Tarōbō, the *tengu* of Mt. Atago, who was converted to the good by En-no-Gyōja. Tarōbō is associated with fire, and thus with Jizō. Another famous *tengu* is Kurama-tengu, worshiped on the neighboring Mt. Kurama and associated with both fire and Bishamon, another guardian of the mountain. Ushiwakamaru/Yoshitsune was commonly believed to have acquired his legendary proficiency with the sword by being trained by Kurama-tengu, as were several other legendary swordsmen. A well-known sword defense is called *konoha*, or tumbling leaf, either deriving from the *tengu* or, because of the association between the term and the *tengu*'s forest home, giving them their legendary reputation for swordsmanship.

Like the *kappa* and some other magical beings, *tengu* do not appear in the official myths, at least not in the form they took in popular imagination. For the highly regimented and regulated common people of Japan, the *tengu*, along with some deities such as Namazu, represented the *potential* of freedom and of upsetting the powers that ruled their lives. The parallel between the real *yamabushi* (also called *kebōzu*, or hairy priests) and the mythical *tengu* was both an explanatory and prescriptive myth. The *tengu* were fierce and wild, obeying their own leaders but not anyone else. In a similar vein, many peasants who rebelled against the accepted order when times were bad appealed to their own leaders and to a higher morality, to which the *tengu* subscribed as well. Further evidence can be found in the *tengu*'s female counterparts, the *yama-uba* and the *happyaku bikuni*. Yamabushi female counterparts often acted in a mixed role of Buddhist mendicant nun, medicine woman, diviner, and holy prostitute. Likewise, the *yama-uba* seduced men, promising them a reward if only they could withstand the burden she placed on them. Under the circumstances in which the people lived—oppressive taxes, lack of security in the long term, and victimization by the powers-that-be in various guises—a myth of a free, wild, and uncontrollable spirit provided some comfort. Nonetheless, it threatened to upset whatever security the peasant or villager *did* have. The wild and the civilized existed side by side with very thin barriers between them.

See also Bishamon-ten; En-no-Gyōja; *Yama-uba;* Yoshitsune.

References and further reading:

Bernier, Bernard. 1975. *Breaking the Cosmic Circle: Religion in a Japanese Village.* Ithaca: Cornell East Asian Papers.

Davis, Winston. 1984. "Pilgrimage and World Renewal: A Study of Religion and Social Value in Tokugawa Japan." *History of Religions* 23 (3): 71–98.

Goodin, Charles C. 1994."Tengu: The Legendary Mountain Goblins of Japan." *Furyu: The Budo Journal* 2. Text in http://www.seinenkai.com/articles/tengu.html.

Joly, Henri L. 1967. *Legend in Japanese Art.* Tokyo: Charles E. Tuttle Co.

TENJIN

The deity of scholarship and learning. In the ninth century, Sugawara Michizane (845–903), a brilliant scholar and official in the Heian court, was charged falsely with a treasonable offense as result of a power struggle. He was exiled from Heian-kyō, the imperial capital (modern Kyoto), to Chikuzen in Kyushu. After his death, the capital was struck by plague and famine, as well as thunderstorms that destroyed many buildings. Sugawara appeared to the emperor, as well as others, in dreams as a *goryō* (angry spirit). The emperor canceled the edict of banishment and reinstated Sugawara in his court rank, declaring him a divinity. When the afflictions did not end, he promoted Tenjin in the official ranking of *kami,* and the afflictions ceased.

A number of shrines were established to honor Tenjin as patron deity of scholarship: There are a number of famous Tenman-gu shrines, including in Kyushu and Kyoto. Minor Tenjin shrines are also often found on the grounds of Hachiman (the *kami* of culture) shrines, and visitors, particularly students doing their university entrance examinations, will often tie petitions for success to branches of trees planted near the Tenjin shrine.

Tenjin is a prominent example of a *goryō,* an angry *kami* who has a cause for grievance (unlike, for example, Susano-wo). His appeasement and deification, insofar as the authorities were concerned, was merely correcting an improper situation. The case also illustrates the thin boundary between political reality and religion that existed in the Japanese system. The difference between humans and *kami* is a very narrow one, more a difference of degree than of kind. Humans can

Sugawara Michizane riding his ox into exile before his elevation to Tenjin, deity of learning (The Art Archive/Private Collection Paris/Dagli Orti)

achieve *kami*-hood, and *kami* can become disturbed and rough, almost demonic, under sufficient provocation. The point is further emphasized by the fact that portrayals of Tenjin during his *goryō* phase show him in the form of a red *oni*, lightning sprouting from his body and striking onlookers and buildings. The continuation deity-human-demon is clearly illustrated here.

See also *Goryō*; Hachiman.
References and further reading:
Borgen, Robert. 1994. *Sugawara no Michizane and the Early Heian Court.* Honolulu: University of Hawaii Press.
Murayama, Shuichi, ed. 1983. *Tenjin shinko* [Tenjin belief]. Tokyo: Yuzankaku.
Ueda, Masaaki, ed. 1988. *Tenman tenjin: goryo kara gakumonshin e* [Tenman Tenjin: From Vengeful Ghost to God of Learning]. Tokyo: Chikuma Shobo.

TENSON (RYUKYUS: OKINAWA)
Mythical founder of the first Okinawan kingdom. He was reputed to have ruled for seventeen thousand years on Okinawa. His name is written with the same

characters as Ninigi (no-mikoto), Amaterasu-ō-mikami's grandson. This may simply be the result of Japanese or Okinawan attempts to increase the legitimacy of this legendary founder in Japanese eyes. He divided humanity into five classes: Ruler, high priestesses, nobles, local priestesses, and peasants. In some accounts he is named as Tenteishi.

> *See also* Amaterasu-ō-mikami; Ninigi-no-mikoto.
> *References and further reading:*
> Herbert, Jean. 1980. *La religion d'Okinawa*. Paris: Dervy-Livres. Collection
>   Mystiques et religions. Série B 0397–3050.
> Lebra, William P. 1966. *Okinawan Religion: Belief, Ritual, and Social Structure.*
>   Honolulu, University of Hawaii Press.
> Robinson, James C. 1969. *Okinawa: A People and Their Gods.* Rutland, VT:
>   Charles E. Tuttle Co.

TENTEISHI (RYUKYUS; OKINAWA)
See Tenson.

THUNDER DEITIES
A large category of important named and unnamed deities associated with death, protection, and fertility, often simply addressed indifferently as "Kaminari-sama" (Sir thunder). Among the important named thunder deities are Ajishiki-takahikone, Takemikazuchi, and Raiden. Thunder was a feared natural phenomenon associated with both death and fertility. Because by thunder the Japanese also meant lightning, thunder is also related to the concept of diamond (*see* Jewels). At the other extreme, thunder is also related to snakes, which are, at least in the classical mythic histories, associated with death and the underworld.

The various myths concerning thunder deities show them to be a varied lot in both nature and characteristics. The eight snake/thunder deities that emerged from the body of the dead Izanami in Yōmi are clear representations of death and corruption. Presumably because of their habitat and occasional poisonous nature, snakes were considered the denizens of the world of the dead. Their association with thunder is less clear but may be result from a similarity to the shape of lightning.

Takemikazuchi, a warrior *kami* who subdued Ōkuninushi and his sons, later became associated with the cult of the Kashima Daimyōjin, a deity who protects against earthquakes. When that association began, and whether Takemikazuchi was the original deity worshiped at Kashima, is difficult to tell. Nonetheless, the duality between thunder and earthquakes was noted by the early Japanese, and the associated deities—Takemikazuchi and Namazu—became fixtures of myth.

A demon flees from Raijin, the Thunder God. (HIP/Art Resource, NY)

There is also the figure of Raiden. Represented in iconography by a taloned demon banging on drums, Raiden is clearly influenced by Buddhist tradition. The stories told about him—his incessant crying (the cause of thunder), his fondness for human navels—are, like the stories about the *raiju*, a complex of "Just so" stories and presumably local myths that have lost their original explanation. Ajishikitakahikone-no-kami, a son of Ōkuninushi, had a petulant outburst at a funeral and is therefore credited with being the baby whose crying (while he is being taken up and down a ladder) is the sound of thunder. The *raiju* is another personification of thunder, this time in the form of a weasel- or cat-shaped animal that leaps onto trees and marks them with fiery claws. Lightning burns on trees are said to be formed by a *raiju*'s claws. One other reminder of the thunder deities needs to be mentioned: their offspring from human women. The myth of the strong man (or woman) who is a child of the thunder deity (name usually unspecified) can be found throughout Japan in both local and Great Tradition form. The offspring generally favor their male parent: They are wild, powerful, and uncontrollable but essentially can be tamed by the application of the Buddhist Law (Dōjō-hōshi) or by "natural" social obligations of society (Musashibō Benkei).

These three aspects of the thunder deity myth—association with death, association with protection, and explanation of natural phenomena—are combined in popular imagination. The classic myth histories describe a large number of thunder deities, and the addition of other myths from nonclassical and later sources indicates that thunder was a major concern; indeed, it is one of the most important deity characters in Japanese mythology. Viewed as a myth complex rather than as individual myths, we can see that thunder deities are among the category of deities that are most intimate with humankind, in all senses of the word. They are controllable *if only one knows how to approach them*; they are vastly powerful but able, and willing, to impart some of that power to humans; and they interact with both humans and deities and as such, serve as useful emissaries and go-betweens. Moreover, they are quintessentially connected both to the heavens *and* to the earth, thus both to the divine and pure, and to the mortal and polluted.

See also Ajishikitakahikone-no-kami; Benkei; Dōjō-hōshi; Izanami and Izanagi; Jewels; Raiden; Stones; Takemikazuchi-no-kami.

References and further reading:

Aston, William G., trans. 1956. *Nihongi.* London: Allen and Unwin.

Joly, Henri L., and Inada Hogitaro. 1963. *Arai Hakuseki's the Sword Book in Honchō Gunkikō and the Book of Samé Kō Hi Sei Gi of Inaba Tsūriō.* New York: Charles E. Tuttle Co.

Ouwehand, Cornelius. 1964. *Namazu-e and Their Themes: An Interpretative Approach to Some Aspects of Japanese Religion.* Leiden, the Netherlands: E. J. Brill.

Philippi, Donald, trans. and ed. 1968. *Kōjiki.* Tokyo: Tokyo University Press.

TOKOYO-NO-KUNI
See Underworld.

TOYOASHIHARA-NO-CHIAKI-NO-NAGAIOAKI-NO-MIZUHO-NO-KUNI
"Land of the plentiful reed plains and the fresh rice-ears"; in other words, the Japanese islands. These were the first lands created by the *kami* and given to the divine descendants of Amaterasu-ō-mikami. Often referred to as *Ashiharanakatsukuni* or *Toyoashi-no-hara-no-kuni* or Central Land of the Reed Plains, which is how it is referred to in this volume.

> *See also* Amaterasu-ō-mikami; Yamato.
> *References and further reading:*
> Aston, William G., trans. 1956. *Nihongi.* London: Allen and Unwin.
> Philippi, Donald, trans. and ed. 1968. *Kōjiki.* Tokyo: Tokyo University Press.

TOYOUKEBIME (ALSO TOYOUKE-Ō-MIKAMI; TOYOUKE-NO-KAMI)
See Food Deities.

TSUKIYOMI-NO-MIKOTO
The moon deity, penultimate of Izanagi's children. He was destined to rule over the night as his sister, Amaterasu, was to rule over the day. In a myth recounted in the *Nihonshōki* but not the *Kōjiki* (where it is told of Susano-wo), he was sent by his sister to visit Ukemochi-no-kami, *kami* of food. The goddess offered him food taken from her own mouth. The *kami* was enraged by this seeming insult (she offered him food polluted by her mouth, rather than fresh food), and he immediately killed her. Amaterasu heard of the incident and was incensed that he had killed the *kami* of food. She subsequently banished her brother to be the *kami* of the moon so that she, as *kami* of the sun, would not see his face again.

It seems that the authors of the *Nihonshōki* were retelling two origin myths: the myth of the separation of day/sun and night/moon, and the origins of humankind's food. There is also a third theme that touches on this story: The paradox between men, as pure, or at least potentially pure creatures, and women, as polluting, or at least potentially polluting creatures.

> *See also* Izanami and Izanagi; Susano-wo; Ukemochi-no-kami.
> *References and further reading:*
> Aston, William G., trans. 1956. *Nihongi.* London: Allen and Unwin.

UGAJIN
Female fertility *kami* often identified with Benzaiten. She appears as a woman-headed white snake and is associated with rivers and particularly with the Heavenly River (Milky Way). In some cases she is represented as part of Benzaiten's

headdress. Ugajin may be a Japanese representation of the *naga*, the serpent deities who protected the Buddha and stored some of his treasures (that is, teachings) in their heads. However, given that native Japanese inclination to adore/fear serpents, this seems like a later interpolation.

See also Benzaiten; Snake.

References and further reading:

Frank, Bernard. 1991. *Le pantheon bouddhique au Japon.* Paris: Collections d'Emile Guimet. Reunion des musees nationaux.

UKEMOCHI NO KAMI

See Food Deities.

UMINAI-GAMI AND UMIKII-GAMI (RYUKYUS)

The sister and brother deities who, together, created the Ryukyu Islands. As is true with other Ryukyuan mythical figures, they are barely personified, and the myth is vague and lacks detail. They are comparable to the Japanese Izanami and Izanagi, albeit without the detail. Formal positions in the Okinawan kingdom were modeled on the sibling pair: a sister-brother pair were respectively the chief priestess and the chief ruler in traditional Okinawa, before the importation of the Confucian patriarchal system in the fourteenth century. Even so, the position of the sister has always been ritually higher than that of the male of the pair.

See also Izanami and Izanagi.

References and further reading:

Herbert, Jean. 1980. *La religion d'Okinawa.* Paris: Dervy-Livres. Collection Mystiques et religions. Série B.

Lebra, William P. 1966. *Okinawan Religion: Belief, Ritual, and Social Structure.* Honolulu, University of Hawaii Press.

Sered, Susan Starr. 1999. *Women of the Sacred Groves: Divine Priestesses of Okinawa.* New York and Oxford: Oxford University Press.

UNDERWORLD

A complex term used here to synthesize three related but different concepts in Japanese mythology: Yōmi, Jigoku, and Tokoyo. In crude terms, the first two represent the world of the dead in Shintō, and hell in Buddhism. The third is a concept linking the two, but it is also equivalent to Never-never land, the Land of Cockaigne, Hi Brasil, and Fiddler's Green: a land of wondrous plenty and magic. Examined in detail, however, none of the Japanese concepts fit precisely with the Western concepts.

Yōmi is perhaps the easiest to deal with. It is the land of the dead. When Izanami died giving birth to Kagutsuchi, the fire *kami,* she arrived in the land of Yōmi, from where her loving husband tried to rescue her. Because he disobeyed

Demon skewering heads of the damned, from Jigoku-zoshi (Wheel of Hell), *late twelfth-century Japanese. (The Art Archive/Lucien Biton Collection Paris/Dagli Orti)*

her orders not to observe her, they fell into dispute, settled only when Izanagi escaped to the land of the living. Izanami then reigned as the personification of death until their son Susano-wo was banished there for mourning his mother more than was appropriate.

Yōmi is described as a dark and gloomy land, usually "down below," where the dead continue their existence amidst centipedes and rot and other polluting things. Yōmi does not appear to be attached to any idea of sinfulness or punishment, and aside from its general gloominess, there is no specific idea of hell as any more than a continuation of existence. Though the way out is barred by the Heavenly Rock Barrier, it is clearly identified as a place accessible from the land of Izumo.

With the emergence of Buddhism in Japan, the idea of Jigoku (hell) was added to the concept of Yōmi, and Susano-wo became identified with Gozu-tenno, lord of hell and bearer of pestilence and disease, and with Emma-Ō, king of hell and its chief magistrate. In Jigoku, the Buddhist hell, the sinful and unrepentant dead are tormented by demons until the time of rebirth. The demons are managed by ten kings headed by Emma-Ō. Jigoku is reached by a river, the Shozukawa, and after crossing it, the dead are deprived of their clothes by Dat-sueba or his female counterpart, Shozuka-no-baba. In the dry river bed of Sansu no kawa, the souls of little children build cairns of pebbles as their penance. They are aided by Jizō-bosatsu, the sound of whose ringed-staff both offers them comfort and frightens off Shozuka-no-baba.

The two reasonably clear images portrayed by the concepts of Yōmi and Jigoku are, however, bridged by the third concept, Tokoyo-no-kuni. Tokoyo is variously described as a land of wonders across the sea, as a place where the dead go, and as a realm under the sea. Access is via known entrances in the land of Izumo.

Tokoyo is also the land across the sea where an important category of *kami*—the *marebito*, or visiting kami—come from, including Sukunabikona and Ebisu. It is also the far-off land where Tajima-mori, a servant of Emperor Suinin, went to fetch the fruit of the seasonless fragrant tree as medicine. This fruit of Tokoyo gave rise to the *tachibana* (Japanese orange) of today. Moreover, Tokoyo is also the source of saké (rice wine), the medicine *par excellence*, the secret of which was brought by Sukunabikona, deity of magic and healing, when he came to help establish the world. The concept could therefore also imply a realm of magic and power. To complicate things further, Tokoyo is the realm to which the son of Tamayori-hime and Hikohohodemi returns. It is identified as the realm of Tamayori-hime's father, Owatatsumi, the dragon king of the sea. The Tokoyo concept was embraced in Buddhism as well, where it is seen as the Land of the Blessed, ruled by Kannon, and lying somewhere to the southeast of Cape Muroto in Shikoku. From Tokoyo the ancestors would return from time to time to visit their descendants. These associations firmly anchor Tokoyo as a marine domain.

The multiple associations of Tokoyo with death, the sea, and blessings mean that at least in ancient Japan, the three realms were conflated, or that the boundaries between the three were very thin. This is reinforced by Ryukyuan myth: On Ishigaki Island in the southern Yaeyama Group of the Ryukyu Islands is a cave that leads to *niiru*, the underworld. Two monstrous giants, Akamata (Red) and Kuromata (Black), emerge from the cave from time to time, bringing with them the typhoons that assail the world, and punishing wrong-doers. The underworld is a good and bad place at the same time: The ancestors come from there, bringing good, but evils and *akuma* come from there as well. And the idea that blessings can be acquired from Tokoyo/the sea is reinforced by the Urashimatarō legend, as the fisherman goes to the dragon king's palace, which might be in Tokoyo. Finally, the relationship between the land of the dead and the realm of the sea is evident in the complex position of Susano-wo, who, delegated to rule the sea, has become ruler of the underworld as well.

The concept of a far land of wonders, usually an island, should not be surprising in the Japanese case. Though Tokoyo is often mentioned as being off the southeastern coast of Cape Muroto in Shikoku (in Buddhist tales) and is reachable from Izumo, on the other side of Honshu, it is also the kind of never-never land that people have always speculated about in many cultures. Whether the concept derives ultimately from a religious myth (the land of the dead) that was adopted by popular culture, or whether it was a popular myth about the land of plenty (which can be found in many cultures) adopted for religious purposes, does not matter. What is significant is that there was a miraculous source for good (and bad, or at least, upsetting) things in society. Indeed, Japanese official and popular experience throughout Japan's history was such that many strange and potentially useful things—concepts, people, and material goods—did come from Korea and China, and starting in the fifteenth century, from Europe. These same things, and same persons, were also often dangerous, upsetting to the normal order, and threatening in their arrival. The very foundations of Japanese culture were based on the importation of Chinese ideas, and later, by Emperor Ōjin in particular, of whole families and clans of craftsmen and experts from Korea (this was important enough to have Ōjin deified as Hachiman, *kami* of culture). These imports forced a wholesale rearrangement of archaic Japanese society, just as the importation of Buddhism some years later, the arrival of the Mongols centuries later, and the arrival of the Europeans almost a millennium later did. Thus visits from the outside became embedded in Japanese myth as both opportunities and threats, and these mysterious far-off lands were the source of blessings and miracles, as well as evils and upsets. The myth of Tokoyo was thus reinforced from time to time by the actual appearance of gifts from Tokoyo, that is, from overseas. For the Japanese peasant and commoner (and sometimes even the elite) those lands were no less fabulous than the fabled Tokoyo.

See also Datsueba; Emma-ō; Gozu-tenno; Hachiman; Izanagi and Izanami; Jizō; Ryūjin; Shozuka-no-baba; Sukunabikona; Susano-wo; Urashimatarō.

References and further reading:
Aston, William G., trans. 1956. *Nihongi.* London: Allen and Unwin.
Joly, Henri L. 1967. *Legend in Japanese Art.* Tokyo: Charles E. Tuttle Co.
Jones, Hazel J. 1980. *Live Machines: Hired Foreigners and Meiji Japan.* Tenterden, UK: Paul Norbury Publications.
Kōnoshi, Takamitsu. 1984. "The Land of Yōmi: On the Mythical World of the Kōjiki." *Japanese Journal of Religious Studies* 11 (1): 57–76.
Philippi, Donald, trans. and ed. 1968. *Kōjiki.* Tokyo: Tokyo University Press.
Ouwehand, Cornelius. 1964. *Namazu-e and Their Themes: An Interpretative Approach to Some Aspects of Japanese Religion.* Leiden, the Netherlands: E. J. Brill.

URASHIMATARŌ

The Japanese Rip van Winkle. Urashimatarō was a poor fisherman who found two boys tormenting a turtle on the beach. He rescued the animal. The following day he was invited to ride the turtle's back to the dragon king's palace under the sea. Upon arrival, he was greeted, feasted, and entertained by the dragon king's daughter. After some time (often described as several years) he yearned to return home, notwithstanding the princess's entreaties. As a parting gift, she gave him a jewel box.

Arriving at his village, he saw that everything was changed. His house and family had disappeared. No one remembered him except one old woman who recalled that she had been told, in her childhood, of Urashimatarō's disappearance. Despondent, Urashimatarō opened the jewel case. A mist enveloped him, and he suddenly changed into a white-bearded old man. In some versions, the box also contained a feather, which changed him into a crane (symbol of felicity); as the crane flew away, it was greeted by the dragon king's daughter in the form of a turtle (symbol of long life).

The theme of Urashimatarō is a common one around the world. Two elements are significant: the concept of the dragon or sea king's home under the waves, with clear connections to Ryūjin and to Owatatsumi-no-kami and Ho-ori-no-mikoto, on the one hand; and the association of the turtle and the crane, symbols of marital felicity, longevity, and good wishes, which feature on the Takarabune (Treasure ship) as well. For fishermen in Japan as elsewhere, the sea was the provider of its bounty, but, at the same time, it was also a source of danger, and of loss of fishermen and those who lived by its shores.

See also Ho-ori-no-mikato; Owatatsumi-no-kami; Ryūjin; Takarabune.
References and further reading:
Joly, Henri L. 1967. *Legend in Japanese Art.* Tokyo: Charles E. Tuttle Co.

USUSUMA MYŌ-Ō

One of the heavenly kings responsible for purification from material pollution. He is invoked by menstruating women, those who are ill, and those with other bodily afflictions. He is, in consequence, also the guardian of the privy. He is portrayed as multiarmed, with flaming hair and flames spurting from every pore. He is sometimes portrayed as bearing a trident.

Ususuma is venerated in Tendai and Shingon esoteric schools of Buddhism, and particularly in Zen monasteries, mainly at the entrance to meditation halls, where he ensures the purity of the premises by his presence.

See also Myō-ō, p. 54.
References and further reading:
Frank, Bernard. 1991. *Le pantheon bouddhique au Japon.* Paris: Collections d'Emile Guimet. Reunion des musees nationaux.
Getty, Alice. 1988. *The Gods of Northern Buddhism.* New York: Dover Publications.

WAKA-USH-KAMUI (AINU)

Deity of the waters. Her name means "Water-dwelling kamui." Also called Petorush-mat (Watering-place woman), she is responsible for all fresh water. While sitting at her hearth (the *kamui* have hearths and homes like humans, and they engage in the same tasks, in this case, needlework) she received a message from the culture hero Okikurmi that a famine had broken out among the humans. With the last of his resources, he had brewed wine and sent a winged *inau* to supplicate the goddess. The goddess then invited the *kamui* of the River Rapids, the *kamui* of game, of fish, of the hunt (Hashinau-uk Kamui), and Kotankor Kamui (Domain-ruling *kamui*) to a feast. While dancing and singing with the *kamui* of River Rapids, to entertain her guests, she told them of the humans' plight.

"The humans do not respect the deer when they come to visit (that is, spirits wearing their deer guise, as a present to the humans)" said the game *kamui*.

"The humans do not respect the salmon, killing them any old way, instead of by properly beating them with a fish maul," said the fish *kamui*.

Kotankor Kamui, the domain-ruling *kamui*, was angry too, for a woman's hair had fallen into the wine of the offering.

"I am so sorry," said the goddess quickly, "I am so stupid, that hair fell from my head while I was dancing."

While they were dancing, the two goddesses sent their souls to the storehouses of the *kamui* of game and of fish and let the deer and the salmon out, so that they swarmed once again in the land of the humans. The gods went on with the feast, not wishing to make a scene. After the feast, Waka-ush Kamui sent a dream to Okikurmi, telling him what had happened, and warning him to treat the game and fish respectfully. She also told him to apologize to the two offended deities, and to her assistant, the goddess of the River Rapids, by offering them *inau* and wine. This he did, ensuring the *kamui*'s delight, as well as enhancing Waka-ush Kamui's reputation and prestige (because she had gotten offerings for the other gods).

Hokkaido is covered by a web of lively streams and rivers, and it is not surprising that the Ainu, whose *kotan*, or corporate domains, centered around river valleys, felt that the waters were worthy of particular respect. The myth retold here, from a *kamui yukar*, also shows the interdependence and exchange between the Ainu and their gods. A god's power and reputation rested on the amount of offering s/he received, just as human lives depended on treating the *kamui*, in their guise as food, in a properly ritualized manner.

See also Hashinau-uk Kamui; Kotankor Kamui; Okikurmi.
References and further reading:
Munro, Neil Gordon. 1962. *Ainu Creed and Cult*. London: Routledge and Kegan

Paul; London and New York: K. Paul International, distributed by Columbia University Press, 1995.

Philippi, Donald L., trans. 1979. *Songs of Gods, Songs of Humans: The Epic Tradition of the Ainu.* Princeton: Princeton University Press.

WATATSUMI-NO-KAMI

See Owatatsumi-no-kami.

WEAPONS

Many of the Buddhist and Shintō deities are portrayed carrying weapons, which are an essential part of their regalia, and weapons appear in many myths. The carrying of weapons, most notably swords and bows, was a distinguishing mark of the "gentleman" throughout East Asia from earliest recorded history. The Yayoi culture, with its stratified ideas, must have participated in this weapon-bearing ideology. The three most common weapons are swords (which are often named and constitute *kami* in their own right), bows, and *kongō* (a small hand weapon representing lightning). Swords and *kongō* are dealt with in separate entries.

As a general rule, Buddhist deities tend to carry elaborate Chinese pole arms, of which the Chinese had a more varied inventory than did the Japanese. Shintō deities tend to carry a bow or sword, if anything. The main exception here is the jeweled spear, Ama-no-Nuboko, with which Izanagi stirred the sea to bring forth the land.

Bows and arrows feature in a number of myths. Although arrows can slay, they can also bring about good luck, and they even represent some deities, such as Hachiman. Contrary to the impression gained from evocations and imagery of later ages, it was the bow more than the sword that signified the nobleman and the warrior in Heian Japan and earlier. This might be because metallurgy was less developed, or because bows were more effective and less risky weapons (after all, one did not have to see the whites of the enemy's eyes in order to use a bow). Several magical bows and arrows appear in the early myths. The most important arrow is the one that slew Ame-no-wakahiko when he killed the pheasant rather than returning to heaven. Perhaps the most important bow is found in the bow-and-arrow of life, symbols of Susano-wo's nature as *kami* of death and ruler of the underworld, and of the ambiguous nature of Ōkuninushi, who stole them from his father-in-law and is thus wizardly dispenser of both life and death.

A weapon commonly carried by Buddhist deities is the *kongō* (*vajra* in Sanskrit). It consists of a handle with a pile-shaped, rectangular, hexagonal, or octangular spike at either end. *Tokko* have a single spike on either side, *sankō* are triple-spiked, and there are *gokkō*, which are five-pronged. They represent the diamond and the hard piercing truth of the Buddhist Law, as well as the thunderbolt, which creates flashing illumination.

One of the most famous and feared collections of weapons are the seven weapons carried by Benkei, Yoshitsune's hatchetman and majordomo. The weapons he carried differ among sources. In addition to a sword and a *naginata* (a kind of halberd, with a short, broad sword blade attached to a pole) or a *masakari* (broad ax), he also kept a rather unorthodox collection of weapons, almost all of which were common workmen's tools. This may have derived from the minor theme in many myths: the assertions of independence and rebellion by the lower classes.

The importance of weapons as symbols of power is a feature of many myth systems, and Japan's is no different. During most of Japanese history, those who carried arms displayed and exhibited superiority over those who did not. Therefore, even in Buddhism, with its tradition of respect for life (not always adhered to, granted), weapons became symbolic of the *struggle* that Buddhism was engaged in to establish itself. The weapons, of course, were the weapons common to the times, and those that had particular ideological associations, such as swords and bows, both expensive items, and items that needed a great deal of training to use effectively.

From a lengthy historical perspective, the different types of weapons displayed in mythical iconography constitute a form of debate between prevailing trends and mythical arguments. The primacy of the *kami* and the foundation myths is elaborated by the representation of archaic weaponry: straight mallet-headed swords and long bows. Later, the historical period is presented in the form of curved *tachi* and compound long bows. Buddhism weighs in with Chinese broad-bladed halberds and *kongō*. Commoners contribute the weapons available to them in the form of adapted daily tools and staves. And the various strongmen, Benkei, Kintoki, and the *oni*, carry massive weapons that demonstrate their position, straddling the worlds of order and disorder. The debate is not about supremacy but more about the place of these many concepts within the ideological/mythical world the Japanese were constructing.

See also Kongō; Swords.

References and further reading:

Ouwehand, Cornelius. 1964. *Namazu-e and Their Themes: An Interpretative Approach to Some Aspects of Japanese Religion.* Leiden, the Netherlands: E.J. Brill.

Stone, George Cameron. 1961. *A Glossary of the Construction, Decoration, and Use of Arms and Armor.* New York: Jack Brussel.

YAKUSHI NYŌRAI

The Buddha in his appearance as Master of Remedies. Yakushi Nyōrai is the Buddha of the Pure East (in counterpoise to Amida Nyōrai, Buddha of the Pure West), the Land of Pure Beryl. He represents the quality of the Buddha as the great healer to the illness of suffering engendered by attachment to illusion. Yakushi Nyōrai has a luminous body the color of beryl (green) or lapis lazuli (deep blue) and is the guardian of the suffering body. Yakushi is particularly efficacious when appealed to for illnesses that affect the eyes. He is also generally worshiped at hot springs, and therefore, by association—because hot springs were places of both healing and relaxation—at places of entertainment.

Yakushi is usually portrayed holding a pot of medicine in his left hand, with his right hand raised in a gesture of appeasement. Yakushi (like Amida) is associated with light, and he may be accompanied by a number of followers representing space, stars, and other bright objects.

See also Amida Nyōrai.

References and further reading:

Eliot, Sir Charles Norton Edgcumbe. 1959. *Japanese Buddhism.* London: Routledge and Kegan Paul.

Frank, Bernard. 1991. *Le pantheon bouddhique au Japon.* Paris: Collections d'Emile Guimet. Reunion des musees nationaux.

Getty, Alice. 1988. *The Gods of Northern Buddhism.* New York: Dover Publications.

Joly, Henri L. 1967. *Legend in Japanese Art.* Tokyo: Charles E. Tuttle Co.

Okuda, Kensaku ed. 1970. *Japan's Ancient Sculpture.* Tokyo: Mainichi Newspapers.

YAMA-NO-KAMI

Mountain deity. There are a great number of these, some mentioned in the *Kōjiki* by name. Japanese myths and rituals will quite often refer to a, or the, mountain *kami* without specifying the name. Most important, the eponymous Yama-no-kami leaves his home in the mountains in the spring and is enticed down to the plains by the invitation of the farmers, where, for the summer season, he assumes the name and guise of Ta-no-kami to protect the crops and ensure a bountiful harvest.

Mountains were considered the main residence of the deities in both Shintō and Buddhist belief. The willingness of these mountain deities to leave their places of residence and aid humans in their work required a great deal of effort on the part of humans and reaffirmed both the tie between humans and deities and the fragility of those ties: The harvest was never guaranteed, and the deities always required proper propositioning and propitiation.

The idea of itinerant deities has wider distribution in the idea of *marebito*.

The Yama-no-kami deigns to descend from his seat for a while to help humankind. But he is there, in the fields, only for a brief while before departing for his home in the mountains. Many Shintō rituals are thus constructed on the idea that humans need to entice the far-off *kami* to be human guests for a short while, bringing with them gifts of their presence and what their presence might provide, that is, the bounty of the harvest.

Though the "itinerant" agriculturally oriented Yama-no-kami is the most commonly found, another Yama-no-kami is worshiped by hunters, woodcutters, charcoal gatherers, and other mountain workers. In this myth the Yama-no-kami was believed to be female, represented as an elderly woman whose twelve offspring are the twelve months of the year.

See also Inari; *Marebito;* Mountains; Ta-no-kami.

References and further reading:

Aston, William G., trans. 1956. *Nihongi.* London: Allen and Unwin.

Havens, Norman, trans. 1998. *Kami.* Tokyo: Institute for Japanese Culture and Classics, Kokugakuin University.

Ono, Sokyo. 1962. *Shinto: The Kami Way.* Rutland, VT: Charles E. Tuttle Co.

Philippi, Donald, trans. and ed. 1968. *Kōjiki.* Tokyo: Tokyo University Press.

Seiffert, Geneviève. 1983. *Yanagita Kunio: Les Yeux précieux du serpent.* Publications Orientalistes de France.

Stefansson, Halldor. 1985. "Earth Gods in Morimachi." *Japanese Journal of Religious Studies* 12 (4): 277–298.

Yoshida Mitsukuni, Tanaka Ikko, and Sesoko Tsune, eds. 1985. *The Culture of Anima: Supernature in Japanese Life.* Translated by Lynne E. Riggs and Takechi Manabu. Hiroshima, Japan: Mazda Motor Corp.

Yoshida, Teigo. 1981. "The Stranger as God: The Place of the Outsider in Japanese Folk Religion." *Ethnology* 20 (2): 87–99.

YAMATO

Ancient province of central Japan and the original home of the Japanese ruling house. Jimmu Tenno, the first emperor, traveled east to subdue the lands and founded his kingdom in what is now the Nara Plain in central Japan, which was known as Yamato. By association, however, the term has come to mean the Japanese people and Japan as a whole. The term *Nihon* used today in Japanese for Japan (from which the English "Japan" originates) is a sinitic term, and traditional Japanese will still sometimes refer to their country as Yamato.

A large portion of both the *Kōjiki* and the *Nihonshōki* are devoted to the political, ritual, and military expansion of this Yamato state. By dint of clever marital alliances, political maneuvering, and sheer military power, the Yamato state grew throughout the fifth and sixth centuries C.E. to dominate most of Honshu and the littoral of the Seto Inland Sea. This expansion and consolidation continued until the Heian period, during which the three major islands of Japan came under imperial rule. The ruling family of the Yamato state became the imperial house of Japan, whose descendant still sits on the throne today.

YAMATO-TAKERU

Born Wousu-no-mikoto, Yamato-takeru is one of the major heroes of Japanese myth associated with the conquest of Japan by the Yamato. His nickname means "Hero of the Yamato." The usual dates of his life are given as 70–130 C.E., though if he existed, those dates are probably a guess by later commentators.

The third son of Emperor Keikō, Wousu-no-mikoto, was a wild and fierce youth. While still a boy, he was ordered by his father to admonish his older brother for not appearing before their father (the brother was ashamed because he had married two maidens destined as concubines for the emperor). Wousu-no-mikoto caught his older brother in the toilet and tore him apart, throwing the bits away, after which he calmly reported his deed to his father. Fearing for his own life, the emperor directed his son to subdue two mighty men, the Kumasō-takeru in the far west. Equipping himself with women's garments and a short sword, the boy hero set forth. Arriving at his destination, he found that the Kumasō-takeru and their warriors were completing the construction of a pit dwelling and preparing for a feast. When the feast started, the prince combed down his long hair (because he was a boy, his side-locks had not yet been shaved) and dressed in his aunt's clothes. Mingling with the women, he joined the festivities. The two Kumasō-takeru had the young "maiden" sit between them. At the height of the feast, the hero-prince drew forth his blade and killed the elder Kumasō-takeru. The younger victim fled but was caught at the ladder out of the pit dwelling, where the prince thrust the blade through his body. In a line that could be credited to a Schwarzenegger film, Wousu-no-mikoto then said, "Don't remove the sword, there's something I want to say." The youthful hero told his opponent that he had been sent to kill the Kumasō-takeru. The dying victim then bestowed the name Yamato-takeru-no-mikoto on his killer for his bravery. Following the assassination, Yamato-takeru subdued the country to the west.

On the way home Yamato-takeru directed his attention to Izumo. He made himself an imitation sword of wood, then falsely befriended Izumo-takeru, a hero of Izumo. At an opportune moment, after they had relaxed with a swim, he suggested to his host that they exchange swords, and then suggested that they practice fencing against one another. Izumo-takeru was unable to draw the imitation from its sheath, and Yamato-takeru drew and killed him. After singing a satirical song, he then subdued Izumo and returned home to report.

His (apparently still fearful) father next ordered the hero of Yamato to pacify the East, giving him one servant and a spear (the *Nihonshōki* indicates, in an alternative view, that this was a sign of the emperor's trust and confidence in his son, not an attempt to kill him). Stopping at the Grand Shrine of Ise, where his aunt (the emperor's sister) was the high priestess, Yamato-takeru complained of his treatment by his father: He had been sent without an army, and without a chance for rest to subdue first to the west, then to the north, and now to the east. His aunt provided him with the sword Kusanagi (originally the property of Susano-wo and later of Amaterasu, and a sign of the youth's future role as emperor) and a bag that he was to open only in an emergency. He then proceeded to the East and subdued the people there.

In Suruga, near Mt. Fuji, he was tricked by the local ruler into going into a wide plain of grass, which the foe set on fire. Opening his aunt's bag, he found fire-making implements with which he set a counterfire, using the sword (whose name means "Grass-cutter") to clear a space for himself. He then killed the treacherous ruler and all his clan, setting fire to his house.

While crossing the sea, Yamato-takeru's boat was tossed by the waves. His wife, Ototachibana-hime (the myth seems to have skipped a period of time, because he is referred to from this point on as the emperor) threw her eight sleeping mats onto the waves and followed in sacrifice (some people say she did this to spite her husband, who had told her a woman's place was on the mats!); by her sacrifice, she calmed the waves. When the hero reached land, he remembered his wife's sacrifice and exclaimed, "*Azuma wa ya* (Oh, my wife!)" as a consequence of which the eastern provinces of Japan were known as Azuma. Yamato-takeru then proceeded to subdue the Emishi people. On his way back to the capital, while he sat to eat his rations, he saw a white deer, which he killed by striking it in its eye with some wild garlic he was eating.

On his way he stopped and married a woman at Owari. Leaving his sword Kusanagi with her, he climbed Mt. Ibuki to capture the deity of the mountain with his bare hands. The deity appeared as a white boar, but it evaded the hero by causing a hailstorm that battered Yamato-takeru into a daze. Weakened, he struggled to Nobo, where he died. While he was being mourned by his wives and children, his spirit turned into a white bird.

The myth of Yamato-takeru is a myth that elaborates on the growing power of the Yamato state. It also represents a general myth pattern similar to the myth of Arthur in Western Europe. In fact, so great are the similarities that Littleton has argued that both myths derive from a similar source, perhaps a now-vanished culture of central Asia, from which it spread eastwards and westwards to Britain carried by Sarmatian mercenaries in the Roman army. Yamato-takeru is thus the greatest mythical hero of the state religion and emperor cult. The myth both provides a record of the expansion of the empire and continues the practice of providing names for known (at least at the time) geographical features.

See also Amaterasu-ō-mikami; Susano-wo; Swords.

References and further reading:
Aoki, Michiko Yamaguchi. 1974. *Ancient Myths and Early History of Japan: A Cultural Foundation*. New York: Exposition Press.
Aston, William G., trans. 1956. *Nihongi*. London: Allen and Unwin.
De Veer, Henrietta. 1976. "Myth Sequences from the Kojiki: A Structural Study." *Japanese Journal of Religious Studies* 3 (2–3): 175–214.
Littleton, C. Scott. 1995. "Yamato-Takeru: An 'Arthurian' Hero in Japanese Tradition." *Asian Folklore Studies* 54 (2): 259–275.
Philippi, Donald, trans. and ed. 1968. *Kōjiki*. Tokyo: Tokyo University Press.
Sato, Hiroaki. 1995. *Legends of the Samurai*. Woodstock, NY: Overlook Press.
Tyler, Royall. 1987. *Japanese Tales*. New York: Pantheon.
Umehara, Takashi. 1986. *Yamato Takeru*. Tokyo: Kodansha.

YAMA-UBA

Mountain old woman, or mountain witch. A powerful magician, she could be portrayed as a terrifying anthropophagous woman of immense strength whose sharp-toothed mouth is hidden under her hairline, and whose hair turns into serpents with which she ensnares and captures small children to eat, or as a merciful foster mother to many heroes. Men working in the mountains, wandering priests, or defeated warriors sometimes meet the *yama-uba* in the mountains. She sometimes gives them her baby to hold, promising to return soon. The child's weight increases almost beyond endurance. But if the weight *is* endured, when she returns she usually endows her victim with superhuman strength, which becomes hereditary in his family. If the man is unable to bear the weight, it turns into a rock that crushes him. The most famous hero raised by the *yama-uba* is Kintarō (or Kintoki), one of the Shi Tenno (four retainers) of Raikō.

One variation on the *yama-uba* myth is that of the *happyaku bikuni*. The *happyaku bikuni* (eight-hundred year nun) wanders the mountains with everlasting youth. She eats the servants (some say, the nine-holed shellfish) of the sea deity and so remains young. She offers people she meets oracles and protective amulets.

In some ways the *yama-uba* is the counterpart of the *tengu*. The *tengu* are all male, and their dress and manners are mythical reflections of the mountain ascetics—the *yamabushi* or *kebōzu*—who wandered the mountains (itself suspicious behavior in Japanese society: Where do they belong? What group are they members of?). The *yamabushi* visited remote villages to perform rituals, which to the villagers were magical acts. In parallel there were nuns—*bikuni*—who did the same. They ranged in function from traveling holy prostitutes to fortune-tellers and mediums. From the people's experiences with them probably rose the image of the *happyaku bikuni* as well as that of the *yama-uba*. The *tengu* and the *yama-uba* offer men gifts of skills, but only if they are strong and resolute enough to acquire them. At the same time they are wild and uncontrolled individuals who can engender wildness among humans, as the myth of Kintoki shows.

See also Kintoki; Raikō; *Tengu.*
References and further reading:
Bethe, Monica, and Karen Brazell. 1978. *No as Performance: An Analysis of the Kuse Scene Yamamba.* Ithaca, NY: Cornell East Asian Papers.
Davis, Winston. 1984. "Pilgrimage and World Renewal: A Study of Religion and Social Value in Tokugawa Japan." *History of Religions* 23 (3): 71–98.
Grapard, Allan G. 1991. "Visions of Excess and Excesses of Visions: Women and Transgression in Japanese Myth." *Japanese Journal of Religious Studies* 18 (1): 3–22.
Ouwehand, Cornelius. 1964. *Namazu-e and Their Themes: An Interpretative Approach to Some Aspects of Japanese Religion.* Leiden, the Netherlands: E. J. Brill.
Yoshida, Teigo. 1981. "The Stranger as God: The Place of the Outsider in Japanese Folk Religion." *Ethnology.* 20 (2): 87–99.

YAOYOROZU-NO-KAMIGAMI
The "eight-hundred ten-thousand-many *kami*," or eight million deities. The term is used to indicate the multitude of *kami,* many unnamed, some worshiped only locally, that comprise the Shintō pantheon. Many *kami* worshiped are not named except by title, and the use of the terms allows for great inclusiveness in descriptions of the pantheon. It indicates that the *kami,* whether known or unknown, permeate Japan and affect everything that happens there. This idea is related to the concept that Japan is eminently the land of the *kami,* and therefore that the boundaries between the Japanese, as a people, and their *kami* are multistranded.

See also Divine Descent; Divine Rulership.

YŌMI
See Underworld.

YOSHITSUNE
A cultural hero and warrior (b.1159–d.1189) during the Gempei war (1180–1185). Minamoto-no-Yoshitsune, born Ushiwakamaru, was the younger brother of Minamoto-no-Yoritomo, who became the shogun. Not much is definitely known about his real life, though it is clear he was a successful general on the Minamoto side, and responsible for many of their military successes.

In myth, Yoshitsune looms large as the perfect knight, *sans peur et sans reproche.* His father had been killed rebelling against the Taira overlords, and Yoshitsune, a handsome young boy, was sent as an acolyte to the temple on Mt.

Panoply of Yoshitsuné.

Samurai warrior as he wears and displays his full array of arms and armor of
Yoshitsune. (Kean Collection/Getty Images)

Kurama. While there, he was taught fencing by the *tengu*, whose master took a fancy to the boy. After his training, he escaped from Mt. Kurama, killing four robbers on his way to Heian-kyō, the capital. There he defeated the fearsome warrior-monk Benkei, using nothing but his fan and flute, thus making Benkei his loyal servitor for life. Joining his elder brother's cause, he fought in many battles. Perhaps the most famous is the cavalry charge at Ichinotani, where he led his troops down what was considered an impassable slope. At the battle of Dan-no-Ura, where the Taira were finally defeated, Yoshitsune jumped over eight boats, landing in the ninth, to avoid the attentions of Noritsune, the strongman champion of the Taira.

Yoshitsune eventually incurred his suspicious brother's hostility for his popularity and success. He went into hiding again, and, as one major myth tells, on his way to Northern Japan he and his party disguised themselves as *yamabushi* on pilgrimage. At the San no Kuchi barrier, they were detained, only saved by Benkei's quick thinking: He beat the young Yoshitsune for being an intractable servant, thus convincing the gate keeper to let them pass. The story is recounted in a famous *Kabuki* play, *Kanjinchō*.

Finally, after some time of wandering, Yoshitsune, Benkei, and Yoshitsune's wife were surrounded by Yoritomo's forces and burned to death in their castle. However, one myth recounts, the brave Benkei dressed himself in his master's distinctive armor and died, while Yoshitsune himself escaped from Japan, eventually becoming a Mongol prince known as Temujin (in some accounts, Temujin's father), who in time became known as Genghis Khan, founder of the Mongol empire.

The Yoshitsune myth is known by virtually all Japanese, and elements of it—for example, the servant episode—are the staple of theatrical productions in *Nōh* and *Kabuki* theater. The idea of Benkei's loyalty to his lord, and indeed of Yoshitsune's loyalty to his lord and brother notwithstanding the provocation he endures, is a major icon of Japanese normative beliefs in loyalty and hard work.

See also Benkei; *Chūshingura*; Heroes.
References and further reading:
McCullough, Helen Craig, trans. 1966. *Yoshitsune: A Fifteenth-Century Japanese Chronicle* (Gikeiki). Stanford: Stanford University Press.
Sieffert, Rene. 1995. *Histoire de Benkei.* Paris: P.O.F.
Waley, Arthur. 1957. *The Nō Plays of Japan.* ["Kumasaka," "Eboshi-ori," and "Benkei on the Bridge."] New York: Grove Press.

YUKI-ONNA

Snow woman. She is a tall white spirit in the form of an elderly woman. She may be an image of the *kaze-no-kami* (the *kami* of colds) and can sometimes be seen by people who are performing *kangeiko* (cold-weather austerity, during which men in manual trades, usually apprentices, run naked from their homes to pray at shrines) during the *daikan,* the period of greatest cold during the first two weeks of the second month.

Like the *yama-uba,* the *yuki-onna* may be a good or bad omen, depending on the individual's stamina, strength, and most importantly determination. *Kangeiko* is still practiced in Japan, largely by apprentices in traditional trades and martial arts schools. The tinkle of the bell that practitioners hang from their sashes (like sumo wrestlers, they dress only in a *mawashi,* or broad-sashed loincloths) is one of the most evocative midwinter sounds in Japan. The concept of fortitude and self-discipline in adverse circumstances is intrinsic to Japanese culture. There are a number of ways of expressing it, such as *misogyi* (purification under mountain waterfalls) and fire-walking. The *yuki-onna* and her relative (?) the *yama-uba* are expressions of this cultural concept. The cold threatens and even kills, but being able to overcome it implies the potential for personal growth and reward.

See also *Yama-uba.*
References and further reading:
Joly, Henri L. 1967. *Legend in Japanese Art.* Tokyo: Charles E. Tuttle Co.

YUSHKEP KAMUI (AINU)

The spider goddess. She is also known as Ashketanne-mat (Long-fingered woman). She is often the familiar of women shamans, serving as guardian and guide. She is also invoked by birthing women, because with her long legs and pincers she is able to pull out the newborn safely. In one myth she was wooed by Poronitne Kamui, a giant demon who lived beyond the cloud horizon. Warned by a friendly deity, she prepared a trap for her unwelcome suitor. Poronitne Kamui turned up, but Yushkep Kamui had turned herself into a reed and set her servants in ambush. The demon searched for his prize, but while digging up the embers of the hearth he was popped in the eye by Chestnut Boy, who had hidden there. Falling backwards in surprise, he was jabbed by Needle Boy, then stung by Hornet Boy in his other eye. His hand was bitten by Viper Boy, his head thumped by Pestle Boy, and, as he was escaping, Mortar Boy fell onto his head from above the lintel. The dying demon fled back to his homeland. Yushkep Kamui lived on calm and undisturbed.

As in most Ainu myths, women are supreme in their own domain, and the very domestic implements that help them in their daily lives are also weapons if they are attacked by men. Though Ainu women were formally subordinate to men in most spheres, they had their own responsibilities and areas of autonomy. Most crucially, they controlled marriage and the choice of partners through the secret *kut* girdles they wore. As a consequence, few Ainu men were willing to cross them.

References and further reading:
Philippi, Donald L., trans. 1979. *Songs of Gods, Songs of Humans: The Epic Tradition of the Ainu.* Princeton: Princeton University Press.

ZAŌ-GONGEN

The protective deity of Mt. Zaō, one of the peaks used extensively by the Shugendō ascetics for pilgrimage and ascetic practices.

Zaō-gongen was revealed to En-no-Gyōja, the original *yamabushi*, during the Heian period. While meditating in Yoshino, En-no-Gyōja solicited the aid of the local guardian spirit. The spirit of Shakyamuni appeared to the sage, but he rejected him, saying that he himself had not sufficient merit to approach the state of Buddhahood. The spirit of Kannon then appeared to him in the form of the Thousand-hands Kannon, but the sage rejected her as well, saying that her approach was too gentle for the evil world he found himself in. Maitreya then appeared, and En-no-Gyōja rejected him in turn, saying that the time of the Buddha of the future had not yet come: He needed a figure to help in the immediate battle against evil. As a consequence, he was immediately vouchsafed the view of the giant figure of Zaō-gongen, whom he adopted as his patron.

Zaō-gongen is usually portrayed as a violent deity, one foot raised to stamp down evil. He carries a *kongō* thunderbolt in one hand and wears a flaming crown. Three giant statues (each over 23 feet tall) of him can be seen at his main temple, Kinbusen-ji in Yoshino. Many pilgrims, not all of them *yamabushi*, participate in his rituals, intended to drive out evil. Zaō-san is today still a *yamabushi* pilgrimage mountain.

See also Atago-gongen; En-no-Gyōja; *Kongō*; Konpira-daigongen.
References and further reading:
Earhart, H. Byron. 1970. *A Religious Study of the Mount Haguro Sect of Shugendo.* Tokyo: Sophia University Press.

TABLE OF MINOR DEITIES

Minor deities are defined here as those for whom there are few mythical sources—for example, a deity mentioned in the *Kōjiki* or *Nihonshōki* without any particulars, or a deity integral to a story without any details, or a deity whose myths are restricted to one area or community. The various mythical sources—*Kōjiki, Nihonshōki, Engishiki,* and others—name several hundred deities, some without explanation. Scholars such as Motoori attempted to order this information, often based on little more than a reading, often highly imaginative, of the deity's name. The same can be said of Buddhist deities. The following table is merely a brief sample of some deities who are related in some way to the myths described throughout this volume, but for whom there is no further significant information. A few names have been added as examples of the breadth of interests of mythological figures.

NAME	DESCRIPTION
Amatsumara	A smith deity who made the mirror that enticed Amaterasu-ō-mikami from her cave. He is worshiped as patron *kami* of smiths.
Amatsuhiko-no-mikoto	Ninigi-no-mikoto's father, and son of Amaterasu-ō-mikami. He was directed to descend to the Central Land of Reed Plains to assume control in the name of the heavenly deities. He declined in favor of his son, Ninigi-no-mikoto, and remained in heaven.
Amatsumikaboshi	*Kami* of the evening star. Also known as Amenokagasewo. One of the deities born from the blood of Kagutsuchi-no-kami, the fire *kami* slain by his father Izanagi. Identified with Ajishikitakahikone.
Amenomikumari	A pure-water deity. One of the eight born of Haya-akitsu-hiko. *Kami* with *kumari* (rushing water) in their names are generally associated with pure streams and therefore purification.
Amenominakanushi	One of the first "single" and "hidden" deities of the creation.
Amenooshikumone	A youthful *kami* who brings the purification water for the enthronement rituals of the emperor. He manifests as a snake.
Amenotokotachi	One of the five heavenly deities who came into being as separates (that is, with no female counterpart).
Anan (Sanskrit: Ananda)	One of the Buddha's earliest disciples, and the youngest among them. Blessed with a phenomenal memory, he was able to recite all of the Buddha's sermons he had heard, and as such was the source of much of the literature that became the Buddhist sutra.

Ashuku Nyōrai	The lord of the paradise of extreme bliss. He helps purify the mind in order to engage in the search for the Buddhist Law.
Bon-ten	The Japanese representation of the Hindu deity Brahma. Protector and defender of the Buddhist Law.
Ekibiogami	A *kami* of disease and pestilence.
Haniyasu-hiko	One of the deities who came into existence, along with his spouse/sister, Haniyasu-hime, from the feces Izanami voided after dying while giving birth to the fire deity. The two are the *kami* of earthworking.
Haniyasu-hime	Spouse and sister of Haniyasu-hiko. Both came into existence from the feces Izanami voided after dying while giving birth to the fire deity.
Hosho Nyōrai	The Buddha of the South.
Hōsō-no-kami	*Kami* of smallpox. Appears in numerous guises, some of which may well be related to the Indian Durga. Smallpox was a terrible killer in all premodern societies. The vast number of deities, usually female, whose protection against this illness is sought is evidence of this.
Izuna-gongen	Guardian deity of Mt. Izuna. Under the impulse of Shugendō, the *kami* of Mt. Izuna (north of modern-day Nagano, in north-central Honshu), which may have been an Inari, was redeified as a syncretic *gongen*. The deity is the guardian of the fertile Nagano Plain. Like most *gongen*, the local *kami* was subsumed into the syncretic form as a strong and vigorous protector.
Kanayama-hiko	The male *kami* of metals. He was one of the last born of Izanami when she died. He and his sister, Kanayama-hime, were born of her mouth.
Kanayama-hime	The female *kami* of metals. She and her brother, Kanayama-hiko, were born of the death throes of Izanami.
Kayanohime-no-kami	"Miscanthus plains princess," a deity of the plains. One of the many children born by Izanami before the fatal birth of Kagutsuchi-no-kami.
Kisagai-hime	A deity (Ark-shell princess) who was sent to revive

NAME	DESCRIPTION
	Ōkuninushi after he had been killed by his brothers.
Kukunochi-no-kami	A tree *kami* born of the mating of Izanagi and Izanami.
Kuninotokotachi-no-kami	One of the first deities to emerge at the beginning of the world.
Mari-no-kami	Three-headed *kami* of *kemari*, or traditional football.
Musubi-no-kami	The *kami* of marital fate. He binds the feet of those destined to be married with red thread. He is also known more poetically as Gekka-ō, or "Old man under moon." Probably of Chinese origin influenced by Buddhist ideas of fate.
Nakatsu-hime	Emperor Ōjin's wife, and mother of his successor, Emperor Nintoku. She is deified as *kami* of the Yashiro-guni (the Eight Islands, one of the names for Japan in the *Kōjiki*).
Poiyaunpe (Ainu)	Ainu culture hero extolled for his fighting against the *Repunkur* (Sea people: the traditional enemies of the Ainu, or Yaunkur [Land People]) in Ainu epics). Sometimes identified with Okikurmi.
Shinatsuhiko-no-kami	*Kami* of the wind. One of the children born to Izanagi and Izanami before Izanami's death. In another more popular representation inspired by Buddhism, he is named Fujin.
Shodo-shōnin	A founder of Ryōbu Shintō about whom many miracle tales are told. He established Nikko shrine in the mountains north of what is today Tokyo.
Taishaku-ten	The Japanese representation of the Hindu deity Indra. Protector and defender of the Buddhist Law.
Takitsu-hime	A female *kami* of rainfall.
Toyoukebime (also Toyouke-o-mikami; Toyouke-no-kami; Uganomitama-no-kami)	A food deity who is enshrined at the Outer Shrine of Ise–jingû.
Umugi-hime	"Clam princess." Sent with Kisagai-hime to bring Ōkuninushi back to life after he had been killed by his brothers.

4

ANNOTATED PRINT AND NONPRINT RESOURCES

BOOKS AND ARTICLES

Aston, William George. 1905. *Shinto: The Way of the Gods.* London: Longmans, Green, and Co.

An early and rather laudatory description of Shintō. Aston was one of the earliest foreign scholars in Japan. The book is an excellent exposition of the Great Tradition view of one aspect of Japanese religion.

Aston, William G., trans. *Nihongi.* 1956 London: Allen and Unwin.

A translation of the second of the major works on Shintō mythology. Unfortunately, Aston's translation is both abridged (he did not include elements that he found repetitious or conflicting, or perhaps just boring) and bowdlerized (he steers well clear of all sexual and scatological words).

Batchelor, John. 1971. *Ainu Life and Lore: Echoes of a Departing Race.* Tokyo, Kyobunkwan, and New York: Johnson Reprint Corp.

A description of the vanished way of life of the forest-dwelling Ainu of Hokkaido. Batchelor was a doctor in Hokkaido at the turn of the century, and his report, though somewhat colored by his missionary zeal, is sympathetic and authentic.

Dykstra, Yoshiko Kurata. 1986. *The Konjaku Tales: Indian Section (Tenjiku-Hen) Part 1/Part 2 from a Medieval Japanese Collection.* Osaka: Kansai University of Foreign Studies.

A translation of the *Konjaku-Monogatari,* including many of the heroic and Buddhist myths discussed in this book.

Ehrich, Kurt S. 1991. *Shichifukujin: Die Sieben Glücksgötter Japans.* Recklinghausen, Germany: Verlag Aurel Bongers.

If you read German—the most detailed exposition of the place of the Shichi Fukujin in Japanese religious and mythical thought.

Frank, Bernard. 1991. *Le pantheon bouddhique au Japon. Collections d'Emile Guimet.* Paris: Reunion des musees nationaux.

An illustrated guide to one of the world's greatest collections of Buddhist art. The Emile Guimet collection is explored with detailed descriptions not only of the images and illustrations but also of their meanings and iconography.

Goldsbury, Peter. 2001. "Touching the Absolute: Aikido vs. Religion and Philosophy." http://www.aikidojournal.com/articles/.

An easily accessible paper dealing with Takemikazuchi-no-kami and his relationship to the soul of an important martial art.

Goodin, Charles C. 1994. "Tengu: The Legendary Mountain Goblins of Japan." *Furyu: The Budo Journal* 2. Text in http://www.seinenkai.com/articles/tengu.html.

A good description on the Internet of the history and nature of *tengu.*

Hakeda, Yoshito S. 1972. *Kukai.* New York: Columbia University Press.

The biography of the priest Kūkai, better known as Kōbō Daishi. It places his life and works in the context of his times, the politics of the court, and the countryside he worked in.

Herbert, Jean. 1967. *Shinto—At the Fountain Head of Japan.* London: George Allen and Unwin Ltd.

A very detailed description, with illustrations, of all the major elements of Shintō, including some of its myths.

Iwasaka, Michiko, and Barre Toelken. 1994. *Ghosts and the Japanese: Cultural Experience in Japanese Death.* Logan: Utah State University Press.

A detailed discussion, including representative myths and legends, of Japanese stories and beliefs about ghosts. The discussion is far-ranging and relates Japanese myths to thinking and literature about ghosts in other cultures.

Joly, Henri L. 1967. *Legend in Japanese Art.* Tokyo: Charles E. Tuttle Co.

A detailed glossary, including many illustrations, of the major mythical themes in Japanese art. The entries are very brief and the orthography is old-fashioned, but the number of entries is enormous and very broad.

Kamata, Toji. 2001. "The Topology of Oni and Kami in Japanese Myth." http://homepage2.nifty.com/moon21/.

A paper discussing the nature of *oni* as strange beings and outsiders in Japanese thought.

Kayano, Shigeru. 1985. *The Romance of the Bear God: Ainu Folktales [Eibun Ainu minwashu]*. Tokyo: Taishukan Publishing Co.

A collection of Ainu folktales taken from the Ainu *yukar*. The author, an Ainu himself, is the first Ainu to have been elected a member of the Japanese Diet (parliament).

Kitagawa, Hiroshi, and Bruce T. Tsuchida, trans. and eds. 1975. *The Tale of the Heike [Heike monogatari]*. Tokyo: University of Tokyo Press.

A translation of one of the major epic stories in Japan: the rise and particularly the fall of the Heike. The story is full of lively characters and an impending sense of doom as they struggle their way to Dan-no-Ura and final dissolution.

Littleton, C. Scott. 1995. "Yamato-takeru: an 'Arthurian' Hero in Japanese Tradition." *Asian Folklore Studies* 54 (2): 259–275.

Littleton argues that the similarities between the Arthurian tale, particularly Arthur's two swords (from the stone and from the Lady of the Lake) and the myth of Yamato-takeru and his two swords, are related. These two myths may have originated with a Central Asian culture, brought eastwards and westwards by these people in early historical times.

Mayer, Fanny Hagin, ed. and trans. 1985. *Ancient Tales in Modern Japan: An Anthology of Japanese Folk Tales*. Bloomington: Indiana University Press.
———. 1986. *The Yanagita Kunio Guide to the Japanese Folk Tale*. Bloomington: Indiana University Press.

Mayer is a well-known translator and collaborator with Yanagita Kunio, the father of Japanese folklore studies. In these two books she translates myths largely taken from the "Little Tradition" and collected over several decades by Yanagita.

McCullough, Helen Craig, trans. 1959. *The Taiheiki*. New York: Columbia University Press.
———. 1966. *Yoshitsune: A Fifteenth-Century Japanese Chronicle [Gikeiki]*. Stanford: Stanford University Press.
———. *The Tale of the Heike*. Stanford: Stanford University Press.

Three excellent translations of major literature from what we have called here the Age of Heroes. These constitute feats of loyalty and daring-do, complete with heroes and villains. *The Tale of the Heike* was a staple of bards during the Kamakura period. All of these give a rounded picture of the lives of warriors during the Middle Ages of Japanese history. Extensive notes clarify the difficult concepts.

Munro, Neil Gordon. 1962. *Ainu Creed and Cult.* London: Routledge and Kegan Paul. Reprint, London: Kegan Paul International, 1995.

Another description of Ainu mythology and religion. Partly based on first-hand research, partly on earlier writings.

Nakamura, Kyoko Motomuchi. 1997. *Miraculous Stories from the Japanese Buddhist Tradition: The Nihon Ryoki of the Monk Kyokai.* New ed. Richmond, VA: Curzon Press. Text at http://campross.crosswinds.net/books.

Mythical stories about wondrous events, miracles inspired by the boddhisattvas, and good and bad deeds repaid. This straddles the divide between the Great Tradition and the Little Traditions and, in effect, is an example of the Great Tradition co-opting Little Tradition stories for its own ends.

Ohnuki-Tierney, Emiko. 1969. *Sakhalin Ainu Folklore.* Anthropological Studies, 2. Washington, DC: American Anthropological Association.

A detailed description, no longer in print, of the Ainu of what is now Russian Sakhalin.

Ono, Sokyo. 1962. *Shintō: The Kami Way.* Rutland, VT: Charles E. Tuttle Co.

A description by a Shintō priest and professor of the antecedents and nature of Shintō. Heavily biased toward the Great Tradition view of things.

Philippi, Donald, trans. and ed. 1968. *Kōjiki.* Tokyo: Tokyo University Press.

An excellent annotated translation of one of the major myth cycles of Japan. The book is a detailed translation, with extensive notes and a comprehensive index. Lengthy discussion of the place of the *Kōjiki* in Japanese literature and history.

Philippi, Donald L., trans. 1979. *Songs of Gods, Songs of Humans: The Epic Tradition of the Ainu.* Princeton: Princeton University Press.

An annotated and footnoted recording, partly in verse, of major Ainu *yukar.* The range of *yukar* includes both those dealing with the gods and those dealing with humans and their relationship to their environment.

Sansom, Sir George. 1976. *Japan: A Short Cultural History.* Tokyo: Charles E. Tuttle Co.

A detailed description and analysis of the effects of Japanese historical processes on the development and changes in Japanese culture. An excellent background book by an eminent historian and specialist of things Japanese.

Statler, Oliver. 1984. *Japanese Pilgrimage.* London: Picador.

An easy and fascinating read that includes the highlights of Kōbō Daishi's life and miracles and his eighty-eight-station pilgrimage route in Shikoku.

The descriptions are unparalleled, and the author weaves the story of his own pilgrimage into the historical and geographical background.

Takeda, Izumo, Miyoshi Shoraku, and Namiki Senryu. 1971. *Chushingura, the Treasury of Loyal Retainers: A Puppet Play.* Translated by Donald Keene. New York: Columbia University Press.

A detailed translation of the *Chūshingura*, which depicts one of the major myths of Japanese mythology, a myth that has shaped much of how the Japanese see themselves. The concepts might be alien, but the translator has provided a series of notes to ease recognition.

Tyler, Royall. 1987. *Japanese Tales.* New York: Pantheon.

A collection of over two hundred translated tales and stories from Shintō and Buddhism, from both Great and Little Traditions. Many of the tales appear in other forms elsewhere, but this collection provides a sampling of almost every genre and period.

Wehmeyer, Ann, trans. 1997. *Kojiki-den [Motoori Norinaga], Book 1.* East Asia Series, no. 87. Ithaca: Cornell University Press.

A difficult-to-read, detailed exposition of Motoori's thinking and interpretation of the *Kōjiki.* Some of what he writes may sound strange to modern ears. Worth dipping into if only to see the foundations of modern Japanese nationalistic thought.

Yanagita, Kunio. 1954. *Japanese Folk Tales.* Translated by Fanny Hagin Mayer; illustrated by Kiichi Okamoto. Tokyo: Tokyo News Service.

An easy-to-read collection of tales collected by Yanagita, the father of Japanese folklore studies. Most of these illustrate themes of the Little Tradition in Japan.

VIDEOS

Chūshingura. 1962. TohoScope, directed by Hiroshi Inagaki.

The story of the forty-seven *rōnin.* Lengthy three-hour drama of revenge climaxing with the raid of Lord Kira's mansion and its aftermath.

Kwaidan—Kaidan (Ghost Story). 1964. TohoScope, directed by Masaki Kobayashi.

A collection of Japanese ghost stories originally assembled by Englishman Lafcadio Hearn. Includes the myth of the *yuki-onna.*

Those Who Tread on the Tiger's Tail [Tora no o fumu otokotachi]. 1945. Academy Ratio. Directed by Akira Kurosawa.

The tale of Yoshitsune at the Ataka barrier. Based on the *Kabuki* play *Kanjinchō*.

WEBSITES

Web pages can be a useful source of information regarding Japanese mythology. However, because there is no quality control on the Web, you should be aware that some information may be misleading or incomplete. Some sites seem to have uncritically accepted data, and as a consequence, information may be dubious. Moreover, because the Web is fluid and always incomplete, new sites will appear and old ones disappear even in the period between writing and publication. Also to be considered is that many of the relevant sites are in Japanese—an obvious barrier for scholars lacking Japanese language skills.

Samples of four types of relevant sites are reviewed here. Sites dealing specifically with mythology include some useful universal glossaries. In the Japanese case, these must be used carefully. For example, *Encyclopedia Mythica* (http://www.pantheon.org) uses the term "God of ___" freely, which is more than misleading in the Japanese context. Sites about Japanese religion may have brief notations of mythological stories or narratives, or other relevant data. Many of these are in Japanese. The third type are sites that contain bibliographical information and even partial fragments of texts, in translation or the original Japanese. Finally, not dedicated to mythology, some sites have illustrations of Japanese artworks that depict figures from mythology.

General Japan

Japan Glossary
http://www.wsu.edu:8080/~dee/GLOSSARY/JAPGLOSS.HTM

Useful glossary of Japanese concepts, including some in the area of myth.

Japan Guide.com
http://www.japan-guide.com/e/

A general guide to Japan, including a lengthy annotated section on Japanese religions and deities. The text, in English, is well annotated with hyperlinks, making it a comprehensive and useful site for those with little knowledge of Japan.

Nihongo.org
http://www.nihongo.org/english/

A site dedicated to Japanese culture, serving mainly as a gateway. Useful starting point for exploring Japanese culture and language through a multitude of links.

PMJS (premodern Japanese studies)
http://www.meijigakuin.ac.jp/~pmjs/trans/

A site cataloging translations of Japanese premodern texts including stories, plays, poetry, and, of course, myths. Some of the entries include gateways to either translated texts or the original Japanese texts. Essential for anyone seriously interested in studying traditional Japanese culture.

Buddhism

Japanese Buddhist Corner
http://www.onmarkproductions.com/html/buddhism.shtml

Excellent, well-illustrated, and linked site on the various aspects of Japanese Buddhism. In addition to a judicious and clear description of all mythological aspects of Japanese Buddhist deities, there is a wealth of photographs of *tengu* masks, deities statues, paintings, and other graphical elements. Clearly a labor of love and possibly the single best website devoted to Japan.

Mibu-dera temple
http://www.yamanakart.com/egg-p/mibu/index.html

Excellent web page of this famous temple. Pages include pictures of statuary and religious painting and, most important, brief synopses of *Nōh* plays performed at the temple. Those with mythical connections include *Funa Benkei* (Benkei's boat), the fox spirit Tamamo-no-mae, Raikō, and the spider.

Sacred Books: Buddhism
http://www.sacred-texts.com/bud/index.htm

Excerpts and full texts of a number of central Buddhist texts including the Lotus Sutra, and an introduction to Zen Buddhism by Daisetz Suzuki.

Shintō

Cyber Shrine
http://www.kiku.com/electric_samurai/cyber_shrine/

Photographs of Shintō shrines, some of which (e.g., Shiragi, Izumo Taisha) are mentioned in the myths recounted in this volume.

Institute for Japanese Culture and Classics, Kokugakuin University
http://www.kokugakuin.ac.jp/ijcc/wp/

Japanese university website in English dedicated to various aspects of Shintō. Academic papers online, as well as the most comprehensive annotated and hypermarked glossary on Shintō anywhere on the web. Extremely useful for any scholarly activity.

Itsukushima Shrine
http://www.hiroshima-cdas.or.jp/miyajima/english/jinja/noshock.htm

A site dedicated to the shrine of Benzaiten at Itsukushima. This "floating shrine" is considered one of the three most beautiful sites in Japan and is a world heritage site. Includes a detailed description and history.

Sacred Texts: Shintō
http://www.sacred-texts.com/shi/

Excerpts from a number of Shintō texts, including:

- Excerpts from the Chamberlain 1882 translation of the Kōjiki; names of deities are translated, sometimes with peculiar results
- Excerpts from the Aston translation of the Nihongi
- The Engishiki
- Lafcadio Hearn's retelling of Japanese legends and ghost tales
- The Book of Tea

Though some of the translations are old and out of date, they nonetheless provide an opportunity to study the original texts.

Shintō Online Network Association
http://www.jinja.or.jp/english/index.html

A site dedicated to publicizing Shintō shrines. Excellent photographs accompanied by text explaining many aspects of Shintō, including some myths.

Mythology in Art and History

Ancient Izumo Culture
http://inoues.net/yamataikoku/study/bunkaten.html

Japanese language site. Plentiful pictures and text try to recreate the life of the Izumo people. Photos of models of Izumo buildings, based largely on recent archaeological findings, are included (though the estimate of a ninety-six-meters-tall shrine need not be taken seriously), as well as those of the actual bronze swords and bells found in recent archaeological excavations.

Japanese Gods and Goddesses
http://www.artelino.com/articles/japanese_gods_and_goddesses.asp
http://www.artelino.com/articles/japanese_mythology.asp

> Brief depiction of some of the mythological characters. Accompanied by photographs of depictions of those mentioned in painting and sculpture.

Koma-inu Library
http://www.komainu.pos.to/

> The website of the All-Japan Koma-inu Library. A wonderful site (in Japanese) with photographs of *koma-inu* from all over the country. Hypermarked map shows localities of temples and shrines with *koma-inu.*

Orihime, Kengyuu, and Tanabata: Adapting Chinese Lore to Native Beliefs and Purposes
http://www2.gol.com/users/stever/

> Paper describing the Tanabata myth and its astronomical correlates. Includes a page of photographs from the Tanabata celebration.

Shintō and Japanese Mythology
http://www.geocities.com/blackthornraven/

> Superficial but well-illustrated site including brief descriptions of some myths.

Tengu: The Legendary Mountain Goblins of Japan
http://www.seinenkai.com/articles/tengu.html

> Brief description of the *tenguū* in art. Includes a number of pictures of depictions of *ūtengu* and a brief essay on *tengū* in history and art.

Myths and Glossaries

Encyclopedia Mythica: Japanese Mythology
http://www.pantheon.org/areas/mythology/asia/japanese/articles.html

> Part of a comprehensive online mythological glossary that lists most Japanese mythological figures. Brief explanatory descriptions are given of each entry. Unfortunately, little attention has been paid to ensuring accuracy or to dealing with the differences in conception between Japanese and Western concepts, such as the *kami*/god distinction.

Ghosts, Demons, and Spirits in Japanese Lore
http://www.asianart.com/articles/rubin/

> A brief paper discussing various supernatural beings in Japanese mythology. Some picture files. Good as a generalized introduction to the subject of supernatural beings in Japan.

Japanese Myth
http://www.st.rim.or.jp/~cycle/myrefe.html

> A Japanese site in English. It includes an illustrated and hyperlinked genealogy of the principle Shintō *kami,* as well as a portal to a number of myths, including Susano-wo and Kōnōhanasakuya-hime.

Japanese Mythology
http://www.windows.ucar.edu/mythology/japan.html

> Page with four Japanese myths from a site relating astronomical bodies and human myths regarding them.

Japanese Mythology
http://www.interq.or.jp/www-user/fuushi/e-myth-a.htm

> Several myths retold from the *Kōjiki* (e.g., rabbit of Inaba). Somewhat eccentric in retelling, because the Japanese author has a somewhat shaky command of English.

The *Kami* of Shintō
http://zen.quasisemi.com/myth/home.htm

> Idiosyncratic website by a game-player. Includes a lengthy glossary of Japanese mythological terms. However, the spelling is erratic, and the content is largely derivative.

Myth—Japan
http://ancienthistory.about.com/library/bl/bl_myth_asia_fareast_japan.htm

> From the History Net. Gateway to several mythical stories and sites. Includes a retelling of the Izanami and Izanagi myth and a brief genealogy of the principle *kami.*

Myths and Legends in Miyazaki
http://www.harapan.co.jp/english/miya_e/myth/myth_index.htm

> Myths of Miyazaki prefecture in Japan, one of the putative sites of Himuka, where Ninigi-no-mikoto came to earth. Somewhat eccentric translation and editing of myths from the *Kōjiki* relating to Miyazaki prefecture.

Out of the Cave and into the Light
http://www.lyricalworks.com/stories/amaterasu/amaterasu.htm

A retelling of the Amaterasu foundation myth in folktale form. Includes pages on exegesis and meaning of the myth and similar myths from other cultures.

GLOSSARY

akuma   Personified evil. That is, beings, sometimes undefined, who bring afflictions to humankind.

amatsu-kami   The heavenly deities. Those deities who came into existence out of the void, or who were created or born of these deities.

avatar   A reflection or expression of a particular Buddha that has (semi-) independent existence and personifies a limited set of characteristics of that Buddha. The closest Western analogy are the angels and *sephirot* of the Jewish Kabbalah.

bikuni   Wandering nun. The *yamabushi*'s female counterparts; some became "wives" of settled *yamabushi* in villages while others wandered on their own or as part of groups of *yamabushi*.

boddhisattva   Someone capable of achieving Buddhahood immediately, but who has decided to delay this state in order to assist in the salvation of others. The title *-bosatsu* (Japanese rendition of the Indian term *boddhisattva*) is appended to a number of deities and saints, such as Jizō-bosatsu, the patron of lost children.

-bosatsu   See *boddhisattva*.

bunke   Branch family of a *dōzoku*.

bushi   The class of individuals throughout medieval and premodern Japanese history who had the right to bear arms and fight in the service of their lords. Their status was publicly indicated by the right to wear two swords. *Bushi* included *samurai* (retainers) and unattached *rōnin* (wave-men). During the Heian period their status was well below that of the *kuge*, or court aristocrats.

butsu   Japanese form for Buddha, meaning enlightened. It is appended to the names of those entities who have freed themselves from the Wheel of Being and have entered into a state of nirvana where they are no longer subject to reincarnation and human passions. In practice in Japanese mythology, the title is applied to a few main venerated beings: Amida-butsu, Shaka-butsu.

daimyō   The lord of a feudal domain in the period from the Gempei wars to the end of Tokugawa rule in 1868. The title, which broadly means "great name," is perhaps equivalent to the Western baron. During the Edo period (1600–1868) the title was regularized, and only lords with an income of 10,000 *koku* (one *koku* is the amount of rice needed to sustain one man for one year, equivalent to 180 liters of rice) and above could call himself *daimyō*.

daishi   Usually an honor applied to a great Buddhist priest or innovator who has exhibited persistent efforts to preserve and extend the Law, such as Kōbō Daishi.

Daizōkyō   "Great Storehouse of Writings." The compilation of Buddhist texts, including sutras, legal treatises, and other matter. This is roughly comparable to the Bible combined with the writings of the church fathers, the prayer books, and the rules of monastic and other orders.

Daoism   A philosophical system based heavily on Chinese traditional religion and incorporating many of its ideas and concepts. Elucidated in two main books—the *Dao-de-jing* and the *Zhuangzi*—and myriad lesser volumes, it supposes a necessary connection between natural and human ways. Many of its ideas became incorporated into Japanese religions, particularly Zen.

dōzoku   An association of households bound by descent from a common stem or main household and held together by ritual and economic tie, and most particularly by the obligations between branch houses and the stem house.

fuda   A strip of paper with the name of a *kami* or Buddhist deity inscribed on it. Usually placed in the household *kami* shelf of Buddha-shelf.

goryō   Vengeful spirits of people who have died from false accusations or from transgressions committed against them. The most widely known *goryō* is that of Sugawara Michizane, subsequently deified as Tenjin-sama.

Great Tradition   The traditions of the literary elite. Generally focused on themes of national unity, power, and the "proper" order of things.

-*gu*   Suffix for the name of some Shintō shrines. Hachiman and Tenman (Tenjin-sama) shrines are usually labeled such, for example, Tenman-gu.

gyōja   An ascetic who practices austerities, usually in isolation, in order to gain magical powers.

hiko   Prince. A common suffix of many Japanese male *kami* as well as the sons of emperors.

hime   Princess. Applied to female deities and women of high rank.

honji-suijaku   The theological idea, evolved in the Heian period, that Japanese *kami* were local expressions of the Buddhas, who were the universal expression of the *kami*. This idea formed the basis for Ryōbu Shintō.

honke   Main, or stem, family of a *dōzoku*. The Imperial family is sometimes considered the *honke* of the Japanese people, who are viewed in their entirety as a sort of "super *dōzoku*."

hum   The final word. The sound that brings about the end of the universe. The last word of the Buddhist creed *"Om ma ne pad me hum."*

ie   The fundamental building block of Japanese society, *ie* consists of the current occupants of a household—spouses and their children—and all deceased ancestors and unborn descendants. Where no children are born, *ie* members will adopt outsiders to continue the *ie;* thus it does not correspond exactly to non-Japanese concepts of family.

Immortals   A group of sages from Chinese mythology who, following the Daoist concept of "the Way," have found immortality. Six such immortals, including Lotse, are denizens of Heaven, though not a part of the heavenly bureaucracy. The idea was also translated into the Japanese experience, albeit as a minor theme.

in   Japanese pronunciation of the Sanskrit "om." See *om*.

inau   Used in Ainu culture, a stick representing the deity formed by shaving strips off a wand but leaving them intact at the top. Different forms of shaving and curling represented different *kamui*. The *inau* itself was an offering to the *kamui*, a representation of the *kamui*, and a *kamui* itself, mediating between humans and the *kamui*. *Inau* were generally placed in a row on the northeast side of the house, forming a sort of sacred fence.

-ji   Suffix indicating a Buddhist temple, for example, Enryakuji.

jingū   A central Shintō shrine. There are a few shrines with this title in Japan, the main ones being the shrine to Amaterasu-ō-mikami at Ise (Ise-jingū) and the new shrine to the Meiji emperor in Tokyo (Meiji-jingū).

jinja   A Shintō shrine. Shrine names might also end with the term *-jingū, -gū, -taisha*, or *-miya*.

kamui   Ainu deity. The word is related to the Japanese *kami*.

kamui yukar   "God Epic." An Ainu song, of varied length, which tells a tale, usually in first person, about a deity and its adventures. These were sung as both entertainment and ritual during Ainu feasts.

kang   Ryukyuan deity. The word is related to Japanese *kami*.

kebōzu   Hairy Buddhist priest. A name given colloquially to the *yamabushi* and other Shugendō practitioners because they acted as priests and yet did not shave their heads as other Buddhist priests did.

kōji   Buddhist practitioner who does not become a monk. In a traditional Buddhist story, Yuima-kōji was so eloquent in telling the Law that the Buddha sent Monju-bosatsu to visit him when Monju was ill. Yuima and Monju are therefore often represented together.

kotan   Domain. Ainu families and clans each controlled a domain, usually a river valley or stream, which was their main hunting and gathering ground. Such *kotan* were sanctified by custom and defended vigorously. *Kotankor Kamui* was the deity of the domain, ensuring that the Ainu used their usufruct rights wisely.

kunitsu-kami   The Earthly deities. Those deities who were bound to the Earth or were born there. Usually associated with a particular location. It is likely that these were the deities of polities assimilated or conquered by the Yamato. The most powerful among them is probably Ōkuninushi, who seems to have been a chief deity among the Izumo, the Yamato's main rivals.

kut   A narrow (one to two inches) woven girdle worn by Ainu women. Each matrilineage (women owning descent by birth from a common ancestress) had a specific design and way to tie the *kut*. The *kut* were a secret. Many men were unaware of them, or professed to be unaware. Each mother instructed her daughters in the proper weaving. A woman could not have the same *kut* as her mother-in-law. Thus marital negotiations were the responsibility of the women of the community, which afforded them a great degree of power.

Little Traditions   The traditions of local communities, often of the powerless and the illiterate. These traditions may show an overall cultural continuity from one place in a culture to another but differ widely in details.

lotus   A water plant that grows without soil and produces a large flower with an enchanting scent. In mythology, the lotus flower, bud, and sometimes seed represent the Buddhist Law, which like the lotus has no earthly roots. A number of Buddhist deities—Kannon is one prominent example—carry a lotus branch or flower.

mana   A religious concept deriving from most Polynesian religions. Mana is an impersonal immanent power that humans and gods possess to differing degrees. It is both beneficial (when handled correctly, with rituals and respect) and dangerous (when mishandled). Anthropologists use the term to identify similar concepts from other parts of the world.

mandara   Mandala (Sanskrit). A picture illustrating, in visual/cartoon form, the main Buddhist principles. They usually show the major Buddha (of whichever sect drew the *mandara*) surrounded by lesser Buddhas and items representing esoteric concepts of the sect. There are a large number of them, the two most important ones in Japan being the Diamond *mandara* and the Womb *mandara*.

marebito   Wandering visitors. A term usually applied to mysterious *kami* who arrived from afar, sometimes from the land of Tokoyo. Many Shintō rituals are addressed to *marebito*, who are mysterious, powerful, and, most important, visit only to leave again.

matsurareru kami   Named *kami* that are celebrated and recognized as individuals.

miko   A shrine maiden in Shintō shrines. Miko perform sacred dances, assist at rituals, and in some cases perform divination or enter into possession trances. They are different from female *kannushi* (priests) since this is usually a temporary position from which they retire upon marriage.

mitama   Spirit, soul, or nature, usually of a deity. Each deity has three *mitama: aramitama* (rough and wild), *nigimitama* (gentle and life-supporting), and *sakimitama* (nurturing).

mudra   A hand gesture used in esoteric Buddhism. There are several hundred of these, some with exoteric meanings such as compassion or protection, others with more esoteric meanings.

Nembutsu   The formula "*Namu Amida Butsu* (Hail the Buddha Amida)" repeated as an act of faith by followers of Amidist sects in Japan. Frequent repetition is considered a sure path to salvation.

om   The first word. The sound that brought forth the universe. Also the first word of the Buddhist creed "*Om ma ne pad me hum.*"

rakan   Arhats. A stage in Buddhist progression where one is free of all passions, this state has been achieved by all of Shakyamuni's original disciples. In Japanese belief, however, the term is applied to only sixteen named individuals, more or less equivalent to the Apostles.

ramat   Ainu spirit, usually of a *kamui* (deity).

rōnin   Masterless *bushi* who did not owe loyalty to a lord. The word means "wave-man," meaning someone who is unattached, wild, free.

Ryōbu Shintō   Two schools Shintō. A theological concept that held that Shintō and Buddhist deities are both to be worshipped, and which fused both religions into one. Abolished formally by Meiji-era government edicts. See also *honji-suijaku.*

samurai   Members of the *bushi* class who were retainers of a lord. The word means "temple guard," and the position originated during the Heian period when *samurai* were sent to serve *kokubunji* (provincial temples).

sarariman   "Salary man." A white-collar worker in modern Japan. Sometimes extolled as the modern *samurai*, whose loyalty is to his firm rather than a feudal lord.

seishin-ichi   The idea that Buddhist and Shintō deities were one and the same; a simplified concept of *honji-suijaku.*

-sennin (rishi)   Hermit. Sage. Immortal (Daoist). Usually applied to individuals such as famous abbots, hermits, or wonder workers. The title is appended to the names of sages, usually of Chinese Daoist origins.

seppuku   Honorable suicide. An option available to members of the *bushi* class who had transgressed in certain ways, had lost in battle, or who wished to follow their master into death. The acceptable method was a self-inflicted abdominal cut (hence the popularly vulgar name *harakiri*) followed by beheading by a trusted friend or retainer.

shakujō   A staff topped by four to twelve steel rings set in a stupa-shaped capital. By thumping on the floor the rings sound, and the carrier can announce his presence, thus allowing insects and other small animals to remove themselves from harm. The sound also dispels evil. Carried by Jizō in the netherworld, it calls the souls of unborn and dead children to him, where he can offer them his mercy and aid.

-shonin   A title applied to important Buddhist abbots and senior priests, particularly those known for piety and the working of miracles. The best known is Nichiren, founder of the Nichiren sect.

Shugendō   A syncretic religious sect still practiced in Japan, based on a mixture of Shingon, Tendi, and Shintō beliefs and practices. Practitioners, generally termed *shugensha* or *yamabushi*, practice group austerities, special magical rituals such as firewalking, and mountain pilgrimages. Shugendō preaches that salvation is to be found in magical words and in purification. Mountain pilgrimages seek to replicate the Buddhist act of ascending Mt. Meru. Shintō *kami* are celebrated as avatars of Buddhist deities, notably Fudō Myō-ō.

shugensha   Shugendō practitioner.

sonja   "Eminent priest." A title bestowed on some Buddhist venerable beings, such as Binzuru-sonja, and on *rakan*, individuals who have almost reached the rank of Buddha.

sumo   A form of competitive wrestling by large, well-fleshed professional wrestlers that remains popular today. In the Heian period it was used as a form of divination. *Sumo* today is still highly ritualized, with the bout taking place in a structure resembling a Shintō shrine, the ring being purified with salt, and each wrestler performing a *shiki*—raising his feet alternatively in the air and bringing them forcefully down, to evoke the power of the earth.

sutras   The canons of the Buddhist law. They consist of a large number of volumes that include the Buddha's preaching, commentaries, records of his life, and various anecdotes concerning him and his activities. There is no agreed-on list, and each Buddhist sect, in Japan and elsewhere, chooses from the collection those books it wishes particularly to expound on.

-ten   A class of deities, many of Indian origin, who function to protect the Buddhist Law.

tsumi   Sin. A very important concept in Shintō, *tsumi* implies a polluting action. In consequence of *tsumi*, the perpetrator is likely to suffer punishment, which can only be avoided by performing purification, such as ablution, fasting, and making offerings to the offended deity/spirit. Even the deities can commit *tsumi,* as witnessed by Susano-wo's destruction of the dikes.

ujigami Clan deity. *Ujigami* are the particular deity worshipped by a household (*ie*) or an extended collection of households (*dōzoku*) as their primary family deity. *Ujigami* will appear in dreams to warn or foretell, and they will protect the family, provided they are worshipped appropriately. Common *ujigami* are Inari, Ryujin, and Fudō Myō-ō. Amaterasu-ō-mikami is, of course, also the *ujigami* of Japan's imperial household.

utaki Okinawan term for a sacred grove in which the priestesses commune with the *kang* using appropriate rituals.

yamabushi "One who sleeps in the mountains": an ascetic and practitioner of Shugendō. *Yamabushi* may be the model for *tengu.*

yashikigami "House deity." The patron deity of a household, particularly of a *bushi* family. *Yashikigami* are usually worshipped in private by members of the family.

yo Japanese pronunciation of the Sanskrit *hum.* See *hum.*

APPENDIX: PRIMARY SOURCES

ENGLISH-LANGUAGE PUBLICATIONS

Ainu Mukei Bunka Densho Hozonkai. 1983. *Hitobito no Monogatari* [Fables of men]. Sapporo: Ainu Mukei Bunka Densho Hozonkai.

Akima, Toshio. 1993. "The Myth of the Goddess of the Undersea World and the Tale of the Empress Jingū's Subjugation of Silla." *Japanese Journal of Religious Studies* 20 (2–3): 95–185.

Anesaki, Masaharu. 1928. *Japanese Mythology.* Mythology of All Races, vol. 8. Boston: Marshall Jones Co.

Aoki, Michiko Yamaguchi. 1974. *Ancient Myths and Early History of Japan: A Cultural Foundation.* New York: Exposition Press.

Aoki, Michiko Yamaguchi, trans. and intro. 1971. *Izumo Fudoki.* Monumenta Nipponica Monographs. Tokyo: Sophia University Press.

Ashkenazi, Michael. 1993. *Matsuri: The Festivals of a Japanese Town.* Honolulu: University of Hawaii Press.

Aston, William George. 1905. *Shinto: The Way of the Gods.* London: Longmans, Green, and Co.

Aston, William.G., trans. 1956. *Nihongi.* London: Allen and Unwin.

Ballon, R. J. 1990. "Decision Making in Japanese Industry." *Business Series* 132. Tokyo: Sophia University Press.

Barker, A. J. 1971. *Suicide Weapon.* London: Pan/Ballantine.

Batchelor, John. 1901. *The Ainu and Their Folk-lore.* London: Religious Tract Society.

———. 1971. *Ainu Life and Lore: Echoes of a Departing Race.* Tokyo, Kyobunkwan, and New York: Johnson Reprint Corp.

Befu, Harumi. 2001. *Hegemony of Homogeneity: An Anthropological Analysis of Nihonjin-ron.* Japanese Society Series. Melbourne: Trans. Pacific Press.

Bellah, Robert. 1957. *Tokugawa Religion.* New York: Free Press.

Bernier, Bernard. 1975. *Breaking the Cosmic Circle: Religion in a Japanese Village.* Cornell East Asian Papers. Ithaca: Cornell University Press.

Bethe, Monica, and Karen Brazell. 1978. *No as Performance: An Analysis of the Kuse Scene Yamamba*. Cornell East Asian Papers. Ithaca: Cornell University Press.

Blacker, Carmen. 1975. *The Catalpa Bow*. London: George Allen and Unwin Ltd.

Bock, Felicia G., trans. 1985. *Classical Learning and Taoist Practices in Early Japan, with a Translation of Books 16 and 20 of the Engi-Shiki*. ASU Center for Asian Studies, Occasional Paper No. 17.

Bock, Felicia Gressitt, trans. and intro. 1970. *Engi-shiki: Procedures of the Engi Era, Books 1–4* . Monumenta Nipponica Monographs. Tokyo: Sophia University Press.

———. 1970. *Engi-shiki: Procedures of the Engi Era, Books 6–10*. Monumenta Nipponica Monographs. Tokyo: Sophia University Press.

Borgen, Robert. 1994. *Sugawara no Michizane and the Early Heian Court*. Honolulu: University of Hawaii Press.

Brandon, James R., and Tamako Niwa, adapters. 1966. *Kabuki Plays*. New York: S. French. [Contains *Kanjincho*.]

Brett, L. Walker. 2001. *The Conquest of Ainu Lands: Ecology and Culture in Japanese Expansion, 1590–1800*. Berkeley and London: University of California Press.

Brightman, Robert A., and David Meyer. 1983. "On Windigo Psychosis." *Current Anthropology* 24 (1): 120–122.

Casal, U. A. 1967. *The Five Sacred Festivals of Ancient Japan: Their Symbolism and Historical Development*. Tokyo: Sophia University and Charles Tuttle Co.

Cuyler, P. L. 1985. *Sumo: From Rite to Sport*. Tokyo: Weatherhill.

Czaja, Michael. 1974. *Gods of Myth and Stone: Phallicism in Japanese Folk Religion*. New York and Tokyo: Weatherhill.

Dale, Peter N. 1986. *The Myth of Japanese Uniqueness*. New York: St. Martin's Press.

Davis, S. Hadland. 1913. *Myths and Legends of Japan*. London: George Harrap. Facsimile edition, New York: Dover Publications, 1992.

Davis, Winston. 1984. "Pilgrimage and World Renewal—A Study of Religion and Social Value in Tokugawa Japan." *History of Religions* 23 (3): 71–98.

De Veer, Henrietta. 1976. "Myth Sequences from the *Kojiki*: A Structural Study." *Japanese Journal of Religious Studies* 3 (2–3): 175–214.

Dumoulin, Heinrich. 1981. *Approaches to the Idea of God as "Father" in Some Popular Religions of Modern Japan*. Translated by T. L. Westow. New York: Seabury.

Dykstra, Yoshiko Kurata. 1978. "Jizo, the Most Merciful: Tales from Jizo Bosatsu Reigenki." *Monumenta Nipponica* 33 (2): 179–200.

———. 1986. *The Konjaku Tales: Indian Section (Tenjiku-Hen), Part 1/Part 2 from a Medieval Japanese Collection.* Osaka: Kansai University of Foreign Studies.

Earhart, H. Byron. 1970. *A Religious Study of the Mount Haguro Sect of Shugendo.* Tokyo: Sophia University Press.

Ehrich, Kurt S. 1991. *Shichifukujin: Die Sieben Glücksgötter Japans.* Recklinghausen, Germany: Verlag Aurel Bongers.

Eliot, Sir Charles Norton Edgcumbe. 1959. *Japanese Buddhism.* London: Routledge and Kegan Paul.

Etter, Carl. 1949. *Ainu Folklore: Traditions and Culture of the Vanishing Aborigines of Japan.* Chicago: Wilcox and Follett Co.

Frank, Bernard. 1991. *Le pantheon bouddhique au Japon. Collections d'Emile Guimet.* Paris: Reunion des musees nationaux.

Getty, Alice. 1988. *The Gods of Northern Buddhism.* New York: Dover Publications.

Glassman, Hank. 1998. "Chujo-hime, Convents, and Women's Salvation." http://www.columbia.edu/cu/ealac/imjs/programs/1998-fall/Abstracts/glassman.html.

Goff, Janet. 1997. "Foxes in Japanese Culture: Beautiful or Beastly?" *Japan Quarterly* 44 (2): 66–71.

Goldsbury, Peter. 2001. "Touching the Absolute: Aikido vs. Religion and Philosophy." http://www.aikidojournal.com/articles/ajArticles/_TouchingTheAbsolute.asp.

Goodin, Charles C. 1994. "Tengu: The Legendary Mountain Goblins of Japan." *Furyu: The Budo Journal* 2. Text in http://www.seinenkai.com/articles/tengu.html.

Grapard, Allan. 1982. "Flying Mountains and Walkers of Emptiness: Toward a Definition of Sacred Space in Japanese Religion." *History of Religions* 20: 195–221.

———. 1991. "Visions of Excess and Excesses of Visions: Women and Transgression in Japanese Myth." *Japanese Journal of Religious Studies* 18 (1): 3–22.

———. 1992. *The Protocol of the Gods: A Study of the Kasuga Cult in Japanese History.* Berkeley: University of California Press.

Grayson, James H. 2002. "Susa-no-o: A Culture Hero from Korea." *Japan Forum* 14 (3): 465–488.

Grotenhuis, Elizabeth ten. 1999. *Japanese Mandalas: Representations of Sacred Geography.* Honolulu: University of Hawaii Press.

Guthrie, Steward. 1980. "A Cognitive Theory of Religion." *Current Anthropology* 21 (2): 181–204.

Hakeda, Yoshito S. 1972. *Kukai.* New York: Columbia University Press.

Hardacre, Helen. 1989. *Shinto and the State: 1868–1988.* Princeton: Princeton University Press.

———. 1994. "Conflicts Between Shugendō and the New Religions of Bakumatsu Japan." *Japanese Journal of Religious Studies* 21 (2/3): 137–166.

Havens, Norman, trans. 1998. *Kami.* Tokyo: Institute for Japanese Culture and Classics, Kokugakuin University.

Herbert, Jean. 1967. *Shinto—At the Fountain Head of Japan.* London: George Allen and Unwin Ltd.

———. 1980. *La religion d'Okinawa.* Collection Mystiques et religions, Série B. Paris: Dervy-Livres.

Hori, Ichiro. 1968. *Folk Religion in Japan.* Chicago: Chicago University Press.

Isomae, Jun'ichi. 2000. "Reappropriating the Japanese Myths." *Japanese Journal of Religious Studies* 27 (1–2): 15–41.

Iwasaka, Michiko, and Barre Toelken. 1994. *Ghosts and the Japanese: Cultural Experience in Japanese Death.* Logan: Utah State University Press.

Jolivet, Muriel. 2000. "Ema: Representations of Infanticide and Abortion." In M. Ashkenazi and J. Clammer, eds., *Consumption and Material Culture in Contemporary Japan.* London: Kegan Paul International.

Joly, Henri L. 1967. *Legend in Japanese Art.* Tokyo: Charles E. Tuttle Co.

Joly, Henri L., and Inada Hogitaro. 1963. *Arai Hakuseki's the Sword Book in Honchō Gunkikō and the Book of Samé Kō Hi Sei Gi of Inaba Tsūriō.* New York: Charles E. Tuttle Co.

Jones, Hazel J. 1980. *Live Machines: Hired Foreigners and Meiji Japan.* Tenterden, UK: Paul Norbury Publications.

Kamata, Toji. 2001. "The Topology of *Oni* and *Kami* in Japanese Myth." http://homepage2.nifty.com/moon21/oniB.html.

Katō, Genchi. 1908. "The Ancient Shinto Deity Ame-no-minaka-nushi-no-kami Seen in the Light of To-day." *Transactions of the Asiatic Society of Japan* 36: 139–162.

Kawai, Hayao. 1995. *Dreams, Myths, and Fairy Tales in Japan.* Einsiedeln, Switzerland: Daimon.

Kayano, Shigeru. 1985. *The Romance of the Bear God: Ainu Folktales* [*Eibun Ainu minwashu*]. Tokyo: Taishukan Publishing Co.

Khanna, Anita. 1999. *The Jataka Stories in Japan.* Delhi: B. R. Publishing.

Kitabatake, Chikafusa. 1980. *A Chronicle of Gods and Sovereigns: Jinno Shotoki.* Translated by H. Paul Varley. New York: Columbia University Press.

Kitagawa, Hiroshi, and Bruce T. Tsuchida, trans. and eds. 1975. *The Tale of the Heike* [*Heike monogatari*]. Tokyo: University of Tokyo Press.

Kitagawa, Joseph M. 1987. *On Understanding Japanese Religion.* Princeton: Princeton University Press.

Kiyota, Minoru, ed. 1987. *Japanese Buddhism: Its Tradition, New Religions, and Interaction with Christianity.* Los Angeles: Buddhist Books International.

Kobayashi, Sakae. 1992. *Religious Ideas of the Japanese Under the Influence of Asian Mythology.* Nishinomiya, Japan: Kansei Gakuin University.

Kodama, Sakuzaemon. 1970. *Ainu: Historical and Anthropological Studies.* Sapporo: Hokkaido University School of Medicine.

Komatsu, Chikō. 1989. *The Way to Peace: The Life and Teachings of the Buddha.* Kyoto: Hōzōkan Publishing Co.

Kōnoshi, Takamitsu. 1984. "The Land of Yōmi: On the Mythical World of the *Kōjiki.*" *Japanese Journal of Religious Studies* 11 (1): 57–76.

Kornicki, Peter F., ed. 1996. *Religion in Japan.* Cambridge: Cambridge University Press.

Kreiner, Josef, ed. 1993. *European Studies on Ainu Language and Culture.* Munich: Iudicium-Verlaag.

Kubota, Hideki, and Inoue Hiroko. 1995. *Tune of the Yakumo-goto: Myth and the Japanese Spirit.* Nishinomiya, Japan: Yakumo-goto Reminiscence Society.

Kurosawa, Kōzō. 1982. "Myths and Tale Literature." *Japanese Journal of Religious Studies* 9 (2–3): 115–125.

Lebra, William P. 1966. *Okinawan Religion: Belief, Ritual, and Social Structure.* Honolulu: University of Hawaii Press.

Littleton, C. Scott. 1995. "Yamato-takeru: An 'Arthurian' Hero in Japanese Tradition." *Asian Folklore Studies* 54 (2): 259–275.

Macgovern, William Montgomery. 1922. *An Introduction to Mahayana Buddhism, with Especial Reference to Chinese and Japanese Phases.* London: Kegan Paul and Co.

Manabe, Masahiro, and Kerstin Vidaeus. 1975. "The Old Fox and the Fairy Child: A Study in Japanese Folklore." *Journal of Intercultural Studies* 2: 5–28.

Matisoff, Susan. 1978. *The Legend of Semimaru, Blind Musician of Japan.* Studies in Oriental Culture, no. 14. New York: Columbia University Press.

Matsuda, Kaoru. 1994. *"Ketsueki-gata to Seikaku" no Shakai-shi* [Social history of "blood type and personality"]. Revised edition, Tokyo: Kawade Shobo Shinsha, 1994.

Matsumoto, Nobuhiro. 1928. *Essai sur la mythologie japonaise.* Paris: Librairie Orientaliste Paul Geuthner.

Matsunaga. Alicia. 1974/1996. *Foundations of Japanese Buddhism.* Los Angeles: Buddhist Books International.

Mayer, Fanny Hagin, ed. and trans. 1985. *Ancient Tales in Modern Japan: An Anthology of Japanese Folk Tales.* Bloomington: Indiana University Press.

———. 1986. *The Yanagita Kunio Guide to the Japanese Folk Tale.* Bloomington: Indiana University Press.

McCullough, Helen Craig, trans. 1959. *The Taiheiki*. New York: Columbia University Press.

———. 1966. *Yoshitsune: A Fifteenth-Century Japanese Chronicle [Gikeiki]*. Stanford: Stanford University Press.

———. 1988. *The Tale of the Heike*. Stanford: Stanford University Press.

McCullough, William H. 1973. "Spirit Possession in the Heian Period." In S. Ota and R. Fukuda (eds.), *Studies on Japanese Culture—1*. Tokyo: Japan P.E.N. Club.

Mori, Masato. 1982. "Konjaku Monogatari-shi: Supernatural Creatures and Order." *Japanese Journal of Religious Studies* 9 (2–3): 147–170.

Morrell, Robert E. 1982. "Kamakura Accounts of Myōe Shōnin as Popular Religious Hero." *Japanese Journal of Religious Studies* 9 (2–3): 171–198.

Munro, Neil Gordon. 1962. *Ainu Creed and Cult*. London: Routledge and Kegan Paul. Reprint, London: Kegan Paul International, 1995.

Nagai, Shinichi. 1968. *Gods of Kumano: Shinto and the Occult*. Tokyo: Kodansha International.

Nagatsuka, Ryuji. 1972. *I Was a Kamikaze: The Knights of the Divine Wind*. Translated by Nina Rootes. London: Abelard-Schuman.

Naito, Hatsuho. 1989. *Thunder Gods: The Kamikaze Pilots Tell Their Story*. Translated by Mayumi Ichikawa. Tokyo and New York: Kodansha International.

Nakamura, Kyoko Motomochi. 1983. "The Significance of Amaterasu in Japanese Religious History." In Carl Olsen (ed.), *The Book of the Goddess, Past and Present*. New York: Crossroad.

———. 1996. *Miraculous Stories from the Japanese Buddhist Tradition: The Nihon Ryoki of the Monk Kyokai*. New ed. Richmond, UK: Curzon Press. Text at http://campross.crosswinds.net/books/Miraculous.html.

Naoe, Hiroji. 1984. "A Study of Yashiki-gami, the Deity of House and Grounds." In R. Dorson (ed.), *Studies in Japanese Folklore*. New York: Arno Press.

Naumann, Nelly. 1974. "Whale and Fish Cult in Japan: A Basic Feature of Ebisu Worship." *Asian Folklore Studies* 33: 1–15.

Nishida, Masaki. 1994. "The Mythological World of Jomon Culture." In Takashi Irimoto and Takako Yamado (eds.), *Circumpolar Religion and Ecology: An Anthropology of the North*. Tokyo: University of Tokyo Press.

Norbeck, Edward. 1955. "Yakudoshi: A Japanese Complex of Supernatural Beliefs." *Southwestern Journal of Anthropology* 2: 105–120.

Nozaki, Kiyoshi. 1961. *Kitsune: Japan's Fox of Mystery, Romance, and Humor*. Tokyo: Hokuseido Press.

Oguma, Eiji. 2002. *The Genealogy of Japanese Self-images*. Translated by David Askew. Melbourne: Trans Pacific Press.

Ohnuki-Tierney, Emiko. 1968. *A Northwest Coast Sakhalin Ainu World View.* Thesis, University of Washington. Abstracted in *Dissertation Abstracts* 29 (1969) no. 12, pt. 1: 4494-B.

———. 1969. *Sakhalin Ainu Folklore.* Anthropological Studies 2. Washington, DC: American Anthropological Association.

———. 1974. *The Ainu of the Northwest Coast of Southern Sakhalin.* New York: Holt, Rinehart, and Winston.

———. 1988. *The Monkey as Mirror.* Princeton: Princeton University Press.

Okuda, Kensaku, ed. 1970. *Japan's Ancient Sculpture.* Tokyo: Mainichi Newspapers.

Ono, Sokyo. 1962. *Shinto: The Kami Way.* Rutland, VT: Charles E. Tuttle Co.

Ouwehand, Cornelius. 1964. *Namazu-e and Their Themes: An Interpretative Approach to Some Aspects of Japanese Religion.* Leiden, the Netherlands: E. J. Brill.

Philippi, Donald, trans. and ed. 1968. *Kōjiki.* Tokyo: Tokyo University Press.

Philippi, Donald L., trans. 1979. *Songs of Gods, Songs of Humans: The Epic Tradition of the Ainu.* Princeton: Princeton University Press.

Rabinovitch, Judith N. 1986. *Shōmonki: The Story of Masakado's Rebellion.* Monumenta Nipponica Monographs. Tokyo: Sophia University.

Reader, Ian. 1993. *Japanese Religions Past and Present.* Folkstone, UK: Japan Library.

Røkkum, Arne. 1998. *Goddesses, Priestesses, and Sisters: Mind, Gender and Power in the Monarchic Tradition of the Ryukyus.* Oslo/Boston: Scandinavian University Press.

Roberts, John M., Saburo Morita, and L. Keith Brown. 1986. "Personal Categories for Japanese Sacred Places and Gods: Views Elicited from a Conjugal Pair." *American Anthropologist* 88 (4): 807–824.

Robinson, James C. 1969. *Okinawa: A People and Their Gods.* Rutland, VT: Charles E. Tuttle Co.

Rohlen, Thomas P. 1974. *For Harmony and Strength: Japanese White-Collar Organization in Anthropological Perspective.* Berkeley: University of California Press.

Ross, Floyd Hiatt. 1965. *Shinto: The Way of Japan.* Boston: Beacon Press.

Sadler, A. W. 1970. "Of Talismans and Shadow Bodies: Annual Purification Rites at a Tokyo Shrine." *Contemporary Religions in Japan* 11: 181–222.

Sakurada, Katsunori. 1980 (1963). "The Ebisu-gami in a Fishing Village." In R. Dorson (ed.), *Studies in Japanese Folklore.* New York: Arno Press.

Sansom, Sir George. 1976. *Japan: A Short Cultural History.* Tokyo: Charles E. Tuttle Co.

Sasaki, Kiyoshi. 2000. "Amenominakanushi no Kami in Late Tokugawa Period

Kokugaku." Tokyo: Institute for Japanese Culture and Classics, Kokugakuin University. http://www.kokugakuin.ac.jp/ijcc/wp/cpjr/kami/sasaki.html# para0060.

Sato, Hiroaki. 1995. *Legends of the Samurai.* Woodstock, NY: Overlook Press.

Scholem, Gershom G. 1965. *On the Kabbalah and Its Symbolism.* London: Routledge and Kegan Paul.

Seiffert, Geneviève. 1983. *Yanagita Kunio: Les Yeux précieux du serpent.* Paris: Publications Orientalistes de France.

Sered, Susan Starr. 1999. *Women of the Sacred Groves: Divine Priestesses of Okinawa.* New York and Oxford: Oxford University Press.

Shimizu, A. 1987. "*Ie* and *Dōzoku:* Family and Descent in Japan." *Current Anthropology* 28: 85–90.

Shioya, Sakae. 1956. *Chūshingura: An Exposition, Illustrated with Hiroshige's Coloured Plates.* 2d ed. Tokyo: Hokuseido Press.

Sieffert, Rene. 1995. *Histoire de Benkei.* Paris: Publications Orientalistes de France.

Sjoquist, Douglas P. 1999. "Identifying Buddhist Images in Japanese Painting and Sculpture." *Education About Asia* 4 (3), available at http://www.aasianst. org.

Smith, Robert J. 1974. *Ancestor Worship in Contemporary Japan.* Palo Alto, CA: Stanford University Press.

Smits, Ivo. 1996. "An Early Anthropologist? Oe no Masafusa's 'A Record of Fox Spirits.'" In Peter F. Kornicki and I. J. McMullen (eds.), *Religion in Japan: Arrows to Heaven and Earth.* Cambridge: Cambridge University Press.

Smyers, Karen. 1999. *The Fox and the Jewel.* Honolulu: University of Hawaii Press.

Statler, Oliver. 1984. *Japanese Pilgrimage.* London: Picador.

Stefansson, Halldor. 1985. "Earth Gods in Morimachi." *Japanese Journal of Religious Studies* 12 (4): 277–298.

Stone, George Cameron. 1961. *A Glossary of the Construction, Decoration, and Use of Arms and Armor.* New York: Jack Brussel.

Stone, Jacqueline Ilyse. 1999. *Studies in East Asian Buddhism.* Honolulu: University of Hawaii Press.

Takeda, Izumo, Miyoshi Shoraku, and Namiki Senryu. 1971. *Chūshingura, the Treasury of Loyal Retainers: A Puppet Play.* Translated by Donald Keene. New York: Columbia University Press.

Tcherevko, K. E. 1973. "Chinese Heterography and Formation of the Japanese Written Literary Language: On the *Kojiki* Material of the Year 712." In S. Ota and R. Fukuda (eds.), *Studies on Japanese Culture—2.* Tokyo: Japan P.E.N. Club.

Teeuwen, Mark, and John Breen, eds. 2000. *Shinto in History: Ways of the* Kami. London: Curzon Press.

Toshimasa, Hirano. 1980. "Aruga Kizaemon: The Household, the Ancestors, and the Tutelary Deities." *Japanese Journal of Religious Studies* 7 (2–3): 144–166.

Tucker, John Allen. 1999. "Rethinking the *Akō Rōnin* Debate: The Religious Significance of *Chūshin Gishi.*" *Japanese Journal of Religious Studies* 26 (1–2): 1–38.

Tyler, Royall. 1987. *Japanese Tales.* New York: Pantheon.

_____. 1990. *The Miracles of the Kasuga Deity.* New York: Columbia University Press.

Vance, Timothy J.1983. "The Etymology of *Kami.*" *Japanese Journal of Religious Studies* 10 (4): 277–288.

Visser, Marinus Willem de. 1913. *The Dragon in China and Japan.* Amsterdam: J. Müller. Reprinted Wiesbaden: M. Sändig, 1969.

———. 1931. *The Bodhisattva Kokuzōō in China and Japan.* Amsterdam: Verhandelingen der Koninklijke Akademie van Wetenschappen. Afdeeling Letterkunde. Nieuwe Reeks.

Waley, Arthur. 1957. *The Nō Plays of Japan.* New York: Grove Press.

Warner, Denis, Peggy Warner, and Sadao Seno. 1982. *The Sacred Warriors: Japan's Suicide Legions.* Cincinnati: Van Nostrand Reinhold Company.

Watanabe, Shoko. 1968. *Japanese Buddhism: A Critical Appraisal.* Rev. ed. Tokyo: Kokusai Bunka Shinkokai.

Wehmeyer, Ann, trans. 1997. *Kojiki-den* [Motoori norinaga], *Book 1.* Cornell East Asia Series, Number 87. Ithaca: Cornell University Press.

Wilson, William R., trans. 1971. *Hōgen Monogatari: Tale of the Disorder in Hōgen.* Monumenta Nipponica Monographs. Tokyo: Sophia University Press.

Yamamoto, Kōshō, and Shinshō Hanayama. 1966. *A History of Japanese Buddhism.* Translated and edited by Kōshō Yamamoto. Tokyo: Bukkyo Dendo Kyokai.

Yamashita, Hideo. 1996. *Competitiveness and the* Kami *Way.* Aldershot, UK: Avebury.

Yanagita, Kunio. 1954. *Japanese Folk Tales.* Translated by Fanny Hagin Mayer; illustrated by Kiichi Okamoto. Tokyo: Tokyo News Service.

———. 1970. *Senzo no hanashi* [About our ancestors: the Japanese family system]. Translated by Fanny Hagin Mayer and Ishiwara Yasuyo; compiled by the Japanese National Commission for Unesco. Tokyo: Japan Society for the Promotion of Science [distributed by Kinokuniya bookstore].

———. 1975. *The Legends of Tono* [translated, with an introduction, by Ronald A. Morse]. Tokyo: Japan Foundation.

———. 1983. *Nihon no mukashibanashi.* [Contes du Japon d'autrefois]. Translated by Genevieve Seiffert. Paris: Publications orientalistes de France.

Yoshida, Mitsukuni, Tanaka Ikko, and Sesoko Tsune, eds. 1985. *The Culture of Anima: Supernature in Japanese Life.* Translated by Lynne E. Riggs and Takechi Manabu. Hiroshima: Mazda Motor Corp.

Yoshida, Teigo. 1981. "The Stranger as God: The Place of the Outsider in Japanese Folk Religion." *Ethnology* 20 (2): 87–99.

JAPANESE-LANGUAGE PUBLICATIONS

Higa, Choshin. 1991. *Okinawa no shinko yogo* [Okinawan religious terminology]. Naha-shi: Fudokisha.

Ikeda, Yasaburo, ed. 1978. *Origuchi Shinobu: marebito ron* [Origuchi Shinobu's theory of *marebito*]. Tokyo: Kodansha.

Kubo, Noritada, ed. 1978. *Okinawa no gairai shukyo: sono juyo to hen'yo* [Okinawan imported religion: its extent and incorporation]. Tokyo: Kobundo.

Kubo, Noritada Sensei Okinawa Chosa Nijunen Kinen Ronbunshu Kanko Iinkai hen. 1988. *Okinawa no shukyo to minzoku: Kubo Noritada Sensei Okinawa chosa nijunen kinen ronbunshu* [Okinawan religion and people: the collected works of Professor Kubo Noritada]. Tokyo: Daiichi Shobo.

Kubo, Noritada. 1971. *Okinawa no shuzoku to shinko: Chugoku to no hikaku kenkyu* [Okinawan and Chinese believers and beliefs: a comparative study]. Tokyo: Tokyo Daigaku Shuppankai.

Matsumoto, Nobuhiro. 1956. *Nihon no shinwa* [Japanese mythology]. Tokyo: Shibundo.

Minzokugaku Kenkyujo, ed. 1951. *Minzokugaku jiten: Yanagita Kunio kanshu* [Ethnological dictionary]. Tokyo: Tokyodo.

Miyata, Noboru, ed. 1998. *Shichifukujin shinkō jiten* [Dictionary of Shichi Fukujin mythology]. Tokyo: Ebisu Kosho Shuppan.

Miyoshi, Fumio. 1973. *Ainu no rekishi: kami to daichi to kariudo to* [Ainu history: gods, lands, huntsmen]. Tokyo: Kodansha.

Namahira, Emiko. 1977. "An Analysis of 'Hare' and 'Kegare' in Japanese Rites of Passage." *Minzokugakku Kenkyu* 40: 350–368.

Ono, Susumu. 1997. *Kami.* Tokyo: Sanseidō.

Origuchi, Shinobu. 1954–1959. *Origuchi Shinobu zenshū* [Origuchi Shinobu: the complete works]. 32 vols. Tokyo: Chuo Kōronsha.

Ōshima, Tatehiko. 1990. *Daikoku shinkō* [Daikoku beliefs]. Tokyo: Yūzankaku Shuppan.

Sano, Kenji, ed. 1991. *Kokuzo shinko* [Kokuzō beliefs]. Tokyo: Yuzankaku.

Shiga, Gō. 1991. *Nihon no kamigami to kenkoku shinwa* [Japanese deities and national foundation]. Tokyo: Yūzankaku Shuppan.

Takahashi Yōji, et al., eds. 1989. *Nihon no kami* [Japan's deities]. Tokyo: Heibonsha.

Takioto, Yoshiyuki. 1996. *Kami to shinwa no kodaishi* [Ancient history of deities and mythology]. Tokyo: Iwata Shoin. [Includes reprint of "Teisei Izumo fudoki" revised by Senge Toshizane and published in 1806.] Umehara, Takashi. 1986. *Yamato-takeru.* Tokyo: Kodansha.

Yamaori, Tetsuo, ed. 1996. *Nihon bunka no shinso to Okinawa* [Japanese culture and Okinawa]. Nichibunken sosho, no. 12. Kyoto: Kokusai Nihon Bunka Kenkyu Senta.

Yasuda, Yoshinori. 2001. *Ryū no bunmei, taiyō no bunmei* [Dragon culture, solar culture]. Tokyo: PHP Shinsho.

Yoshino, Hiroko. 1979. *Hebi: Nihon no hebi shinkō* [Serpent: Japanese snake beliefs]. Tokyo: Hosei Daigaku Shuppankyoku.

Yanagita, Kunio. 1933. *Mukashibanashi saishu no shiori* [A guide to legend collecting]. Tokyo: Hagiwara Masanori hatsubaijo Azusa Shobo.

———. 1943. *Shintō to minzokugaku* [Shintō and ethnology]. Tokyo: Meiseido.

———. 1949. *Mukashibanashi to bungaku* [Legends and culture studies]. Tokyo: Sogensha.

———. 1953. *Nihon no mukashibanashi* [Japanese legends]. Tokyo: Kadokawa Shoten.

———. 1968–1971. *Teihon Yanagita Kunio shu* [Collected works of Yanigata Kunio]. Tokyo: Chikuma Shobo.

INDEX

ABOUT THE AUTHOR

Michael Ashkenazi (Ph.D. Anthropology, Yale 1983) has taught anthropology in several countries. He is the author and editor of numerous articles and several books, including *Matsuri: Festivals of a Japanese Town* (University of Hawaii Press), and coauthor of *The Essence of Japanese Cuisine* (Curzon Press/ University of Pennsylvania Press).